UNSHAKABLE FAITH

"When I was a youngster, the easiest place to snore was in history class. We were made to memorize dates and disconnected places and people. In the skillful hands of John Perry, history reads like a novel. Booker T. Washington and George Washington Carver come to life as Perry tells their stories. I knew the accomplishments of these men but I didn't know what drove them. Perry gets us inside Washington's head and underneath Carver's heart. You will love this intimate portrait of godly pioneer educators."

DR. RICHARD ALLEN FARMER
RAF MINISTRIES, INC.

"John Perry is an excellent writer whose work is consistently both entertaining and insightful. I highly recommend him as an author."

ARKANSAS GOVERNOR MIKE HUCKABEE

"Though the journey of Booker T. Washington and George Washington Carver from slavery to the heights of national renown affords us a remarkable testimony of individual achievement, the greatest legacy of the men was not so much what they accomplished themselves, but what they helped thousands of others accomplish. John Perry has beautifully captured that legacy of selfless sacrifice in a must-read profile of these pioneering American heroes."

GEORGE GRANT, PH.D.
PROFESSOR OF MORAL PHILOSOPHY, BANNOCKBURN COLLEGE

"John Perry's well-researched and engagingly written *Unshakable Faith* retells an American story that desperately needs a retelling today, of two Christian men whose names and successes should be honored by all believers."

MARK GALLI
EDITOR, *CHRISTIAN HISTORY*

UNSHAKABLE FAITH

BOOKER T. WASHINGTON &
GEORGE WASHINGTON CARVER

A BIOGRAPHY BY JOHN PERRY

Multnomah Publishers® *Sisters, Oregon*

UNSHAKABLE FAITH
published by Multnomah Publishers, Inc.

©1999 by John Perry
International Standard Book Number: 1-57673-493-5

Cover image by Ron Morecraft/the i spot
Photographs courtesy of the Tuskegee University Archive
Design by Kirk DouPonce

Scripture quotations are from:
The Holman Christian Standard Bible
©1999 by Broadman & Holman Publishers
Used by permission. All rights reserved.

Multnomah is a trademark of Multnomah Publishers, Inc.,
and is registered in the U.S. Patent and Trademark Office.
The colophon is a trademark of Multnomah Publishers, Inc.
Printed in the United States of America

For information:
MULTNOMAH PUBLISHERS, INC.
POST OFFICE BOX 1720
SISTERS, OREGON 97759

Library of Congress Cataloging-in-Publication Data:
Perry, John, 1952–
    Unshakable faith / by John Perry.
       p. cm.
    ISBN 1-57673-493-5 (alk. paper)
    1. Washington, Booker T., 1856–1915. 2. Carver, George Washington,
    1864?–1943. 3. Afro-Americans Biography. 4. Washington, Booker T.
    1856–1915—Religion. 5. Carver, George Washington. 1864?–1943—Religion.
    6. Afro-American educators Biography. 7. Afro-American agriculturists
    Biography. I. Title.
E185.96.P378 1999
920'.009296073—dc21
{B}   99–4335
                                                                                    CIP

00 01 02 03 04 05 — 10 9 8 7 6 5 4 3 2 1

This book is dedicated to Matt Jacobson and David Shepherd—
friends, encouragers, life models for me
as Christian husbands, fathers, and businessmen.
As long as iron sharpens iron, I will treasure them.

TABLE OF CONTENTS

ACKNOWLEDGMENTS

This book is the work of many hands. Once again, Matt Jacobson served as midwife and chief advocate in the project's early stages. Later on Don Jacobson, my editor and friend Tracy Sumner, and others at Multnomah helped hammer the book into shape, cheering me on even as the clock ticked on and the candle burned low.

I owe a special word of gratitude to Cynthia Wilson and Loretta Robinson, at the archive of the Hollis Burke Frissell Library on the Tuskegee campus, for guiding me through the Washington and Carver collections there, and for their courtesy, efficiency, and unerring sense of when to show up with hamburgers.

I'm grateful to Professor Sheridan Howard Settler and Dr. B. D. Mayberry, former colleague and student, respectively, of Dr. Carver, as well as once again to Cynthia Wilson, for their patient hours of conversation, which added a vital dimension to the story in this book.

Thanks also to Wes Driver, who was with me on this one from the beginning, for the countless hours of library research, Internet cruising, and trips back and forth to Tuskegee in a car nobody as tall as he is should have to ride in.

This book could never have been written without the enthusiastic support of my family: Charles, Olivia, and my dear Susan Ann, God's greatest gift to all three of us. I thank them for their kind words, sincere prayers, and smiles that never failed to encourage and delight.

PREFACE

History is a mirror, and sometimes the image it reflects is far from flattering. But the more shocked we are at the past, the more hopeful we can be that we have learned from it. More than 135 years after Emancipation, race relations remain an issue that prompts a hair-trigger response from people at every point on the ideological scale. But it's only by facing the facts—uncomfortable as they may be—that we can understand our past and rely on it to guide our future.

To see the truth in history, we have to resist the temptation to hold past actions accountable to contemporary standards. Cynthia Wilson, assistant to the archivist at the Hollis Burke Frissell Library on the Tuskegee campus, speaks for many modern American blacks when she says of Booker T. Washington's ever conciliatory tone, "I can't imagine he would say something like that, and then I have to press myself back and say it's the context, and realize the time period I'm talking about, and I'm taking my 1990s views and looking at an 1890s situation."

To understand how far their faith brought Washington and Carver, we have to have an accurate picture of the world they lived in. They were "niggers" or "colored" or "Negroes" (the actual name of the race, though still offensive to some). To modern ears these words have a savage ring, but they truly recall a savage time.

Booker T. Washington and George Washington Carver lived in an era when discrimination was the law of the land. Not only were they not allowed by conductors to ride on railroad cars with white people, in some states it was against the law. It was against the law for a white nurse to touch a black hospital patient, whether she was willing to or not. They and their generation watched as the Supreme Court, along with one state legislature after another, gradually stripped the power and meaning from the three constitutional amendments passed in the aftermath of the Civil War to bring blacks equality, to the point where they were all but useless.

And yet they refused to be bitter. As Ms. Wilson wisely notes, "Bitterness serves no purpose. You can't implement change from a position of bitterness. You can only get wrapped up in the bitterness." Based on the model of Christ, whose guidance they freely and openly sought, Washington and Carver held fast to humility, hard work, self-help, and a commitment to reconciliation. Later generations would chafe at their accommodating stance. But Washington and Carver left a legacy of inspiration and success few have equaled.

Millions of Americans alive today can hardly imagine a time when black citizens were denied a table at a restaurant or a seat in a theater because of the color of their skin. I have lived all my life in the South. I remember as a child seeing the "colored" waiting room at the bus station, segregated rest rooms at the shopping centers, the "white" and "colored" drinking fountains at the grocery store, and being warned to "get out of the pool if those niggers get in." Those days are long gone, but their legacies still haunt us. In the late 1980s, I went into a white tablecloth restaurant in Louisiana and was seated by the hostess. Thirty minutes later I still didn't have a menu or a glass of water. I finally got up and left and learned shortly thereafter that a business associate traveling with me, who was Pakistani, was a little too dark for their taste.

As William Faulkner said, "The past is never dead. It's not even past." The image in the mirror is a haunting one, ancient yet still before us. While the laws that so challenged Booker T. Washington and George Washington Carver exist now only in history books, many of the preconceptions, assumptions, and obstacles they faced are as fresh as today's headlines.

By seeing what they did, with God's help let us see what we can do.
Soli deo gratia.

John Perry
Independence Day, 1999
Nashville, Tennessee

"I would permit no man, no matter what his colour might be, to narrow and degrade my soul by making me hate him."
BOOKER T. WASHINGTON

"Divine Love is destined to rule the world, I believe, despite the many things that often irritate and depress us."
GEORGE WASHINGTON CARVER

"Do not stand still and complain, but go forward—mere fault-finders accomplish little."
TUSKEGEE CHAPEL FLYER, 1899

Here is My Servant whom I have chosen,
My Beloved in whom My soul delights;
I will put My Spirit upon Him,
And He will proclaim justice to the nations.
He will not argue or shout,
And no one will hear His voice in the streets.
He will not break a bruised reed,
And He will not put out a smoldering wick,
Until He has led justice to victory.
The nations will hope in His name.
MATTHEW 12:18–21,
HOLMAN CHRISTIAN STARDARD BIBLE

CHAPTER ONE

INDEPENDENCE DAY

T he journey by train had been full of new sights, especially the last few minutes along the spur between Tuskegee and the whistle stop on the main line at Chechaw, five miles to the north. As the coach came to a halt in a cloud of hissing steam, an earnest young passenger looked out the window at the modest buildings surrounding the rail yard, raising his gaze to the ramshackle houses beyond. Past the houses he could see rows of young cotton plants nurtured by the spring sunshine, emerging from soil as black as night.

The young man had grown up in Virginia and West Virginia— tobacco country. Traveling south from the James River, with a detour through West Virginia to bid good-bye to his family, he had seen the ancient Appalachians give way to rolling foothills; and their vast and familiar stands of virgin hardwood, interspersed with fields of tobacco, corn, wheat, and vegetables, give way to field after field of cotton. The last five miles had given him his first good look at what awaited him at the end of the line in Tuskegee, the smallest county seat in Alabama, where he had been invited to start a school for his people.

"His people," in the polite parlance of nineteenth century public discourse, were, in another nineteenth century term, "Negroes," though

Booker Taliaferro Washington was as much white as black. His mother was a slave, as he had once been, and his father, an unidentified white neighbor of their owners. Such unions and such children had been commonplace in the Virginia countryside twenty-five years earlier when Booker was born. Under the circumstances, no one would have expected the father to come forward and acknowledge his child, and he never did. Washington's broad nose and full lips revealed a slave's heritage, but his relatively light skin, the reddish tint of his hair, and the piercing gray of his eyes told the careful observer that this was a mulatto—half black by birth, all black under the law of the day.

Washington had been a standout student at Hampton Institute, near Newport News, Virginia, one of the first and most successful colleges set up for former slaves after the Civil War. A committee of men he had never met, appointed under the Alabama state legislature to found a school for black pupils, had hired Washington to serve as principal at Tuskegee. There were just over 435,000 black residents in Alabama, about a third of the total population. Until sixteen years earlier they had had no more right to a public education than a cow or a chair or any other piece of property. Now the world was a different place. They were entitled by law to an education, and many of them were hungry for it. Mr. Washington had come to see whether he could give it to them.

Washington met with the three-man committee that had sent for him. All three men were Tuskegee residents, two white and one black. Washington learned from them that although the state legislature had passed an act "to establish a Normal School for colored teachers at Tuskegee," they had allocated only two thousand dollars per year for its operation. This modest amount was expressly reserved to pay the teachers' salaries (as soon as there were teachers to pay), leaving Washington to begin his school without land, buildings, books, or supplies.

The chairman of the committee was a prominent local merchant named George Washington Campbell. The other members were M. B. Swanson, also a merchant, and Lewis Adams, a tinsmith and former slave who was recognized by both black and white as a leader of Tuskegee's black community. Campbell was surprised at Washington's youthful appearance; although the new arrival sported a luxuriant handlebar moustache, Campbell later recalled that "he looked like he was about eighteen years old...so young that we did not know whether we were able to take him or not." On the strength of Hampton's recommendation, however, the committee resolved to give Washington a chance.

When he stepped off the train on a June day in 1881, Booker Washington expected to head a school for blacks, not build one from scratch. But seeing the task before him, he addressed this unexpected challenge with the enthusiasm born of a lifetime of hard work and his own thirst for knowledge. His immediate plan was twofold: to write for advice and assistance to his mentors at Hampton and to assess the specific conditions in the surrounding community to find out what kind of school his new neighbors needed most.

On June 25, 1881, he sent a postcard to the treasurer of Hampton Institute, General James Fowle Baldwin Marshall, describing Tuskegee as "a healthy and pleasant location—high and hilly." The card continued with a note of optimism, "Think I shall like it. Will open school 1st Monday in July," and followed with a request for the addresses of text-book publishers. Three days later he wrote to Frank C. Briggs, business manager at Hampton, again mentioning his intention to begin classes the first Monday in July and asking him to forward any spare supplies— maps, globes, handwriting charts, or whatever else he could scrape together. "I think," he added, "Miss Lothrop has a great many library books which she does not use or care for. These would make an excellent beginning for my library. You know what I need and *any thing* that you can send me I will be thankful for."

Booker Washington spent much of the month of June traveling around Tuskegee and Macon County to see what sort of students he could expect and what they would expect from him. What he found in the rural areas was a community of black people who lived much as he himself had lived as a slave: subsistence farmers in dirt-floored shacks who were wholly unskilled, illiterate, and oblivious to events outside their immediate experience, and whose only vague notion of education was that it somehow offered an alternative to a lifetime spent chopping cotton.

He traveled through the countryside in whatever manner he could manage, crisscrossing the county on narrow dirt roads. Occasionally someone would lend him a horse and cart; other times he rode a mule—with a saddle when he could borrow one, or bareback when he couldn't. He spoke in the two black churches in Tuskegee, the Baptist and the African Methodist Episcopal Zion, explaining his purpose and encouraging members of the congregations to enroll for the upcoming term. He spent the nights in the homes of black families. Since his arrival was completely unexpected most of the time, his visits gave him the chance to observe their everyday lives.

His host families usually slept in a single room, sometimes with distant relatives or unrelated members of the household piled in as well. Washington waited modestly outside while the rest of the family got settled, then came in and took his assigned place on the floor or in the corner of someone else's bed. There was seldom any place inside to clean up before retiring. While the others typically went to bed as they were, Washington would go outdoors to a well or some other nearby water source to wash his face and hands.

People wore clothes that to Washington appeared hopelessly filthy and worn out. Except during cold weather, some children up to the age of puberty went around the house and yard completely naked.

The typical meal consisted of fat pork and cornbread, which the family gobbled up unceremoniously on the run with the father of the house eating from his hands on the way to the field, the mother hastily downing hers from a plate on her lap or directly from the skillet, and the children eating outside as they played. Some families ate breakfast sitting around the table during Washington's visits, but their awkwardness convinced him they were doing so strictly in his honor.

After breakfast the whole family left their cabin for the cotton field, where even the smallest children spent the day "chopping" cotton—digging out the weeds between them with a hoe. It was a back-breaking job, required as many as eight or nine times during the growing season. It had been the forced labor of slaves in the region for generations and was now the occupation of their descendants. Only the youngest babies were excused from labor, and they were laid at the edge of the field where their mothers could give them a little attention between finishing one row of cotton and starting the next.

As poor as these people were, and as new as Washington was to the community, he quickly identified practical educational opportunities. He saw that the rural black families he visited lived almost entirely on fat pork and cornbread they could hardly afford because, as he later wrote, it was "bought at a high price at a store in town, notwithstanding the fact that the land all about the cabin homes could easily have been made to produce nearly every kind of garden vegetable that is raised anywhere in the country. Their one object seemed to be to plant nothing but cotton; and in many cases cotton was planted up to the very door of the cabin." Washington believed there was no reason to buy food at inflated prices if they could grow it themselves off the back porch for nothing. He would soon have the opportunity to put this lesson into practice.

He also noticed that what little cash the families had too often seemed to go for frivolous luxuries. People who could not afford clothes for their children or beds for themselves bought sewing machines and clocks. One night at dinner he noticed that "while there were five of us at the table there was but one fork for the five of us to use. Naturally there was an awkward pause on my part. In the opposite corner of the same cabin was an organ for which the people told me they were paying sixty dollars in monthly installments. One fork and a sixty-dollar organ!"

The Alabama legislature expected teachers in the black county schools to improve their own skills at the new normal school in Tuskegee. But seeing black educators firsthand gave Mr. Washington little encouragement that he could help them. Visiting classrooms on his exploratory journey that summer, he found there were no public funds for school buildings for black children, and that what rude classes were available met in churches or abandoned buildings scattered around the countryside. These were often nothing more than tumbledown shanties, unheated in winter.

Bonfires had to be built outside during cold weather, with students and teachers alike leaving their lessons to go out and get warm from time to time.

With few exceptions, Washington found teachers in these schools to be "miserably poor in preparation for their work, and poor in moral character." There was also a shortage of even the most basic supplies. Entering an abandoned log cabin being used as a schoolhouse, he saw five pupils studying from a single book, with two on the front seat, two looking over their shoulders, and behind them "a fifth little fellow who was peeping over the shoulders of all four."

In spite of Washington's depressing account of those first weeks in Tuskegee, he wrote that "there were many encouraging exceptions to the conditions which I have described." He drew a sense of optimism from the few promising students he encountered, the support of the two black church congregations he visited, and his developing relationship with the legislative committee that had brought him here.

Tuskegee had a somewhat more hopeful history of interracial cooperation than the average Southern town. The school committee that hired Washington had itself been biracial from the beginning. The only hardware store in town was owned and operated jointly by a white man and a black. Black craftsmen enjoyed steady and profitable patronage from white customers. Nevertheless, there were white residents of Tuskegee who thought that educating the black race was a dangerous idea and looked upon Washington's activities with considerable skepticism.

There were two reasons for their discomfort. The first was economic: They believed that, once educated, former slaves would no longer be satisfied with menial jobs as farm laborers and household servants at substantially lower wages than whites demanded for the same work. If that were to happen, the legions of affordable cotton choppers would disappear. And at the same time the source of cheap domestic help was drying up, there would be increased competition among the skilled workers and small businessmen from newly minted black teachers, carpenters, merchants, and landowners.

The other concern among white residents was the use former slaves would make of their education. Would they rise up in revenge for generations of bondage? Some citizens doubtless had heard of the bloody riots that had broken out in Southern cities since the end of the war. In Memphis, more than forty black rioters had been killed, nearly seventy wounded, and more than a dozen schools and churches burned. New Orleans had witnessed a similar disturbance resulting in almost forty more deaths. On the other hand, Washington later pointed out, many whites objected to educating blacks because they feared that educated blacks would become indolent dandies, who loafed around the square sporting high hats, gloves, and walking sticks.

Washington avoided any trace of conflict or controversy, focusing on the black residents of Macon County and how he could help them. Both of the churches where he had spoken enthusiastically welcomed Washington and his vision for a school. Black churches were a principal center of social life for their members, in part because they were the only formal institution of any consequence many of them had even known. Church attendance had been permitted, even encouraged, during the slavery era as a way to foster contentment and encourage the Christian attributes of honesty and humility. Justification for teaching black people to read (particularly in states such as Georgia where teaching them was illegal) was that it allowed slaves to read the Bible and thus save their souls and make them docile laborers. Many slaves were taught the apostle Paul's admonishment to the church at Ephesus to "be obedient to them that are your masters." Tragically, slave owners ignored the rest of Paul's instructions: "And, ye masters, do the same things unto them, forbearing threatening: knowing that your Master also is in heaven; neither is there respect of persons with him." How tragic, too, that they ignored the fact that biblical slaves were most often prisoners of war subject to exchange or ransom or indentured servants with specific rights, rather than chattel property.

Both the Baptist and A. M. E. Zion churches had nurtured the faith of black Christians through decades of bondage in Alabama and elsewhere.

In them, Booker Washington found the most enthusiastic audience for his vision of a new school for blacks.

From the Zion Church, Washington finally secured a place to begin his school. Determined to start classes on the first Monday in July, which would be Independence Day, Washington had relied on his energy, resourcefulness, and faith to find a suitable building. What Zion Church offered would have been unbelievably primitive to his fellow students at Hampton, but it was all the poor congregation had, and they offered it gladly.

Washington's first classroom building was a dilapidated two- or three-room shanty on the church grounds, about fourteen by forty feet, made of square cut logs with a wood shingle roof. After the first week of classes, as enrollment quickly grew to the bursting point, the congregation invited Washington to use the church building itself, a somewhat larger and better-kept whitewashed frame structure with two front doors, a peaked roof, and a short, square steeple.

As principal, teaching staff, and janitor rolled into one, Washington prepared his modest schoolroom for opening day. He had no books or supplies and only broken-down furniture. But the floor was swept and mopped until it shone, and the ragged, cast-off chairs and benches were arranged in neat rows with military precision. On July 4, 1881, the "Normal School for colored teachers at Tuskegee" was called into session.

During his travels in Macon County and his presentations before church groups, Washington had encouraged prospective students to come on July 4 for an admissions examination. The school charter called for its students to be trained as teachers, and most of those who appeared at the door of the churchyard shanty that morning were teachers in the dismal schools Washington had seen the previous month. One of the black preachers in town, who was nearly sixty, had come as well, along with a large number of younger children. Washington, probably in consultation with his three-man committee, decided to use his meager resources at first only on students who were at least sixteen and who had some previous schooling.

That first day, the students were about evenly divided between boys and girls, with teachers and their students sometimes standing side by side waiting to be interviewed. Washington observed that, though some of the teachers were nearly forty, "it was amusing to note that in several cases the pupil entered a higher class than did his former teacher." Washington's reaction to some of the students mirrored the way he had felt when sharing a single fork with the family who bought a sixty-dollar organ. These were students who boasted of some rudimentary learning that had no practical application. "The bigger the book and the longer the name of the subject, the prouder they felt of their accomplishment," he observed. "One subject which they liked to talk about and tell me that they had mastered, in arithmetic, was 'banking and discount,' but I soon found out that neither they nor almost anyone in the neighborhood in which they lived had ever had a bank account."

If the school and its pupils were less than Washington had expected when he boarded the train in Virginia, Washington was something of a letdown for a few of the junior students. In addition to looking so young, Washington lacked the long formal coat they thought a professor ought to wear. Furthermore, several of them were convinced that they could write more neatly on the blackboard than he could.

By the end of the first day, Washington had selected an opening enrollment of thirty men, women, boys, and girls. Based on his examination, he gave each one a colored card, the color indicating which of the three grade levels that student would be assigned. The junior class was the most elementary, followed by preparatory B, then preparatory A.

The second morning, instead of assigning lessons or giving a lecture, Mr. Washington had the men and boys form one line, the women and girls another, and walked up and down looking at their clothes. He pointed out missing collars and cuffs, greasy spots, scuffed shoes, and other evidence of insufficient grooming and made it clear that he expected improvement the next day. The students eagerly responded, returning the following morning with clean, new cuffs and collars (paper ones, which cost five cents a package at the general store), clean clothes, and polished shoes (even farm brogans). Inspection was repeated every day thereafter.

Having been introduced to classwork on the first day and grooming on the second, the students moved on to current events on the third.

Following the morning prayer, which began every day of class, Washington began asking individual students what news events were taking place in the country. Though there was a local newspaper called *The Tuskegee News,* few students read it, and if they did it was more likely to be, as one student remembered, about "an account of a big fight or something." Washington wanted them to tell him what was going on in the community or in the state legislature; he wanted them to know about issues that affected their lives, but they had never cultivated any interest in such matters. He warned them that the next day each of them had to come to school with a news item; anyone unprepared would be sent away and not readmitted to class until they had one. Again they enthusiastically rose to the challenge, and the current events quiz became a part of the daily classroom routine.

During opening ceremonies for the school on July 4, Washington had announced his hope "to be able to move to a more commodious place in a short time." The student body grew from thirty to nearly fifty during the first month, with a steady stream of applicants continuing to appear as word of the school made its way from one house or one market to the next through the countryside. What began as a logistical challenge soon threatened to become unmanageable. Teaching three grades of fifty pupils by himself, Washington worked grueling days. As well as being cramped, the old church building leaked so badly that when it rained, students took turns holding an umbrella over their teacher's head as he lectured to keep him from being soaked.

As he traveled around the country in June, Washington had found what seemed the ideal permanent location for his school. It was a hundred-acre plantation owned by a Confederate veteran named William Bowen and his wife, Julia. The place was known locally as the Burnt Farm because its main house had burned years before and had never been rebuilt. Possibly to avoid taxes, the Bowens had sold it in 1875 for twenty-five hundred dollars to a couple in Kansas, who then sold it back to the Bowens for one dollar in 1879. Aside from the charred ruins of the house, there were several outbuildings, about twenty-five acres of cleared land, and the rest in hilly woodlands too steep to plant. Washington and Lewis Adams, the black member of the committee that founded the school, had visited Bowen and agreed to buy the land for five hundred dollars, with two hundred dollars down.

Washington wrote to the treasurer at Hampton, General Marshall, to ask his advice on the purchase. On the second day of class, he received the general's reply encouraging him to go ahead. Washington's difficulty was that the first state appropriation would not be available until October. He wrote again to General Marshall and asked to borrow the two hundred-dollar down payment from Hampton, pledging his own salary as collateral. Marshall replied that it was unbusinesslike for one school to lend money to another but enclosed his own personal check for the amount. Washington dutifully sent him a receipt promising repayment on October 1.

With the down payment made to Bowen, Washington could at last move the school out of the Zion Church building. The new schoolrooms were more numerous but, at least in the beginning, no more weather-proof. The first order of business on the new campus was to repair the old plantation hen house, kitchen, stable, and a small cabin that had once been a dining room. The students set up sawhorses and went to work with Mr. Washington pitching in to show them how and continuing to work alongside them.

Manual labor was not popular among the students. Washington discovered most of them were interested in school because they thought it would bring them higher wages—which among black school teachers averaged twenty-five dollars per month—and, more important, relieve them of physical toil. They equated education with a life of ease. It turned out that persuading them to help with the building renovations was not actually difficult because it was obvious to them that their future education depended on it. Persuading them to tackle Washington's next project proved far more challenging.

Washington wanted to clear some more land on the property to plant cotton, thinking he could grow enough to pay back General Marshall. But the young men who came expecting to be better teachers saw no connection between getting an education and wielding an axe. Besides, Washington could see that many of them "questioned whether or not clearing land would be in keeping with their dignity." So after teaching a full day of classes, Washington himself took up an axe and headed into the woods. The students soon followed and, as one remembered, "cut and cut until they was near dead and there was a lot of cleared land." Washington and the men worked every afternoon until they had cleared about twenty acres and planted a crop. They had missed the cotton season but could still grow winter vegetables.

By November enrollment at the new school had grown to more than eighty. Struggling to keep up with the demand, Washington wrote to Hampton Institute asking for graduates who were willing to come to Tuskegee to teach. The first to arrive was a young mulatto woman named Olivia Davidson, a Virginia native whose mother was said to have been a household servant of General George Armstrong Custer. The young woman's poise and ability had attracted the attention of Lucy Hayes, wife of President Rutherford B. Hayes, who paid her tuition at Hampton. Graduating after only one year, Olivia went on to further study at Framinghan State Normal School near Boston. Two other teachers also arrived from Hampton: John W. Cardwell, to teach at Tuskegee, and Margaret E. Snodgrass came to teach in the local black public school.

Contributions to support Tuskegee dribbled in through the summer and fall of 1881. Students from Hampton sent donations; wealthy northern whites who contributed regularly to Hampton sent money to Tuskegee as well. Olivia Davidson organized "literary entertainments" and a school supper, soliciting donations of food and money door to door with the help of a canvassing committee of fifteen students. Miss Davidson and her committee collected more than one hundred dollars in all from the citizens of Tuskegee, including some whites.

Though Washington owed a great debt of thanks to the northern white benefactors who provided most of the money to keep his school running until the first state appropriation came in, he was most proud of the contribution blacks made to the building fund. To the Hampton students who collected money for his cause he wrote, "That the colored people begin to help each other, is the best evidence of their progress....

Every dollar we can get out of the colored people themselves for educational purposes is worth two coming from elsewhere."

By the following spring the money to buy the Burnt Farm had all been raised, and on April 10, 1882, William Bowen signed his deed for a hundred acres over to the "Trustees of Tuskegee Colored Normal School." Washington was delighted that the land was owned by the school and not, as with Hampton, by the state.

The early success of the Tuskegee school was all the more remarkable for the fact that as recently as two years before, no one would have even considered starting it. The idea for a school for black residents in Tuskegee had come from Lewis Adams, the unofficial leader of and spokesman for Tuskegee's black citizens. Adams had learned tinsmithing as a slave, and after Emancipation he had built a successful business making and selling cooking utensils and tin roofing to customers both black and white. It was to Adams that two white Democratic candidates came before the 1880 election to suggest a deal. The Fifteenth Amendment to the Constitution, which gave former slaves the right to vote, had transformed the legislative landscape across the South. Black Republican candidates—some of whom were nearly illiterate and had little understanding of government—were elected by blacks who were voting for the first time and who had a deep-seated distrust of white men regardless of their qualifications. These two white men wanted to be elected to the state legislature. They knew they had to have the black vote to win, and they knew Lewis Adams could deliver it for them. One of the two, Wilbur Foster, a wounded Confederate veteran and lawyer, was running for a seat in the state senate; his friend Arthur Brooks was a candidate for the state house of representatives.

They asked Lewis what he wanted in exchange for encouraging blacks to vote for them. All he wanted, he said, was a free school for blacks in Tuskegee. The white candidates agreed, and with Macon County support, Foster and Brooks were elected to the legislature. True to their word, the men introduced legislation on November 16, 1880, establishing the school Adams had requested and appropriating two thousand dollars for teachers' salaries. The act named a three-member commission—Adams, Thomas B. Dryer, and M. B. Swanson—to oversee the school. The act was approved by both houses of the Alabama legislature and signed by Governor Rufus W. Cobb on Abraham Lincoln's birthday, February 12, 1881.

By that Christmas, Booker T. Washington had been hired, the school begun, surplus supplies and equipment received from Frank Briggs at Hampton, and classes with an enrollment approaching one hundred moved to temporary quarters on the Bowen land.

As hopeful as Washington was of giving his students a practical education, he insisted that any successful curriculum had to include instruction in personal habits and religious training. If he only taught them geography and arithmetic, he feared, their progress would be slowed by the bad influences that reasserted themselves every afternoon and evening.

Christmas in the homes of Tuskegee's blacks was a sobering sight for Washington. His faith as a Christian had carried him through many crises and disappointments in life. Though he was strongly nondenominational, Washington read his Bible every day and held prayers in his classroom twice a day. Christmas was a day of joy and thanksgiving for him, filled with religious significance. It seemed to him that his new neighbors had little understanding of what the day commemorated or how they should celebrate.

Some of the most disturbing practices Washington observed in the homes and cabins he visited around the holiday were those left over from Christmas celebrations during slavery. Christmas was often the only holiday slaves had all year. The vacation lasted from a day or two to a full week. Because it was one of the few times slaves were allowed off their owners' land in large numbers, many slaves were married at Christmas, and it was a time to celebrate weddings, anniversaries, and to visit with children and other relatives owned by neighboring families.

Washington later wrote:

> The male members of the race, and often the female members, were expected to get drunk.... Persons who at other times did not use strong drink thought it quite the proper thing to indulge in it rather freely during the Christmas week.... The sacredness of the season seemed to have been almost wholly lost sight of.

Washington visited poor families who probably worked as share-croppers on the plantation of their former owners. In one cabin he noticed that "all that the five children had to remind them of the coming of the Christ child was a single bunch of firecrackers." In another home he found "nothing but a new jug of cheap, mean whiskey, which the husband and wife were making free use of, notwithstanding the fact that the husband was one of the local ministers."

From the first Christmas his school was in session, Washington made a particular effort to teach his students the true meaning of Christmas and appropriate ways to observe it.

Once he had secured the land for his school, Washington decided that his next step would be to establish an agricultural program. Eighty-five percent of Alabama's black residents earned their living as farmers; Washington felt strongly that practical training in farming was part of his responsibility to his students. Besides, farming duties gave the students a way to work off their living expenses, which almost none of them could afford for the whole school year even with free tuition. (In fact, enrollment had stalled at around eighty because as new students continued to arrive, others came to Washington with tears in their eyes to announce that their board and expense money had run out, and they would have to quit.) Furthermore, as he pragmatically observed, "we wanted something to eat."

As with his tree-clearing plans the previous fall, at first Washington met resistance from the students, who still were suspicious about any "school" that would put them back in the field. But again Washington's spirit won them over. He had planned to plant cotton for sale but soon discovered that the land was too sandy for a healthy crop of it and sowed vegetables and grain instead.

With the spring planting underway in 1882, Washington turned his attention to funding a permanent building for the school. He was eager to see his pupils enjoying comfortable, modern facilities; eager as well to establish a boarding school so he could guide the social development of the students as well as their book learning. A girl who could read Greek but knew nothing about how to set a table properly, Washington thought, would have but little success in the world.

In less than a year, Washington had become a respected member of the Tuskegee community. His school enjoyed broad support in Macon County, and he had even been appointed the only black member of the county school textbook selection committee. The local newspaper, which had originally opposed establishment of the school, proudly carried the news that Washington was beginning a campaign to raise money for a new building with six classrooms, an assembly hall, offices, library, and dormitories for boys (in the basement) and girls (in the attic). The total cost would be about three thousand dollars, with a tenth of that required to prepare the foundation and lay the cornerstone.

Washington scheduled the laying of the cornerstone as part of a ceremony commemorating the last day of class. (Since there were no seniors, there was no "graduation" as such.) The event drew a large crowd of blacks and whites, some who rode into town from the outlying plantations and farms hours ahead of the appointed ten o'clock starting time. The weather was clear and mild as the crowd gathered at the African Methodist Episcopal Zion Church where the first classes had been held. After an hour and a half of recitations, the students, parents, visitors from Hampton Institute, local officials and townspeople marched through town to the new school property. When they arrived at the site where the students had dug the foundation for the new building, many laid souvenirs beneath the spot where the cornerstone would be placed.

Waddy Thompson, the superintendent of Macon County schools, gave an address praising Washington's work, calling him an "able and efficient Principal," and declaring, "No defense is cheaper to a community or commonwealth than education.... Expenditures for education will lessen the demands for charity and correction." Thompson concluded by wishing Washington Godspeed and trusting that "this building and its labors may indeed prove a blessing to his race."

After the speech there was a country style "dinner on the ground," a picnic under the trees made up of food and refreshments the merrymakers had brought with them. After lunch, past the heat of the day, the crowd returned to the church for more recitations. Then Reverend C. C. Petty, a pastor from Montgomery's largest black church, gave an inspiring address, followed by a speech from a white Tuskegee pastor. Reverend Petty's words in particular drew Washington's thoughts to the miracle he was witnessing:

"I thank God for what I have witnessed today," Petty said, "something I never saw before, nor did I ever expect to see it. I have seen one who but yesterday was one of our owners, today lay the cornerstone of a building dedicated to the education of my race. For such a change let us all thank God."

As shouted echoes of amen resounded through the crowd, Washington reflected on the fact that only about sixteen years before, "no Negro could be taught from books without the teacher receiving the condemnation of the law or of public sentiment.... About the corner-stone were gathered the teachers, the students, their parents and friends, the county officials—who were white—and all the leading white men in that vicinity, together with many of the black men and women whom these same white people but a few years before had held a title to as property."

The proceedings concluded with all present joining in to sing the doxology:

> *Praise God from whom all blessings flow,*
> *Praise Him all creatures here below,*
> *Praise Him above ye heavenly host,*
> *Praise Father, Son, and Holy Ghost.*

As the last note died away to be replaced by a heartfelt cheer, dignitaries, students, and visitors alike crowded around Washington and his staff of two—John Cardwell and Olivia Davidson—shaking hands, wishing them well, and calling down all of heaven's blessings on them and their enterprise.

Students began construction of the building immediately, and Miss Davidson traveled north in hopes of using her contacts to secure donations for it. Though the state provided an annual appropriation, none of it was for land or buildings. Any classroom for the black students at Tuskegee would come only through a combination of student labor and generous philanthropy.

Washington worried constantly about failing. He feared that if his school failed, it would be a sign that black people were incapable of educating themselves. He later said:

> I knew that, in a large degree we were trying an experiment—that of testing whether or not it was possible for Negroes to build up and control the affairs of a large educational institution. I knew that if we failed it would injure the whole race. I knew that the presumption was against us. I knew that in the case of white people beginning such an enterprise it would be taken for granted that they were going to succeed, but in our case I felt that people would be surprised if we succeeded. All this made a burden which pressed down on us, sometimes, it seemed, at the rate of a thousand pounds to the square inch.

Washington's students were so poor that even with free tuition many of them could not afford room and board for more than a few months at a time, nor could their families spare them from working in the fields or at labor because the money was needed at home. He wanted to hire the best teachers he could get and have adequate facilities for his students to live on campus, but the shortage of money was an unending concern.

Olivia Davidson was a young woman of great intellectual gifts and with a subdued yet tenacious spirit. She had been born to a slave woman on a Virginia plantation in 1854. Her father was almost certainly white, and Olivia herself was fair-skinned enough to pass for a white person. After completing her studies at Hampton and in Framingham, Massachusetts, she was advised by well-meaning friends to live as a white among the strangers of the North. She declined, saying she was proud to be a black woman and had no plans to forsake her race. (Though she, like Washington, was a mulatto—and therefore as much white as black—she fell under the laws and traditions that categorized people as "colored" or "Negro" if they were as much as one-eighth black.)

Combining her pride in Tuskegee and its mission with the poise she acquired at Framingham, Olivia made a favorable impression on prospective donors. After a stop at Hampton on her first fundraising trip, she traveled to Boston by coastal steamer. Her first donation was a check for fifty dollars from a lady she met on board. After arriving in New England, Olivia walked from door to door through affluent neighborhoods soliciting contributions. Usually, her ring was answered by a servant who invited her to wait in the hall, then took her calling card up to the lady of the house. Some days yielded hundreds of dollars, while others produced nothing. The work was grueling, and on at least one occasion the lady she called upon came into the entry hall to find Olivia sound asleep on the sofa. Some nights she was so exhausted by her work that she fell into bed fully dressed.

Her checks from progressive white New Englanders were a godsend to Washington, who often received them just in time to pay a debt or purchase critical supplies for the building under way. General Samuel Chapman Armstrong, founder and president of Hampton Institute, continued to send personal contributions and guarantees from Hampton. Local merchants donated some supplies; townspeople gave what money they could, and those without money to give offered days of labor or contributions in kind. One old former slave arrived at a fundraising rally with a big hog. Standing in the midst of the crowd, he announced he had raised two fine hogs and was donating one of them to the building fund. Washington remembered the old black man's closing challenge that any black person "that's got any love for his race, or any respect for himself, will bring a hog to the next meeting."

At the end of April, Washington followed Olivia Davidson north on a fund-raising trip of his own. He had proven himself to the white leadership of Macon County and now set out to see whether he could be as convincing to the white New Englanders for whom the legacy of slavery and the question of black education were abstractions for the most part. En route to Farmington, Connecticut, he carried a letter of introduction from Henry Clay Armstrong, Alabama state superintendent of schools, with endorsements from Governor Cobb, George W. Campbell, and Waddy Thompson, recommending Washington as "a *gentleman*," with hopes that "he may meet with success in this enterprise."

Washington met with businessmen, philanthropists, and ministers to explain his mission and solicit contributions. Some refused (including one of the Merriam brothers, publishers of Webster's dictionary, who said he was "too poor" to help Washington), and many gave gifts of two to five dollars. Occasionally, Washington would get a check for a hundred dollars.

Washington was alternately optimistic and gloomy about his efforts, though always buoyed by invitations to speak, which were extended frequently by churches and community groups. His approach to "the Negro problem"—how whites and blacks could coexist peacefully in the post-slavery era—was novel and appealing because it assigned responsibility for educating blacks to blacks themselves. Black audiences heard responsibility and empowerment in his words; whites saw a solution that cost little, promised much, and indicated early signs of success.

Washington and Olivia Davidson continued to travel separately, canvassing different cities and sending contributions back to Tuskegee. Washington met with John Fox Slater, a Connecticut textile merchant who had recently endowed his Slater Fund for Negro Education with a million dollars. The industrialist explained the fund and told Washington there was a fair chance Tuskegee would receive something from it. By the time they returned to Alabama, Washington and Davidson had collected more than three thousand dollars—enough to finish their new building—plus a pledge of tin for the roof from Phelps, Dodge and Company in New York.

Washington came back to Tuskegee a married man. His bride was Fanny Norton Smith, a recent Hampton graduate. They were married on August 2, 1882, and moved to a large house near the Tuskegee campus where Fanny set up housekeeping and provided room and board for teachers.

Washington had met Fanny when she was his pupil in West Virginia. He was the teacher in the black Tinkersville community in Malden, and she was the only girl out of eighty or more pupils in the day school. Her light brown skin and high cheekbones gave evidence of an Indian branch on the family tree. Washington had given her special tutoring to help her secure a scholarship to Hampton. She worked to earn her expenses, and spent the 1878–79 and 1879–80 school years teaching to work off her debt to the school, reenrolling in the fall of 1880. She had saved the money by walking three miles each way to her teaching job every day.

Construction of Tuskegee's first building continued through the summer with students donating their labor, and contributions continuing to come in from near and far. The students had changed their opinion of work, at least as it related to the new classrooms. The previous fall their teacher had picked up an axe and headed for the woods himself in an effort to convince them they should help clear land for planting when they thought they should be learning how to keep away from manual labor instead. Washington's unwavering vision was for his students, boys and girls alike, to see intellectual development as a companion to practical skills, not a substitute for them.

The message was beginning to take hold. Students could see that without their work, they would not have any sort of school. In addition, their labor gave them the satisfaction of paying their board and expenses. Early every morning a team of students, all in clean clothes and properly groomed, assembled at the building site. There were no overalls to be seen, no ragged work clothes. These men and boys worked in crisp white shirts, some with neckties; their hats were brushed and their shoes shined. Carpentry work was as noble as any other pursuit, and these eager students were dressed for the part.

A Tuskegee merchant provided some lumber on credit with the rest cut on the property by students. The black townspeople continued to bring in a handful of eggs, a chicken or two, or whatever they had, to contribute to an enterprise that had become a great symbol of progress in their eyes. Barrels of donated clothing came from the North. Sometimes Miss Davidson would select a pair of socks from one of them to give to a student worker who was obviously in need; most were sold to raise money. Student-craftsmen toiled long days through the hot Alabama summer without pay or the hope of pay, sweat dripping from their eyes and soaking their clothes. They were building the future; no task was too hard.

Well-meaning critics warned Washington that a building put up by inexperienced students was likely to be rough, rickety, and uncomfortable. There was some truth in their predictions: Blackboards made by students during the previous year seldom had squared corners or finished edges. But they had served their purpose, had cost little, and had given a class of young carpenters experience and confidence. Washington was determined to stick with his idea. "I told those who doubted the wisdom of the plan that I knew that our first building would not be so comfortable or so complete in its finish as buildings erected by the experienced hands of outside workmen, but that in the teaching of civilization, self-help, and self-reliance, the erection of the building by the students themselves would more than compensate for any lack of comfort or fine finish."

The structure was named Porter Hall in honor of Alfred Haynes Porter, a Brooklyn industrialist who had made the largest single gift to the building fund. As it went up on the outskirts of Tuskegee, the amateur construction crew made various modifications in its design. True to the predictions of some, the building had some deficiencies. There were rooms for the students, but no dining hall for them to eat in; no kitchen and no laundry to produce the clean clothes Washington considered a part of their education. The girls' dormitory was still planned for the top floor, but the lower floor, where the boys were to have been quartered, was reconfigured into a dining hall, kitchen, and laundry. Boys would be boarded in private homes and hotels around the campus.

By the time its tin roof was installed, Porter Hall was taller than the courthouse and was, in fact, the tallest building in the county. It was far from handsome; some said it looked more like a barn than a school building. But it was the symbol of pride and accomplishment Washington so wanted. And it was a permanent home for the school he envisioned, a warm, dry place to teach and learn.

Porter Hall was still unfinished when the new school year began, and almost a hundred students squeezed into the old buildings on the first day of class. As summer gave way to autumn, Washington began developing the idea of holding a Thanksgiving service in the second floor chapel of Porter Hall as a way of marking the official completion of the project. He invited Robert C. Bedford, the white minister of a black Congregational church in Montgomery, to preach a sermon that day. Washington and Bedford, who was from Wisconsin, had never met, but Bedford's sympathy with Washington's wish that blacks improve and educate themselves made him an enthusiastic participant in the Thanksgiving service. He later joined Tuskegee's board of trustees.

Most blacks in Macon County had never been to a Thanksgiving service. Though the first Thanksgiving observance was shared by the Pilgrims and Indians at Plymouth Colony in 1621, it had been observed only sporadically until President Washington issued a national proclamation in 1789 declaring it a day of prayer and thanksgiving to God by people of every religious denomination. The ecumenical aspect of the day appealed to Booker Washington's nondenominational Christian beliefs. It would have additional meaning for his black audience, in that it was President Lincoln who had established a national Thanksgiving holiday in November, first celebrated in 1863, the year of Emancipation.

The student laborers had missed their early fall target date for completing Porter Hall and, in spite of great effort, the building was still unfinished on Thanksgiving Day. Nevertheless, the chapel was finished enough to hold a service, and students, parents, visitors, and guests once again assembled to mark a milestone in the history of the school. Citizens of both races took delight in the building, admiring its unpainted walls and unadorned exterior. Plain though it was, designed and built by amateurs, Porter Hall would serve the students of Tuskegee for more than twenty years. To Washington and the rest of the grateful assembly, the sight of this building made it a day of Thanksgiving they would never forget.

CHAPTER TWO

The Promised Land

One of the dilapidated original outbuildings on the Bowen property, used by the school for several months as a classroom, had once been the plantation kitchen. The sight of this simple building must have awakened bittersweet memories in Booker T. Washington's heart. For it was in a similar place on a plantation near Hale's Ford, Franklin County, Virginia, that Booker was born. He thought the year was 1858 or 1859, though the family Bible of his owner recorded the birthdate as April 5, 1856. He remembered his childhood home as a log slave cabin fourteen by sixteen feet with a dirt floor, a few pieces of primitive furniture, and a small square hole in one corner near the floor for the family cat to slip in and out. In the center of the room, covered with a few boards, was a storage pit for the master's sweet potatoes.

The most prominent feature of Booker's first home was an enormous fireplace where a great fire burned year round. Jane, Booker's mother, was the plantation cook. Her cabin doubled as the kitchen where she prepared three meals daily for her owner, James Burroughs, his wife, and the seven of their fourteen children still living at home, as well as meals for all the slaves. With unglazed windows and a small, ill-fitting door on sagging hinges, the cabin was drafty in winter in spite of the ever-present fire.

Summer turned the whole room into a furnace as Jane toiled at her pots and skillets.

Booker was the second of Jane's three children. He had an older brother, John, and a younger sister, Amanda. Neither Booker nor his brother ever knew who their father was or whether the same man had fathered them both. Jane never mentioned the subject to Booker; he never even knew his father's name. The man was almost certainly a white neighbor of the Burroughs's. One possibility was Thomas Benjamin Ferguson, a twenty-five-year-old bachelor who lived across the road from Jane's owner and who was notorious for his drunkenness and immorality. Another man with both opportunity and inclination was Thomas's father, Josiah, who was known to have fathered a number of mulatto children, some by slave mistresses.

A third prospect, the one most frequently cited by Booker's descendants in later years, was Benjamin Hatcher, James Burroughs's nephew. Ben was a business partner with his brother-in-law, John Cardwell Ferguson, Josiah's older son. Ferguson and Hatcher employed a number of slaves in their tobacco and blacksmithing businesses. According to some members of the family, Jane once ran away from the Burroughs farm and was detained by Hatcher at his house. By the time the Burroughs got her back, she was pregnant.

Booker never expressed any resentment toward his father. "Whoever he was," he later wrote, "I never heard of his taking the least interest in me or providing in any way for my rearing. But I do not find especial fault with him. He was simply another unfortunate victim of the institution which the Nation unhappily had engrafted upon it at that time."

The Burroughs farm was not a classic Virginia plantation with field after field surrounding a white-columned mansion. The family home was a log house covered in weatherboarding with three rooms downstairs and two in the eaves. The property was a 207-acre tract near Hale's Ford, where the family raised tobacco as their main cash crop.

There was a regular rhythm to the season beginning when delicate tobacco plants were coaxed up from seeds in early spring. Transplanted, then carefully tended as the days grew longer and warmer, the plants grew until late summer or early fall when their large, limp leaves turned from dark green to light green and yellow, lower leaves changing first followed by upper ones in turn. The leaves were then carefully picked, tied into "hands," and hung in curing barns until around Christmas, when their sale afforded the opportunity of settling cash accounts with the merchants in Hale's Ford and buy a few modest luxuries as well.

Burroughs also raised vegetables, cereal grains, flax, and a few cows, sheep, and hogs for the family's use, making them very nearly self-supporting, though far from wealthy. They also owned ten slaves, including Booker (valued in 1861 at $400), his mother ($250), his brother and sister ($550 and $200, respectively), and his mother's half-sister Sophia ($250).

By 1860, Booker's mother had married Washington, a slave owned by Josiah Ferguson, and given birth to Booker's sister Amanda. In keeping with laws and customs of the time, Jane and Washington continued to live with their respective masters even after their marriage, visiting each other with permission of both owners during the Christmas holidays and at other times by request. Jane and her three children made their home in the kitchen cabin, where the children slept each night atop a pile of rags on the same dirt floor where all three had been born. Washington, considered a malcontent by his owner, was hired out at various times for labor in saltworks, tobacco factories, and on a railroad construction crew. The children eagerly awaited Washington's Christmas visits, anticipating the stories he always told them about his adventures in far off places.

Her duties at the hearth left Jane little time to tend to her own family, and Booker and his siblings seldom ate a meal together. Rattling around in surroundings that were always greasy, smoky, and dirty, the children scrounged a bit of cornbread or bacon whenever they could. Booker sometimes ate the boiled corn he was given to take out to the hogs. He also occasionally helped himself to one of the sweet potatoes stored so tantalizingly close in the pit beneath his cabin floor, and roasted it in the giant fireplace. One of his earliest memories was of his mother waking him, John, and Amanda in the middle of the night to eat a chicken she had stolen from the master's yard and cooked while they slept.

The one time each year Booker and the other slaves had plenty to eat was in early December when hogs were killed to supply salt pork for the year. The sides of meat were scalded in large vats, then butchered and salted in huge wooden troughs. Masters were expected to share the meat generously with their slaves; those who did not were considered skinflints by whites and slaves alike.

Booker was a young boy at the time of Emancipation, still too young to work in the fields. (The Burroughs did not grow cotton, which protected their slaves from the harsh work of plantations farther south.) Booker cleaned the yards, carried water to men working in the fields, and took corn once a week to be ground at a mill three miles from the farm. On these trips Booker walked beside the horse carrying corn in a large sack draped across its back. Often the corn would shift to one side in the sack and tumble off the horse. Too small to lift the sack himself, Booker waited—sometimes hours—for a passerby to help him. When this made him late in returning home, he knew he could expect a tongue-lashing or worse when he finally arrived. He was flogged on occasion, and he had seen grown slaves tied naked to trees and flogged for the slightest infractions. The master's power was absolute, and without his mercy the slave had no recourse whatever.

Booker also had other duties from time to time. Occasionally he was summoned to the master's house to fan the flies in the dining room while the family ate. Then, as always, he wore his only article of clothing: a long homespun flax shirt. Putting it on new was one of Booker's most vivid memories of his years as a slave. It was coarse and torturously scratchy. Seeing his misery, Booker's brother, John, wore the shirt for him as a favor until it softened with wear. It was only during his last year or so of slavery that Booker had a pair of shoes. They had hickory plank bottoms and leather tops; he received them in his Christmas stocking and took great pride in clunking around in them.

Another of Booker's occasional chores was to accompany one of his owner's daughters, Laura Burroughs, to the rural Franklin County school-house where she taught. Booker would ride behind her, bring her horse back to the farm for the day's work, and return with it after school so she could ride home.

Though Booker played with his master's children, he was not allowed to learn with them because it was against the law in Virginia to teach a slave to read. Booker watched his playmates through the schoolhouse window, consumed with curiosity about what they were doing, and all the more interested because it had the allure of forbidden fruit.

Two boyhood experiences made Booker aware that he was something called a slave. The first was bits and pieces of information he picked up from the white people's dinner conversation about the prospect of war as he stood fanning flies from their plates. The second was overhearing his mother's prayers late at night for President Lincoln and freedom. Though no slaves in the household could read, news about Lincoln's election in 1860 and the resulting prospect for war traveled faster through the black community than through the white.

A prime source for recent news came from whichever slave went to Hale's Ford to pick up the mail. Standing in Asa Holland's general store, where the mail came in from the county seat at Rocky Mount, an attentive listener could gather a great deal of information from the whites as they stood around trading opinions about what they had read in the newspaper and in their own letters that day. On his way to deliver the mail to the own-er's house, the messenger would inevitably stop at the slave cabins first, giving his own people the latest news ahead of their masters.

Fort Sumter was shelled in April of 1861, and the battle between North and South began. Three months later, James Burroughs died. His sons soon went off to fight for Virginia, five of them in the Franklin Rangers under General Robert E. Lee's great cavalry commander, General Jeb Stuart. The women of the household were left largely on their own to supervise and discipline the slaves, tend to the tobacco business, and learn to manage without coffee, sugar, and other accustomed luxuries.

The first two Burroughs men to ride with the Franklin Rangers gave their lives for the cause. Billy was killed in battle at Kelly's Ford on the Rappahannock in the spring of 1863, and his brother Frank died a Union prisoner. Ben was wounded at Gettysburg, and the youngest brother, Edwin, was wounded at Nance's Shop, a small settlement in Virginia, shot in the rump as he ran from the battlefield. Tom Burroughs survived unharmed and eventually became a successful businessman and landowner after the war.

Though there was no fighting near Hale's Ford, Union troops began marching through the area in the spring of 1865. Booker's brother, John, had driven the women of the household to church on the first day Yankees were spotted. When word came that the Northern scouts were visible up the road, John later recalled, "The preacher stopped preaching and everybody got down to praying. I never heard so many people praying at one time before or since." The soldiers, about a hundred in all, passed by without disturbing the service. More astonishing to the worshipers, the invaders didn't even steal their horses.

At the same time war was tearing at the fabric of American society, it also divided Virginians. Appalachian mountaineers of western Virginia had petitioned the Continental Congress for permission to form their own government as early as 1776. When the Virginia state legislature voted to secede from the Union in 1861, many westerners loyal to the Union began a concerted effort to separate themselves from the Confederacy. West Virginia was admitted to the United States on June 20, 1863, and immediately became a natural haven for escaped slaves.

One well-traveled black man who had his sights on freedom in the west was Booker's stepfather, Washington. He had been working at the salt furnaces in the Kanawah River Valley during the early months of the war. When it became clear that the valley would soon be part of West Virginia—a separate, free state—Washington's owner brought him back to work at a chewing tobacco factory in Lynchburg. In 1864, General David Hunter led a Union raid on the Lynchburg area. When he returned to Northern territory, many slaves went with him, including Washington, who returned to work in the Kanawah furnaces as a free man.

On the Burroughs plantation, rumors began flying through the slave cabins that freedom was soon to come. One day word came that something big would happen the next day. Early the following morning, all slaves were ordered to the main house. The Burroughs explained to the slaves that they were now free. A stranger from the Union read the Emancipation Proclamation aloud to the assembled group. As the meaning of the words sank in, Booker's mother, with tears of joy running down her cheeks, leaned over and kissed him and her other children. "She explained to us what it all meant," Booker later remembered, "that this was the day for which she had been so long praying, but fearing that she would never live to see."

Slaves who had moments ago been property, who had defended their master's land and livelihood against Northern invaders, hiding livestock in the woods and burying silver in the garden out of a mixed sense of loyalty, confusion, and fear, found themselves free in an instant to do as they pleased. The initial reaction was "wild rejoicing," but exhilaration soon changed to concern as the former slaves considered how to find their place in the world and how they would earn a living.

Booker's impression of the moment remained burned into his memory and influenced his behavior for the rest of his life. Looking back years later, he wrote:

> In a few hours the great questions with which the Anglo-Saxon race had been grappling for centuries had been thrown upon these people to be solved. These were the questions of a home, a living, the rearing of children, education, citizenship, and the establishment and support of churches.

Booker's stepfather soon sent for his wife and children, and the family left the Burroughs farm, their friends, Virginia, and the only world they had ever known for a new life of freedom.

It was about two hundred miles from Hale's Ford to the salt furnaces of Malden, West Virginia, on the Kanawah River, where Washington worked filling barrels with salt for shipment to commercial meat packers. Washington, or "Wash" as he was more often known, somehow procured a wagon and two horses for his family's move. They loaded their small stock of household goods on board, and Jane climbed up as well. Unable to walk long distances, she rode the whole way; her children alternately rode with her in the wagon and walked. Most nights they cooked over a campfire and slept under the stars. One night Jane found an abandoned cabin and, settling the household inside, built a comforting fire in the fireplace. The heat aroused a snake sleeping in the chimney. It dropped into the room, scattering the family and forcing them outside once again.

Jane found her husband living not in the black settlement of Tinkersville, but in an integrated neighborhood in Malden proper. Washington was known locally as Wash Ferguson. Typically slaves were given first names by their masters and had no family names at all. After Emancipation many of them adopted the last names of their owners; this Wash had done.

As poor as his home in Virginia had been, Booker's new one was even worse. Cramped and bare as it had been, the farm cabin at least caught fresh breezes and the welcoming smells of the countryside—wildflowers, clover, fresh-turned earth, the lilies planted around the walks of the master's house. His new home was jammed in among a crowded cluster of others, and surrounded by reeking outhouses and standing sewage. At the farm there had been room to spread out, room to play, and friends to play with. Their new neighborhood was packed with disagreeable examples of both races, and Booker recalled later that, "drinking, gambling, quarrels, fights, and shockingly immoral practices were frequent."

The combination of a disastrous flood in 1861 and four years of war had greatly reduced the once-impressive salt works at Malden. Availability of salt from new sources closer to the meat packing plants further west had also hurt their business. But the business lumbered on, as much through inertia as anything else. Water from salt springs was piped into furnaces, boiled, and the salt residue collected at the end of the day. Wash soon had both John and Booker working with him, often beginning as early as 4 A.M., and pocketed their meager wages himself to help support the family.

Two incidents during Booker's time at the salt works further raised his curiosity about reading and learning, which had been so aroused as he watched his white playmates in Hale's Ford studying in a schoolroom that was off-limits to him. The first was the regular practice of the foreman of coming around at the end of each work day to mark Wash's identifying number on the barrels of salt he had packed. His number was "18," and by watching the foreman write it on the barrels every day, Booker soon learned how to write it himself. He didn't know any other numbers or letters or exactly what "18" meant, but he wrote it anyway for practice. It was the first writing experience of his life.

The second event was his mother's purchase of a Webster's blue-backed speller for him. Somehow Jane Ferguson had scraped together enough money for one and gave it to him. He saw it as the key to his dream of getting an education. But try as he might, he couldn't make heads or tails of the lessons. There were all sorts of word combinations, but no matter how hard he studied, Booker could not figure out on his own how the letters went together or how to pronounce them. He enlisted his mother's help, but even the two of them together could not deduce from Webster's lessons how spelling worked.

Booker's frustration was relieved by the appearance of a young black man from Ohio, where educating blacks was not illegal. As soon as the black residents of Malden learned the newcomer could read, they persuaded him to read the newspaper aloud to them every day after work. Seeing the man holding his newspaper high in the middle of an excited and appreciative crowd made Booker envious and all the more eager to learn. The boy became one of the regulars, stopping by to hear the news on his way home from the salt works.

Not long afterward, Lewis Davis, another young black Ohioan, arrived in town and agreed to set up a school for blacks. Without any support from the white residents or the government, black families raised the money to pay the young man and took turns boarding him in their homes.

Reverend Lewis Rice, pastor of the African Zion Baptist Church in Tinkersville, invited the community to turn his home into a schoolhouse, removing the bed from his bedroom and replacing it with benches for thirty or more students. Though illiterate himself, Rice recognized the value of an education for newly freed slaves and worked enthusiastically to establish schools for them.

Reverend Rice was also Booker's first pastor. Booker had grown up hearing his mother pray, but evidently he had not had any formal religious training until one Sunday morning when an old black gentleman interrupted him during a game of marbles with his friends in the middle of the main street. The man warned the boys that they should be in church instead of playing marbles on the Sabbath and exhorted them to mend their ways and follow Jesus. Young Booker was so convicted by the message, he stopped playing marbles on the spot and followed the old man to worship.

The church was Reverend Rice's, meeting in the same bedroom that would shortly hold the school. Booker began attending regularly, and his whole family soon followed. Reverend Rice baptized Booker a short time later, and the young boy quickly got involved in every aspect of the church.

Booker hoped to begin school under Mr. Davis in Reverend Rice's converted bedroom/church/schoolroom, but Wash decided he could not afford to let his son quit working. Booker passed the school every day on the way to and from the salt furnaces, longing to join the other students but recognizing it was all but impossible. The whole time class was in session, Booker worked with his stepfather, pounding salt into wooden casks with mallets so each cask would make its required weight. From his position in the packing shed, he could watch the other children going to and from class.

Day after day, Booker longed to join Mr. Davis's class, and he was overjoyed to hear that Davis planned to open a night school for adults. To his delight, Booker was accepted for admission. He spent his days at the shipping dock with anticipation, knowing that every stroke of his mallet brought him closer to class time. Even after a long and tiring day at the furnace, Booker was an eager and animated student. Still he wanted more time for study than night school allowed, and his mother wanted it for him. After repeated requests from both Booker and Jane, Wash finally agreed to allow Booker to go to day school. But the boy had to work from 4 A.M. until 9 A.M., when school began, then return to the furnace after school and work two more hours.

This presented a daunting logistical challenge. Booker had to work until nine o'clock every morning, and school, which was a mile from the salt works, started at the same time. That meant he was late to class every day. He solved the problem in the short run by sneaking into the salt works office and moving the clock hands forward half an hour. He was never caught, but the foreman eventually locked the clock in a glass case.

It was in school that Booker, as a boy of ten or so, finally acquired his full name. When he was a slave his name was just Booker, perhaps after Bowker Preston, his mother's first owner. In fact, his name had been originally written "Bowker" in one inventory of James Burroughs's property, then scratched out and "Booker" written instead. He got his last name when he enrolled in school and Mr. Davis asked him his father's name. "Washington," the boy replied. And so Booker Washington became his name. Some time later he added the middle name Taliaferro (pronounced "Tolliver") after a prominent family from Rocky Mount, Virginia, that his mother admired. Booker once said that his mother gave him Taliaferro as a second name when he was a baby but had stopped using it.

It wasn't long before Wash Ferguson changed his mind about his son's schooling and compelled him to return to the salt works full time. Booker resumed his night school attendance and sought out other educated people in addition to Mr. Davis to help him with his lessons at the end of the day.

As the salt industry continued its gradual decline in the Kanawah Valley, Booker was reassigned from the packing shed to the coal mine that supplied fuel for the furnaces. Salt packing had been hard and monotonous work; coal mining was all that and dangerous besides. Fatal gas explosions were common underground, and there was a constant threat of cave-ins. When his lamp blew out, Booker would find himself stranded in pitch-darkness until someone came along who could relight his lamp. Still determined to learn, he took his blue-backed speller into the mine shaft with him and read by lamplight whenever he could steal a moment.

One day at work he overheard the news that the mine owner's wife was looking for a new houseboy. Booker resolved to apply for the job at once. Though he was only eleven or twelve and had absolutely no experience as a household servant, the boy was convinced it would give him educational opportunities he was unlikely to find working in a hillside coal mine and living in a fetid Malden shack.

General Lewis Ruffner owned both the mine and the salt works. Ruffner had served in the Virginia legislature and originally opposed the establishment of West Virginia but had also served in the legislature of the new state as a delegate to its constitutional convention. Lewis was the first white child born in Charleston, and his family was among the first to develop the salt springs and coal mines of the region. His second wife, Viola, had come from Vermont after his first wife's death to serve as governess for his children, and later accepted his offer of marriage.

Her Northern reserve was in stark contrast to the effusive and outgoing personalities shared by the general and his household. The general's children thought she was cold and overbearing and disliked her intensely. To some extent she returned the sentiments and felt profoundly unhappy and uncomfortable around them.

Viola Ruffner was a stickler for detail. Her own son was a cadet at West Point, and her Yankee coolness made her appear fearfully exacting. It was likely more than appearance, as she had gone through an alarming number of houseboys since her arrival in Malden without finding one who could satisfy her demands. When he interviewed for the job and for a while afterward, young Booker shook involuntarily in fear whenever he was in her presence. Nevertheless, he eagerly accepted the job at a salary of five dollars per month, which went directly to his stepfather.

Booker's keen intellect and powers of observation allowed him to meet Viola Ruffner's standards when so many others had failed. He realized she had notions about behavior, cleanliness, manners, and propriety that she saw no reason to change. He began to see there were predictable ways of pleasing her, and that if he was diligent about maintaining her unwavering standards, she would be satisfied. Booker recalled later that he learned first of all that his new employer "wanted everything kept clean about her, that she wanted things done promptly and systematically, and that at the bottom of everything she wanted absolute honesty and frankness. Nothing must be slovenly or slipshod; every door, every fence, must be kept in repair."

From being literally terrified of her, Booker gradually came to admire Mrs. Ruffner and her sense of order. Eventually he became the most satisfactory houseboy she had had since moving to Malden. There were rough spots along the way, though, and several times Booker, weary of Mrs. Ruffner's constant correction, ran away. Once he shipped out on a riverboat for Cincinnati as a dining steward. It didn't take long for the captain to realize his new waiter knew nothing about serving at table. Booker was fired, but he persuaded the captain to let him ride on to Cincinnati and back to Malden, where he returned to Mrs. Ruffner and begged her forgiveness. Eager to have her most promising servant back, Viola Ruffner accepted his apology and put him to work immediately.

Booker's occasional departures from the Ruffner household reminded him of what an advantage it was for him to be there. For one thing, he was surrounded by books. His mother had barely managed to come up with the money for his one speller, and in the Ruffner house books seemed to line the walls of every room. Mrs. Ruffner allowed Booker to read when he had finished his duties and even gave him some books, which the boy proudly shelved in his own "library" made out of a wooden crate.

Booker was also attracted by the very standards of punctuality and cleanliness that seemed so daunting at first. Wash Ferguson's shack and the entire rancid neighborhood around it were periodically flooded by the Kanawah River, sending residents scurrying like rats through the mud and filth to salvage their meager belongings. In the Ruffner house, one of the finest in Malden and positioned on high ground, everything was clean, orderly, and correct. When he began his service as a houseboy, Booker went back to the Ferguson cabin every night; later he began spending the night at the Ruffner home and eventually moved in with them permanently.

The Ruffners' trust in Booker grew, and he was steadily given more responsibility. Viola had a big vegetable garden and taught Booker how to cultivate it, gradually leaving the whole job largely to him. Booker took the surplus vegetables into town to sell and, to his employers' delight, accounted for every penny collected in sales and brought the leftovers back.

Viola Ruffner encouraged Booker in his studies by going over his lessons with him and by allowing him to attend Mr. Davis's school once in a while. Booker made further progress by hiring students for a few pennies to come by the Ruffner home at night and teach him what they had learned in school that day. While he was learning grammar and spelling, Booker found he was learning how to get along in the world as well. He felt the first small sense of assurance that even a former slave could make a success of himself, and he began to think commitment and hard work could transport him to a higher station in life, in spite of people's presumptions and perceptions of his race. Mrs. Ruffner taught him both by word and deed that "the difference in social conditions is principally the result of intelligent energy."

Booker began to identify more with the fine surroundings and polite manners of the Ruffners and their friends than with the lifestyle of his own family and their neighbors. He wasn't attracted to them because they were white, but because they represented his newly formed ideal of order, responsibility, and propriety.

Still, he was a black boy in a time and place when black boys were not particularly welcome among many of the small town elite whose lives Booker found so appealing. Three weeks before Christmas in 1869 the Ku Klux Klan came to the defense of a white man in Malden who had lost a fight with a black man, then been served with a warrant for swearing publicly at him after losing. The Klan boasted that the black man would never appear in court to testify. As the black man and his friends approached the courthouse the next day, the white man and his supporters ordered them to leave. A short gun battle followed, which attracted the attention of General Ruffner. White and black retreated in opposite directions, and the general, with Booker following behind him, led the blacks back in an attempt to restore order. As he began to address the whites, the general was knocked unconscious by a thrown brick and the gunfire resumed, surrounding Booker with scenes of race-induced hatred. Miraculously, no one was killed, the mob shortly dispersed, and a grand jury eventually disposed of the matter.

Booker refused to accept his race as a stumbling block to improving himself, but it was his race that kept him out of any school other than Mr. Davis's modest operation in Reverend Rice's bedroom. The federal government was putting a program in place to fund schools for black people, but the idea was none too popular in Malden. The Freedmen's Bureau, a government agency to aid former slaves, had sent a white representative named Charles W. Sharp to tour the Kanawah Valley and meet with local boards of education about setting up schools for their black citizens. The board in Malden explained that it had spent all its money building schools for white children and had none left for blacks.

Sharp got a two-hundred dollar grant from the Freedmen's Bureau for each of three proposed school buildings and raised one hundred ten dollars more from black residents of Tinkersville and Malden. The school board as a group was unmoved, though Sharp found he could convince individual members of the value of black education when he spoke with them privately. The trouble was that no matter what they promised him confidentially, in board meetings they always came out against supporting schools for blacks. "Some favor the education of freedmen in theory," he observed, "but do not choose to encounter the violent prejudice of the community, by any positive action." By 1868 the black residents had built a school building of their own and supported it mostly by public subscription. What government funding there was had been partially diverted by the school board, which underreported the number of black pupils in order to reduce the amount of money given to them. Funding was based on the number of pupils reported. The lower the reported enrollment, the less money went to black schools and, probably, the more available to white schools.

Back when he still worked in the coal mine, Booker had heard about a school in Virginia for black students called Hampton Normal and Agricultural Institute. Underground one day, he overheard two miners talking about the fact that Hampton was a place where poor but worthy students could work out the cost of their education. Booker had no idea where or how far away it was, but Hampton became a place he thought about often. Viola Ruffner had detected in him a particular determination "to emerge from his obscurity." Hampton would be the key.

Booker's thinking about Hampton intensified after his teacher, Mr. Davis, left for a position in Charleston, West Virginia, and was replaced by a Hampton graduate named Henry Clay Payne. The new teacher quickly learned that Booker was on fire with ambition to somehow go to Hampton. Mr. Davis, only eighteen when he started teaching, had struggled to keep ahead of his best pupils. The contrast between him and Payne, a polished institutional graduate, must have made Booker's ambition burn all the brighter.

Booker confided in his mother, who half-heartedly encouraged him in his dream but had no way of helping him achieve it. She was frail now and in poor health, keeping house for John, Amanda, Benjamin (a foundling they had taken in), and Wash as best she could and earning a few cents here and there by taking in laundry. Jane Ferguson could hardly imagine something so foreign to her experience as leaving home to go to school. The only thing that interested her about it was the intense desire Booker had to go there.

Some time in the summer of 1872, Booker made his decision. He had never been away from his family before. His job with Mrs. Ruffner was by far the best he'd ever had. He had almost no money. He didn't even know where he was going or how long a trip it was. But he was going to Hampton Institute to get an education. They welcomed black students there and gave them a way to earn an education even if they were poor. Booker was willing to leave behind everything he had ever known for that kind of chance.

The one aspect of leaving that tore at Booker's heart was the fear that he would never see his mother again. She was sick and worn with a lifetime of hard work, most of it as a slave, and Booker later wrote that she feared her son was wasting his time and money on a wild goose chase.

Booker had managed to save a little money over the wages that were sent to his stepfather. His brother John gave him what he could. In a surprising and touching gesture, black townspeople began dropping by the Ferguson cabin in the days before Booker's departure to present him with a few coins, a handkerchief, or anything else they could give to help him on his journey. All of them were illiterate; many were old and had lived their most productive years as slaves. In young Booker they saw the future and the hope of a brighter day. Freedom had been the answer to a lifetime of prayer, but freedom alone could not bring independence. Along with education, perhaps it could.

Young Booker began his trip with a flourish, boarding the Chesapeake & Ohio Railroad in Charleston. He had no idea that nearly five hundred miles separated the Kanawah Valley from Hampton Institute, near Newport News on the James River. The railroad only went part of the distance then, but the hopeful student's money ran out even before the rail line did. After that he walked along the line for days at a stretch, his travel on foot relieved occasionally by kind-hearted conductors who let him ride a while for free. At the end of the line a stagecoach met the rail passengers to carry them on eastward. Booker used some of his remaining money to buy a ticket for part of the way, then he walked or hitched rides on passing wagons or stages.

It was after a long day aboard a stagecoach that Booker had what he considered his first direct personal experience with discrimination. The stage stopped at an inn for the night, and the passengers lined up at the desk to be assigned their rooms. Booker was sharply refused admission and spent the chilly Appalachian September night pacing up and down trying to keep warm. His reaction was one more of surprise than anger; besides, he was too excited about getting to Hampton to let the innkeeper's rejection upset him. "This was my first experience in finding out what the colour of my skin meant," he remembered more than a quarter of a century later. "My whole soul was so bent upon reaching Hampton that I did not have time to cherish any bitterness toward the hotel-keeper."

Eventually Booker came to Richmond, once the capital of the Confederacy, eighty miles or so from Hampton. He had never seen a big city before, and he arrived late at night, tired, hungry, and without a penny. He tried to find a place to sleep, but no one would let him in without paying. Carrying his cheap satchel in his hand, he walked the streets not knowing which way to turn, tormented by the aroma of fried chicken and apple pie from roadside food stalls. Discouraged and physically spent, he finally squirmed under an elevated wooden sidewalk and slept fitfully, with the tread of shoes on the boards inches above his ears, using his satchel as a pillow.

He awoke at daylight, desperate for a meal, and saw in the distance a vessel at the dock where men were offloading a cargo of pig iron. Booker approached the captain and asked if he could earn enough money unloading pig iron to buy some breakfast. The captain agreed; the boy set to work, and soon he had enough to purchase a meal that he said ever afterward was the best breakfast of his life. Impressed with the boy's work, the captain invited Booker to return after breakfast and work some more. This he gladly did and continued to sleep under the sidewalk in order to save enough to get to Hampton as soon as possible. After a few days, he figured he had what he needed, thanked the captain for his kindness, and started out on the last leg of his trip.

On October 5, 1872, Booker Washington walked onto the campus of Hampton Institute with a few spare clothes, fifty cents cash, and his burning desire to learn fully intact. Though it would have seemed small and unimpressive to many, the three-story brick Academic Hall appeared to Booker to be the most wonderful building he had ever seen: a fine school dedicated to the education of poor but eager black students. At the sight of it, all the difficulties and sacrifices he endured in his weeks on the road melted away to nothing. It gave him a renewed sense of hope that the end of his journey would be the beginning of a great future. He would, as Viola Ruffner had said, "emerge from his obscurity." He knew he would. Nothing would prevent him from equipping himself to accomplish the most possible good in the world.

As he stood there, a stranger on campus, dirty and rumpled from weeks of travel, hundreds of miles from anyone or anything he knew, he thought not of the past but only of the future. "I felt that a new kind of existence had now begun," he later wrote, "that life would now have a new meaning.

"I felt that I had reached the promised land."

CHAPTER THREE

THE FORCE THAT WINS

The first person in authority Booker Washington met on the Hampton campus was Mary Mackie, a stern New Yorker in charge of assigning new students to classes. She was unimpressed with his bedraggled appearance, and only his innocent earnestness kept her from turning him away altogether. He hovered expectantly while she processed admissions for several other students, desperately hoping he would get the same chance as these other newcomers.

After a while, Miss Mackie suddenly looked up at Booker and said, "The adjoining recitation room needs sweeping. Take the broom and sweep it." Here was one task that, even as weary and apprehensive as he was, Booker could have done almost in his sleep. Mrs. Ruffner had given him advanced instruction in sweeping and plenty of opportunity to practice. He saw this as his one chance to make an impression on Miss Mackie, and he went determinedly to his work.

He swept the room three times, dusted four times, moved the furniture to clean in the corners, and even swept and dusted the closet floors. When he finished, he reported back to Miss Mackie, who came in to inspect his efforts. She looked in the closets and corners and ran her handkerchief along the woodwork and over the furniture. There was not a speck of dust anywhere. She looked at the boy and said quietly, "I guess you will do to enter this institution."

It was the most joyful moment of Booker's life. On the strength of his performance with the broom and dust cloth, Booker was offered a job as janitor in order to work off his expenses. Except for a short stint at the school sawmill, it was the only job he would have during his three years at Hampton. He enjoyed the work because he knew how to do it well and because it brought him into daily contact with well-mannered, well-educated whites. It was similar to the way his work in the Ruffner house had exposed him to their standards and lifestyle as opposed to the coarse ways of his own family and neighbors. He was attracted to the refined tastes of the teachers and was soon drawn particularly to the figure of General Samuel Chapman Armstrong, founder and president of Hampton Institute.

The institute was a result of General Armstrong's lifelong passion for leading and educating minority races. He had been born to missionary parents in the Hawaiian Islands in 1839. His father, a Princeton graduate, was a Presbyterian pastor who later became Hawaii's minister of education. Armstrong moved to the United States in 1860 and there saw similarities between the problems of educating blacks and the challenges his parents had faced while teaching native Hawaiians over a span of thirty years.

To the general, Hawaiians had seemed backward and poorly equipped to succeed in the 1850s, just as the former slaves seemed destined to fail in the late 1860s. Armstrong unflinchingly embraced the prevailing assumptions that dark-skinned people (whether from the Pacific or the Potomac) were backward compared with whites, their civilizations less developed. But Armstrong did not consider them innately inferior to whites, rather simply behind them on the scale of social and intellectual development.

Sociologists of the day attributed this apparent disparity to a variety of social and biological factors, but to Armstrong, there was a simple truth in the fact that both Hawaiians and American blacks were expected to do in only a few years what their white counterparts had taken centuries to accomplish. For example, until the Englishman James Cook landed in Hawaii in 1788, the concept of a written language—essential for collecting and distributing knowledge beyond what one person could remember—was completely unknown there. Black Americans were in a comparable situation since many of them were forbidden by law from learning to write.

General Armstrong believed that knowledge alone was useless unless it was combined with moral training, personal hygiene, and practical life skills. Comparing Polynesians and blacks, Armstrong wrote, "Of both it is true that not mere ignorance, but deficiency of character is the chief difficulty, and that to build up character is the true objective point in education." And on another occasion, "The best of sermons and schools amount to little when hearers and pupils are thriftless, live from hand to mouth, and are packed at night either in savage huts or in dirty tenement houses."

Armstrong was a student at Williams College in Massachusetts when the Civil War began. After graduation he enlisted in the Union army and assumed command of the 9th U.S. Colored Troops, made up of white officers and black enlisted men. Before his discharge from the army as a twenty-six-year-old brigadier general, Armstrong wrote to offer his services to General Oliver O. Howard, head of the Bureau of Refugees, Freedmen, and Abandoned Lands (known informally as the Freedmen's Bureau). This agency of the war department was responsible for the welfare of newly freed blacks. Though at first Howard thought he was too young and refused his application, Armstrong finally secured a job with the bureau in Virginia.

Picking his way through the government bureaucracy over the next couple of years, Armstrong realized that help for the black race was unlikely to come from ineffective clerks and politicians with no practical understanding of the needs they were supposed to address. He had seen schools for native Hawaiians based on a bedrock curriculum of manual skills and moral instruction; he was convinced that intellectual education was helpful only after those deficiencies were addressed and corrected.

The general claimed there were other similarities in the situations of Hawaiians and blacks. By the time Armstrong's father came to the islands in 1830, the unsteady kingdom that had been formed from a host of tribal regions only twenty years before was already being influenced and undermined by American sugar interests. Native Hawaiians saw their ancient culture disappear and their rights to self-government along with it. Likewise, until 1865, most American blacks could not vote, own property, serve as a juror, swear a deposition, or do anything else they were suddenly expected to do for themselves—and do well—once the war was over.

In 1869, with assistance from the American Missionary Association and some wealthy Northern donors, General Armstrong established Hampton Institute to encourage blacks to get an education built on moral instruction, discipline, and practical skills.

From the beginning, Armstrong set a high value on order and regularity. This emphasis sprang partly from his military training and his belief that teaching responsible habits was as important (or more important) than teaching arithmetic. It also made coeducation less of a problem. Both girls and boys were accepted as boarding students, and keeping them busy every waking hour reduced the risk of temptation.

Boys and girls lined up every morning for inspection. They had to be cleanly and neatly dressed and appropriately groomed. Booker found it difficult to keep his clothes sharp at first. He had one suit, which he wore every day to class and to his work as a janitor, then washed every night. Eventually he received more clothes, given to him from the barrels of donated clothing that arrived from the North.

The daily schedule reflected Armstrong's determination to keep his pupils fully occupied:

5:00 A.M.	Rising bell
5:45	Personal inspection
6:00	Breakfast
6:30	Prayers
8:00	Inspection of quarters
8:30	Roll call and exercises
8:50	Classes: reading, natural philosophy, arithmetic, grammar, geography, bookkeeping
10:20	Recess
10:40	Classes: writing, arithmetic, grammar, history, algebra, elocution
12:15 P.M.	Dinner and rest

1:30 P.M.	Roll call
1:40	Classes: spelling, arithmetic, grammar, geography, natural philosophy, history, civil government, moral science
4:00	Cadet drill
6:00	Supper
6:45	Evening prayers
7:15	Study
9:30	Retiring bell

In spite of the daunting schedule, Booker managed to work enough to pay his monthly board of ten dollars. His tuition of seventy dollars a year was paid by a Massachusetts supporter of Hampton at General Armstrong's recommendation.

Like many young students, Booker Washington struggled over what he should do with his life. He knew he wanted to use his natural gifts to uplift members of his race but could not decide, now that he was in school at last, what the specific goal of his education should be. One of his teachers remembered that "to help his people was uppermost in his thoughts," and at one point he wanted to be a lawyer. Booker told his teacher he felt the black community especially needed lawyers, "faithful men to plead their cause when injustice was likely to be done them."

Booker also explored the idea of becoming a minister. Since the day he had been chastised for playing marbles on Sunday, he had been a stalwart churchgoer. On the advice of Miss Nathalie Lord, a teacher at Hampton who hired him on occasion to row her boat on the river, Booker began setting aside fifteen minutes every day to read the Bible. The two of them and a couple of classmates met regularly before the noon meal in the corner of a classroom to read to each other. Though they had time for only a few verses during each session, by the end of the year they had read much of the New Testament, including the four gospels, Acts, and Paul's epistles.

Up to this time, Booker's religious training had been shaped by the prayers of his mother, the emotional, simplistic teachings of Reverend Rice in Malden, and earlier, the teachings of former slaves whom he later remembered as self-proclaimed laypreachers more interested in avoiding the heat of the cotton patch than preaching the Word. These daily Bible readings encouraged Booker to look deeper into his faith and seek answers on his own. He also attended Miss Lord's Sunday school every week, and afterward, stayed with a few others to pray for students who had not accepted Christ.

Whether he became a lawyer or a preacher, Booker knew he would benefit from participating in the Hampton debating societies. Though he was only a teenager and some of his fellow pupils were as old as forty, he was one of the outstanding speechmakers of the group. His modest nature prompted him to cultivate a natural, personable style in sharp contrast to the stiff and bombastic delivery most speakers preferred. And his gift for observation produced a steady stream of inside jokes and wry remarks that kept audiences entertained.

At the end of his first year at Hampton in the spring of 1873, Booker could not afford to go home as most students did, and he was unable to get one of the few summer caretaker jobs that would have allowed him to stay on campus until the fall. Somehow he had ended up with two coats and decided to raise some money by selling one of them. An old black man came to Booker's room to look at the coat, and the boy was overjoyed when the man announced he would buy it. The feeling was short lived; the man announced he would pay Booker "five cents, cash down" on the coat and installments on the balance whenever he could.

After more searching, Booker finally got a job as a restaurant waiter in nearby Fortress Monroe, famous then as the site of the historic battle between the two Civil War ironclad warships *Monitor* and *Merrimack*. Unlike his brief stint on the Cincinnati riverboat, Booker kept this job for the duration of the summer. He had owed the school sixteen dollars at the end of the year and hoped to earn enough during the summer to settle his account before the fall term began. He was disappointed to find that his wages were so low he couldn't save enough, even by living as frugally as possible and doing his own laundry. One day in the restaurant he found a ten dollar bill. Unflinchingly honest and not one to feel that he "deserved" anything, Booker felt it only proper to show it to the owner, who explained that since the money was lost in his restaurant it belonged to him.

In spite of his remaining debt, Booker was allowed back for his second year at Hampton, promising to pay as he was able. He went back to his job as a janitor in Academic Hall. The second year of school was an extension of the first: daily inspections, classes, drill, prayer, and study. He continued to learn by watching others as well as by working on his lessons. He marveled at General Armstrong's energy and commitment and developed a similar admiration for some of the Hampton donors who came to visit.

Of all he learned that year, Booker claimed that the most valuable of all was "an understanding of the use and value of the Bible." He credited Miss Lord's Bible study and Sunday school classes for his newfound appreciation of Scripture. His daily reading became a habit; whenever he was at home, he read from the Bible every morning for the rest of his life.

After his second year at Hampton ended, Booker went back home for the first time since leaving his family's cabin for the Charleston train station almost two years earlier. Between what he had saved and what his mother and brother John could send him, he had just enough to get to Malden by rail and stagecoach. From a campus atmosphere swirling with the promise of a better life, Booker returned to an environment of hopeless decay. The local salt industry had continued to decline, and all the furnaces were closed. The coal mines were also closed because of a strike.

Booker's homecoming was a bright spot in the weary lives of Tinkersville and Malden blacks. The same townspeople who had given Booker what money and gifts they could to send him on his way now welcomed him back with invitations to dinner and eager requests to tell them what he had seen and learned. He addressed enthusiastic crowds at the African Zion Baptist Church and other places in town. He called on General and Mrs. Ruffner and accepted their heartfelt congratulations.

What he most longed for, however, was a job that would pay enough to get him back to Hampton in September. Unemployment was high because the furnaces and mines were shut down, and Booker went farther and farther from the Ferguson cabin in search of work. One night, after yet another unsuccessful day of job hunting, he found himself too exhausted to walk all the way back to Malden and stopped for the night about a mile from home. In the middle of the night he was awakened by his brother John, who had come in search of him with the sad news that their mother had died. Booker was heartbroken that he had not been with her at the end, and that she had not lived to enjoy whatever benefits his education might bring.

With Jane Ferguson's death, responsibility for running the household fell to her daughter, Amanda. She was only about twelve, but Wash Ferguson had no inclination to take on cooking, cleaning, and mending chores—he saw that as women's work—and there was no money for a housekeeper. What little sense of order there was in the house descended into chaos as Amanda tried in vain to keep up with her duties.

During these trying times Viola Ruffner frequently invited Booker to visit and gave him odd jobs to do. Her assistance, along with a coal mining job in a nearby community and a little money from John, allowed Booker to travel back to Hampton to begin his third year of study.

Three weeks before classes were to begin, Booker was surprised to receive a letter from Miss Mary Mackie, the first person he had met at Hampton and the one who admitted him to school on the strength of his performance with a broom and dust cloth. She asked him if he could return to school two weeks early to help her get the buildings ready for the new term. He left for Hampton at once.

To his amazement, Miss Mackie, a proud and taciturn member of a prominent New York family, intended to work alongside him, a black teenage janitor, to prepare the rooms. It was a lesson he never forgot, as he wrote later:

> Miss Mackie was a member of one of the oldest and most cultured families of the North, and yet for two weeks she worked by my side cleaning windows, dusting rooms, putting beds in order, and what not. She felt that things would not be in condition for the opening of school unless every window-pane was perfectly clean, and she took the greatest satisfaction in helping to clean them herself.

Miss Mackie did not have to do these menial jobs, but she didn't consider that kind of work "beneath her"; she saw the tasks as important and useful. Her example gave Booker a ringing respect for black schools that taught the "dignity of labor," and little patience with those that did not.

Before the year was out he had completely abandoned his original assumption that intellectual education should replace manual training. At Hampton he realized, "I not only learned that it was not a disgrace to labour, but learned to love labour, not alone for its financial value, but for labour's own sake and for the independence and self-reliance which the ability to do something which the world wants done brings."

Here, too, he affirmed in his own mind "the fact that the happiest individuals are those who do the most to make others useful and happy." The former slave boy had been replaced by a new man of great promise. "Amid Christian influences I was surrounded by an atmosphere of business, and a spirit of self-help that seemed to awaken every faculty in me and cause me for the first time to realize what it means to be a man instead of a piece of property."

Booker earned a prominent part in the commencement exercises the day of his graduation from Hampton in 1875, debating the issue of whether Cuba should be annexed by the United States. He argued that the island nation, then fighting for its independence from Spain, should be left alone to develop a system of self-government for the time being and that America had all it could handle in assimilating and caring for four million emancipated slaves. "Before we risk a war for Cuba," Washington declared, we should "redeem ourselves from the meshes of the last war." A reporter for the *New York Times* wrote that Washington "carried the whole audience, both white and black," and was "enthusiastically applauded." At the end of the day, humble as he was, Washington seemed to glow with a sense of satisfaction and accomplishment. To one fellow student he looked like "a conqueror who had won a great victory."

Back in Malden there were still no jobs, even for conquerors. Booker Washington traveled north in search of work and found something that put his past experience to use: waiting tables in a resort hotel. His restaurant job in Virginia had been in a relatively unassuming hotel where most of the guests were visiting wounded relatives at a nearby military hospital. This job was in one of the grand vacation palaces frequented by the Northern elite, possibly the United States Hotel in Saratoga Springs, New York. It was an imposing resort with more than a thousand rooms, each with running water and electric lights. The guests enjoyed strolling along European-influenced piazzas almost half a mile long.

In a repeat of his first experience as a waiter aboard the Cincinnati riverboat, Washington proved unsuitable for the task. Not knowing how to serve a formal table, he was upbraided by his well-heeled customers to the point where he retreated to his room confused and embarrassed. He was demoted to busboy on the spot, but through diligent work and observation he was promoted to his former position after a few weeks.

When the season ended at Saratoga, Washington returned to Malden hoping to teach and found that the patrons of the black school in Tinkersville had already elected him teacher there. He was examined by the white county school superintendent and authorized to teach at a salary of about thirty dollars per month, ten dollars less than the average salary for white teachers. It was the accepted practice at that time for there to be four pay scales: one for white men, one for white women, one for black men, and one for black women. Booker, however, was eager to take the job, which gave him a pay raise from what he received at Hampton.

He found lodging in a two-room house next to the railroad tracks in Malden and took in a fellow Hampton graduate as a boarder. In the spirit of his experience at Hampton, Booker arrived at school at eight in the morning and frequently worked until ten at night, convinced that his students needed more than "mere book education" in order to succeed. He emphasized punctuality, good manners, and personal cleanliness—keeping hair combed and clothes clean. Regular bathing and tooth brushing were a novelty for some of the pupils, but they soon learned its importance from Mr. Washington. On the subject of tooth brushing, Washington was convinced that "there are few single agencies of civilization that are more far-reaching."

Once an impoverished student himself, Washington well knew how important night school was to students who had to work to pay their expenses. He soon opened a night school of his own to accommodate adults who wanted to learn but who had to work all day. In a short while he was crowding up to ninety pupils into the schoolhouse during the day, and about ninety more for night school. Some of them were over fifty, with little promise of progressing, but Mr. Washington welcomed and encouraged them.

Washington taught upwards of two hundred students every day in various grade levels. There was no assistant, so he handled all the preparation, teaching, assignments, and testing on his own. Even that much work failed to satisfy the community's thirst for knowledge and Washington's desire to deliver it. He also set up a reading room and a debating society and taught Sunday school twice every week: once at Father Rice's Baptist Zion Church and again at a little community two or three miles distant. Eager for other Malden residents to follow in his footsteps at Hampton, he offered private tutoring to a select few scholars he thought had the best chance of being admitted there.

The two years he taught at Malden were some of the happiest of Booker's life. He was by all accounts an excellent teacher—articulate, patient, and an inspiration to his students. Following the Hampton model, he instituted military drill for the boys (using sticks for rifles) and inspected his students' dress and grooming every morning. Though he was only in his early twenties, Mr. Washington became a revered presence in town. Both blacks and whites looked forward to hearing his speeches at the school graduation exercises or to seeing him sitting beside Father Rice at the monthly business meetings of the church, taking minutes and advising the elderly pastor on points of order. Washington also excelled in the debating society meetings and was invariably victorious as the "closer" in competitions with other local groups.

His popularity as an orator intensified Washington's interest in politics and the law. At sixteen, before leaving for Hampton, he had been the secretary of the local Republican party (in part because he was one of only a handful of members who could read). He had shone in debates at Hampton and in Malden and had his letters on political issues published in local newspapers. During the summer of 1877, he took a position on the question of which city should become the capital of West Virginia. Wheeling had been the first capital in the west after the partition of old Virginia, then Charleston, then Wheeling again. Reports of Washington's public appearances called him the "champion of Charleston" and complimented his good style, expressive ability, and use of anecdotes.

It wasn't the study of law that finally drew Booker Washington away from his beloved classroom in Tinkersville and the debating societies of Malden, but his decision to enter Wayland Seminary in Washington, D.C., to prepare for the ministry. Wayland was sponsored by the American Baptist Home Mission Society and opened in 1867 to supply black preachers for congregations in the surrounding states.

The nation's capital was an attractive place for ambitious black men in 1878. During Reconstruction they were drawn by relatively good public schools, relatively lenient laws concerning the rights of blacks, and the government programs set up to help them adapt to their new lives as free people. Hopeful though he was at the beginning of his year at Wayland, Booker T. Washington looked around after a few months and concluded his new vocation was a mistake.

Part of the problem was the atmosphere on campus and the attitudes of the students. Hampton had taught Washington the value of strict routine and of lessons learned by earning one's own way through school. His seminary classmates, both men and women, seemed to him too fond of clothes and expensive carriage rides and too little aware of the worth of their training because someone else was footing the bill. He felt they "knew more about Latin and Greek when they left school, but they seemed to know less about life." More worrisome was Washington's concern that after a comfortable stint at Wayland, graduates would not want to go to the South, where the weather was hot and the people desperately poor, thus denying Washington's native region the black leadership it so badly needed.

The discomfort spilled over into his views of the city at large. Washington, D.C., was notorious for its immorality. Booker found that black girls who had developed a taste for the finer things in life were lured into prostitution to support their lifestyles. He found black men who made triple his teaching salary working at government jobs, yet were deeper in debt at the end of every month than they had been the month before.

Federal programs intended to lift former slaves out of poverty and give them a fresh start were, in Booker's view, draining them of their ambition and incentive to work and rendering them dependent on the government for everything. He wrote later that he wished he could move these people to the countryside and "plant them upon the soil, upon the solid and never deceptive foundation of Mother Nature, where all nations and races that have ever succeeded have gotten their start."

Another annoyance for Booker may have been whatever denominational indoctrination was included in his seminary studies. His church in Malden and the seminary were both branches of the Baptist church, and he had been secretary and de facto assistant to Father Rice. His impatience with religious dogma was never far beneath the surface, though, sometimes rising to a considerable degree of passion. In his commencement debate at Hampton, one of the reasons he gave for why America should not annex Cuba was that an influx of Cubans would increase the power of the Roman Catholic Church.

Whatever the reason for his dissatisfaction, Washington gave up his studies and returned to Malden. Once again he was out of a job. When he had left the school at Tinkersville, the school had elected his brother John to take his place. (In return for John's support of their family while Booker went to Hampton, Booker had returned the favor by helping pay John's way. The two of them later paid the way for their adopted brother, Benjamin.)

As he reconsidered the prospect of a career in politics or law, Washington was surprised to receive a letter from General Armstrong inviting him to speak at the Hampton commencement the following May. He arrived early to write and practice his remarks and noted with satisfaction how his life had changed in the five years since he had traveled from Malden to Hampton the first time. Then he had arrived dirty, unknown, and almost penniless. His first duty had been to sweep a classroom. This time he was there by invitation of the school president to present a keynote address to the commencement audience.

He titled his speech "The Force That Wins," identifying that force as one "that requires not education merely, but also wisdom and common sense, and heart bent on the right and a trust in God." The key to success, he told his listeners, was not in planning and talking about noble deeds but in doing them. Washington's presentation was a huge success. One listener remembered it as a compelling appeal for the graduates to "believe in patient, unostentatious, consecrated labor in their efforts to help their race."

Washington returned to Malden to try to figure out what to do next. Within a few weeks he was surprised once again to receive another letter from General Armstrong. This one offered him a teaching position at Hampton for twenty-five dollars a month. Washington jumped at the chance. The Hampton faculty had originally been all white; he would be one of a growing number of black graduates invited to return as instructors.

Late that summer, Washington retraced the journey he had made in May and spent time at Hampton preparing for his new role. One of his tutors was the school chaplain, a Yale graduate and former Presbyterian pastor named Hollis B. Frissell, who strongly endorsed General Armstrong's belief that hard work and self-sufficiency would bring blacks the greatest advances in society.

The general wanted Washington to teach night classes since there were a large number of students who had to drop out of day school because they could not afford their expenses. Booker was a product of the Hampton night school, a testament to its success, and had set up his own at Tinkersville with impressive results. Washington agreed and held class from seven until nine-thirty each night. At first only a handful of pupils attended, but the number grew eventually to about three dozen in spite of the fact that the students arrived for class after working from 7 A.M. until 6 P.M., boys in the sawmill and girls in the laundry.

Washington was concerned that after such a long day his students would be sleepy and inattentive and prepared himself to keep them alert with probing questions and clever jokes. The truth was that these boys and girls were eager to learn and that a long day of anticipation actually made them more, not less, lively during class. Their industry was such that most of them made enough money after one year of night school to pay for two years of day school.

Some time early in his Hampton teaching career, Washington received another invitation from General Armstrong, this one of a more peculiar sort. About two years earlier, federal authorities had selected Hampton for an experimental program to give Native Americans an education in the ways of the white man. The teacher supervising the program for the school had left, and Armstrong asked Washington to be their "house father," live in their dormitory, keep an eye on them, and instruct them in the social graces.

The first of the group to arrive had come in 1878 from a federal prison in Florida, where they were taken after being captured in the last of the Native American uprisings in the West. Others—both young men and women—came later from western reservations. General Armstrong felt confident that the educational techniques he had developed for the Hawaiians and the American blacks would be useful to American Indians, who in Armstrong's eyes suffered from a similar lack of civilizing influences and moral instruction. He hoped in time to assimilate them into the mainstream of white society the same as he expected to do with the other "darker races."

On his first night as a Hampton student, sleeping on a proper bed for the first time in his life, Washington had wondered why there were two sheets on his bed. One night he slept on top of them, the next night beneath, until someone showed him how to crawl between the two. Washington saw that experience magnified and multiplied in his new charges.

He was the only non-Indian resident of the Wigwam, a three-story frame building built as a dormitory for Native American boys. Where young Booker had been confused by the bed sheets, these residents were strangers to any bed at all. Most of them had never lived in a building, but in a teepee. They had never worn clothing, but wore skins, blankets, and moccasins instead. They had never seen forks or spoons or other table-ware and saw no point in going to all the trouble when fingers worked just as well and were easier to wash.

Washington learned that the things they despised most were having their long hair cut, wearing clothing (especially underwear), and giving up smoking (which they had taught European settlers in the first place). He also felt a mutual sense of mistrust at first. American Indians, naturally patrician and self-assured, considered themselves superior to whites and far superior to blacks, who had been slaves of whites. Native Americans themselves had owned black slaves. Washington, on the other hand, initially considered his charges to be "wild and for the most part perfectly ignorant." However, he had seen firsthand what was possible in transforming "disadvantaged races" at Hampton and embraced his responsibilities with confidence and enthusiasm.

Washington's eagerness was enhanced by "the general feeling that the attempt to educate and civilize the red men at Hampton would be a failure." It made him doubly determined to succeed. In time, he gained their confidence, though not necessarily their close friendship. They always referred to him formally—and somewhat derisively—as "Mr. Booker T. Washington."

Washington sympathized with the men and felt compassion for them. They had been involuntarily uprooted from their lives, families, and customs—some at gunpoint—and were being compelled to adapt to unfamiliar and unwanted urban lives. He came up with the idea of letting them spend Saturdays in the open, reporting that after a lifetime of fresh air and outdoor activity they could not be cut off from such pursuits "too abruptly without serious injury to their health."

The first week they pitched a tent at the beach, cooked supper on an open fire, participated enthusiastically in racing and other active pursuits, and even made a half-hearted attempt at staging a war dance. The next week they played football. Monitoring the transition, Washington later wrote with unintended irony that "no white American ever thinks that any other race is wholly civilized until he wears the white man's clothes, eats the white man's food, speaks the white man's language, and professes the white man's religion."

The experience of discrimination in white society made Hampton students generally tolerant of their Native American classmates and their strange ways. Washington noted this tendency with delight, wondering if any white school in the country would welcome "more than a hundred companions of another race in the cordial way that these black students at Hampton welcomed the red ones." (Being described as "red" was something the native students never understood. Cardinals and raspberries were red; obviously they were not.)

In an article for the magazine *Southern Workman,* published by Hampton, Washington described one of the Indian students after three years at school:

> His long hair and moccasins he has long since forgotten, and instead of the weak, dirty, ignorant piece of humanity that he was, with no correct idea of this life or the next—his only ambition being to fight the white man—he goes back a strong, decent, Christian *man,* with the rudiments of an English education, and hands trained to earn himself a living at the carpenter's bench or on the farm.

Though Washington was in charge of the Native American students, a trip with one of them reminded him of the convoluted situation regarding race in America. One of them fell ill, and Washington had to escort him to the Department of the Interior for treatment. On the coastal steamer from Norfolk to the District of Columbia, Washington waited until most of the passengers had finished eating before entering the dining room with his student. The student was seated at once, but the waiter refused to serve Washington. At the hotel where he was supposed to take the student, the Native American was again admitted but his black teacher was not.

In May of 1881, General Armstrong received a letter that would change the course of Booker T. Washington's life. The letter was from Moses Campbell, who had written at the request of his uncle, George W. Campbell, a successful merchant and banker in Tuskegee, Alabama. He explained that his uncle had recently become chairman of a board of commissioners charged with starting a school for blacks and was looking for a qualified white man to serve as principal. Hampton was a well-known and respected school for African-Americans that had been organized and led by whites. Campbell had written there as well as to other schools to see if any of them could recommend someone for the job in Tuskegee.

General Armstrong was impressed with Booker Washington on many levels. He had been a hard working and excellent student. The handful of pupils Washington had sent from his school at Tinkersville had been so well prepared that they started Hampton with the second year curriculum. His work as the dormitory supervisor for the Native Americans proved his compassion and sensitivity to members of a race even farther from white society's norms than his own.

Soon afterwards, Armstrong sent for Washington to report to his office. There he asked if Washington thought he could fill the position. The young teacher said he was willing to try. On May 31, General Armstrong wrote Campbell that the only man he could suggest was "one Mr. Booker T. Washington, a graduate of this institution, a very competent capable mulatto, clear headed, modest, sensible, polite and a thorough teacher and superior man. The best man we ever had here." Sensitive to the fact that the Tuskegee trustees were expecting a white man, Armstrong inquired, "Is his being colored an objection?... I am confident he would not disappoint you. I know of no white man who could do better." The general closed by requesting an "answer by night telegram at my expense if satisfactory."

The next Sunday night, a telegraph messenger entered the chapel during evening services and handed an envelope to General Armstrong. He opened it, glanced at its contents, then called for the attention of the assembled students. The telegram was from the Tuskegee trustees, and Armstrong read it aloud:

"Booker Washington will do. Send him."

CHAPTER FOUR

CAST DOWN YOUR BUCKET

I n his first year and a half at Tuskegee, Booker T. Washington proved
the wisdom of the school trustees' decision. He had come expecting
to begin with a fully equipped campus and instead had started literally with nothing. But by the end of 1882 he had a hundred acres of land;
a sturdy and serviceable building that, though admittedly unattractive,
was the biggest building in town; classrooms full of eager students; the
support and even admiration of the community; and bold plans for the
future.

His wife, Fanny, settled into the community and took up her duties as
official hostess of the school. Washington had met her when she was a student in his school at Tinkersville. As feelings of affection had begun to grow
between them, he chose her as one of the select group of star pupils preparing for admission to Hampton Institute. Like Washington, she was a diligent and hard-working student; unlike him, she was average in her
academic performance. She was admitted to Hampton at least partly on
account of his endorsement, but once there she completed the three-year
program and graduated.

In its second year, Tuskegee had four teachers including
Washington. By the 1883–84 school year there were nine. In 1884,

Washington organized a night school along the model that had served him so well at Hampton. He also continued to expand the choices of trades the students could learn, fully convinced that economic independence was more important in raising the living standards and expectations of his race than intellectual pursuits. The catalog of courses for that year listed housekeeping and sewing for girls, and farming, carpentry, printing, blacksmithing, and brickmaking for boys.

Brickmaking gave both Washington and his students alike a series of lessons in patience and humility. Eager to continue his building program, Washington had an eye for quality and wanted his buildings to have the solidity and elegance of brick. Brick was considerably more expensive than wood, and some friends of the school advised Washington to continue building wooden structures in order to make his money go further. Another difficulty was that, while there were plenty of sawmills in Tuskegee owned by merchants who would extend credit to the school, there was not a brick kiln in all of Macon County.

Washington saw it as an opportunity. Bricks would make a better looking, more substantial building; moreover, the school could start a brickmaking operation and supply the whole county without competition, thus providing a regular source of badly needed cash. Instead of making do with what the community had to offer, he and his students would make something the community needed and learn a marketable trade in the process.

Neither Washington nor hardly anyone else in town knew anything about making bricks, but they soon learned that the kaolin clay on campus was ideal for the purpose because it was easily pliable and had a rich, red color. While this raised Washington's spirits, students stiffly resisted the idea of making bricks. Just as they had when Washington wanted to clear land for planting two years before, his pupils protested that they had come to school to get away from manual labor. They expected to trade backbreaking work in the sun for a life of study, contemplation, and physical ease. Leading by example once again, Washington waded into knee-deep mud to dig clay himself. Students and other faculty members soon joined in.

Washington set out to construct a first-class dormitory for a hundred students that would include a students' parlor and reading room, library, a proper kitchen, dining room, and laundry to replace the poorly designed ones in the basement of Porter Hall. Using student labor, he figured the cost at about eight thousand dollars with startup cost to establish the brick kiln at only two hundred dollars. General Armstrong agreed to lend him the money to equip a brickyard.

The land adjoining the school property was owned by Edward T. Varner, whose wife boarded many of the Tuskegee boys. Varner had once operated a brickyard, and he still had all the necessary equipment. He was impressed with Washington's plans and agreed to give him all his brick molds, barrows, and other equipment. Elated, Washington had them transported to the clay pit on campus and prepared to get to work.

In spite of the initial enthusiasm Washington had inspired, brick-making proved to be a much harder sell to the students than clearing timber had been. Most of the boys knew how to handle a saw, but molding bricks was completely foreign to their experience. It was also muddy, dusty, hot, and monotonous. Faced with the prospect of standing in mud up to their knees for hours at a time, day after day, a number of students quit school instead.

The first day, the remaining crew molded fifty bricks in the used wooden molds Mr. Varner had donated. Gradually, their skill and efficiency improved to the point where they were molding five thousand bricks a day. When they had a stock of twenty-five thousand, they stopped to fire them in their wood-burning kiln, built in place around the bricks on site. Washington and his students nervously awaited the results. The kiln was a failure; something was wrong with its design or construction, and the whole firing of twenty-five thousand was worthless.

Gamely, Washington supervised the construction of a second kiln and tried again. Once again the kiln failed. Washington wanted to make a third attempt. This time it was even harder to persuade the students to participate, and many did so only grudgingly. Teachers were embarrassed, too, at having promoted an unpopular project that failed so completely. Drawing on the same persuasive powers that had brought the school so far in such a short time, Washington induced them to clean up the mess, build another kiln, and have a final go.

The firing took a week. This time, only hours from the time when the bricks would be fully fired, the kiln collapsed. His teachers advised Washington to forget it; without professionals to build and tend the kiln, they argued, his efforts were obviously in vain. Besides, he had used up his two hundred dollars from General Armstrong—and more—on wood and materials for three kilns, and there was nothing more to spend.

Washington had a gold pocket watch that had been a gift from one of his New England benefactors. He took the train to Montgomery and pawned the watch for fifteen dollars. Returning to Tuskegee and the clay pit, he rallied his teachers and students for one more try. They cleared away the rubble and ashes of the third kiln and built a fourth. This time they were completely successful, and at the end of the week they had the great satisfaction of seeing stack after stack of perfectly cured bricks needed to begin work on the new building, which they christened Alabama Hall.

Washington reflected later on the lessons the experience had taught him about the relationship between blacks and whites in the South when he wrote:

Many white people who had had no contact with the school, and perhaps no sympathy with it, came to us to buy bricks because they found out that ours were good bricks…. The making of these bricks caused many of the white residents of the neighborhood to begin to feel that the education of the Negro was not making him worthless, but that in educating our students we were adding something to the wealth and comfort of the community. As [whites] came to us to buy bricks, we got acquainted with them; they traded with us and we with them. Our business interests became intermingled….

My experience is that there is something in human nature which always makes an individual recognize and reward merit, no matter under what colour of skin merit is found. I have found, too, that it is the visible, the tangible, that goes a long way in softening prejudices. The actual sight of a first-class house that a Negro has built is ten times more potent than pages of discussion about a house that he ought to build, or perhaps could build.

Within a few years, Tuskegee brickmakers were turning out more than a million bricks a year and selling them throughout the community. The one casualty of the business was Washington's pocket watch. Before he could get back to redeem it, his time limit had expired and the watch had been sold.

As the pace of growth at Tuskegee accelerated, Fanny Washington was confined to bed for the birth of her first child. Though she was not actually a teacher, she was often listed on the official roster as one. She was an active if unheralded participant in the life of the school, keeping the Teachers House as a residence for faculty and assisting her husband in his duties.

Fanny gave birth to a daughter, Portia, in 1883, and may never have fully recovered from the delivery. She died the following year at the age of twenty-six after less than two years of marriage; some reports attributed her death to childbirth complications, others to "consumption of the bowels," and still others to injuries sustained in a fall from a farm wagon at Tuskegee.

Washington had loved his former pupil deeply and wrote eloquently of her to their friends at Hampton after her death. Her neatness and attention to detail "taught our students many valuable lessons. Her heart was set on making her home an object lesson for those about her, who were so much in need of such help."

Washington's mother-in-law, Celia Smith, came down from Malden to give what support she could and help take care of little Portia. She had not been particularly eager for Fanny to marry this ambitious and unproven teacher, but sharing the tragedy of her daughter's death brought them closer. After a while, homesick for the West Virginia mountains, she returned home, leaving Washington, always circumspect about his private life, to move forward on his own.

There was a natural basis for attraction between Booker T. Washington and one of his first staff members, Olivia Davidson, whose title by now was Lady Principal. Like both Booker and Fanny Washington, Miss Davidson was a mulatto, lighter skinned than either of them and with high cheekbones that indicated a trace of American Indian blood. She shared Washington's passion for education and his preference for the practical over the theoretical. She was a rarity in that she was one of the few people in Washington's professional circle who was actually more highly qualified to teach than he was: She was a college graduate; he was not, as Hampton, like Tuskegee, was a kind of secondary school. She had also proven herself an outstanding fundraiser, making regular trips to New England to take advantage of the connections she had made during her college days in Boston.

Miss Davidson and her employer again saw eye to eye in their desire to combine school subjects with moral instruction. An effective teacher, she believed, had a responsibility to show even farm women the value of modesty in dress, articulate conversation, decent furniture (even if it were nothing more than old crates covered in calico), and flower gardens. She encouraged farmers' wives to be upstanding models for their children and to do away with the unnerving custom of having the girls sleep in the same room with the men and boys.

In 1885, the same year Alabama Hall was completed, Booker Washington and Olivia Davidson were married. They had worked closely together for four years, and their personal relationship seemed a logical extension of their shared commitment to the Tuskegee mission. Olivia continued her productive trips to Boston and Hartford, charming Yankee industrialists and philanthropists with her poise and beauty. In a letter Robert C. Winthrop, chairman of a philanthropic fund established by George Foster Peabody, wrote that he was "greatly impressed by her intelligence & address. I did not dream that she was of the colored race, until she told me so. She would do credit to any race." He gave her five hundred dollars from the Peabody Fund and added a twenty-five dollar check of his own.

The new Mrs. Washington was one of several Tuskegee officials who went north regularly on behalf of the school. Booker T. Washington himself was away frequently, working to keep donations coming in so Tuskegee might continue its growth. No matter how much money came in, there was always some new building, new field of study, or unexpected need to absorb every penny. As the school's financial affairs became more complicated, Warren Logan, another of Washington's first faculty members and a fellow Hampton graduate, became the treasurer, and Washington's brother, John, who had graduated from Hampton and gone to work for the United States Corps of Engineers, came to Tuskegee to serve as business manager.

To improve the efficiency of his fundraising, Washington hired a full-time agent to work in Boston (whose wealthy citizens, Washington wrote, had a "fine and Christlike spirit"); and a second, based in Beloit, Wisconsin, to solicit in Chicago, St. Louis, and points west. The Wisconsin representative was none other than Washington's old friend, Reverend Robert C. Bedford, the Montgomery pastor who had preached at Tuskegee's first Thanksgiving service in 1882.

By the time he married Olivia, Washington had begun to realize he could not maintain his previous degree of involvement in Tuskegee. He was teaching in the classroom, preaching at chapel, making all the important administrative decisions, and making fundraising trips to the North. In 1885 he suffered a physical collapse and spent ten days in bed. Borrowing money from a friend, Mrs. Washington sent her husband to a special physical fitness course at Harvard, where, over several weeks, he and his fellow students—many of them medical doctors—practiced calisthenics and studied health and physiology. He returned much renewed and attacked with relish the issues that awaited his attention.

Mrs. Washington well knew the value of good health. In spite of her energy and success in fundraising, she suffered from a mysterious and chronic aliment doctors were never able to diagnose. She herself had collapsed more than once during her years at the school, but she endured sickness with her customary pleasant manner. Her first child, Booker Junior, was born in Boston during a fundraising tour. Her second, Ernest Davidson Washington, was born in Tuskegee when her husband was raising money up north. Her delicate constitution was further weakened by a complicated delivery. Days after Ernest's birth, a house fire sent Olivia, clutching her newborn, running outside into the predawn chill of a February morning.

When she did not recover her health, Washington took her to Massachusetts General Hospital in Boston. For three months he put Tuskegee planning and fundraising completely aside to stay with her. Regaining consciousness only intermittently, she slipped slowly away until May 9, 1889, when she died quietly in her hospital bed.

Washington, now twice a widower and with three small children, was devastated at her loss. Moreover, Tuskegee had lost its best fundraiser. Her refined manner and classical knowledge had played well in the parlors of Tuskegee's most enthusiastic benefactors. School income had dropped during the months of her confinement and illness, and Washington had stopped soliciting while she was in the hospital. He had barely enough money to get her body back to Alabama for burial beside Fanny and had to ask for a loan of three hundred dollars from General Armstrong to see Tuskegee through the summer.

The 1880s were years of great change in the American political landscape, and it was during and just after his marriage to Olivia that Booker T. Washington started gaining public attention outside Alabama and his circle of prominent Northern contacts. He was already cultivating a reputation as an articulate, polished spokesman for the black race when he was invited to speak at the national meeting of the National Educational Association in Madison, Wisconsin, in the summer of 1884.

His message to the four thousand delegates who heard him speak on July 16 was that racial harmony was an achievable goal and that the goal was within reach at Tuskegee. He pointed to the cooperation between white and black citizens of the county in building the school. A white man donated tools to start the brickyard, and whites bought the bricks because they were an excellent product. Both a former slave and a former slaveholder served on the state commission that founded Tuskegee. Another former slaveholder was at the moment working on the construction of a new building under the supervision of a black master carpenter.

The country was roiling in the aftermath of Reconstruction over questions of black economic and social opportunity. Playing to his audience,

Washington declared that good schoolteachers and money to attract them would prove "more potent in settling the race question than many civil rights bills"; and that, "Brains, property, and character for the Negro will settle the question of civil rights." Washington admitted that improvement of the black man's condition depended on cooperation from Southern whites. He strongly believed, however, that assisting high-achieving blacks was in the interest of whites and saw the appropriate division in society not as black versus white, but industrious, well-meaning whites and blacks together versus the lazy, intemperate, and unproductive members of both races.

Washington's speech was enthusiastically received. He encouraged a sense of hope and optimism in blacks who heard that equality was not so unbelievable and distant a dream after all, while at the same time relieving the minds of whites who feared that educating blacks would lead to trouble. He was a visionary who saw a future in which, with patience and diligent application, blacks could earn the respect of whites, be awarded the same economic opportunities, and prove that they were deserving of equal treatment under law. He was also a realist who saw that three centuries of conditioning pitting black against white would not soon be reversed and that social assimilation was for the present impossible.

These two points—that blacks should be awarded economic and legal equality because they could prove they deserved it; and that as long as they were treated as civic equals, they should humbly resign themselves for the present to "separate-but-equal" social segregation—were the cornerstones of his position on race relations. Time, black achievement, and Christian humility were the tools that would eventually lead to a culture where industry and ability, not race, were the only markers separating one class from another.

Under the circumstances, it was a highly optimistic and unlikely scenario. Unfortunately for Washington and the hopeful millions for whom he spoke, while he was developing programs and policies to help blacks reap the fruits of emancipation, many whites at every level were desperately working to get the top back on what they saw as a Pandora's box of horrors and nail it shut.

Civil rights laws and the efforts to foil them had produced a protracted high-stakes game of cat and mouse that blacks and their allies were losing. The Lincoln administration had fired the first salvo with the Emancipation Proclamation. Within months after the surrender at Appomattox, the Thirteenth Amendment was added to the United States Constitution abolishing slavery in the reunited nation. But the amendment gave former slaves and other blacks no protection against discrimination.

The Fourteenth Amendment of 1868 was written specifically to protect the civil rights of blacks, despite the ambiguous tone of its language:

> No State shall make or enforce any law which shall abridge the privileges or immunities of citizens of the United States; nor shall any State deprive any person of life, liberty, or property, without due process of law; nor deny to any person within its jurisdiction the equal protection of the laws.

The seceded states were required to ratify the amendment before they were readmitted to the Union.

In 1869, the Louisiana state government awarded a slaughterhouse monopoly to a company in New Orleans on grounds that doing so was in the best interest of public health and safety. Competing butchers sued, citing the "equal protection" clause of the Fourteenth Amendment. Eventually in 1873, the case was heard by the Supreme Court, which ruled that the Fourteenth Amendment did not protect the butchers from a restraint imposed by their state government.

Though the case had nothing to do with race, lawmakers readily applied it to situations where blacks were denied protection from discrimination by state laws. Later rulings further diluted the power of the Fourteenth Amendment, limiting its reach to Americans outside the jurisdictions of state governments, such as residents of the District of Columbia. By 1885 court rulings had generally declared federally mandated equal protection a violation of states' rights. And even if states could be held accountable, privately owned businesses—such as railroads and universities—were free to discriminate.

As the power of the federal law was drained away, social attitudes also deteriorated. In the national elections of 1866, Republican blacks by the hundreds were elected to positions in the Congress, state legislatures, and courts—voted into office by newly enfranchised blacks while whites were still barred from the ballot box as conquered aliens. There was a vindictive streak in the U.S. government's policy, and its results were alarming. Through no fault of their own, very few black office holders knew anything about government or the law. Their performance played to Southern whites' worst fears about wild renegades of an inferior race bent on destroying three hundred years of agrarian society.

As whites reclaimed their voting power and grappled to reassert political control with claims of states' rights and with the reenergizing of the Ku Klux Klan, the number of blacks in office declined to nearly nothing, with only a handful of capable black legislators holding their positions into the 1890s.

Toward the end of the 1880s, policymakers became bolder about specific acts of discrimination against blacks. Railroads, which had sometimes separated blacks from other passengers and sometimes not, officially barred blacks from white coaches. Washington lobbied not necessarily for the right to ride with whites, but for "Negro" coaches to be as clean and spacious as those for whites, which they almost never were. He also thought black passengers who paid a first-class fare should have a first-class car, whether with whites or not.

Emboldened by the weakening of the Fourteenth Amendment, states began to define voting requirements in ways that kept blacks from qualifying—residency, literacy, payment of a poll tax—in some cases going so far as to rule that state political parties were "voluntary associations of citizens" that could limit membership any way they pleased.

Against these formidable odds, Booker T. Washington continued to promote self-help for blacks and patience and accommodation with whites, all the while successfully walking the tightrope that preserved and uplifted his school.

Washington was becoming more and more well known outside the South, inviting comparison with the most famous black public figure of the day, Frederick Douglass. Douglass was in his late sixties by the time Washington appeared on the national scene, and his life had been an exciting one. Escaping from his master, Douglass fled to England where sympathetic friends purchased his freedom. As a freedman he spoke out for women's rights and the abolitionist movement, retreating to Canada as the Civil War approached. Douglass had tried to establish black industrial schools along the model of Hampton and Tuskegee before the war without success.

One critical difference between Washington and Douglass—and between Washington and other prominent blacks with whom he would share the spotlight—was Washington's strongly held Christian beliefs. His experience both at Hampton and at Tuskegee supported a long-held conviction that Christian morality and the habits it encouraged were indispensable to a thorough and lasting education. The ramshackle A. M. E. Zion Church had been the school's first benefactor, and Washington's frequent speaking engagements in churches were an important continuing source of donations.

The daily chapel service in Porter Hall was only one of a host of religious events Washington encouraged at Tuskegee. There was also a weekly preaching service that teachers and students alike were expected to attend as well as Sunday school, Friday prayer meeting, a YMCA chapter, and other Christian social and charity groups.

In 1888, Washington hired the first school chaplain, a Congregationalist minister from Nashville named John William Whittaker. Reverend Whittaker also taught grammar and composition and made the rounds of Northern cities in search of donations. After three years, Whittaker accepted a position with a congregation in New Orleans but later returned and spent more than thirty years serving Tuskegee in various capacities.

Friday night prayer groups evolved into somewhat of a cross between a tent revival and a seminary class discussion with students and teachers alike speaking out, their voices overlapping in their excitement, singing, praying, or reciting Scripture. Washington took pride in the fact that many students dated their Christian conversion from one of those Friday nights.

After their conversion experience, students were asked to sign a duplicate form, keeping one copy and returning the other to Chaplain

Whittaker. The wording of the form surely reflected Washington's own private religious beliefs. Headed "My Pledge," it read:

> I thank God that I was led by the Spirit to accept Christ. I am glad I am a Christian, and I promise:
>
> 1. That, as soon as I can, I will join the church of my choice, and by word and deed help to build up the kingdom of Christ on earth.
>
> 2. That I will, daily, think of, or read some portion of the Bible, and will pray, in private each day of my life, closing each prayer with this verse:
>
> "Lord Jesus, I long to be perfectly whole;
> I want Thee forever to live in my soul;
> Break down every idol, cast out every foe:
> Now wash me and I shall be whiter than snow."
>
> —Amen

In keeping with his desire to educate the whole student, Washington took advantage of any chance to relate the chapel service to the students' daily lives. In one case, he had tried without success to get students to bring tools in from the fields at the end of the day. None of them had learned to do it at home, and they had no interest in doing it at Tuskegee; they left plows, hand tools, and everything else outside in all weather. Washington caused a "mild sensation" at one evening prayer service by calling out the forgetful students' names and announcing that the rest of them would wait to begin the service until they had put away their tools and returned, confident they would "be more benefited by prayer and song after having done their work well than by leaving it poorly done." Lessons like that worked "a noticeable betterment" in the way students tended to their duties.

In addition to Hampton, Washington began turning to Fisk University in Nashville, Tennessee, as a reliable source of good teachers. Attending the Fisk commencement exercises in 1889, he met Margaret James Murray. The two sat across from each other at the dinner table, where she respectfully reminded him that she had written Tuskegee asking for a job. He hired her and, recognizing her maturity and skill, promoted her at the beginning of her second year's employment to supervisor of women's programs, making her the second "Lady Principal."

Maggie Murray was born the daughter of a slave and an Irishman. After Emancipation, her mother got a job as a laundress in Macon, Georgia, and married a brick mason. Neighbors of the family, a Quaker brother and sister, took Maggie into their home, sent her to school, loaned her books, and taught her their religious beliefs. When she was fourteen, her Quaker guardians asked her if she would like to be a teacher. When she said she would, they sent her to the local magistrate to take the teachers' examination. She passed and was assigned to teach in the classroom where she had been a student the day before. Five years later, she enrolled at Fisk, working through the preparatory school in five years and the college curriculum in four.

Miss Murray and Mr. Washington shared a range of interests. She was intelligent, deeply religious, always impeccably groomed, and adored tidiness. There was also an attraction of opposites. He was reserved in public, she was frank; he was imposing in looks, she was full-figured and stood four feet ten inches; she was proudly Quaker and indirectly accused staunchly nondenominational Washington of sympathizing with Unitarians.

Washington proposed to her in 1891, but Maggie put him off, unsure of her feelings for his three young children and definitely at odds with John Washington, who thought she was influencing his brother's behavior for the worse and had no reservations about telling her so. Finally she consented, and she and Washington were married in the fall of the next year. Maggie immediately tackled her responsibilities by accompanying her husband on his next long fundraising trip. At home she had plenty to learn as well. She was suddenly the mother of three children, but she had never even dressed one.

Washington spent little time with his family. As much as he loved them, he put in long hours on school business, corresponding with an ever-increasing circle of politicians, newspapermen, educators, and intellectuals. He also gradually began leading a dramatic double life in pursuit of education and respect for his race. On one hand he was a conciliatory member of the African-American race who was warmly embraced by whites for urging blacks to prove themselves worthy of respect. On the other, he was a forceful, even aggressive, agent of change, working out of the public eye to influence policy, control access to information, shape popular opinion, and outmaneuver his opponents.

In both his public and private life, Washington took his own advice that the one way for black Americans to achieve equal status with whites was to concentrate on the essentials of success, "that his pillar of fire by night and pillar of cloud by day shall be property, economy, education, and Christian character." But the two sides of Booker T. Washington interpreted that advice in very different ways.

More than any other factor, Washington lived his double life as a result of the backlash against Reconstruction. He had to remain in the good graces of his white friends, Northern and Southern, in order to support Tuskegee even as the popular endorsement for black equality plummeted. Yet he also had to respond to the increasing political and social hostility of the times without appearing confrontational, which would make it awkward or unattractive for wealthy whites to keep endorsing him.

The changing climate of opinion was obvious. For example, in 1884, Washington had been applauded by thousands at the National Education Association convention after an impressive and compelling defense of black education. At the association's annual meeting in 1890, however, Southern white members threatened to form their own separate Southern Education Association unless the national organization agreed to exclude blacks. One speaker in favor of the proposal warned members against "the menace of Negro rule." Segregation and discrimination of every kind were growing more common and more aggressive.

Washington began quietly building a network of influential editors of black publications, legal advisors, and others in positions to oppose the segregationist tide, but always in a private way that maintained his public relationships. He also competed for resources against others in the field of education for blacks, in one case working secretly to keep a white-run school for blacks from moving to Montgomery, only forty miles from

Tuskegee. When his effort failed, he wrote to Tuskegee treasurer Warren Logan with customary resolve, "We will waste no time worrying over it but throw our energy toward making Tuskegee all the better institution."

Of the handful of nationally recognized blacks other than Washington, more of them were using stronger language against the growing threat. T. Thomas Fortune, a former slave who was an influential New York publisher and editor, railed in an 1890 speech against the government's halfhearted and ineffectual support of equality:

> Loyal in every condition to the flag of the Union—as slave, as contraband of war, as soldier, and as citizen—we feel that we have a right to demand of the government we have served so faithfully the measure of protection guaranteed us and freely granted to the vilest traitor who followed Robert E. Lee.

Frederick Douglass, whom Washington had heard as a teenager, had spent his life fighting to free the blacks. In a pamphlet titled "I Denounce the So-called Emancipation as a Stupendous Fraud," he vilified whites for depriving blacks of their natural rights for generations, then exploiting them as freedmen through a tenant farming system designed to keep them in ignorance and poverty. The same whites who had once coaxed work from the blacks with the whip "now get their labor by a mean, sneaking, and fraudulent device," paying the average tenant farmer eight dollars a month in paper scrip good only at a store owned by the white landowner.

A dramatic illustration of Washington's increasingly delicate situation came on the evening of June 8, 1895, when a black lawyer and former Tuskegee student named Thomas A. Harris appeared on Washington's doorstep, his leg shattered by gunshots from a mob of whites intent on running him out of town. Harris had passed the Alabama bar exam in 1890 and practiced law in Tuskegee. Considered "impudent" and "obnoxious" by some whites—who could tolerate a black carpenter or tinsmith, but felt threatened by the idea of a black lawyer—Harris further displeased them by boarding an itinerant white preacher who was visiting black churches in the area. An angry crowd of whites forced the minister to leave town and later wrote Harris warning him to be gone as well by a certain day and time.

Harris's son was on his way back from the post office with the warning letter when the deadline passed. After reading the letter, Harris was walking across the street to ask his white neighbor's advice when the mob turned the corner at the end of the block. The neighbor was shot in the throat and Harris in the leg before he could get away. White doctors in town refused to treat Harris. His son finally carried him to Washington's house and asked for help. Washington refused to admit them.

The black press condemned Washington as a hypocrite, and a prominent black pastor, Francis J. Grimké, wrote him a letter expressing his sadness and disappointment at Washington's decision. Washington replied with a long letter explaining what he had done and why. "Personally I could not take the wounded man into the school and endanger the lives entrusted by their parents to my care to the fury of some drunken white men." Nor did he feel obliged "to shelter them in all their personal troubles any more than you would feel called on to do the same thing."

He also revealed to Grimké what no one else had known: Washington had arranged for Harris to escape from town and had secured and paid for medical treatment. "I do not care to publish to the world what I do," he wrote, "and should not mention this except for this false representation. I simply chose to help and relieve this man in my own way...." That way, he ministered to a fellow black without raising the hackles of the white population.

This incident was an example of how Washington was becoming an expert at presenting a soothing, accommodating public face while jockeying to influence issues behind the scenes.

As differences between Washington and other black public figures grew more obvious and pronounced—his accommodation versus their confrontation—Washington was seen more and more by whites as the supreme champion of safe, gradual change. His speeches to Northern audiences radiated reconciliation and confidence. To black listeners, he emphasized the value of industry and hard, honest work. To whites he focused on the benefits to them of a gainfully employed and productive black population. He believed that "persons who possess sense enough to earn money have sense enough to know how to give it away.... Rich people are coming to regard men and women who apply to them for help for worthy objects, not as beggars, but as agents for doing their work."

Washington was constantly concerned about the image of Tuskegee as a black-operated institution. If he failed, it would be seen as proof that the race couldn't take care of itself. All the more reason, then, to celebrate the victories, even when they were long in coming. Once Washington called on a prospective donor in Stamford, Connecticut. After walking two miles through a rainstorm, he arrived at the man's house and was grudgingly granted an interview, but he left empty-handed. Two years later back in Tuskegee, Washington opened a letter and read, "Enclosed I send to you a New York draft for three thousand dollars, to be used in furtherance of your work. I had placed this sum in my will for your school, but deem it wiser to give it to you while I live. I recall with pleasure your visit to me two years ago." It was by far the largest donation he had ever received.

In the spring of 1894, his notoriety brought Washington an invitation to participate in the Cotton States and International Exposition in Atlanta the next year. His first assignment was to help lobby the U.S. House Appropriations Committee for money. His eloquent appeal, applauded by legislators and his fellow committee members alike, helped persuade the committee to budget two hundred thousand dollars for the event.

As they made plans for the exposition, organizers decided to include a Negro building in order to showcase the advances blacks had made in the thirty years since the end of the Civil War. Exposition organizers asked Washington to take charge of the exhibit but he declined, citing his duties at Tuskegee. They did, however, persuade him to speak at the opening ceremonies. Some members opposed inviting a black man to speak but were overruled by others who thought it was fitting since black progress was a featured theme.

The vote to invite Washington to be the black keynote speaker was unanimous. One of his first thoughts on receiving the official invitation was that he might have one of his former owners in the audience. Again he faced the conundrum of remaining faithful to blacks while retaining his friendships with whites. No black person had ever been invited to speak at such a large and important gathering on the same platform with whites. The exposition committee gave him no guidelines on what to say.

Washington's experience and instincts told him he had to strike a balance in his speech, as he wrote later:

> I was also painfully conscious of the fact that, while I must be true to my own race in my utterances, I had it in my power to make such an ill-timed address as would result in preventing any similar invitation being extended to a black man again for years to come. I was equally determined to be true to the North, as well as to the best element of the white South, in what I had to say.

Washington began drafting his speech just when preparations for the new school year were at their peak, forcing him to divide his time between a flurry of administrative responsibilities at Tuskegee and work on his remarks. He was alternately encouraged and depressed as the date of his speech drew closer. Southern white papers voiced their discontent that a black man was going to be allowed so prominent a position in the ceremony. Various black colleagues and friends made suggestions on his script. He practiced it aloud in front of Maggie, and the day before leaving for Atlanta, presented it to the teachers at Tuskegee at their request. Their approval helped ease his apprehension a little.

On the morning of September 17, Washington, Maggie, and the three children took the train to Atlanta. Aboard the coach and on platforms at stations along the way, Washington overheard people discussing him and his speech. The big question was how he could appeal to a mixed audience of Northern whites, Southern whites, and blacks all at the same time.

A welcoming committee met Washington and his family at the Atlanta station and escorted them through the teeming city to their hotel. To Washington, Atlanta seemed "literally packed...with people from all parts of the country, and with representatives of foreign governments, as well as with military and civic organizations." Newspapers were full of stories anticipating tomorrow's opening.

Washington slept little that night, and he rose before dawn to read over his speech one last time. It was his custom to pray for God's blessing before every public appearance. On this occasion he prayed on his knees, kneeling on the hotel room floor in the first quiet light of a late summer morning as his wife and children slept nearby.

A committee came to the hotel to escort Washington to the opening procession. Though they began the parade early in the morning, the southern sun was beating down on them by the end of their three-hour journey through the packed streets of the city. For Washington, the draining effect of the heat was further compounded by the sight of thousands of spectators packed into the exhibition hall where he would speak, with thousands more standing outside. One of Washington's white friends, William H. Baldwin Jr., general manager of the Southern Railroad and a Tuskegee trustee, was so nervous on Washington's behalf that he couldn't sit still inside but paced nervously back and forth along the grounds in front of the building until the ceremonies were over.

Because of the crowded streets, the speakers arrived on the platform an hour late. Seeing them begin to appear onstage at last, the restless crowd cheered—until Washington walked in. The sight of him produced a sudden and uneasy quiet, and one spectator heard a nearby member of the audience ask gruffly, "What's that nigger doing on the stage?"

Rufus B. Bullock, former governor of Georgia, was the master of ceremonies, introducing the various speakers and occasional musical numbers from the Twenty-second Regiment Band led by Victor Herbert, who later became famous as the composer of *Babes in Toyland* and other popular operettas.

The audience applauded "The Star Spangled Banner," answered "Dixie" with a chorus of blood-curdling rebel yells, and more or less politely endured "Yankee Doodle." Governor Bullock stood and began another introduction: "We shall now be favored with an address by a great Southern educator." A wave of applause began, but stopped abruptly when Washington rose from his chair. Bullock continued: "We have with us today a representative of Negro enterprise and Negro civilization." The applause resumed, especially in the black section of the segregated audience.

Facing the crowd, Washington had the sun in his eyes and moved around on the platform to find a more comfortable position. No spot was better than another, and after a moment, he stood still, faced into the rays of sunlight streaming in through the windows, and began:

> One-third of the population of the South is of the Negro race. No
> enterprise seeking the material, civil, or moral welfare of this sec-

tion can disregard this element of our population and reach the highest success.

Washington went on to thank the exposition leadership for including blacks, which afforded his race an opportunity to begin "a new era of industrial progress," rooted not in the political posturing and misdirected interests of Reconstruction days, but in skills and industries that would transform blacks from illiterate subsistence farmers into financially responsible, morally upright, self-made citizens worthy of merit.

He then employed a metaphor he had heard during a Thanksgiving service in a Washington, D.C., church two years before:

A ship lost at sea for many days suddenly sighted a friendly vessel. From the mast of the unfortunate vessel was seen a signal, "Water, water: we die of thirst!" The answer from the friendly vessel at once came back, "Cast down your bucket where you are." The distressed ship sent its frantic cry again and got the same response, and again a third time. In desperation the captain lowered buckets to the sea, and drew up sparkling clear water flowing from the unseen mouth of the Amazon River nearby.

To my race I would say…"Cast down your bucket where you are"—cast it down in making friends in every manly way of the people of all races…. Cast it down in agriculture, mechanics, in commerce, in domestic service, and in professions…. Our greatest danger is that in the great leap from slavery to freedom we may overlook the fact that the masses of us are to live by the production of our hands, and fail to keep in mind that we shall prosper in proportion as we learn to dignify and glorify common labour and put brains and skill into the common occupations of life; shall prosper in proportion as we learn to draw the line between the superficial and the substantial…. No race can prosper till it learns that there is as much dignity in tilling a field as in writing a poem.

Washington had been a gifted orator at Hampton. In the intervening twenty years he had honed his presentation skills to a masterful degree. Skeptical whites were drawn gradually yet steadily into his words, and their intermittent applause grew louder and more sustained. His intense grey eyes shone back at the sun, his face was startlingly illuminated by the rays of afternoon light, now nearly horizontal, streaming into the hall. In spite of the heat, he was impeccably dressed in suit, vest, and high collar. His manner was confident—respectful yet authoritative. His voice had no trace of black dialect, none even of the Southern drawl so familiar to many of his white listeners. His pronunciation and inflection were refined, cultured, patrician, and hinted vaguely of Virginian gentility. He rolled his Rs in the declamatory fashion of the day, clipped his consonants with precision, and formed the distinctive "ou" sounds of the James River speech he had heard as a student.

Having addressed his own race first, Washington turned to the whites, repeating his advice:

> "Cast down your buckets where you are"…among the eight mil-lions of Negroes whose habits you know, whose fidelity and love you have tested in days when to have proved treacherous meant the ruin of your firesides…among these people who have tilled your fields, cleared your forests, builded your railroads and cities, and brought forth treasures from the bowels of the earth…in our humble way, we shall stand by you with a devotion that no for-eigner can approach, ready to lay down our lives, if need be, in defense of yours, interlacing our industrial, commercial, civil, and religious life with yours in a way that shall make the interests of both races one.

A New York reporter described him on the platform as "straight as a Sioux chief.… The sinews stood out on his bronzed neck, and his muscu-lar right arm swung high in the air." He raised his hand with the fingers extended wide.

"In all things that are purely social we can be as separate as the fin-gers"—here he drew his fingers together and made a fist—"yet one as the hand in all things essential to mutual progress."

The audience rose as one as wild cheers shot up to the ceiling and cas-caded down the walls in a "delirium of applause." Ladies waved hand-kerchiefs as their escorts flailed the air with hats and walking sticks. When the uproar had tapered off enough, Washington continued.

He said that black and white should—must—pull together for the common good of the South, but integration at various levels had to develop at a natural and comfortable pace.

> The wisest among my race understand that the agitation of questions of social equality is in the extremest folly, and that progress in the enjoyment of all the privileges that will come to us must be the result of severe and constant struggle rather than of artificial forcing. No race that has anything to contribute to the markets of the world is long in any degree ostracized.

He ended with a prayer that sectional differences and racial animosities would be blotted out and that the South would determine "to administer absolute justice, in a willing obedience among all classes to the mandates of law. This, then, coupled with our material prosperity, will bring into our beloved South a new heaven and a new earth."

Again the hall exploded in cheers and applause. Women threw handkerchiefs and flowers at the stage. Governor Bullock dashed across the platform to shake Washington's hand in front of the audience. Washington was engulfed by well-wishers of both races as he left the room and was met by enthusiastic crowds the rest of the day wherever he went. The Atlanta *Constitution* printed the entire text of Washington's speech the next day, declaring it was "an event in the history of the race.... His speech could not have been excelled." Clark Howell, editor of the *Constitution*, called it "a revelation." The Boston *Transcript* reported, "The sensation that it has caused in the press had never been equaled."

The speaker following Washington, Judge Emory Speer, had been billed as the principal speaker of the opening festivities. He declared that the race problem in the South "does not exist" and that all Southerners wanted was "white control of local affairs."

Most news dispatches did not even mention his name.

CHAPTER FIVE

BRINGING THE
MASSES UP

Washington's electrifying speech at the Cotton States Exposition made him a national figure. Educational and political insiders had known of him for a decade, and so had a large and growing network of friends, colleagues, and correspondents in the South. "Cast down your bucket where you are" brought him a wider spotlight and unprecedented acclaim.

In the days after his appearance in Atlanta, newspapers continued their commentary on his words and the public response to them. The Boston *Transcript* declared that Washington's speech "seems to have dwarfed all the other proceedings and the Exposition itself." Washington sent a copy of the speech to President Grover Cleveland, who, from his home in Buzzard's Bay, Massachusetts, had pressed a telegraph key to inaugurate the Atlanta festivities. Days later, Washington received the president's reply, dated October 6, in which he wrote that Washington's words "cannot fail to delight and encourage all who wish well for your race."

The New York *World* dubbed Washington a "Negro Moses" whose words marked "a new epoch in the history of the South." The dispatch also reported the reaction of blacks in the audience:

A ragged, ebony giant squatted on the floor in one of the aisles, watched the orator with burning eyes and tremulous face until the supreme burst of applause came, and then the tears ran down his face. Most of the Negroes in the audience were crying, perhaps without knowing just why.

In the longer term, the response from blacks was much more reserved and ambiguous than the white reaction had been. The initial burst of pride in seeing one of their own speaking at so important an event gradually gave way to a feeling that Washington had given away too much. Washington was evidently willing to accept social segregation in exchange for economic and political equality—"In all things that are purely social we can be as separate at the fingers, yet one as the hand in all things essential to mutual progress," he had said.

Thomas Fortune had spoken out strongly in the past against whites' lukewarm opposition to racial inequality. But over time he had changed his opinion of Washington's approach and became one of his strongest supporters. As editor of the New York *Freeman,* Fortune declared Washington to be heir to the mantle of Frederick Douglass (who had died earlier in the year) as the black man's national spokesman. Yet the black Atlanta *Advocate* strongly opposed Washington's tactic:

Prof. B. T. or Bad Taste Wash. has made a speech and written a letter, yes he has written several letters to President Cleveland and his other white friends.... The white press style Prof. Bad Taste the new Negro, but if there is anything in him except the most servile type of the old Negro we fail to find it in any of his last acts.

Washington stood fast, unshaken in his conviction that "the time will come when the Negro in the South will be accorded all the political rights which his ability, character, and material possessions entitle him to," and that these rights "will not come in any large degree through outside or artificial forcing, but will be accorded to the Negro by the Southern white people themselves, and that they will protect him in the exercise of those rights."

Magazines, newspapers, and speakers bureaus showered him with offers. One tendered a contract for fifty thousand dollars, or two hundred dollars plus expenses per appearance. Washington turned them all down, insisting his life's work was at Tuskegee, and that his duties on the Institute's behalf made a speaking tour impossible.

Tuskegee had continued its rapid growth through the first half of the 1890s. In 1891 the name was changed to Tuskegee Normal and Industrial Institute to emphasize a course selection heavy on the practical skills Washington insisted were the foundation of black self-reliance. By 1895 Tuskegee trained its students in bricklaying and plastering, blacksmithing, carpentry, printing, millworking, dressmaking, and millinery (the design and making of women's hats), as well as farming and brickmaking. There were also several shops: wheelwright, foundry and machine, tin, shoe, carriage trimming, painting, plumbing, and a canning factory. A boys' dormitory was built and named Armstrong Hall in honor of Washington's great mentor and benefactor at Hampton; it was renamed Olivia Davidson Hall in 1892.

With the girls in Alabama Hall and the boys in Davidson, Washington at last realized his vision for a boarding school that could draw students from across the South into a carefully regimented environment combining book learning, practical skills, refined personal habits, and religious instruction. This all-encompassing approach, Washington believed, kept the students from returning home to bad influences and old habits that would make their education useless.

The Practice Cottage was also built around this time. This one-story frame building looked like a private home. Groups of five senior girls took turns living in the cottage and running it as their own household. They did all the housekeeping and washing, sewing and mending, tended a few chickens and pigs, made menus, did the shopping, cooking, and serving, kept a budget from a regular operating allowance, and attended academic classes.

Religious education grew in importance during this same time, though not without controversy. Washington considered most African-American preachers tragically unprepared for their calling: They were poorly educated, lightly motivated, and too often in it just for the steady income. He stated his case at the 1890 commencement exercises of Fisk University in Nashville, claiming, according to one listener, that "out of four hundred colored Baptist churches in Alabama only about fifteen intelligent pastors could be found."

Washington's detractors claimed he made the statement in order to loosen the purse strings of the Northern philanthropists who kept Tuskegee afloat. Their perception was that the philanthropists believed that the more illiterate black people were, the more money they needed. Later that summer, the Fisk speech was published in the black press as "The Colored Ministry: Its Defects and Needs." Washington made the point that very few black ministers had a seminary degree, and that while many of them were intelligent and earnest, they were unqualified to lead their flocks. "I have no hesitancy," he wrote, "in asserting that three-fourths of the Baptist ministers and two-thirds of the Methodists are unfit, either mentally or morally, or both, to preach the Gospel to any one or attempt to lead any one."

Washington's solution was a Bible training school "on a thoroughly Christian but strictly undenominational basis" to teach would-be ministers the nuts and bolts of preaching, counseling, song leading, and witnessing.

Every minister and church leader in a position to know the truth, knew Washington was absolutely right. The senior bishop of the African Methodist Episcopal Church affirmed he had "not overstated, but rather understated the facts." Nevertheless, Washington's frankness was widely condemned by black organizations, at least one of which went so far as to send a "missionary" to warn parents not to send their children to Tuskegee. (Washington later noted with wry humor that this "missionary" had a son at Tuskegee who remained enrolled throughout the controversy.)

Washington never backpedaled, never softened or modified his remarks. He later wrote:

I knew I was right, and that time and the sober second thought of the people would vindicate me.... My experience with [black ministers], as well as other events in my life, convince me that the thing to do, when one feels sure that he has said or done the right thing, and is condemned, is to stand still and keep quiet. If he is right, time will show it.

Putting action to the word, Washington founded the Phelps Bible Training School at Tuskegee with the help of Olivia and Caroline Stokes, wealthy sisters who shared Washington's desire for training black clergymen through a program Olivia described as "simple, direct, and helpful." In 1892 the sisters donated money to build Phelps Hall, a three-story frame building with a wide wrap-around porch, to house Bible students, offices, classrooms, a chapel, and library. True to the sisters' directions, Phelps Hall was simple and unadorned, reminiscent more of a military barracks than a college building.

Religious training remained an educational cornerstone for all the students at Tuskegee. The weekly march into chapel had become a tradition. Every Sunday all students lined up for inspection in their school uniforms—military-style dress for boys and complementary skirts and jackets for girls. By this time enrollment was approaching 750, which made the march to chapel a grand-looking event for campus visitors and town residents. In time it became a local tradition to watch the procession every week.

One of Tuskegee's most popular and enduring programs began in February of 1892 when Washington hosted a "Tuskegee Negro Conference" for local farmers, ministers, and other interested parties. Washington saw black farmers being crushed by the sharecropper system, and he was convinced that the problem, like so many others, could be solved by education and hard work.

Sharecropping was an unequal partnership in which landowners held oppressive economic power over their tenants. Owners lent tenants money at ruinous interest rates of 25 to 30 percent until their crop was harvested. At harvest time, the crop often brought less money than what the tenants owed for the year. The tenant then borrowed against the next year's crop for money to live on, getting deeper in debt every season. To make matters worse, owners typically kept all the accounts—most sharecroppers were illiterate—and set the sale price of crops and the purchase price of goods tenants had to buy during the year. Washington was convinced the black farmer had "natural sense" that only had to be nourished and directed in order to work out from under the system.

About seventy-five people were invited to the conference; between four and five hundred showed up, many of them farmers looking for a way out of the economic cycle of sharecropping. In the morning session, Washington invited men and women to tell the group how many people lived in their communities, how many mortgaged their crops, who the landowners were, and otherwise describe their local situations. He also asked them about housing, educational facilities, and churches. The news was not encouraging. Eighty percent of the farmers had mortgages, schools were in session only three months a year, and church services were held in ramshackle cabins or out of doors.

The group spent the afternoon looking for solutions. The issues were daunting and the people unaccustomed to such deliberations, but by the end of the day, Washington was both surprised and pleased with the results. "Self-respect," they concluded, "will bring us many rights now denied us." Far from seeking help from the government or the white establishment, they set ambitious goals for their own advancement:

> We urge all to buy land and to cultivate it thoroughly; to raise more food supplies; to build better houses with more than one room; to tax themselves to build better school houses, and to extend the school term to at least six months; to give more attention to the character of their leaders, especially ministers and teachers; to keep out of debt; to avoid lawsuits; to treat our women better; and conferences similar in aim to this one be held in every community where practicable.

The Negro Conferences became a centerpiece of Washington's solicitations for money. They were highly visible, obviously popular, and appealed to the Northern whites' interest in helping black citizens help themselves. The farmers and tradesmen and their wives who attended the meetings weren't looking for a handout, but for a way out of the circle of debt perpetuated by the sharecropping system.

Washington wrote of the success of the conference to General Armstrong at Hampton, delighted at how the participants "saw and realized their miserable condition," "wanted light," and "realized that education was their only salvation." Surely they were guided in their conclusions by the predispositions of their host, but the meeting had in fact injected a true note of hope and confidence into a bleak and corrupt situation.

Armstrong was the guest of honor at the Negro Conference of 1893, though it was a bittersweet time for the general and his famous former pupil. After five years of declining health, the once robust, energetic general was partially paralyzed, unable to walk, and had trouble speaking due in part to a series of strokes. Armstrong had visited Tuskegee briefly in 1887 and wrote to Washington that he would like to come again. Both men knew it would be his farewell visit.

General Armstrong, accompanied by a member of the Hampton staff, took the *New Orleans Limited* as far as Chechaw, still the nearest mainline stop to Tuskegee. The crack-limited trains didn't schedule stops at any except the larger stations, but the Western of Alabama Railroad made an exception in honor of their distinguished passenger. The Tuskegee Railroad ran a special train to Chechaw and back, at no charge, to meet the *New Orleans Limited* and bring Armstrong back to town. It was late at night when Armstrong was bundled into a carriage for the mile ride to campus. As he approached the Tuskegee entrance, hundreds of pine knots were lighted on cue, held by Tuskegee students who had stood quietly in the dark on either side of the road waiting to surprise their honored visitor. The whole campus seemed to flash to life in a blaze of wavering torches, their resinous fragrance carried along on the southern night air.

Armstrong expected to stay in Washington's home since his health was too poor to travel around the campus. But it was soon clear that a great many people wanted to see him and wanted him to see their departments, fields, workshops, and other fruits of their labor, which was inspired at least indirectly by his educational legacy. General Armstrong wanted to see it all, and so John Washington fashioned a sedan chair for him—a sturdy, canopied chair with handles for four bearers. Students took turns carrying Armstrong up and down the hilly Tuskegee campus. After a few days, they traded the sedan chair for a wheelchair, which took one student to manage instead of four. Students competed for the honor of wheeling the old gentleman around.

Though Armstrong had not spoken in public since his latest stroke, he eagerly accepted an invitation to address the Negro Conference. Before hundreds of expectant onlookers in the chapel of Porter Hall, four students lifted him up into a chair onstage. In spite of his slurred speech, he persevered with resolute determination, speaking with "characteristic energy and pith" for forty minutes, stopping from time to time to ask his audience if they could understand him; they answered with a roar of affirmation and applause.

General Armstrong spent two months at Tuskegee. After he returned to Hampton, a buoyant Washington was inspired to redouble his effort in the cause of black education that was so near to his mentor's heart. He later wrote, "If a man in his condition was willing to think, work, and act, I should not be wanting in furthering in every possible way the wish of his heart."

Armstrong gave a glowing report of his visit. He had not spoken at Hampton in more than a year on account of his infirmity; his experience in the chapel at Porter Hall gave him the confidence to speak to his own students again. He told them, "If you find something not right in the world, act as Mr. Washington has. He couldn't work a miracle, but he got the people together to see what is the matter and not spend their time in blaming others, but see what they can do to improve themselves." A few weeks later, the old soldier passed away.

By 1895, Booker T. Washington headed an institution with a student enrollment approaching one thousand from more than twenty states, Africa, and the West Indies. The campus covered more than five hundred acres, including an old former Macon County plantation where experimental farming was underway. More buildings had been built with student-made bricks and student laborers, and others were planned. That year Tuskegee's first telephones and first consolidated plumbing system were installed.

The majority of students still came from poor families, and few could pay their tuition and board. Most enrolled on the five-year plan, working during the day and going to night school for the first two years to earn enough money to pay for three more years of day school.

Income from students' work and the annual state appropriation met only a fraction of Tuskegee's operating costs. The rest was covered by contributions, the largest of which were from Northern individuals and foundations that endorsed Washington's approach to education of blacks. Though he had permanent representatives in several cities to call on donors and keep the Tuskegee name and mission in front of them, Washington was the one donors always wanted to see. He had learned something of poise and presentation from Olivia Davidson when they traveled together in the earliest days of the school and had honed his own presentation skills over the years to masterful results.

Prospective contributors wanted to see Washington because he was becoming famous. His appearance at the Cotton States Exposition had catapulted him onto the national stage. Here was a black man who was articulate and humble, looking not for a handout but a means for helping his people succeed on their own. In describing his technique, Washington said, "I think that the presentation of the facts, on a high, dignified plane, is all the begging that most rich people care for."

To keep Tuskegee solvent, Washington spent six months a year on the road, much of it in and around Boston, expanding the circle of contacts he and Miss Davidson had established over nearly fifteen years. Not only Boston, but the North in general had always been a greater source of capital than the South, where wealth was in land and property more than in stocks and bonds and business. The agrarian South supported a barter economy where relatively little money changed hands. What money wealth there was had been lost during and after the war in the devaluing of Confederate currency and bonds, confiscation of lands, foreclosures, insufficient manpower to plant and harvest crops, and taxation (Southerners were assessed back taxes for the years they were citizens of the Confederacy).

One of the earliest organizations begun specifically to fund black education was the Slater Fund, which became a model for many later foundations with varying degrees of interest in the same goal, including the

Ford Foundation, Carnegie Foundation, Phelps-Stokes Fund, George Peabody Fund, and General Education Board.

Samuel Slater, the founder of the Slater fortune, was born in England in 1768 and became an apprentice in a textile mill. At the age of twenty-one, he sailed for America after memorizing the design of the revolutionary new Arkwright machinery for carding and spinning cotton into thread. Importing drawings of the equipment was illegal, which made Slater the only source of this valuable information. Reconstructing the plans from memory, Slater built copies of the Arkwright equipment and started a company that became the foundation of the American textile industry.

The Slater Fund was founded by Samuel Slater's descendants in 1882 for the "uplifting of the lately emancipated population of the Southern states, and their posterity, by conferring upon them the blessings of Christian education." Its endowment was one million dollars, and its first president was former U.S. President Rutherford B. Hayes, a supporter of black rights who, as commander in chief, had removed the last of Federal troops from Southern states at the end of Reconstruction.

Like many donors, the Slater Fund gave preference to organizations that were already established, particularly if they had demonstrated success at reaching their stated goals. For demonstrated results, no institution could outshine Tuskegee. The more money Washington raised, the more he could accomplish; the more he accomplished, the more he could raise.

Some blacks continued to think Washington drained off so much money that the others were denied their proper share. These accusations appeared with increasing frequency in the black press and came most often from those who disagreed with Tuskegee's emphasis on trades and practical skills. Kelly Miller, an essayist whose views moved in and out of accord with Washington's over the years, felt higher intellectual education was essential to the development of the black race. He agreed that practical training was important to the masses, but he also believed naturally gifted blacks should receive an education in literature, mathematics, science, and so forth, in order to prepare them to be leaders. He chafed at what one commentator called the "philanthropic predilection for industrial education" because, in Miller's words, industrial and intellectual education together were "essential to the symmetrical development of any people."

As a result of his travels, his presentations before foundations and boards, and the ongoing commentary about his Atlanta speech, Washington's star continued to rise. What he called the greatest surprise of his life came in the form of a letter dated May 28, 1896, from Charles W. Eliot, president of Harvard University. In it, Eliot invited Washington to the upcoming Harvard commencement exercises in order to receive an honorary Master of Arts degree. Washington was overwhelmed. His former life passed before him in a flood of memories. He later recalled:

> My life as a slave on the plantation, my work in the coal-mine, the times when I was without food and clothing, when I made my bed under a sidewalk, my struggles for an education, the trying days I had at Tuskegee, days when I did not know where to turn for a dollar to continue the work there, the ostracism and sometimes oppression of my race—all this passed before me and nearly overcame me.

The exercises were held the morning of June 24. Washington assembled with the other guests who were to receive honorary degrees, including Dr. Alexander Graham Bell, and marched to the Sanders Theater on campus for the ceremony. Observing a long-standing tradition, none of the students knew who were receiving honorary degrees until they appeared onstage. Washington was welcomed by a reaction the *New York Times* described as "vociferous and long-continued."

A dinner that evening concluded with speeches by Massachusetts Governor Roger Wolcott, Massachusetts Senator Henry Cabot Lodge, President Eliot, and Washington. In his remarks, Washington applauded Harvard for making "the mansions on yon Beacon Street feel and see the need of the spirits in the lowliest cabin in Alabama cotton fields or Louisiana sugar bottoms," and doing so "not by bringing itself down, but by bringing the masses up."

With words that must have gratified Washington, one Boston newspaper reported:

It has been mentioned that Mr. Washington is the first of his race to receive an honorary degree from a New England university. This, in itself, is a distinction, but the degree was not conferred because Mr. Washington is a coloured man, or because he was born in slavery, but because he has shown, by his work for the elevation of the people of the Black Belt of the South, a genius and a broad humanity which count for greatness in any man, whether his skin be white or black.

This was the point Washington had labored to make for fifteen years: Through diligence and patience, excellence will eventually be recognized and rewarded regardless of race.

Celebrated as he was at Harvard, Washington faced a far different reaction at the Tuskegee graduation ceremony the same year. Among the commencement speakers was Alabama Governor William C. Oates. The speaker immediately before the governor was John Dancy, a conservative black leader who was the customs inspector in Wilmington, North Carolina. Dancy was very much in sympathy with Washington's views on self-help and black people's need for patience. In his speech he heaped praise upon the Northern contributors whose money kept Tuskegee going, and when he finished, he received an animated and sustained ovation.

Observing the excitement of his predominately black audience, Governor Oates read a sinister component into it. To him, it seemed that Dancy had somehow stirred the rebellious instincts so many Southern whites feared simmered just under the surface in the black population. Striding to the front of the platform, the governor waved the pages of his prepared remarks at the audience and spoke off the cuff and from the heart:

I want to give you niggers a few words of plain talk and advice. No such address as you have just listened to is going to do you any good; it's going to spoil you. You had better not listen to such speeches. You might as well understand that this is a white man's country, as far as the South is concerned, and we are going to make you keep your place. Understand that. I have nothing more to say to you.

As the governor left the rostrum, there was a nervous rustle from the crowd. The other guest speakers were too shocked and surprised to respond right away. Washington, apparently unruffled, stood and broke the heavy silence: "Ladies and gentlemen, I am sure you will agree with me that we have had enough eloquence for one occasion. We shall listen to the next speaker on another occasion, when we are not so fagged out. We will now rise, sing the doxology, and be dismissed." And they did.

It was Governor Oates's view of the race issue, and not President Eliot's, that was being codified into law in the United States. Legal rulings continued to chip away at equality for black Americans. A Civil War and three constitutional amendments were supposed to have established a framework for equal treatment of blacks. Much of the potential for change went unrealized as a result of the legal transformation of the Fourteenth Amendment (court opinions in favor of states' rights and private corporations' freedom to distinguish citizens and customers on the basis of race).

Perhaps the heaviest blow to hopes of black equality came with the 1896 United States Supreme Court ruling known as Plessy vs. Ferguson. A railroad passenger named Homer Plessy sued to stop the enforcement of a Louisiana state law requiring separation of the races on public transportation. Plessy charged that the law violated the Thirteenth and Fourteenth Amendments and that it stamped blacks with a "badge of inferiority." The Supreme Court ruled eight to one in favor of Louisiana, claiming the law reflected "established usages, customs, and traditions of the people." The Court further ruled that forced segregation did not automatically mean blacks were inferior and that "if this be so, it is not by reason of anything found in the act, but solely because the colored race chooses to put that construction upon it."

Thus was born the "separate but equal" precedent that legalized racial segregation at the federal level. A noteworthy but seldom mentioned fact in the case was that Plessy was seven-eighths white, yet still legally a Negro.

In 1896, Tuskegee began construction of its first chapel. The first permanent building on campus, Porter Hall, included a chapel. As the student body grew, church services were moved to the Pavilion, an ungainly but large barn-like building of rough lumber with a tar paper roof. The Pavilion had been built in 1886 for exercises commemorating the fifth anniversary of the school, which two thousand people had attended.

The Porter Hall chapel was still big enough for evening devotionals and Friday night Bible study, and the Pavilion was ample for the Sunday services. But, ever mindful of the power of appearances, Washington longed for a chapel building that reflected the value he put on religious training.

On March 30, students broke ground for a new chapel that would stand as a symbol of the preeminent importance of religion in campus life. It would also fill a host of practical needs for worship and meeting space.

Robert R. Taylor, a member of the Tuskegee staff since 1892, designed the chapel. He was the embodiment of Washington's educational mission. He was valedictorian of his architecture class at MIT and that institute's first black graduate. The chapel building was conceived as the figurative and literal center of campus life. Taylor's plans called for a brick building in the shape of a Greek cross with seating for twenty-five hundred. The exterior was the Victorian interpretation of gothic architecture, popular then not only for churches but also for commercial buildings and fine private homes.

In keeping with Washington's ever-present emphasis on black accomplishment, the construction was done completely by blacks, and chiefly by Tuskegee students. All 1.2 million bricks for the project were made on campus and all bricklaying and plastering done by students under the guidance of school faculty. Steam heating was installed by the school's plumbing and machine department instructors and their classes. The completed building was 154 feet, 6 inches long and 106 feet wide; the hammer beam ceiling of yellow pine had a clear span of 63 feet and peaked 48 feet, 6 inches from the floor. At the front of the room was a chancel area large enough to seat the entire 88-member faculty and a choir loft for 150.

When completed, it was the biggest, tallest (105 feet to the tower cross), finest building in Macon County. It was also the first building in the county to have electric lights. In spite of its size, it was filled to capacity for commencement, the annual Negro Conferences, and other important celebrations.

The Negro Conferences continued to be a success. Because of the crowds that attended, Washington organized the presentations into two days, one for farmers and one for tradesmen and other workers. The surge of discriminatory state laws being passed throughout the South were economically affecting the tradesmen. Traditionally, the majority of bricklayers, stone masons, carpenters, blacksmiths, tinsmiths, and other skilled tradesmen had been blacks—some slave and some free—and had served a mostly white clientele. While farmers struggled to take advantage of new opportunities, the tradesmen worked to halt the erosion of their employment opportunities in the face of new legal challenges.

Black farmers were still looking for ways to get out of debt and achieve some level of independence from their landlords and sharecropping. Debt management and dedication, common themes at the conferences, were ways they could achieve those goals. Another source of hope for the farmers was in learning techniques for improving crop yields. The more income they could squeeze from their few acres, the sooner they could work off their debt and get land of their own, improve their living conditions, and leave a legacy of self-reliance for their children.

In 1896, trustees of the Slater Fund offered to establish an agricultural school at Tuskegee, which Washington expected to be "the best equipped and only distinct agricultural school in the South for the benefit of the colored people." With this new facility, Tuskegee could research crop selection, crop rotation, fertilizer, planting and harvesting techniques, and other information for farmers in Macon County. Scientific studies would help them get higher yields from their crops. The experiment station could also investigate the economics of farming, giving farmers advice on how much of each plant to grow and how much to spend on fertilizer and supplies.

In spite of its obvious benefit, Washington would not be able to oversee every detail of the new school's operation the way he already did so much. Always worried about Tuskegee's appearance in the eyes of the world, Washington was inclined to keep a firm hand in every detail of its management. When he was on the road speaking and soliciting funds, he had daily reports sent to him about attendance, discipline problems, productivity of the brickyard, harness shop, and other enterprises.

Washington thought the school was organized so "the daily work of the school is not dependent on the presence of one individual." Warren Logan, a Hampton graduate who was Washington's first faculty member after himself and Olivia Davidson, was treasurer of Tuskegee and the chief executive in Washington's absence. Nevertheless, Washington held the reins of leadership tightly even when he was away in Boston or Washington, D.C., reading Logan's daily reports and answering with a steady stream of directives and commentary.

One observer told Washington, "As I have watched you running from one end of the country to the other with no time for recreation or rest, with no vacation or quiet days or recuperation, I have wondered and with my wife often discussed the fate of Tuskegee and its wonderful work, should you overtax your strength and succumb to the inevitable laws of Nature."

At a meeting with Washington in New York, Slater Fund trustees informally suggested he look for a white man to head the agricultural school since there was "no colored man in the country fitted for such work." True, there were any number of white teachers who could do the job, but to this point all of Tuskegee's teachers and staff had been black, and Washington hoped to keep it that way as a testament to black enterprise and accomplishment.

Inquiries early in the spring of 1896 led him to the single black graduate student at Iowa Agricultural College in Ames, Iowa. This man was, like the chapel architect Robert Taylor, a living example of Washington's ideal black achiever—a man who excelled in his field to the point where his abilities overcame white prejudice against him. The man had not entered college until he was nearly thirty, and he was forced at first to eat in the kitchen with the cooks because blacks weren't allowed in the dining hall. He soon proved his worth, however, and after graduation was offered a position as assistant professor of agriculture while continuing his graduate studies. He was an accomplished botanist and a gifted painter. He was still trying to decide whether to devote his life to studying plants or painting them when he received an offer from the black Alcorn Agricultural and Mechanical College in Mississippi to be a professor there.

As he weighed the decisions of art versus science, white school versus black, and graduate study versus teaching, the student received a letter from Booker T. Washington of the famous Tuskegee Normal and Industrial Institute inviting him to take a new position there as director of the agriculture school and the state agricultural experiment station.

This enterprising scholar, George Washington Carver, found himself with a lot of thinking to do.

In his first reply to Washington on April 3, 1896, Carver reported he planned to finish his master's degree in scientific agriculture the next fall and didn't want to take any new position until then, although, he wrote, "I expect to take up work amongst my people and have known and appreciated the great work you are doing." He had put off accepting the appointment at Alcorn because of some interesting experiments that were underway in Iowa.

Two days later Carver wrote again. He had weighed Washington's offer more carefully and, on second thought, decided he might be willing after all to adjust his schedule to accommodate Tuskegee's. "Of course I should prefer to stay here until fall as then I will receive my master's degree, but should I get a satisfactory position I might be induced to leave before."

On April 12, Carver requested more information on Tuskegee and the proposed agricultural school and told Washington, "It has always been the one great ideal of my life to be of the greatest good to the greatest number of 'my people' possible and to this end I have been preparing myself for these many years; feeling as I do that this line of education is the key to unlock the golden door of freedom to our people." Still struggling with his decision, Carver closed by saying, "At the next writing I hope to give you a more definite answer. May the Lord bless you and prosper your work."

Five days later Washington replied with a formal offer of employment. Washington was very proud of the fact that Tuskegee had an all-black faculty, and he appealed to Carver's sense of pride in his race: "If we cannot secure you, we shall be forced perhaps to put in a white man. The salary would be one thousand dollars a year. This perhaps to you may not seem a large salary, but from the first we have made a policy of trying to get teachers who come not only for the money but also for their deep interest in their race." The school, Washington continued, had excellent facilities and the pick of black students in the South: Half of last year's applicants had been turned down because there wasn't enough room for them. New agricultural buildings built with the Slater Fund donation would be the best in the region.

The salary was not an issue with Carver. Iowa State offered him a raise in his assistant's pay to stay there, and another job offer on the table included a thousand dollar salary plus a house. Carver replied, "I expect, as I have already stated, to go to my people and I have been looking for some time at Tuskegee with favor. So the financial feature is at present satisfactory." His biggest concern was that there be room at Tuskegee for cabinets holding the plant collection he had assembled over a period of years and would be moving with him.

Confirming their agreement, Carver wrote to Washington again on May 16:

> I am looking forward to a very busy, pleasant and profitable time at your college and shall be glad to cooperate with you in doing all I can through Christ who strengtheneth me to better the condition of our people.... Providence permitting I will be there in November. God bless you and your work.

CHAPTER SIX

TRUST IN GOD AND PRESS ON

George Washington Carver, like his new employer, was born a slave in a state where the division over slavery was particularly bitter. Booker T. Washington's home state of Virginia was literally broken in two over the issue in 1863, when West Virginia split off as a result of anti-slavery sentiment in the Appalachians. Carver's home state did not split, but by the time he was born, the very name of Missouri was a symbol of dashed hopes for compromise and unity.

Missouri was admitted as a state in 1821 only after a long congressional argument over slavery. There had been slaves in Missouri Territory; when Missouri statehood was first proposed, the U.S. House of Representatives voted to allow slavery to remain for the present on the condition that it be gradually phased out. Southern states were able to block the proposal, producing a stalemate that lasted until Maine applied for statehood. Legislators agreed to admit Maine as a free state and Missouri as a slave state. They reached a further compromise that there would be no slavery in the rest of the land in the Louisiana Purchase above 36°30' North Latitude.

This "Missouri Compromise" remained in delicate balance until California was admitted as a free state in 1850. This gave the free states (those where slavery was illegal) a sixteen to fifteen lead, a source of irritation that flared up four years later with the establishment of Kansas and Nebraska as territories. In organizing the territorial governments, Senator Stephen Douglas of Illinois inserted a legislative provision that allowed citizens of those territories, which were supposedly in the free part of the Louisiana Purchase according to the Compromise, to vote on the question of slavery themselves. Signed into law by President Franklin Pierce, the Kansas-Nebraska Act declared the Missouri Compromise "inoperative and void."

Bloody battles broke out intermittently between pro- and anti-slavery forces in Missouri, fighting that intensified in 1857 with the conclusion of an eleven-year lawsuit waged by a St. Louis slave trying to win his freedom. Dred Scott was the slave of an army surgeon and accompanied him to Minnesota Territory. They later moved back to St. Louis; after his master died there, Scott claimed he was free because he had been living in Minnesota, a free territory.

Eventually the United States Supreme Court heard the case. Though each of the nine justices wrote his own opinion, the court ruled in essence that Scott was still a slave. The justices claimed that because he was black, the federal court had no jurisdiction over him since a Negro could not be a U.S. citizen under the Constitution. Furthermore, a slaveowner's constitutional right to due process made the Missouri Compromise unconstitutional since it deprived him of his property without a trial: Across the state line, his property suddenly wasn't his any more. Scott and his Minnesota-born wife were finally awarded their freedom a little more than a year before Scott's death in 1858. But the Dred Scott decision deepened the profound division over slavery that soon gave birth to the Confederacy.

It was in the southwestern corner of this troubled state of Missouri that Moses Carver and his wife, Susan, lived on 240 acres near the tiny settlement of Diamond Grove. Carver had almost one hundred acres in cultivation or pasture and raised a little bit of everything from hay to honey, including potatoes, wheat, oats, corn, and garden vegetables. He also had a fruit orchard, a herd of oxen, and a few hogs, cows, and mules. Moses was a hard-working man known both for his friendliness and his eccentricity. He had a pet rooster that perched on his shoulder. Though he had the character traits usually associated with Christianity—generosity, compassion, thrift, humility—he never went to church. He loved animals, particularly horses, and was a respected dealer in racehorses.

Moses and Susan had no children of their own. But soon after they moved to Missouri, Moses' brother Richard died, and his three children, Albert, Daniel, and Sarah Jane, went to live with Uncle Mose and Aunt Sue. They grew up as the Carvers' own, helping with chores as youngsters, then taking on more strenuous and responsible jobs as the years passed. By the time the children began leaving to establish their own homes in the early 1850s, Moses and Susan were only in their mid-forties, both strong and healthy. Still, it was clear they could not run such a large farm by themselves. They hired one farm hand and might have hired more if they could have found them. But workers were scarce. The lure of cheap or free land in the West tempted anyone to move out there and set up a homestead.

Though the Carvers were strong Union supporters who opposed the idea of secession, Moses Carver eventually decided a slave had become an economic necessity. On October 9, 1855, he bought a thirteen-year-old black girl named Mary for seven hundred dollars. Her duties were likely to keep house, tend the vegetable garden, take care of the cows, and tend the poultry yard.

Four years to the month after her purchase, Mary gave birth to a son named James. The father's identity was never known. Some claimed he was one of the two slaves of the Carvers' neighbor Colonel James Grant. Others believed the father was the Carvers' white hired man; still others thought he was another white man in the community. Most people who saw him, including the census taker who visited the Carver farm in 1860, believed the baby was a mulatto, strengthening the probability that the father was not a slave.

Mary became pregnant again within weeks of James's birth; her second son, who was fully black, was born July 12, 1860. He was named George. Though born less than a year apart, there were dramatic differences between the boys. Jim gained weight at once and grew into a robust, active toddler, but George was small and sickly from the beginning. George was almost surely born prematurely and with severe respiratory problems. Gathering what simple remedies she found on a frontier farm, Mary tended him as best she could.

George never knew who his father was. Some said he was a slave on a neighboring farm who was killed not long after George was born. Walking beside a load of logs pulled by oxen, he fell under the heavy cart and was crushed to death by the wheels. His mother never told him whether or not that man was his father.

The outbreak of the Civil War threw Missouri, a slaveholding Union-leaning border state, into a panic, particularly the southwestern part where Moses Carver lived. Far from the relative order of the big cities along the Missouri River—Westport (later Kansas City), Jefferson City, and St. Louis—Diamond Grove and all of Newton County became a crossroads for desperate characters. Slaveholders were running south to secessionist Arkansas; abolitionists were liberating slaves from their masters by force and taking them northwest to freedom in Kansas. Adventurers, outlaws, and opportunists were heading in both directions, as well as due west into Indian Territory.

Neosho, seat of Newton County, was commandeered alternately by Unionists and Confederates. Although Federal sympathizers took control of the state government in July 1861, bands of Confederate irregulars and vigilantes continued to terrorize the countryside for years afterward. The winter of 1863–64 was the coldest Missouri winter anyone could remember. That year the Arkansas River at Fort Smith was frozen so thick that entire companies of men, horses, and wagons could cross at once.

One icy November day in 1863, a small band of outlaws appeared at Moses Carver's farm. The men may have been stealing slaves to sell in Arkansas, where the price paid for them had multiplied fivefold since the beginning of the war. They might have been kidnapping them to turn in to Union authorities for a bounty. Whatever their aim, they came to take the slaves and anything else they could.

Moses was out working in the field and had Jim with him. Mary and

George were in the slave cabin only a few feet away from the Carvers' log house. Some of the attackers captured Mary and George while others dragged Moses from the field; Jim was able to run away unseen and hide in the brush at the edge of the field. The invaders may have known Moses was a horse trader and demanded he turn over his gold to them. Like many men in that time and place, Moses buried his gold to keep it safe in just such circumstances. Moses refused to tell them where the gold was. Enraged, they hung him by his thumbs from a walnut tree. When he still refused to tell, they retrieved a shovelful of blazing coals from the cabin fireplace, yanked the shoes from his dangling feet and pressed the coals to his bare soles. Still he refused.

Waiting no longer, the thieves took Mary and George and disappeared into the woods. Moses' wife and hired hand rushed to get him down from the tree. As soon as he could, Carver hired a Union Army scout stationed at Neosho, Sergeant John Bentley, to bring Mary and George back. Sergeant Bentley formed a search party and took up the fugitives' trail. Riding through the woods in the bitter cold, the searchers found evidence of the robbers but never caught them. In the small hours of the morning they came to an abandoned cabin. Inside they found little George alone. The men gave up the chase and returned to Neosho. Sergeant Bentley took George to his house for the night and laid him down to sleep in the same crib with his own son William.

The next morning, Sergeant Bentley took George back to the Carver farm and reported Mary was lost for good. Moses had offered forty acres and a horse for the return of his slaves. Since the sergeant found one but not the other, Moses kept his land but gave the soldier a fine black mare valued at three hundred dollars. There were rumors that Mary was taken to Arkansas; others said she died of exposure. She was never seen again.

Mary and her children had originally lived in the same cabin as their owners. Around the time Jim and George were born, Moses built a second, slightly larger cabin for himself and his wife. Each cabin had a single room with a rock fireplace, a simple door on rude wooden hinges, and window openings with shutters but without glass. They were very close together with just enough room for two people to pass as they walked between them. Now with their adoptive children grown and gone and Mary stolen, Uncle Mose and Aunt Sue moved Jim and George into their house to raise as their own.

It was an act combining compassion and common sense. The couple felt an emotional bond with the two young boys, who had grown up in their household and shared their sorrow at the disappearance of their mother. Moreover, the Carvers were getting on in years, his brother's children had moved on, and the crops and livestock needed attention.

George's health remained delicate. As Jim grew bigger and stronger, he took on a proportionately greater share of the plowing, clearing, harvesting, and other heavy work. George always seemed to lag behind in physical development and was thin and weak. His premature birth made him likely to catch a cold often and keep it for weeks. He had recurring bouts of whooping cough and may have been sick with it the night of his kidnapping. Bronchitis and tubercular inflammation frequently kept him indoors. As a result, George grew up without learning what other farm boys learned about fieldwork. Instead, his chores were the less demanding ones: hauling water, tending the orchard and vegetable garden, collecting eggs and honey, feeding the livestock. Unlike typical country boys, George spent most of his time in and around the house.

Though his duties were somewhat limited, George developed a keen curiosity about them. He was fascinated by the garden and orchard and began cultivating flowers among the bushes a little distance away from the house. He hid his little garden because, as he later explained, "it was considered foolishness in that neighborhood to waste time on flowers." Growing things gave George great satisfaction, and he soon developed a skill in cultivation that even the neighbors began to notice. They brought him sick plants and asked his advice on caring for them; they sought his opinion on planting and tending their vegetables.

Carver put his skills of observation to work as he watched Aunt Susan attend to her daily housekeeping duties. He learned cooking, laundering, and mending, and added them to his own chores as time allowed. What free time he had he spent alone in the woods looking for flowers to transplant to his secret garden. No matter how careful he was, he would sometimes break plants when he tried to pull them up. He was so sensitive and so attuned to nature that this innocent carelessness sometimes brought him to tears.

Aunt Sue began teaching George to read from a Webster's blue-backed speller. There was a school only about a mile from the Carver farm, but George wasn't allowed to go there. It was the Locust Grove School, held in the only public meeting house in the community, which served as the schoolhouse Monday through Friday and became the church on Wednesday night and Sunday morning.

Methodist, Baptist, Campbellite, and Presbyterian ministers took turns riding up from Neosho on horseback to hold Sabbath services there. The preacher for the week would come on Friday afternoon and spend the weekend with a member of the congregation. He'd make his pastoral rounds, hold Sunday worship, and return home after a Sunday dinner provided by his host. Wednesday nights and whenever there were five Sundays in a month, the people were on their own, though several aspiring evangelists who lived in the area jumped at the chance to preach then.

One memorable amateur was a local farmer named Bennie Woods, who convinced himself that he was called to preach whenever he had half an invitation. The afternoon before he was scheduled to speak, everybody within a mile of his barn lot could hear him rehearsing from the top of a large stump sawed flat, gesturing as wildly as the interpretation of his subject required. After one particular sermon had been underway for a full hour and a half, Bennie punctuated his sensational climax by seeming to spit on the floor and stamp his foot on the spot. This relieved his nervous tension for a few minutes, after which he repeated the performance. The boys all referred to him as "spit-and-step-on-it."

Locust Grove was also where traveling companies of actors and other kinds of entertainment were staged. One of George's friends remembered a hilarious performance of "Ten Nights in a Barroom" and the star of the production with "his red wig and blackened face, as a slave, hiding in a barrel, disclosing his presence in his fright by raising his head, much to the merriment of the children, including George among us in the front row."

George was welcome at Locust Grove for the comedy productions and for church on Sunday and Wednesday night, but he was not welcome to go to school. He may have been allowed to attend for a while, but after parents of some of the other pupils complained, he was forced to withdraw. Heartbroken, he resumed his studies at home with Aunt Sue and found solace in the peace, order, and solitude of his flower garden.

In spite of his rejection from school, George delighted in Sunday school and church. As soon as he was old enough, he regularly excelled at reciting Bible verses. The congregation's admiration for George was mixed with guilt for excluding him from attending school in the same building the rest of the week.

The Carvers never went to church, but George was so keenly interested in learning—whether about the Bible or about spelling—that he went by himself even as a very young boy. George's Sunday school teacher, Flora Abbott, particularly appreciated his dedication. She encouraged him to come to church even if he had to walk the mile from the Carver cabin alone. And she was the one who introduced George to Christianity and the Bible.

Mrs. Abbott constantly stressed the fact that "the Lord heard and answered the prayers of a child just as surely as He did that of their parents," recalled one of her students. George eagerly committed Bible verses to memory. Some he learned from Mrs. Abbott, who handed out little cards with Scriptures on them, a listing of the chapter and verse, and a tiny picture of a bird or flower in the corner—colorful gifts young George treasured. Other verses he learned with help from his little blue speller. George had an extraordinary gift for memorizing and reciting verses, which encouraged Mrs. Abbott even more. She nurtured his interest and even presented him with a small book as a reward for his work.

Mrs. Abbott prayed with and for her young charges and taught them to pray before her. George took her lessons to heart, especially during the school day. Longing to be in class with his friends, he wandered alone in the woods, picking flowers, carefully observing the plants and animals around him, and praying to God for a chance to learn about them. He soon formed the habit of getting up before daybreak and going into the woods at the edge of the yard. There he fell to his knees facing east, and as the first glinting of sunrise sparkled through the trees he prayed simply and earnestly, dedicating himself to doing God's will.

Besides being an expert on teaching the Bible to children, Mrs. Abbott was a gifted singer who gave most of them their first exposure to music. George had an advantage over some of his fellow students because Uncle Moses was a locally renowned fiddle player, and George had heard him often at dances and picnics. Even so, George was fascinated at Mrs. Abbott's singing, and by the duets she sang with her oldest son, Henry. George began singing too, and learned to pick out tunes on the church piano.

George always collected plant and animal specimens on his morning walks. At first he smuggled them inside the Carver cabin, but after Aunt Susan encountered one unexpected creature too many, she started making him empty his pockets before coming in. He built a pen outside for his frogs, though he did persuade Aunt Sue to let him keep his rock collection by the hearth until it got so big she was afraid it would collapse on them. The Carvers, including George, often ate game meat, but George had no interest in hunting, especially after accidentally killing a bird with a rock. Holding the bloody body in his hands, he looked at it with a remorse he long remembered.

For someone so young, George felt a remarkably wide range of emotions and empathy for living things. But he hid his intellectual gifts with a shyness that came from his physical frailty. Though he ran and played with neighborhood children and the Carvers' great-nieces and -nephews, he seldom took part in races, wrestling matches, or other competitive games, preferring to stand off to the side and watch.

Left on their own, white and black children played as equals. Without the preconceptions of their parents weighing on them, boys and girls judged each other by strength and speed, who could hold their breath the longest, and who had the brightest, best marbles to play with. Color wasn't a factor until later in life.

George's playmates teased him for staying on the sidelines; still he stayed put, grinning sheepishly, noticeably thinner and smaller than the others, with a delicate head and large, inquisitive eyes. He answered their remarks with silence or with a word or two or with unilateral acts of kindness: One day he presented a crippled friend with a pair of crutches he whittled himself.

The older he got, the more George longed to know about the world around him, but there was no one to teach him. Try as he might, there was nothing more he could learn from the McGuffey reader and the Webster's spelling book he had at home. He learned the text of them both almost by heart. "I sought answers to my questions from the spelling book," he later wrote, "but all in vain."

Hope for George's education appeared in 1876 with the arrival in Diamond Grove of a young educated black man named Steven Slane. The Carvers arranged for Slane to tutor George, but soon the student's questions outstripped the teacher's knowledge. About that time Moses Carver learned of a school eight miles away in Neosho that would accept black students. Some time in the fall of 1877 he sent George there to get the education he so longed for.

In Neosho, George boarded with a black couple named Andrew and Mariah Watkins. The Watkinses were devoted Christians who had no children of their own and who lived one lot down from the Negro school. Mrs. Watkins was a midwife and laundress who continued her young boarder's practical and religious education where they had left off in Diamond Grove. George knew how to cook and do laundry from helping Aunt Susan; Mrs. Watkins refined these skills and added knitting and others to the list. Soon George was jumping the fence between school and the Watkins home during recess to come back and help with the wash.

Mariah shared George's interest in plants and, as a midwife, was an authority on the healing properties of herbs, roots, and other natural medicines. She also encouraged George in his reading of the Bible and took him with her to services at the African Methodist Episcopal Church. Unlike the vast majority of former slaves, particularly women, Mrs. Watkins was literate and relatively well read. She had learned from a slave named Libby, whose example she lifted up before George: "You must learn all you can, then be like Libby. Go out in the world and give your learning back to our people. They're starving for a little learning." How well he knew.

Like most slaves, George hadn't had a last name. There was no family structure, no heritage to mark. He had always been called George or, in the style of the day, Carver's George, after his owner. In the years following Emancipation, families established legal households with the wife and children taking the surname the husband had chosen for himself. But this custom had not made its way to tiny Diamond Grove, and George was still only "George." Mrs. Watkins considered this unacceptable, and enrolled him in school at Neosho as George Carver.

Mrs. Watkins gave George another legacy he considered even more important in later years. For Christmas she gave him a Bible, which he carried everywhere with him from that moment forward and read daily for the rest of his life.

George's tutor in Diamond Grove had run out of answers in a matter of months; the teacher in Neosho lasted only a little longer. The black school in the county seat was taught by a black man named Stephen Frost, one of the well-meaning but poorly prepared teachers available to black students in the 1870s. He had an enrollment of up to seventy-five in a ramshackle one-room school. Immediately after the Civil War white teachers had helped organize and run schools for blacks in Missouri and elsewhere. Within a few years, however, whites grew tired of the enormous task of educating former slaves and began refusing to teach black students.

The few black teachers who had been trained in the decade following the war had inadequate educations themselves and were paid substantially less than their white counterparts. Black education was further limited by the flood of applications for admission to black schools; many would-be students had no instructor at all. The result was that the black school in Neosho was academically anemic but typical of what was available.

One day Mr. Frost—the students called him "Professor"—called George to the blackboard to work an arithmetic problem. When he finished, the teacher told him the answer was wrong. George worked the problem again and got the same answer. Frost insisted George had made a mistake. After school he took the problem home to Mrs. Watkins, who sent him to show it to a white teacher in town. When the white teacher told George his answer was right, he got her to put her signature on the page in support of his solution. The next day he brought the paper to school and showed Professor Frost. Suddenly the professor agreed that George's answer was right after all.

George received his graduation certificate on December 22, 1876, after about a year of study. A neighbor considered him "the smartest boy I ever saw in my life." Once again the slightly-built youth had quickly outpaced his teachers' knowledge and was left wondering where he could go next to keep learning.

The end of his schoolwork in Neosho marked the beginning of a vagabond period in George Carver's life. Desperately thirsty for knowledge and shut out of all conventional public schools because of his race (though strictly by local custom and not by law—those laws were still ten years in the future), he heard of a Neosho family that was traveling to Fort Scott, Kansas, where there was a school both whites and blacks could attend.

Days later George was on his way to Kansas with them. Because their wagon was full of household goods, he traveled most of the seventy-five miles on foot. George and his hosts made their trip at the beginning of what became the largest migration of blacks in the post-Reconstruction years. A former slave from Tennessee named Benjamin "Pap" Singleton promoted "Sunny Kansas" as a place where emancipated blacks could get free land and a fresh start. He distributed flyers to steamboat dockhands and train porters, who handed them out all over the South. A poor southern growing season in 1878 further swelled the ranks of adventurers heading north and west.

Black leaders disagreed on whether uprooting people from the South was a good idea. The dean of Howard University Law School in Washington thought it was good for the people who left by giving them a new start and helped those who remained by reducing the competition for employment. Frederick Douglass disagreed, arguing that the whole scheme was dreamed up by the railroads to increase passenger traffic and that blacks should not abandon a region where they had a near monopoly on laboring jobs.

The citizens and government of Kansas willingly and compassionately accepted this inflow of settlers at first, but as more and more came, their patience in providing resources to newcomers was soon exhausted and their modest assistance programs overwhelmed. Between 1870 and 1880 the black population in the state grew from 17,000 to 43,000. (When Kansas became a state in 1861, there had been 635 free blacks in a population of about 110,000.)

Arriving at Fort Scott, George set out to find a job to earn enough money for school. His skill at housekeeping work quickly landed him a place with Mr. and Mrs. Felix Payne, who were looking for a "hired girl" but agreed to give this earnest teenage boy a chance. Payne was a blacksmith and hired George to do the cooking and other household chores for his wife. George also worked part time at Isaac Stadden's grocery store across the street and did laundry for guests of the Wilder House, Fort Scott's finest hotel and the only brick building in town.

As soon as he could afford it, George started school, continuing with his various jobs as his classwork allowed. Whenever his money ran out, George dropped out of school long enough to get a little ahead, then picked up his studies again. He learned quickly and excelled at his lessons in spite of his intermittent attendance.

George Carver's pleasant and promising months in Fort Scott ended with a brutal shock. On March 26, 1879, a black man named William Howard was arrested and charged with raping a twelve-year-old white girl. After sunset that evening, as a thousand people watched, thirty masked men took Howard from the county jail and hanged him from a lamp post. Then they dragged the body down the street, stopping directly in front of the Payne house to crack the lifeless skull on the curb until its brains fell out as George watched from the window in horror. The mob continued on, dragging the mangled corpse to a pile of boxes soaked in kerosene and setting it on fire. The headline in the next day's *Fort Scott Monitor* screamed "TREMENDOUS TRAGEDY—A Mad Mob Drags the Demon Down to Death."

Though he had had some firsthand experience with discrimination, especially in school, George had been raised by whites and moved comfortably between black and white households, working and living in both. Such hateful, mindless cruelty of white people toward black was unimaginable to him.

The lynching of William Howard affected George so profoundly that he left Fort Scott as soon as he could, resettling a few miles distant to attend school in Paola, Kansas. He found lodging with a black couple named Lucy and Ben Seymour in nearby Olathe, serving as their "hired girl" as he had for the Paynes. He attended school with Lucy Seymour's nieces, Sally and Geneva Cross, and did odd jobs for their father, who was a barber.

The stone schoolhouse in town, called the "Old Rock," had been built as a workshop by a stonecarver who specialized in tombstones. The mason leased the lower floor to the school; upstairs was rented by the Masonic lodge. Just after the Civil War, blacks and whites had attended school together. By the time Carver arrived the classes were segregated.

In spite of his intelligence, George was older than his classmates because he had started school so late. The gangly teenager now towered over his fellow elementary school students. Slightly built and shy as ever, he tended to watch the other children play at recess rather than join in their games. There was no playground at the Old Rock; children played in the public square. Occasionally one of the boys would coax George into a game of marbles. More often than not, George's attention would wander from the game to an interesting leaf blowing across the square. As other players waited impatiently for George to shoot, he would kneel in position examining the edges of the leaf.

"Come on and shoot!" his friends shouted, growing more impatient.

"Look at how the shadows make a pattern there," he would reply, suddenly oblivious to the game, the boys, and everything else around him. He put particularly interesting specimens in his pockets or between the pages of a book and took them back to class, continuing the love of collecting he first showed by sneaking frogs into Susan Carver's kitchen.

Adding to his duties in the Seymour house and his work at the barber shop, George began teaching Sunday school at the Methodist church. He also took up playing the accordion and often sat in the open window of his room at the end of the day playing for passersby.

In the spring or summer of 1880, the Seymour family moved from Paola to Minneapolis, Kansas, more than 150 miles west along the

Solomon River. By July, George had followed them there and once again resumed his search for an education and the means to pay for it. Between July and December he secured three loans (probably an original loan and two renewals) totaling $253.90, and with the money opened George Carver's Laundry in an abandoned shack. The shack, in a ravine known as Poverty Gulch, had been deserted long before by a white family and was badly run down. Putting his domestic skills to work in his own interest for once, George soon made the place not only functional as a laundry but reasonably attractive to the amazement of the townspeople.

George did laundry for customers of Sutton & Son General Store, trudging up out of his ravine with freshly washed, ironed, and folded clothes in a laundry basket on his back, and returning with the new week's load. There was a big, elegant vase in the dry goods department of the store that was always full of flowers. One day George asked if he could buy it for a small down payment and work out the rest of the cost in washing.

"You must be crazy," replied John Sutton, the "& Son" of the enterprise, "to think of taking that vase to your hovel shack down in the creek bottom." Crazy or not, George persevered; and, of course, he got his vase.

The public school in Minneapolis was a two-story frame building with two classrooms per floor. White and black students attended classes together. Now twenty years old and self-employed, George enrolled in the eighth grade. His classmates were catching up with him in height, and though he was older than everybody else, he did not look it. The illusion was enhanced by the fact that his voice had never changed. The whooping cough, lung infections, and other illnesses so common in his early years had permanently affected him. As well as being high pitched, his speech was soft and weak; he frequently lost his voice altogether for days at a time. He was a busy and active young man in spite of colds and frequent bouts of coughing. A doctor once told him he should not expect to live to be twenty-one. Carver remembered later in life that when he heard this somber news, he "trusted in God and pressed on."

George carried over his schoolhouse habits from his Neosho days. He was an outstanding student who kept to himself and spent recess every day on the edge of the schoolyard watching the others play. To supplement his income from the laundry he took a job with Dr. James McHenry, whom Lucy Seymour worked for as a nurse. George cared for the doctor's horses, drove him on his rounds, and carried his large medicine chest in and out of patients' houses.

The Seymours were devout Presbyterians, and, following their example, George joined the racially mixed Presbyterian church in Minneapolis on July 29, 1883. The church was one place George seemed to relax and enjoy mingling with other people. Occasionally he rode home with Chester Rarig, a white schoolmate whose family were members of the congregation. The Rarigs welcomed George at their table for Sunday dinner and enjoyed the accordion concert that inevitably followed whenever he was a guest.

George finished the eighth grade and moved on to the ninth. His laundry business was successful enough that he could afford to invest in two lots of real estate, which he bought for one hundred dollars and sold ten months later for five hundred dollars. After he completed ninth grade, George had an apparent change of heart about graduating from high school. With his real estate profits he moved back to the eastern border of the state, this time to Kansas City, the biggest city he had ever seen. There he enrolled in business school and learned typing and shorthand. He quickly mastered these skills and got a job as a stenographer at the telegraph office in the railroad terminal.

His friend Chester Rarig was with him for at least part of the time he spent in Kansas City. Whereas in Minneapolis George was accepted at school and church by whites, a large restaurant in Kansas City refused to serve him breakfast. When he and Chester walked in and took seats, the waiter came up to Chester and said loudly enough for George to hear, "I'll be happy to serve you but your friend can't eat here."

Both young men rose and left the restaurant. "You stay," replied George quietly when they got outside. "I'll find somewhere else to eat." The scene was repeated more than once in other restaurants, and it clearly embarrassed Chester more than it did George. It was shocking to his white friend that a hungry young man with money in his pocket would be refused service because of his race. After all, George had been conditioned to expect such treatment. Furthermore, he was naturally quiet and accommodating, and if the waiter didn't want to serve him, he would go where they appreciated his business.

George now had a secure job and money in the bank. What he still longed for was more education. After some months in the telegraph office he applied for admission to Highland University, a small coeducational college founded by the Presbyterian church. His acceptance letter was a true delight to George. He immediately made plans to enroll but decided first to visit Uncle Moses and Aunt Susan, his friends back in Diamond Grove.

George's brother had died of smallpox in 1883, and he stopped in Fayetteville to see his grave. Jim had always been the robust, active one, while George was bedridden for days at a time by illness and respiratory problems. Yet it was George who was heading to college, while Jim had lost his life to disease as a young man.

Carver traveled from Kansas City by train. The station agent sold him a half-fare ticket, and the conductor remarked that he was awfully young to be riding by himself. He was twenty-five.

George went to church the next Sunday at Locust Grove, where everyone greeted him happily and noted how much he had grown. George had matured over the year he was gone, still slender but more assured and confident. He told them he was leaving for school in Kansas in a few days but had to come back to see them all. They marveled at his accordion and were even more impressed with the new typewriter he had bought in Kansas City. No one in Diamond Grove had ever seen a typewriter before, and a steady stream of visitors came by the Carver farm to get a souvenir piece of paper with their name or a line or two of something typewritten on it. As one early commentator observed, the contraption "piled an awful stack of words on one page."

Bedford Brown, the father of George's friend Forbes, suggested George join them at home for a hymn singing to celebrate his return. George happily accepted, arriving at their house the following Tuesday afternoon—so early, in his excitement, that the children of the house were still doing their chores when he came to the front door.

He was dressed in a new gray basket-weave suit and sported his accordion, with which he delighted his hosts by performing a selection of hymns and spirituals. The youngest children especially liked the two bells on one side that George could ring in time to the music by pressing a trigger with his thumb. The Browns also got out a prized book of printed music, purchased from a traveling band of entertainers—who sold "Wizard Oil" as well—on the courthouse square in Neosho.

The Browns had learned songs in the book from hearing the traveling singers. They sang them for George, who followed along on his accordion, eventually joining in the singing too with a clear, mellow contralto voice that blended impressively with the others.

At the special request of Mrs. Brown, they closed with "Swing Low, Sweet Chariot," her favorite hymn. When the singing was done, Mr. Brown told George that the family held a devotional service at the end of every day and invited him to stay for it. George accepted with a gentlemanly bow. Mr. Brown read from the twelfth chapter of Romans, explaining that it embodied all the rules necessary for living an upright Christian life:

> Be not conformed to this world: but be ye transformed by the renewing of your mind, that ye may prove what is that good, and acceptable, and perfect, will of God.... We, being many, are one body in Christ...having then gifts differing according to the grace that is given to us, whether prophecy, let us prophesy according to the proportion of faith; or ministry, let us wait on our ministering; or he that teacheth, on teaching;... Be kindly affectioned one to another with brotherly love...rejoicing in hope; patient in tribulation; continuing instant in prayer;... Avenge not yourselves but, rather, give place unto wrath; for it is written, Vengeance is mine; I will repay, saith the Lord.... Be not overcome by evil, but overcome evil with good.

As the last words sounded and the room fell silent, Mr. Brown closed the worn and much-thumbed Bible and placed it on a side table. Now it was time for prayer. Mrs. Brown was in her rocker by the fire; the three youngest children knelt on the floor in front of her with their heads in her lap. The others in the room bowed their heads as they sat. Mr. Brown prayed in the customary simple style Forbes called

...talking with God, not to him. No big words; very simple and personal, and with an assurance in expression that he was being heard and a proper answer would be forthcoming in due time.

He remembered George fully by name, his going in a few days, so far from home in his search for an education, so necessary if he was to succeed in his life's work. Father's closing sentence was always the same: "And may our last days be our happiest is our earnest prayer." There was a quiet moment as we all stood, George searching our faces, then each shook his hand wishing him well. Father was last, near the door, and as he grasped his hand he said: "George, you can go out into the world, and you may make a lot of money. Someone could sneak it from you. You get a good education and no one can ever take it from you."

George walked out the door past the glow of the firelight and into the darkness. They never saw him again.

CHAPTER SEVEN

A GREAT WORK

Brimming with expectation, George Carver rode the train to Highland, north of Kansas City in the very corner of Kansas. After his eight-year sojourn through Neosho, Fort Scott, Paola, Olathe, Minneapolis, and Kansas City, he had finally arrived at a bona fide university where he could satisfy the craving for knowledge that consumed his every waking moment.

His application had already been accepted by mail, so George reported to the office of the president, Reverend Brown, for his class assignment. Brown looked at the polite and eager student before him with an expression of absolute incredulity.

"You didn't tell me you were a Negro," he said. "Highland College does not take Negroes."

Without appeal and in keeping with his past behavior when in a place where he wasn't wanted, George turned around and left the room.

In that instant George Carver's years of study and all his hopes for the future seemed hopeless and wasted. Completely drained and adrift, he found solace where he always found it: in the church. Though he told no one in the small community of Highland what had happened, word of his rejection got around. Church members befriended him, invited him into their homes, and soon learned to appreciate his company. He was well spoken, well read, relatively well traveled, and a skilled entertainer on the accordion.

Soon George was invited into the John Beeler home in his familiar role as general housekeeper. Beeler, who owned an apple orchard south of town, was a fussy eater and a toothless one as well. Early in his stay, George fixed dinner one afternoon when Mrs. Beeler was away. Drawing on his years of experience in the kitchen, he prepared a simple cornbread: a batter of cornmeal, baking powder, egg, and salt, poured into a lard-coated iron skillet, and baked for twenty minutes.

When it was golden brown, the edges just beginning to crust, he pulled the cornbread steaming from the oven and sliced it like a pie. He set a piece on a plate and served Beeler, then stood at the kitchen door to see whether he would eat it. Hesitantly at first, then ravenously, Beeler deftly gummed the cornbread and, with his mouth too full to speak, motioned for more. George exchanged a glance of triumph with Beeler's daughter, Della, who was helping George prepare the meal, and served another piece, and another, and another until the whole cornbread was gone. The two cooks were so delighted they completely forgot the dessert pudding, which had boiled to a poultice-like blob. John Beeler was too full for dessert anyway, and George discreetly threw it away.

Western Kansas was still the American frontier in the 1880s. The Homestead Act of 1862 encouraged settlers to move there with the offer of a free quarter section—160 acres—of land to anyone who would live on it five years. The only cost was a twenty-four-dollar filing fee, payable at the end of the five years. John Beeler's son Frank headed west to Ness County to stake his claim. He opened a store, which soon grew into a settlement named Beeler. After a year or so of cooking and laundering in the Beeler home in Highland, Carver decided he too would become a homesteader.

Carver had been so hopeful of quenching his thirst for knowledge at Highland University, run by his own Presbyterian denomination, that he hesitated to make other plans for fear of disappointment. It took him a year to redirect his thoughts and strike out at last in a new direction. He traveled to Ness County, to the Great Plains of the American Midwest, where there were not even any cities in the familiar sense, much less colleges. He would satisfy his longing for education some other way.

There was a steady circle of adventurers entering and leaving western Kansas. Lured by the promise of free land, hopeful travelers arrived by the thousands. Some were driven away by the solitude, others by the lack of civilized conveniences and entertainment, still others by the harsh winters with biting Canadian winds and snowstorms that Mississippi and Louisiana natives could never imagine. The defeated dreamers headed back east, meeting new settlers on the way to their own dreams, ready to join the hearty homesteaders who remained.

George Carver arrived in Ness County between two crests of the westward immigration wave. The first peaked in 1879 or 1880 in response to widespread organized advertising of the homestead offer. The second came in 1887 and 1888 as the western railroad pushed through, bringing the promise of trade, land speculation, and other commercial enterprises.

Carver came to Eden Township the week of August 14, 1886, where his presence was reported in the *Ness County News,* which erroneously identified him as a "college student in the junior class" at Highland. Surely he felt a pang of sorrow at such news, so wishing it were true.

Carver found lodging and a housekeeping job with George Steeley, a white resident in the township, and he remained there while searching for a homestead claim of his own. Steeley was the county commissioner and lived in a sod house with real glass windows that had come seventy-five miles from the town of Larned on the railroad line. Everybody in the area lived in sod houses, or "soddies," because trees and building stones both were scarce and expensive.

Steeley and Carver got along well, but when Steeley's mother came to visit, she was appalled at having a black person in the house all the time. She barked at him constantly and refused to let him eat meals with the family; he ate alone at the table after they finished. As soon as she left, Steeley and Carver resumed eating together.

George staked his claim to 160 acres of prairie and started building his soddy. Having spent his childhood among the thick, luxuriant woods of Diamond Grove and Locust Grove, he had to readjust his thinking dramatically. Steeley showed him how to cut sod with a plow. Building strips were four inches thick and a foot wide, cut into two-foot lengths. They were stacked up in alternating rows like bricks to a height of nine or ten feet and a thickness of three feet. A tar paper roof was stretched over a frame of sticks, brambles, or precious lumber, then topped with a foot of sod. There was one opening for a door and another for a window. The finished product was windproof and waterproof, warm in winter and cool in summer.

Carver's house was fourteen feet on a side. When he moved in on April 18, 1887, he installed a cookstove (fired with sunflower stalks and sun-dried dung) and a few simple furnishings and found room for his washboard, washtub, flatirons, and accordion. He set to work breaking ground for crops, borrowing most of the tools from Steeley. He planted seventeen acres in corn and vegetables, set out three dozen fruit trees, and bought ten chickens.

While waiting for his first crop, Carver continued to work at the Steeley place, walking to his own soddy every night to preserve his homestead rights. In so isolated a place people were generally hospitable to one another, and George made friends with neighbors who appreciated his articulate and refined manner, his musical skill on the accordion, and his love of nature.

George, they learned, was also a gifted amateur painter. His fascination with plants had prompted him to start sketching them on any stray surface when he was still living back east. Now, surrounded by exotic yucca and other dry-weather plants and with time on his hands, he began sketching and painting more seriously. With his employer's permission he built a sod room onto the side of the Steeley house and began filling it with plant samples he collected. Under his care the flowers bloomed beautifully, a rare and welcome sight in so arid a place. Steeley sometimes invited Carver to take visitors on a tour of his "greenhouse," which he did with obvious pride.

Weather in western Kansas was harsh for growing crops. Water was scarce, and corn that looked promising one July morning could be baked beyond saving in a matter of days. Carver tried four times to dig a well on his land and finally gave up; he carried water three-quarters of a mile from a spring on the Steeley land as long as he lived there. Winters were, if anything, even harsher than the summers, as Carver learned his first year in Ness County. Steeley was away on business, but before leaving he warned Carver about the possibility of a blizzard. If a snowstorm threatened, Steeley said, Carver was to put the livestock in the barn, go inside the house, and not come out for any reason until it was over.

Carver had seen his share of winter weather. But when strange black strips of clouds began advancing from the northwest the next day, he followed instructions. Soon the blizzard came roaring down on him, alone in Steeley's soddy. As an experiment, he tied a rope to the bedpost and stepped outside into the howling wind and blasting snow. He took two steps away from the house, and it completely disappeared in a swirl of white. He held up his hand: It was invisible. He followed the rope back inside, grateful for Steeley's advice. Later he learned that two hundred people, some as far away as Texas, lost their lives that night, some frozen to death only a few feet from shelter.

By the next winter Carver had become a noteworthy citizen of Ness County, starring in its weekend musicales and amazing friends and visitors with his horticultural skill. The *Ness City Times* of December 15, 1887, reported "Geo. W. Carver" had been elected assistant editor of the literary society, indicating the respect the county's best-educated citizens had for him. It also may be the first reference to any middle name for Carver. Evidently, some time between his rejection by Highland College and his elevation to an office in the Ness County Literary Society, he gave himself a new identity.

The remaking of George Washington Carver continued in a newspaper article in the March 31, 1888, edition of the *Ness County News*. The first published announcement of his arrival had mistakenly identified him as a college junior—information the reporter could have gotten only from Carver himself. A year later, a more detailed account of his life repeated the error, though it was otherwise accurate.

Carver had attracted the reporter's attention when he appeared before the district court clerk as a witness for another black man who was filing a homestead claim. The article described Carver as being "by reason of his color and opportunity a somewhat remarkable character."

The report briefly described his early years as a slave and his working and studying in Kansas "until he graduated at high school, bearing with him the honors of his class." The article continued:

> Some time after, he attempted to gain admission to one of the colleges—which one we are not informed—but was defeated by a rebel element of the community. Failing in this he improved every opportunity for private study, which extended to many of the sciences. His knowledge of geology, botany, and kindred sciences is remarkable, and makes him as a man of more than ordinary ability.
>
> He has a fair knowledge of painting, and some of his sketches have considerable merit. He came to Ness County a year and a half ago, taking a claim on which he made final proof last fall. When not employed on another tract which he has entered, he works for Mr. George Steeley, who, being a gentleman of high culture himself, takes great pleasure in encouraging his employee's literary and scientific inclinations. Carver has gathered a collection of about five hundred plants in a neat conservatory adjoining the residence of his employer, besides having a large geological collection in and around the place. He is a pleasant and intelligent man to talk with, and were it not for his dusky skin— no fault of his—he might occupy a different sphere to which his ability would otherwise entitle him.

Even if he had inflated his credentials, Carver was careful not to condemn or even to name the "rebel element of the community"—a Presbyterian college president—that had denied him the education he had wanted for so long. And as far as "occupying a different sphere," his dead-end journey on the road to schooling had left him not sure just what sphere he should occupy.

During brutal winter days when the weather kept him from visiting George Steely, Carver played his accordion and made decorative lace, a legacy of his years as a housekeeper. He also grew even more interested in drawing and painting. He painted on tin cans, newspapers, and any-thing else handy, teaching himself to copy the plants and landscapes around him. He never had an art teacher until a woman named Clara Duncan came out to Ness County to homestead. She had been one of the first teachers at one of the first colleges for blacks in the country, Talladega College. When he found out she was an artist, he asked her to give him lessons. She agreed and showed him how to make a pencil sketch of a rabbit, then critiqued his small still lifes.

To his musical and artistic pursuits, George Carver added an interest in poetry and creative writing. A poem he wrote around 1888 hinted at a renewed interest in the future, the first indication in years that he might look once again for more out of life than a one-room sod hut on the Kansas frontier.

He typed it on his typewriter. Titled "Golden Moments," it started:

> Whilst I was sitting one day musing
> On life's book, each page perusing,
> I heard a whisper softly sighing,
> "Lo! Time's sickle is near thee lying.
>
> The rich and poor, the great and small,
> By this same sickle all must fall.
> Each moment is golden and none to waste.
> Arouse thee then, to duty haste!
>
> O! sit not down or idly stand;
> There's plenty to do on every hand.
> If you cannot prosper in work like some,
> You've at least one talent, improve that one."

And on for thirty-nine more verses.

In the summer of 1888, Carver left his Ness County homestead. Had he lived there five years he would have owned it. Instead, he mortgaged his 160 acres for three hundred dollars and started wandering again. His time on the frontier finally restored the interest in learning that was so wounded by his rejection at Highland College.

He worked his way back east, eventually traveling all the way to Iowa, where he got a job as a cook at a hotel in Winterset. He began attending the Baptist church in Winterset, which welcomed him even though the congregation was virtually all white. The segregation was not forced; the fact was there were very few blacks in Winterset. Once again, as he had in Ness County and Minneapolis, George was drawn to a community that was overwhelmingly white.

Quiet and circumspect, George sat in the back row of the church. Even so, his clear treble voice attracted admiring glances when he joined in the hymn singing. Soon after, George was called away from his work at the hotel one day to meet a distinguished-looking gentleman who had come asking for him. The man introduced himself as Dr. John Milholland and said his wife was interested in meeting Carver. When George arrived at their grand house in Winterset, he recognized Mrs. Milholland as one of the stalwarts of the Baptist church choir. She had heard him singing and wanted to meet the young man with such a beautiful voice. He sang for the Milhollands on the spot, and they promised to invite him back.

Dr. and Mrs. Milholland quickly established a routine of inviting George to their house every week for music and conversation. The more they learned about their new friend's artistic gifts, the more impressed they were. Before long George was stopping by the Milholland house every afternoon on his way home from the hotel.

After a year or so as a cook, George saved enough money to open a laundry and began at last to think about returning to school. The Milhollands strongly encouraged him to develop his obvious gifts, suggesting he enroll at Simpson College, a Methodist school in nearby Indianola. He confided his fear of rejection based on his experience at Highland. They acknowledged that there were no black students at Simpson but continued to insist he pursue his interests in singing and painting. (There had, in fact, been one African-American student at Simpson, but he was gone before Carver arrived. There were three Asian students on campus in 1890.)

Carver may have started taking voice and piano lessons at Simpson even before enrolling as a student. Though his first semester began September 9, 1890, he had started music lessons the previous April. He wrote the Milhollands with delight on April 8, "You will doubtless be surprised to learn that I am taking both vocal and instrumental music [piano] this term. I don't have to pay any direct money for any music, but pay it in paintings." Because he did not have a high school diploma, George was admitted to the select preparatory course while continuing his studies in voice and piano.

After paying his tuition at the beginning of the semester, George had only fifteen cents left over. He spent a dime on cornmeal and the remaining nickel on beef suet, then set about hunting up laundry work from the students so he could afford something else when those meager rations ran out. He made his groceries last a week; by then he had his first customers.

John Morley was beginning his sophomore year at Simpson when Carver enrolled and, like all the other students, was interested in meeting him since he was the only black student at the school. The few black residents of Indianola were accepted as full members of the community, but no one, white or black, expected to see a black student in college. Carver's quiet friendliness, intelligence, and the novelty of his being black gained him a wide circle of friends. As people got to know and appreciate him, the circle expanded rapidly.

Morley went to visit Carver and found him living in a shack whose owner allowed him to use it rent free. The only furniture inside was some empty boxes. George had salvaged a broken-down cookstove from the dump and bought washboards and other laundering equipment on credit. Morley assessed the situation and hired George to do his laundry. He also spread the word at the boarding house he supervised to help pay his own expenses; many of those boys sent George their laundry too.

After more students had made their way to Carver's shack and saw how he lived, they took up a collection and bought him a bed and table and made chairs themselves out of discarded lumber. Certain that, even as poor as he was, Carver would never accept cash handouts from them, students regularly slipped a little money or a concert ticket under his door when he was out.

John Morely felt no superiority over his new friend on account of his race, and other students accepted him as an equal as well. "In young Carver," Morely recalled later in a letter written many years later, "we saw so much beyond the color that we soon ceased to sense it at all.... I felt a special interest in him, realizing how lonesome he must be as the only one of his race among so many who had such numbers of acquaintances and friends."

Carver's long experience living in white communities was useful in finessing potentially awkward situations. His integration as a student was more or less complete, but social integration went only so far. Even in Indianola, where he was welcome in churches and places of business, he crossed to the other side of the street when he saw a girl he knew talking with strangers, so she would not have to speak to him.

During the 1890–91 school year, Carver attended the fall, winter, and spring terms. His course of study reflected the range of his interests: grammar, elocution, algebra, history, etymology, art, voice, and piano. Throwing spelling and punctuation to the wind in his rush to get the thoughts on paper, he wrote excitedly to the Milhollands of his painting and of his feeling of acceptance:

> I am painting flowers now I have nearly finished one very large marine and am painting on an origion design of the cactus and yucca like my teachers only very much larger the canvass is 22 x 48 inches The people are very kind to me here and the students are wonderfully good....

In college at last, surrounded by admiring friends, Carver wrote jubilantly to the Milhollands that God had special plans for him: "I remain your humble servant of God I am learning to trust and realise the blessed results from trusting Him every day.... I realize that God has a great work for me to do." He was active in the church and celebrated the results of a revival, informing the Milhollands of his happiness that "the out look for the upbuilding of the kingdom of Christ is so good. We are having a great revival here. 40 seeking last night and 25 rose for prayers at the close of the service."

Whether out of innocent error or overstatement, he also sent a fanciful report of his progress as a voice student. "I can now sing up to high D and 8 octaves below I have only had one lesson." (With very few exceptions, the greatest opera singers have a practical range of about three octaves; eight octaves is more notes than the entire piano keyboard.)

Carver's art teacher took a special interest in him. Behind the shy exterior she caught glimpses of intense powers of observation and inquiry straining for expression in whatever form they could—painting, singing, collecting plants and rocks. Miss Etta M. Budd recognized great promise in George although she wondered how a black man would make a living as an artist. As well as encouraging him in his painting, Miss Budd praised George's needlework, which he brought for her examination and approval. George also brought her some of his horticultural experiments, plants he had grafted or cross-fertilized.

Miss Budd examined George's plants with a practiced eye. Her father was a professor of horticulture at Iowa State College in Ames, and she realized the extraordinary quality and skill of Carver's work. Before the 1891 school year began, Miss Budd resigned her post at Simpson and moved home to Ames to care for her aging mother. Some time during that summer, she persuaded Carver to enroll at Iowa State and study horticulture under her father.

George was torn between the world of fine arts and the world of science. He loved them both and surely saw opportunities in both directions. Simpson had given his interest in art and music a chance to blossom; perhaps Iowa State would nurture his scientific curiosity to the same degree.

As he had at Simpson, George Washington Carver created a sensation when he arrived at Iowa State. He was the only black on campus, and while he was admitted on the strength of his grades as a Simpson freshman, some of the Iowa students eyed him with suspicion. Carver was by now a seasoned master at avoiding embarrassing moments in his social interaction with whites. He found a sympathetic supporter in Professor James Wilson, who arrived at Iowa State the same year as director of the school's agricultural experiment station.

When Carver reported for his dormitory room assignment, there was some bureaucratic foot shuffling and throat clearing while the administration tried to figure out where to put him. Students lived two to a room, and there were no other blacks enrolled. When Professor Wilson got word of the problem, he said, "Send him to me. I have a room." When Carver appeared in his office, Wilson announced that he was giving up the space for Carver to use as living quarters. Later Carver lived in a campus building where one wing had been converted into rooms for faculty members.

At first, George compared Iowa unfavorably with Simpson. His first day on campus a group of students shouted racial slurs at him. The dining hall manager refused to serve him with the other students and forced him to eat in the basement with the janitors.

Shortly after his arrival at Iowa, George wrote a reflective yet optimistic letter to the Milhollands admitting he did not like it there so far when compared with Simpson "because the helpfull means for a Christian growth is not so good; but the Lord helping me I will do the best I can." He continued expansively on the subject of God's guidance, filled with the hope of finally pursuing his life-long dreams, pouring his heart out to these two friends and Christians who meant so much to him:

> Oh how I wish the people would awake up from their lethargy and come out soul and body for Christ. I am so anxious to get out and be doing something. I can hardly wait for the time to come. The more my ideas develop, the more beautifull and grand seems the plan I have laid out to pursue, or rather the one God has destined for me. It is really all I see in a successful life. And let us hope that in the mysterious ways of the Lord, he will bring about these things we all so much hope for.... Let us pray that the Lord will completely guide us in all things, and that we may gladly be led by him....

Carver and Professor Wilson began hosting Wednesday night prayer meetings. Before long, they started a second group, then a third. Their purpose, as one student explained, was "to pour out to God in prayer our problems, our needs, our hopes, for help." Wilson and Carver recruited new members at the beginning of each term. They got Christian volunteers to go to the train station and escort arriving students to campus, help them get registered and settled, and establish their acquaintance in order to "get them into prayer meetings, etc."

Mirroring his experience at Simpson, he soon won over students and administrators alike through hard work and earnest friendliness. Also, in the eyes of his friends and teachers, George's skill as a botanist surpassed his ability as an artist, and he gradually gained a following of admirers who recognized his extraordinary ability with plants.

Carver did odd jobs for townspeople and faculty members, cutting wood and tending gardens, and he made a little money caring for the college greenhouse and science laboratories. He also sold hominy, a food staple prized for its long shelf life made from corn kernels soaked in lye. To stretch his income he made his own clothes and ate wild plants and mushrooms. A dining hall cook kindly supplemented this fare from time to time with banquet leftovers. Seeing him without writing materials in class because he couldn't afford them, students began saving their pencil stubs for him.

George was a good student, with near-perfect grades in botany and horticulture; his lowest grades in other subjects were 3.2 on a 4.0 scale. He joined the Iowa State College Cadet Corps and was eventually promoted to captain, also serving as company quartermaster and ordinance officer. Carver joined the Welsh Eccentric Society, an organization of young men dedicated to "development in science, literature, and the art of speaking." He quickly became a star member, though, as so often was the case, he and his friends had to devise clever solutions to potentially troublesome social encounters.

On one occasion, the society and the women's literary club jointly hosted a reception for the governor of Iowa. Each man was assigned a literary club member to escort. Of course, there was no black woman in the club for Carver to walk with. Carver's friends quietly and efficiently defused the situation by giving him the honor of escorting the governor.

George blossomed in the attention and affection of his college friends and teachers. Though he had never been athletic, he was welcomed as a trainer and masseur of the school football team. Members of the Welch Eccentric Society delighted in his dramatic and humorous readings and in his guitar playing, which by then had taken the place of the accordion. He also began teaching guitar. He volunteered to make decorations for the society's banquets; members were impressed that "with the aid of some vines and autumn leaves he transformed the room beyond recognition." He presented appreciative students and faculty alike with paintings and sketches.

Even the studious Carver was not above a prank or two. One student later wrote him to ask, "Do you remember the time you chased me all around the backyard with a great butcher knife which you pretended to use in digging up plants?… I hope you have reformed and turned over a new leaf ere this, and no longer chase defenseless freshmen around with knives."

On March 26, 1892, George Washington Carver spoke at the organizational meeting of the Iowa State College Agricultural Society on "The Grafting of the Cactus," illustrating his talk with "several drawings in a very unique and pleasing manner." The following year he conducted impromptu botany field trips as a delegate to the National Students Summer School in Lake Geneva, Wisconsin. Carver impressed other delegates from around the country with his insatiable curiosity about plants. Everywhere he went, he carried an oval tin box with a hinged lid in which to collect field specimens, slung over his shoulder with a leather strap. The two summers he attended, Carver was the only black delegate, prompting comments from Southern students that it was "a little queer that there should be a Negro delegate present."

The World's Columbian Exposition of 1893 brought Carver double honors. This grand event, more popularly known as the Chicago World's Fair, was dedicated on October 12, 1892, in commemoration of the four hundredth anniversary of Columbus's arrival in the New World, and formally opened on May 1 of the following year. The luxuriant artificial lagoons and sparkling white classical buildings (which looked like marble but were actually temporary walls of plaster and jute) celebrated America's progress over the past four centuries.

The star of the show was electricity, still a big-city novelty and unfamiliar to most American citizens. With a single switch, President Grover Cleveland bathed the scene in the miraculous glow of incandescent light, activated fountains fed by electric pumps, and started the circular motion of George Washington Ferris's thrilling new ride, a vertical wheel of iron that carried adventurous passengers 250 feet into the air in large swaying gondolas.

Four of Carver's paintings had been accepted for a state-wide showing in Cedar Rapids, and at least one of them, *Yucca and Cactus*, was chosen for display in the Iowa Building at the World's Fair. "The Lord is wonderfully blessing me," he wrote to the Milhollands in a letter sharing the news. Carver had been invited to the exhibit in Cedar Rapids but did not have enough money to make the trip. When his friends heard of his situation they bought him a new suit and a railroad ticket, ignoring his protestations that he would not accept "charity."

When Iowa Governor Horace Boies visited the World's Fair, Carver traveled to Chicago as a member of the Cadet Corps honor guard. In his letter to the Milhollands, Carver made no reference to the fact that his Iowa friends had rallied around him when he was refused service during a meal sponsored by the Highland Park Methodist Episcopal Church, and again later when, in uniform, he was heckled by onlookers with venomous shouts of "Nigger!"

Safely back on campus, Carver returned to his studies in an atmosphere where people knew and appreciated him. He concentrated his interests more and more in the agriculture department, headed by Dr. Louis H. Pammel. Dr. Pammel, like other faculty members, was impressed by Carver's skill and eagerness. He also saw Carver becoming increasingly interested in Pammel's own scientific specialty of mycology, the study of mushrooms, yeast, mold, and other fungi. After Carver earned his undergraduate degree in agriculture, he began a graduate course of study under Dr. Pammel. He also got enough work taking care of the school greenhouse to quit his other part-time jobs. Pammel praised Carver as "the best collector I ever had in the department or have ever known." The two of them published several articles on mycology together. It was a field rapidly growing in importance as botanists began to identify fungus as a primary cause of plant disease.

Carver started his graduate studies in 1894, still struggling with whether to follow the artistic path or the scientific one—or perhaps a third. In an October 15 letter to the Milhollands, he reported securing a job as assistant station botanist at the state agricultural experiment station on campus. "I intend to take a post graduate course here, which will take two years," he went on. "One year of residence work and one of nonresidence work. I hope to do my nonresidence work next year and in the meantime take a course at the Chicago Academy of Arts and Moody Institute. I am saving all the pennies I can for the purpose and am praying a great deal. I believe more and more in prayer all the time." He envisioned combining his second year of graduate botany with both art school and the Bible college founded five years earlier by the evangelist Dwight L. Moody.

As a graduate student, Carver taught freshman biology courses. Many students considered him their favorite professor, especially because he encouraged them to make discoveries on their own and not depend on him or textbooks for all the facts. Out of respect they began calling him "Doctor Carver" even though he had not yet completed his master's course.

Carver studied under Dr. Pammel's supervision and also worked with Iowa professors who later became Secretaries of Agriculture: James Wilson (who had befriended him his first day on campus and later cohosted his Bible study) and Henry C. Wallace. Wallace's son, Henry A. Wallace, would also serve as secretary of agriculture and later as vice president under President Franklin D. Roosevelt. Young Henry often credited his boyhood nature walks with Carver for beginning his interest in plants, recalling him as the "kindest, most patient teacher I ever knew. He could cause a little boy to see the things which he saw in a grass flower."

His love of botany combined with his deeply held religious beliefs led Carver to look at all life as a gift from God and to see God as "the Creator." He saw the miracle of creation in everything around him and adopted the habit of referring to God as the Creator in his prayers and conversations. Carver also combined science and religion in developing his methods of experimentation, attributing his findings to divine revelation as much as the scientific method. He was well schooled in procedure yet mixed experimental protocol with the intuition that had brought him renown as a "plant doctor" so many years before in Diamond Grove. Carver was confident that God had chosen him for a great purpose and that science and religion were compatible with God communicating to Carver and the rest of the world through his creations as well as through the Bible.

As he neared the halfway point in his two-year graduate program, Carver, so long a wanderer in search of an education and a means of paying for it, was in the unaccustomed position of having more than one offer for continuing his work. In the fall of 1895 he received an offer to join the faculty of Alcorn Agricultural and Mechanical College, a school for blacks in Lorman, Mississippi. At the same time, his friends, professors, and colleagues at Iowa hoped he would remain at Ames after earning his master's degree to pursue his doctorate and join the faculty. Carver was reappointed to his position as assistant director of the agricultural experiment station at a salary equal to what Alcorn offered him to move there. Iowa State president William M. Beardshear encouraged the school to try to keep him, writing, "We would not care to have him change unless he can better himself."

In a letter to Alcorn, Carver's friend Professor Wilson described him as "by all means the ablest student we have here" in his skill at cross-fertilization and plant propagation. He wrote:

> Except for the respect I owe the professors, I would say he is fully abreast of them and exceeds in special lines in which he has a taste.... We have nobody to take his place and I would never part with a student with so much regret as George Carver.... I think he feels at home among us, but you call for him to go down there and teach agriculture and horticulture to the people of his own race, a people I have been taught to respect.... I cannot object to his going.

As he considered whether to stay among his appreciative white colleagues at Iowa or move to the alien land of Mississippi to help other blacks, Carver received a third offer. This came in the form of a letter on March 26, 1896, from Booker T. Washington, founder and president of Tuskegee Normal and Industrial Institute in Alabama.

Washington had risen to fame the year before with his speech at the Cotton States Exposition in Atlanta. But at the same time Washington's personal star continued its ascent and as Tuskegee built a reputation for the quality of its programs and success stories among its students, social and political rights for blacks nationwide were systematically being withdrawn. The black vote had been responsible for creating Tuskegee in 1881; fifteen years later it was almost impossible for blacks to vote in Macon County. By 1896, segregation was the law of the land, and state's rights had trumped constitutional intent in the United States Supreme Court.

If Carver sincerely wanted to "do his people good," as he once told Professor Wilson, this seemed the time, and Tuskegee under Washington's leadership seemed the place.

There were other inducements as well. Washington wrote to Carver that the Slater Fund had given Tuskegee money to establish an agricultural station, but that the fund administrators expressed doubt—mirroring Washington's own history at being called to Tuskegee—that Washington could find a black to head it.

Eager to prove blacks could make it on their own, Washington was willing to go to great lengths to avoid failure in finding a qualified black. He offered Carver a salary of one thousand dollars per year plus board, hoping Carver would not accept just for the money, but hedging his bet just the same. Although Washington wrote it was Tuskegee's policy to seek out teachers "who come not only for the money but also for their deep interest in the race," should the terms fall short, Washington wrote, "we shall be willing to do anything in reason that will enable you to decide in favor of coming to Tuskegee."

By May the two agreed that Carver would finish his master's coursework and thesis, "Plants as Modified by Man," and come to Tuskegee in October. At one time, Carver and another Iowa student had discussed the possibility of being Christian missionaries in Africa. This was a different sort of calling, but Carver determined it was what he would undertake "through Christ who strengtheneth me to better the conditions of our people.... I will accept the offer."

He explained to Washington that he had a large collection of botanical specimens he expected to bring with him. Those he carefully packed. Among his other belongings were a large bouquet of flowers from his old friends at Simpson, a fine microscope (a gift from the students and faculty at Iowa), a few paintings, and two of his most cherished treasures: his mother's spinning wheel and her bill of sale to Moses Carver.

CHAPTER EIGHT

CONFLICT AND ACCORD

Fall classes were already underway when George Washington Carver arrived at Tuskegee on October 8, 1896. He had left Iowa before his master's degree graduation ceremony on November 10 at Booker Washington's request in order to set up the agricultural school as soon as possible. This new venture appeared to fit Carver's plan for the future by giving him a place to conduct his agricultural and botanical research in a way most helpful to blacks. It fit President Washington's future vision by developing practical new ways for black Southern farmers to improve their lives.

These two men shared a belief that a black institution could play a major role in raising the standard of living for black residents of the rural South who were stranded in a subsistence level economy. And they shared a determination to act on that belief.

They also shared similarities from their early years. Carver and Washington were both born slaves. They never knew their fathers. Their owners were unusually compassionate for men of their time and place, far from the stereotype of the linen-suited Southern plantation grandee. Susan and Moses Carver ransomed George from kidnappers and raised him as their own; Elizabeth and James Burroughs supported fourteen children by working alongside the slaves on their land.

Both Carver and Washington followed an inexplicable, irresistible, visceral instinct to seek out an education in the face of almost insurmountable odds. Carver left Diamond Grove for a fifteen-year odyssey that took him at last to Simpson College and Iowa State; Washington gave up his job at the Malden, West Virginia, salt furnace for Hampton Institute and the inspired example of General Samuel Chapman Armstrong.

There was seemingly nothing in their families or situations to encourage or inspire them. They just went. And both saw the hand of divine providence in their decisions.

As talented and ambitious black men, Carver and Washington led similarly convoluted lives. Hailed as an outstanding scholar, Carver crossed the street as a student at Simpson to avoid embarrassing a white classmate. The press in western Kansas singled him out as a model citizen whose prospects were unfortunately hampered by his "dusky" complexion. In Washington's case, even his strongest white supporters shared the prevailing conviction of the day, which didn't see blacks as social equals of whites. Laura Burroughs, whose horse he had led to the school where she taught, once reminded a correspondent, "Not on your life do we believe in social equality."

Carver and Washington had broken through many of the barriers to their race on the strength of their will to succeed, their undeniable intellect and ability, and their faith in God. Now time would tell whether, working together, they could help pave the way for the rest of the race to follow.

Like Booker T. Washington fifteen years before, George Washington Carver arrived at Tuskegee with strong preconceptions about what the school was and what he would do. Like Washington, he found nothing as he expected.

In 1881, Washington had expected to come to town and assume the leadership of a school for Negroes. He was astonished to learn that whatever school there was, he would have to start it from scratch, without land, buildings, teachers, or supplies. On a fall afternoon in 1896, George Washington Carver arrived on a campus renowned for the programs and opportunities it provided, prepared to assume his duties as director of scientific agriculture. To his surprise, he found he had no research laboratory, no equipment, no staff, and no established curriculum.

Within weeks of his arrival, Carver was openly questioning Tuskegee's commitment to him and his agricultural department. He had mentioned, during his negotiations with Washington, a large collection of botanical samples he would be bringing with him. When he got to campus, he was upset by the news that he, like all the other bachelor instructors, would live in a teachers' dormitory two to a room.

On November 27, Carver sent a letter to the Tuskegee finance committee complaining of his quarters and the lack of room for his scientific paraphernalia. He also made it clear he considered his position at Tuskegee a transitory one:

> Some of you saw the other day something of the valuable nature of one of my collections. I have others of equal value, and along Agr. lines.
>
> You doubtless know that I came here solely for the benefit of my people, no other motive in view. Moreover I do not expect to teach many years, but will quit as soon as I can trust my work to others, and engage in my brush work, which will be of great honor to our people showing to what we may attain along science, history, literature, and art.
>
> At present I have no rooms even to unpack my goods. I beg of you to give me these, and suitable ones also, not for my sake alone but for the sake of education. At the present the room is full of mice and they are into my boxes doing me much damage I fear. While I am with you please fix me so I may be of as much service to you as possible.
>
> Also I am handicapped in my work. I wanted a Medical Journal the other day in order that I might prescribe for a sick animal. It was of course boxed up, couldn't get it. Trusting you see clearly my situation, and will act as soon as possible, I remain most Resp. yours, Geo. W. Carver.

At Iowa State, Carver was an outstanding scholar, a popular student teacher, a trustworthy and capable greenhouse manager, a published researcher whose collaboration was highly prized by a leading agricultural scientist, and the source of admiration (mixed, certainly, with some curiosity and prejudice) as the only black student on campus. He had given up the chance to earn his Ph.D. because he decided educating blacks at Tuskegee was more important. He expected deference and respect from his colleagues in his new situation. What he got was just the opposite.

Part of the difficulty was that money at Iowa State was relatively plentiful, while Tuskegee, even after fifteen years, always seemed just ahead of financial ruin. Booker Washington spent six months out of every twelve on the road raising money, supplementing the full-time fundraisers who worked in the East and Midwest. Classroom and dormitory space were always in short supply, and poor students from the countryside always needed help with their living expenses. Finding room for a collection of plants from Iowa was far down the priority list.

Another point of friction was the dramatic cultural difference between Carver's Iowa State and Washington's Tuskegee. Carver had spent most of his adult life in white communities; often he was the only black in his circle of acquaintances. The combination of race and intellect brought him attention and made him newsworthy. He was the first Tuskegee faculty member to have an advanced degree from a white college, and one of the oldest and most experienced at the time of his arrival.

Far from welcoming him, some members of the Tuskegee teaching staff resented Carver sight unseen. His salary was more than twice what the average faculty member earned, even though he had no family to support. His demand for extra space when his peers lived two to a room seemed arrogant and selfish. Most Tuskegee teachers were cut from the same cloth as the man who hired them: young, impeccably dressed mulatto graduates of Hampton or Fisk who respected Washington's insistence on precision, order, and cleanliness. Carver was a full-blooded black who had lived mostly in a white world, dressed for comfort rather than fashion, and descended upon them with his superior air and prima donna demands.

Carver's broad hints to the finance committee that he would not stay long at Tuskegee further alienated him from the leadership of the school. If he was in fact leaving as soon as possible to pursue his painting career, there was no point trying to satisfy him in the short term. Eventually Carver got the space he wanted—an office in one building and two rooms in Rockefeller Hall, the boys' dormitory—and settled in to work.

Professor Carver began by teaching agriculture and dairying. He quickly learned that the Tuskegee reliance on student labor meant things did not always go completely smoothly. Inexperienced help required lots of supervision, which somewhat irritated the new professor, even as he saw the benefit of it. On February 9, 1897, Carver reported to Washington that he was training students to make butter for the dining hall, with the result "that we will get the benefit of their labor without cash and at the same time make it remunerative to them in the way of instructions.... We have enough men if each one would do his duty. Now I am frequently obliged to stop and do work that belongs to someone else.... Of course this cripples my work greatly."

A month later he wrote to his great mentor and friend, Dr. Louis Pammel, at Iowa State. His displeasure of the previous November seemed to have vanished. Far from preparing to leave as soon as possible for his easel and brushes, he confided, "I am enjoying my work very much indeed. The weather is simply superb and as for flowers I never saw anything like it.... I like it so much better than I thought I would at first." His love of music gave him a ready appreciation for the amateur theatricals staged by his fellow teachers. "Our faculty gave an entertainment last night, a farce in one act from the French. I think I have never seen anything rendered so exquisite, and the music was superb." Carver sounded one small note of discord at the end of his letter, his solitary reverie at an end: "Well as someone is coming to bother me I must close for this time." So long accustomed to solitude, whether on the prairie or in the greenhouse, Carver's time was now seldom his own.

One task that particularly intruded on Carver's day was the seemingly endless string of reports he was supposed to make. Between teaching classes and supervising the dairy, he also had to attend faculty meetings and found himself, on top of everything else, having to take time to write a report on the death of a cow, another to request added manpower to pick apples before they rotted, and yet another on milk and butter production. Mr. Washington, Carver quickly discovered, was a stickler for reports. Mr. Carver, Washington realized just as quickly, was not much interested in them.

As supervisor of the dairy, Carver was responsible for seeing that the dining hall had adequate supplies of milk and butter and that they were safe to serve the students. Washington requested daily reports on milk and butter production so he would know the dining steward would not have to spend scarce and precious cash on dairy goods in town that day. The report also told him that the dairy students were progressing, the boys and girls in the dining hall were being cared for, and that all was neat and orderly.

Getting the report in Washington's hands was not a high priority for Carver; his students and his animals came first, paperwork second. Washington pressed for his reports on time. Carver responded by insisting his subordinates in the dairy were causing the delay, and that with so much else to do and no secretary to help him (his reports were all written longhand), he was doing all he could. Far from reducing his responsibilities, Washington steadily added to them, seeing beyond the complaint and frustration to a man whose talents were rare and valuable. In October he appointed Carver to a team assigned to recommend the best use of a large new tract of land the school had received known as the Marshall Farm. Carver led the team and wrote their report. Washington asked Carver for recommendations on new native shrubbery for the campus, put him in charge of building and maintaining fences, and made him responsible for saving the hooves of slaughtered cows to make harness oil.

Whenever he traveled, Washington received detailed daily briefings on happenings at Tuskegee, mailed faithfully by Warren Logan—one of the first teachers hired at Tuskegee after Washington and Miss Davidson, who now served as treasurer—or by Washington's brother, John.

Washington had put his older brother through Hampton, then found him a job at Tuskegee, first as town postmaster, then later as operations manager of the school. Even when the president was away, he sent a steady stream of instructions and questions to everyone back in Alabama, including his chief agriculturist. Instead of being relieved at his absence, Carver had to write detailed letters to Washington in Boston or New York complaining about lazy employees and broken cream separators, but also joyously celebrating the "simply marvelous" sweet potatoes his fertilization experiments were producing.

Bureaucratic and political matters aside, Carver loved being around students who craved learning as much as he did. He commented regularly about students of outstanding ability or potential, such as one Isaiah Hardiman, seventeen, who traveled 533 miles, including 163 on foot, to come to Tuskegee. He left home with seven dollars and still had $2.25 at the end of his trip.

In February 1898 the Alabama legislature approved a fifteen hundred dollar appropriation toward establishing the Tuskegee Agricultural Experiment Station and Agricultural School. With this supplement to the Slater Fund donation, Carver set out to build a showcase operation. One of his goals was to keep in touch with local black farmers and conduct research that would be most beneficial to them. To distribute his results and recommendations, he decided (with Washington's approval) to issue a bulletin, written in plain language, with specific advice for farmers on a particular matter.

In his introduction to Bulletin Number One, "Feeding Acorns," Carver wrote, "We take pleasure in saying that as far as we are able, neither time nor expense will be spared to make our work of direct benefit to every farmer. But few technical terms will be used, and where such are introduced, an explanation will always accompany them." The bulletin reported Carver's research on feeding acorns to cattle, hogs, and chickens. Most farmers bought expensive corn to feed their animals. Carver suggested they gather acorns from the woods and mix them with corn in varying amounts. The practice saved money and made good use of acorns previously wasted. His research showed the animals thrived on the less expensive diet, that chickens produced more eggs as a result, and that cows made richer milk.

The bulletin satisfied Carver's desire to conduct experiments for the benefit of "his people," and fulfilled Washington's wish to give them a practical education that would help them make their way in the world. It was immensely popular with farmers, both black and white. With simple charts, specific recommendations, and an informal, conversational tone, it presented them with a way to save money and improve their products without a cent of capital investment.

Carver produced Bulletin Number Two, "Experiments With Sweet Potatoes," in May to similar acclaim. He raised sweet potatoes in sixteen plots; one had no soil additives of any kind, and the others were each treated with different combinations of phosphate, potash, soda, and lime. Results were carefully tabulated on a chart with photographs of the yields from some plots to underscore the dramatic difference among them. Carver meticulously explained his methods, careful to include his reasons for every step.

The plot with no fertilizer yielded 40 bushels per acre of small sweet potatoes that sold for 25 cents per bushel. The one-tenth acre experimental plot produced a net gain of $2.50. The best plot yielded at a rate of 266 bushels per acre worth 50 cents per bushel which, after deducting the cost of phosphate and potash, left $121.00.

Washington and Carver continued to see Carver's responsibilities from different points of view. Washington expected him to shoulder a full teaching load in addition to his duties in the agricultural department. Carver argued that he shouldn't have to teach, run the agricultural experiment station, and write bulletins all at the same time. Other faculty members got more assistance than he did, he said, more administrative help, more of everything, and were expected to do less with it.

Carver unburdened himself in a long letter to Washington on May 30, 1898. He began by reminding Washington that he "labored early and late and at times beyond my physical strength; have not asked for a private secy. and if you look into my work carefully you will see that I need one quite as much as some who have two." Carver reminded Washington of Carver's special status among whites, and that he continued giving up prestigious opportunities to remain at Tuskegee.

"I had made partial arrangements to enter the Shaw School of Botany, St. Louis, from which I hope to take my doctor's degree," he wrote, "a degree that no colored man has ever taken." Instead, he decided to stay because he felt Washington was sincerely interested in seeing the agricultural department grow since it was a potentially large source of income for the school. "In taking charge of the Agr. Dept. it was my understanding that you wanted it to grow. I have put forth every effort in that direction that time and opportunity would permit." He went back and inserted a comma and the word "means" after "time." It seemed to Carver that in the scramble for scarce resources, he always came up last.

He also protested against administrators with no practical knowledge of his work making decisions that affected the agricultural department. He saw a recurring conflict between theory and practice. "Now Mr. Washington, I think it ludicrously unfair to have persons sit in an office and dictate what I have to do and how I can do it. If I thought things were to run as they have always run I would not stay here any longer than I could get away." He wrote that others "scoffed" at his plans to grow clover; they belittled his sweet potato experiments, then refused to see the results for themselves. A teacher in high authority accused him to his face of "going crazy" when he suggested feeding acorns to the livestock; later Auburn and Mississippi State both praised the results and encouraged farmers to substitute acorns for far more expensive corn.

Clearly disappointed at the lack of respect he received at Tuskegee, Carver also included a quotation from an Iowa State publication heralding his agricultural bulletin on acorns, and concluding that "Mr. Carver surely is and will be a powerful factor in the development of the 'new South.'"

Carver found it difficult to defend his decisions and the results of his projects day in and day out. It was even more challenging when Washington was traveling and Carver had to make his case long distance. A letter to Washington in Boston during the summer of 1898 began, "I am as well as usual and striving hard to make all financial points meet."

Carver wrote at length about personnel difficulties, the shortage of materials and experienced manpower, and his resolve to make the coming school year as successful as possible in spite of all the problems. "Mr. Washington," he added, "I wish you could be here more than you are and look into matters yourself, and not take people's word for it. I know some things would surprise you." He also proudly repeated a story he had heard about one of his staff bragging in town that as fast as Tuskegee was progressing, the white people "were going to sit around and go backward and the niggers were getting away ahead of them."

The relationship between Washington and Carver was shaped largely by an interweaving of two forces, one of conflict and one of accord. The conflict came in Washington's lifelong tendency toward precision and procedure, in opposition to Carver's preference for experimentation and teaching at the expense of writing reports and managing personnel matters.

Washington's view was objective and broad, taking in the whole of the great Tuskegee experiment, yet he was what later generations would call a micromanager. In his resolve to make Tuskegee a showplace for what the black man could do, he worried over the tiniest detail: bits of paper on the campus lawn, a gate with rusty hinges. He knew Negroes had to prove themselves to a higher standard than whites did and stopped at nothing to convince a skeptical world that black people were as worthy and capable as others.

While Washington was learning how to serve at table in the Ruffner home and practicing military drill at Hampton, Carver was living alone in a sod hut on the Kansas prairie—farming, painting, playing the accordion, and collecting botanical specimens. At Tuskegee, Carver lived for experimentation and teaching. He had cut short his academic development for the chance to move to Alabama as head of an agricultural school. It was not a sacrifice he intended to make in exchange for reporting on how many pounds of butter came from the dairy every day.

The daily milk report illustrated the friction generated by these two opposing viewpoints. Washington continued to insist the report be made accurately, completely, and promptly every day; Carver pleaded that he had too much to do, that an assistant was at fault, that ripening fruit and calving cows could not be managed according to a rigid schedule. Washington sent an official, and unequivocal, memorandum to Mr. Carver: "I want the milk report every morning, and on it I want the number of cows milked.... I must insist that it be sent promptly each morning and marked as I have directed."

Though he moved among Rockefellers and Carnegies when he was away, Washington always found time to examine minute details of Carver's dairy operation and send directives on how to improve it. In one memorandum: "I call your attention to the fact that some of the students at the dairy barn complain that they are working now fifteen and sixteen hours a day. If this is true it is entirely too much, and the number of hours should be reduced to ten or something near that." In another he complained that the door fastenings of the dairy wagon were "in a very crude and unsatisfactory condition." He also noted he had seen students leave their farm machinery outside in bad weather "like the common country people." There was no tone of malice in the message, but rather an expression of Washington's consistent concern for the way the public perceived Tuskegee and its students. Being successful was only part of the goal. The success had to show.

Offsetting the conflict that marked their relationship, Washington and Carver shared deeply felt commitments to improving opportunities for blacks and to living Christian lives. In a letter to Washington reciting a litany of difficulties caused by a shortage of tools and assistants in the agricultural school, Carver also praised Washington's work and sent heartfelt encouragement in the wake of criticism by a black poet and novelist named Paul Laurence Dunbar. Dunbar published stereotypical tales of dull-witted rural blacks, who spoke in heavy dialect, and insisted that blacks were unadaptable to urban culture.

Carver wrote:

Mr. Washington, I hope you will not let any such articles similar to that of Paul L. Dunbar give you a moment's uneasiness but simply stimulate you to press on. You have the only true solution to this great race problem. It is only ignorance *mostly* and a bit of prejudice that prompts such articles. Among both white & black, you are living several hundred years ahead of the common herd of both races.... 3 or 4 hundred years from now people will know and honor your greatness much more than now because they will have been educated up to it.... May God bless you & Mrs. Wash. Press on.

(Dunbar did eventually come around and composed the Tuskegee alma mater.)

Carver wrote with boyish enthusiasm about his success at harvest time:

It seems as if we will be able to turn in more to our credit than ever before. The students & teachers have all the green peas they can use, cabbage, tomatoes, squash, some green corn, watermelons, cantaloupes, cucumbers, peaches, grapes, and will soon have sweet potatoes. The teachers have all the honey they can use judiciously.

He also wrote about his frustration over inattentive student workers who mixed the sheep dip improperly, then kept dipping more animals even as the first were dying. His communications had a transparency and subjectivity that laid bare both his admiration for Washington and his displeasure over his rules, strictures, and directives.

For his part, Washington saw the agricultural operation as a keystone to building Tuskegee's future. It carried a high profile, trained students in skills that would make them self-sufficient, helped them work off their living expenses, and reduced cash requirements by supplying food, fodder, livestock, and market produce. The fact that he continued to support his eccentric department head was proof of his respect and confidence, though he never expressed his gratitude as warmly or directly as Carver did. Washington never cultivated friendships as intensely as Carver; besides, Washington had far more on his plate most of the time than worrying about his professors.

In the fall of 1898, Booker T. Washington was invited to speak at the Chicago Peace Jubilee commemorating the end of the Spanish-American

War. His conciliatory position on race relations, combined with the national acclaim that followed his 1895 Atlanta speech, made him a popular figure with both white and black audiences. It also made him a magnet for criticism: from the whites, for overreaching his place as a Negro; from blacks, for being too docile and accommodating in the face of discrimination.

President William McKinley was in Chicago for the festivities and attended Washington's speech. The auditorium was packed with sixteen thousand spectators—so many that policemen had to clear a path through the crowd and escort the speakers to the stage. Washington spoke of the patriotism of the American black in working to free his Cuban brothers, "forgetting his own wrongs, forgetting the laws and customs that discriminate against him in his own country." It was unusually frank language from an orator who thrived on reconciliation. "Until we conquer ourselves," he continued, "I make no empty statement when I say that we shall have, especially in the Southern part of our country, a cancer gnawing at the heart of the Republic, that shall one day prove as dangerous as an attack from any army without or within."

His powerful metaphor raised the ire of Southern newspapermen, ever on the lookout for any hint of insurrection. Clark Howell of the Atlanta *Constitution* was with Washington on one of the two occasions during the week that he had lunch with President McKinley. Nevertheless, his paper opposed the speech, warning that a statement he had made about burying "all that which separates us in our business and civil relations" implied an appeal for the end of social separation as well. A newspaper in Birmingham raised doubts of its own and added to the growing chorus. Washington reaffirmed his view that stewing over the question of social equality was pointless, and that racial prejudice was "something to be lived down, not talked down."

He said:

What is termed as social recognition is a question I never discuss. God knows that both—we, of the black race and the white race—have enough problems pressing on us for solution without adding a social question, out of which nothing but harm would come.... Each day convinces me that the salvation of the Negro in this country will be in the cultivation of habits of thrift, economy, honesty, the acquiring of education, Christian character, property, and industrial skill.

One white Southern commentator responded to Washington's explanation of his remarks with praise: "I think the better class of Southern people feel that you are their Abraham Lincoln, their best friend in watching over the interests of both races and restraining all by your words and life."

Within a month after his Chicago speech, Washington secured a promise from President McKinley to visit the Tuskegee campus during an upcoming trip to Atlanta. McKinley's trip was an example of the way Washington and Carver, despite their differences, could work together for the betterment of race relations in general and the benefit of Tuskegee in particular. Washington's eloquence, notoriety, and acceptance by the white establishment were important in attracting so prominent a visitor. But they were no less important than the fact that McKinley's Secretary of Agriculture, James Wilson, was Carver's friend, admirer, and former professor at Iowa. Wilson had visited Tuskegee at Carver's invitation to dedicate the agricultural building the year before.

Another reason for McKinley's visit was the need to assure the South that the government in Washington had the "race question" under control. A flurry of civil disturbances had raised concerns among Southern whites as to whether or not federal authorities could protect them and their property from what they saw as a violence-prone black population bent on revenge after centuries of forced servitude.

Beginning November 10, a series of race riots in the Carolinas led to the death of nineteen blacks and the forced resignation of the entire Board of Aldermen for the city of Wilmington, North Carolina, along with its mayor and police chief. The incident began with an article by a black journalist suggesting that white women were not always entirely innocent in cases where black men were accused of accosting or raping them—accusations that too often led to lynching. An armed mob of four hundred stormed the newspaper office, destroyed the press, and burned the building to the ground. Blacks in the community rushed to the scene but were ordered to disperse. When they refused, gunfire broke out on both sides.

The same day near Greenwood, South Carolina, a disturbance at an election day polling place reached a flashpoint. Published reports claimed blacks waiting to vote suddenly "opened a fusillade against the store in which the voting was going on." One black suspect named Essex Harrison was confronted by fifteen armed men on horseback, who ordered him "to go toward the pile of four dead Negroes [already killed in the melee]." He started walking; there was a ring of rifles, and Harrison pitched forward dead.

The black assistant postmaster of nearby McCormick, a member of the locally prominent Tolbert family, was ordered out of town on threat of death. He appealed to the governor of South Carolina, claiming the mob had interfered with the operation of the post office and deprived him of his property without cause. His telegram read in part:

> I am a large landowner in the County of Abbeville and also the owner of valuable houses and other real estate in the town of McCormick. My wife is there with our only child, a girl four years old, without my presence and my protection, on account of the action of an armed mob, and my property is without proper care. I have committed no crime....

The governor replied that interruption of postal service was the concern of the postmaster in McCormick, not the state of South Carolina. As far as Tolbert's returning home, the governor's advice was succinct: "If you return home, I will give you all the protection in my power. I don't think it prudent for you to return until the excitement subsides."

In light of all this, McKinley was convinced that a presidential visit would assure America that the deep South was a safe place and that everything was under control.

For students of the Institute and citizens of Tuskegee, December 16, 1898, was a day they would remember the rest of their lives. News of the president's visit excited the white population of the town as much as it did the students. Whites reached out to the school administration with offers to help organize an appropriate celebration, though some pointedly avoided any public connection with the school and offered their help only on the condition that they remain anonymous.

With characteristic diplomacy, Washington later wrote:

I think I never realized before this how much the white people of Tuskegee and vicinity thought of our institution.... Dozens of these people came to me and said that, while they did not want to push themselves into prominence, if there was anything they could do to help, or to relieve me personally, I had but to intimate it and they would be only too glad to assist.

What touched Washington almost as deeply as the president's visit was "the deep pride which all classes of citizens in Alabama seemed to take in our work."

The morning of December 16, President and Mrs. McKinley arrived accompanied by the entire Cabinet except for one, some of their wives and family members, generals from the Spanish-American War, and a horde of newspaper reporters. In session in Montgomery, the Alabama legislature passed a resolution to adjourn and join in the festivities at Tuskegee, accompanied by the governor.

Townspeople decorated the entire mile of roadway between the Tuskegee railroad station and the campus. From his reviewing stand, the president watched the student body march by, with each member carrying a stalk of sugar cane decorated with cotton balls. They were followed by a stream of floats that took an hour and a half to pass, contrasting the old and new ways of dairying, plowing, cooking, and other skills.

The only record of Carver's involvement in the festivities was a memorandum from Washington on November 28 instructing him "to have all the machinery that is to be used in connection with the parade repainted before the President comes."

Among the many speakers that day, the remarks of John D. Long, secretary of the navy, were perhaps the grandest and most sweeping:

A picture had been presented today which should be put upon canvas with the pictures of Washington and Lincoln, and transmitted to future time and generations:... The President of the United States standing on this platform, on one side the Governor of Alabama, on the other, completing the trinity, a representative of a race only a few years ago in bondage.... God bless the orator, philanthropist, and disciple of the Great Master—who, if he were on earth, would be doing the same work—Booker T. Washington.

During a trip to Boston in the spring of 1899, Washington was astonished to learn that a group of his benefactors had raised money to send him and his wife on a European vacation. He had never had a vacation and resisted their suggestion that he take one, fearing that without his fundraising work, donations for the school would dry up. His friends responded by donating enough to keep the school solvent the whole time he was away. As always, Washington was also worried about appearances. He recalled later hearing it said "when people of my race reach any degree of success, they were inclined to unduly exalt themselves; to try and ape the wealthy, and in doing so lose their heads."

His friends prevailed, and on May 10, he and his wife, Margaret, boarded the Red Star liner *Friesland* in New York for a ten-day voyage to Antwerp. This former slave, who once slept on the floor and ate with his hands, was shown to one of the finest staterooms on board. He had heard about "unpleasant experiences" of other black passengers on the high seas but soon found himself a celebrity. As the ship sailed past the Statue of Liberty toward the Verazzano Narrows and the Atlantic, Washington felt the weight of eighteen years as Tuskegee's president slip from his shoulders. It was an unfamiliar feeling for him to realize "I had no engagements; did not have to take a train at a certain hour; did not have an appointment to meet someone, or to make an address at a certain hour." He began sleeping up to fifteen hours a night, a far cry from his previous travel experiences when he "sometimes slept in three different beds in a single night."

The captain invited him to conduct chapel services, which he declined since he wasn't a minister. He did, however, agree to address the passengers and was introduced by a fellow traveler, New Jersey Senator

Sewell. "From the captain down to the most humble servant, we were treated with the greatest kindness," Washington later recalled.

The *Friesland* arrived in Antwerp, where the Washingtons found their hotel faced a public square filled with remarkable and entertaining sights: "...the people coming in from the country with all kinds of beautiful flowers to sell, the women coming in with their dogs drawing large, brightly polished cans filled with milk, the people streaming into the cathedral...." From there they traveled to Rotterdam by canal boat, then to Brussels and Paris, where they were introduced to former President Benjamin Harrison. Washington accepted an offer to speak at the University Club of Paris, which triggered a flood of speaking invitations, most of which he refused, "knowing that if I accepted them all, the object of my visit would be defeated." He did agree to speak Sunday in the American chapel (and gave an "address" rather than a sermon) and attended a reception at the American ambassador's residence.

In Paris, Mr. and Mrs. Washington renewed their acquaintance with a black American painter named Henry C. Tanner, whose paintings were on display in Luxembourg Palace. Washington saw in Tanner another example of the credo he preached at Tuskegee and in his public addresses:

[T]hat any man, regardless of color, will be recognized and rewarded just in proportion as he learns to do something well— learns to do it better than someone else—however humble the thing may be. As I have said, I believe that my race will succeed in proportion as it learns to do a common thing in an uncommon manner; learn to do a thing so thoroughly that no one can improve on what it has done; learns to make its services of indispensable value....

Few people ever stopped to inquire whether Mr. Tanner was a Negro painter, a French painter, or a German painter. They simply knew that he was able to produce something which the world wanted—a great painting—and the matter of colour did not enter into their minds. When a Negro girl learns to cook, to wash dishes, to sew, to write a book, or a Negro boy learns to groom horses, or to grow sweet potatoes, or to build a house, or to practice medicine, as well or better than someone else, they will be rewarded regardless of race or colour. In the long run, the world is going to have the best, and any difference in race, religion, or previous history will not long keep the world from what it wants.

Carolina riots notwithstanding, the eager, optimistic voice of the student of twenty years ago still rang out loud and clear.

Mr. and Mrs. Washington continued on to London, where Washington was besieged with dining and speaking invitations. One of the few he accepted was at the American embassy, where he met many members of Parliament as well as another famous American visitor: Mark Twain. The Washingtons were presented to Queen Victoria at Windsor Castle and accepted her majesty's invitation to tea. Among the guests that day was Susan B. Anthony, a lifelong crusader in America for temperance, abolition, and women's legal rights, including the right to vote. Seeing the two austere, elderly ladies together (the queen was eighty, Miss Anthony a year younger) was an unforgettable moment for Washington; one was the embodiment of tradition and decorum, the other a lifelong advocate of change. "I was deeply impressed," he wrote, "with the fact that one did not often get an opportunity to see, during the same hour, two women so remarkable in different ways."

Washington also met Sir Henry Stanley, the reporter and adventurer the New York *Herald* had sent to Africa to find out whether Dr. David Livingstone was still alive. Their conversation confirmed Washington's belief that repatriating American blacks to Africa, as some had suggested and others had done, was no proper path to racial harmony.

Washington noted with interest the relationship between servant and master in England. Freed of its racial overtones, it seemed to him pleasant and appropriate for both parties. The "servant class" in Britain was long established, as were social strata that people had little inclination to challenge. Late in the nineteenth century, 20 percent of the entire workforce of Great Britain was employed in domestic service. Washington was impressed with the deference that the servants show to their "masters" and "mistresses,"—terms which I suppose would not be tolerated in America. The English servant expects, as a rule, to be nothing but a servant, and so he perfects himself in the art to a degree that no class of servants in America has yet reached. In our country the servant expects to become, in a few years, a "master" himself. Which system is preferable? I will not venture an answer.

The Washingtons sailed for New York from Southampton aboard the *St. Louis* after three months in Europe. On the way home, Washington read a biography of Frederick Douglass in the ship's library. He particularly noted Douglass's description of the way he was treated aboard ship when he had traveled from America to England more than half a century before. Douglass was refused entry to a cabin and spent the entire trip on deck (and this in a sailing vessel, when a fair voyage east across the Atlantic took three to four weeks).

A few minutes after reading the passage, Washington received a visit from a group of passengers requesting he deliver a speech after the next evening's concert. He agreed and was introduced to the packed salon by the governor of New York. To Washington the contrast between his and Douglass's experiences were astonishing, "and yet," he declared, "there are people who are bold enough to say that race feeling in America is not growing less intense!"

Returning to Tuskegee before summer vacation was over, Washington resumed his fund-raising and administrative duties with renewed vigor. Warren Logan had managed the school's affairs in his absence. And, true to their word, Northern benefactors had sent donations sufficient to keep the school current with expenses.

Since first coming to Tuskegee in 1881, Washington and his family had lived in a succession of comfortable yet unpretentious quarters, sometimes managing dormitory space for teachers as well. After his return from Europe, Washington began construction of a fine new house both as a home for his family and as a place to entertain important visitors.

Robert Taylor, the Ivy League architect who had designed the Tuskegee chapel four years previously, designed the house. Washington's home was rather sober on the outside, a very subdued Victorian silhouette with numerous porches and gables but little decoration for decoration's sake. The house was built using school-made bricks and constructed almost entirely by paid student labor. Carpenters, bricklayers, and other workers earned the same wage they would have made for constructing any other campus building.

Inside, Washington applied something of what he had seen in the great homes and palaces of Europe. There was gold leaf on the ceiling trim, Italian marble around the fireplace, comfortable reception and dining rooms downstairs, and five spacious bedrooms upstairs. On the third floor were lodgings for up to eight students who performed housekeeping, serving, gardening, and other chores in the home. Washington added touches of his own. The handrail on the main staircase was positioned much lower than usual so that Mrs. Washington—at four feet, ten inches—could reach it. He installed an electric sauna in his bathroom, modeled after one he had seen overseas. It looked like a chest-high wooden telephone booth with no top. One of its four sides was hinged to make a door. The inside was lined with electric light bulbs, set into mirrors to intensify the heat.

Inside and out, the house was a prime example of Washington's ideal: well designed and well made completely by Negroes, highest quality but never ostentatious by the standards of the day. It had full indoor plumbing and was wired throughout for electricity—the first house in Macon County with indoor toilets or electric lights. And a black man lived there.

—

CHAPTER NINE

AGAINST
THE TIDE

T he 1899–1900 academic year at Tuskegee began with enrollment at
an all-time high of more than twelve hundred students. They came
from all over the South, and many of the young men and women
still arrived penniless, working during the day and going to night school
for two years, then attending day classes for the next three years.

The generation born after Reconstruction had grown up under a con-
fusing combination of legally guaranteed freedom and legally mandated
discrimination. Still, a notice at the head of a chapel flyer titled "Things to
Remember and Practice in 1900" neatly summarized the Tuskegee perspective:

> Do not stand still and complain, but go forward—
> mere fault-finders accomplish little.

By the turn of the century Tuskegee was attracting students from the
Caribbean, Central and South America and Africa as well as the American
South. The annual Farmer's Conference, which Booker T. Washington
had started with promising results in 1890, had grown every year until it
had become one of the largest and most important events in the region.
Both black and white farmers, some with their wives and children in tow,

flocked to the school to learn scientifically tested methods for improving their yields with modest capital investment, explained in everyday language they could understand. Professor Carver continued issuing his agricultural bulletins to great acclaim, with requests for reprints pouring in from Oklahoma, Texas, Mississippi, Georgia, and other states. Individual farmers wrote asking for them, and so did the agriculture departments and libraries of colleges for whites and blacks alike.

Tuskegee graduates developed a reputation for excellence and a strong work ethic. Prospective employers wrote Booker T. Washington frequently asking him to recommend a student to hire as a mason, wheelwright, blacksmith, dairyman, housekeeper, or any of the other trades the school was preparing its graduates for. One gentleman wrote from Montgomery on behalf of his wife seeking a cook and a chambermaid who could also sew. "There are numbers I could get here at very low wages," he admitted, "but I want nice girls who are intelligent and know how to do their work." For those he wrote to Tuskegee.

Morning devotionals and evening prayers remained part of the daily schedule. Washington often presided at these meetings when he was in town, reading from the Bible and delivering a brief homily. There were also Sunday school and chapel services every Sunday morning, which students were required to attend. Neighbors who lived near the campus often joined the fellowship, which, combined with students and faculty, made a congregation of fifteen hundred strong.

In his own way, Professor Carver took an active part in religious affairs on campus. Three years at Tuskegee had made him extremely popular with the students as a teacher, counselor, and friend. His somewhat rumpled appearance was in sharp contrast to the spit and polish of the other male teachers, and it made him approachable in a way the more famous and more reserved Washington was not. Carver was not a gifted orator like Washington or the visiting dignitaries who spoke in chapel; still, his strong personal faith and love of teaching made him an effective, compelling instructor in the Bible class he taught.

Carver saw no conflict between science and religious faith. To the contrary, he told his Bible students that knowing science helped him appreciate God's handiwork all the more. Carver also held frequent private conversations with his Creator. These talks, rather than prayers in the formal sense, were Carver's way of communicating with his Lord. He was in awe of God's power to make the flowers and animals he so enjoyed but spoke to him more as a dear friend than as a deity.

The daily schedule for students in 1899 clearly reflected Washington's admiration of the regimen at Hampton Institute:

5:00 A.M.	Rising bell
5:50	Warning breakfast bell
6:00	Breakfast bell
6:20	Cleaning of rooms
6:50	Work bell
7:30	Morning study hour
8:20	Morning school bell
8:25	Inspection of young men in ranks
8:40	Chapel
8:55	Daily news
9:00 A.M.–12 noon	Morning classes
12:15 P.M.	Dinner
1:00	Work bell
1:30–3:30	Afternoon classes
5:30	End of work day
6:00	Supper
7:10	Evening prayers
7:30	Evening study hour
9:20	Warning retiring bell
9:30	Retiring bell

In response to questions about how he kept a student body of more than twelve hundred both together and "out of mischief," he said there were two answers: first, "that the men and women who come to us for an education are in earnest." Second, "that everybody is kept busy." About the only free time students enjoyed was a few minutes in the evening after supper and Sunday afternoons after church. Because most students wanted to attend Tuskegee so badly and made such sacrifices to be there, few were willing to risk disobeying the rules. Chaperones kept a watchful eye on them in the dining hall, chapel, and other places where boys and girls congregated together. Very occasionally a girl became pregnant; she was sent quietly home.

Washington and Carver shared a devotion to Tuskegee, to teaching, to their faith, and to improving the prospects for members of their race. Yet the misunderstandings and differences between them had festered more or less steadily since Carver's arrival. Carver had expected a fully equipped laboratory, courtesy of the Slater Fund, and found literally nothing with which to begin his work. Moreover, he found himself saddled with enthusiastic but inexperienced student workers who couldn't handle the jobs Carver delegated to them, which in turn got Carver in trouble with the administration.

Washington, on the other hand, seemed to think that in Carver he was getting a precise, well-organized, detail-oriented scientist who could assume responsibility for a large share of hands-on management. The agricultural department was the jewel in Tuskegee's crown in that it was the best means for producing graduates, products, information, and services immediately useful to thousands of black Southern farmers in search of self-sufficiency and financial independence. Washington had handed it over to a man he thought could control it.

Carver's heart was with his students, his experiments, and his classes. He had no interest or skill in administrative duties and was relatively uninterested in the protocol and decorum Washington found essential for making the right impression and fulfilling his mission. Both men were strong willed and convinced they were right. Instead of working out their differences over time, they became more firmly rooted in their separate viewpoints.

As he had from the beginning, Carver wrote asking Washington for more resources to accomplish what was expected of him, while eagerly reciting what he had been able to do in spite of the limitations. One letter from early in the year began, "I send you lists of a few things that would add greatly to the instruction in my Dept. I think you will find some improvement when you return." He went on to describe the various crops under cultivation—oats, rye, wheat, turnips, onions, lettuce, rutabagas—and closed with a promise "to reduce every expense to its lowest minimum." At Washington's request Carver also included specific listings of livestock—reports on mule prices, how many sows had died (and why; Washington always wanted to know why), the number of cows milked and how much milk they gave, and so forth.

Gathering these reports was time-consuming and frustrating for Carver. They took him away from his agricultural work and had to be done with the help of students and hired hands that always seemed below par. But to Washington, often hundreds of miles away in a Boston hotel, these reports were the only way he could keep in touch.

Though Washington and Carver disagreed on the details, Carver shared his employer's interest in saving money. Under Washington's stewardship, Tuskegee had amassed seven hundred thousand dollars worth of land and buildings, all of it debt free, and an endowment of a million dollars. Nevertheless, including faculty members and dependents, the Institute supported or served seventeen hundred people, most of whom were working students or teachers on salary.

The Alabama state legislature still contributed two thousand dollars per year to the campus, and some students paid part or all of their expenses in cash. All the rest of the money came from foundations and wealthy individuals on the strength of the school's reputation and Washington's international prominence. There were many hundreds of Tuskegee mouths to feed, and every dollar collected in New England drawing rooms had to be squeezed to the utmost.

Carver was one of the most enthusiastic money savers on campus. When there was nothing in the budget for laboratory glassware, he made his own. For example, he chilled a discarded whiskey bottle with ice-cold water, then tied a string tight around the middle of it and set the string on fire. The bottle popped neatly in two; the top half became a funnel and the bottom, a beaker.

He worked diligently to make the campus dining hall self-sufficient, supplying meat, vegetables, and milk from his agricultural operations, so that the same ear of corn that taught a farming student planting, cultivation, and harvesting, also fed him, which trained the cooks and dining stewards—all without a cent of expense.

One of Carver's frustrations was that as soon as he got one task right, Washington seemed to bring up something else he had neglected. There was always something else that, in Washington's estimation, needed doing now.

Carver eventually found himself in charge of repairing and refurbishing the toilet facilities on campus (which were notoriously foul), and of supervising repair of all the water wells. The water reservoir on campus was in embarrassingly bad shape, though no one before Carver evidently had the skill or interest to perform an analysis. His report found the water to contain rust, decaying leaves, tadpoles, mosquitoes, and other insects.

Carver was assigned to find land for a new peach orchard. He decided a farm the school was about to buy was ideal, but administrative roadblocks kept him from beginning work on it. Frustrated, he wrote Washington to ask, "In order that I may not be hindered with my plans as I have been frequently heretofore, will you kindly notify me officially that the Gregory field can be used, also stating the amount."

Even though Washington was sometimes exasperated with Carver's shortcomings as an administrator, he genuinely admired his devotion to the school and its mission. While on a speaking and fundraising trip to New York, Washington wrote to Carver thanking him for his work and for his recent thorough reports, to which Carver replied, "I certainly appreciate your very kind letter, it is full of encouragement just at this time when I am feeling very tired." Carver then went on to report happily on the latest progress with radishes, cabbage, potatoes, turnips, beets, kohlrabi, eggplant, tomatoes, corn, English peas, and other crops.

For his part, Carver also acknowledged their differences of opinion about how he should spend his time—whether working on agricultural experiments with advanced students or doing classroom teaching and administrative duties. In a letter to Washington dated March 18, 1899, he wrote: "In regard to the teaching I have always felt as you do about it, and therefore have stuck very close to it, frequently at the expense of the other, and more practical part, but I think I see brighter days ahead, if the Lord allows us to continue this great work."

Washington's interest in the smallest details of Tuskegee's operation inevitably led to oversights. When they involved Professor Carver, Carver took them very much to heart, while Washington acknowledged them and went on to the next matter. Two days before Christmas in 1899, Washington sent Carver a curt memo:

> Mr. G. W. Carver—
> Mr. J. H. Washington [John, Booker's brother] reports that you were tardy at the Directors and Division Instructors meeting Dec. 6th. It is important that these meetings be attended promptly.
>
> > B. T. W.
> > Principal

Carver wrote his astonished reply at the bottom of the page and returned it to Washington's office:

> Mr. Washington—
> I respect your wishes above any other duty. I was detained by *you in your office* and publicly announced the same in the above meeting and asked Mr. J. H. W. to have the kindness to excuse me.
>
> > Very truly,
> > G. W. Carver

As a welcome relief from Tuskegee matters, Carver enjoyed frequent correspondence with his old professor and friend Louis Pammel. The two of them exchanged plant samples, and Carver asked for the professor's advice in preparing scientific papers on their shared specialty—fungus.

In the summer of 1900, Carver returned to Ames for a visit with Professor Pammel and his family, visiting old colleagues and basking in attention and respect that he longed for at Tuskegee but never felt he received. Where in Alabama he was in charge of outhouses, in Iowa he was hailed as a returning hero. He wrote to Washington, then in New York, on July 9, reporting "everyone is very much interested and enthused over the work at Tuskegee.... I am sparing neither time nor expense to take in everything I think of value to us." He also mentioned making "arrangements for my study which will lead up to a PHD degree." As eager as he was to return with information useful to Tuskegee, he still had visions of resuming his own academic studies, though by now he was forty years old.

Back on the Tuskegee campus, Washington had plenty for Carver to take care of. In a three-page memorandum written on September 26, 1900, shortly after the beginning of the school year, he called Carver's attention to a long list of repairs and renovations he expected Carver to see to, including reworking the field terraces, cultivating crop fields closer to the fences, raising more chickens, enlarging the hog run, improving drainage ditches, reducing the size of fields devoted to experimental crops, repairing shabby looking wagon bodies, planting velvet beans (which Washington considered an attractive plant) where campus visitors would see them more, clearing out dead trees, sprucing up the sheep pen, making sure harnesses were "regularly and systematically greased," and building hay racks for the horses and mules. Washington also added a typical admonition: "I repeat what I said in your presence this morning to Mr. Clayton [one of Carver's assistants]. There is entirely too much waste wood in the cow lots, etc. Everything in connection with these lots must be put in first class condition."

While the endless stream of notes, directives, and reminders irritated Carver, they were signs of Washington's sheer force of will and unflinching dedication to the dream that had become Tuskegee. That same force and dedication served Washington and his cause well on the national stage.

As always, Booker T. Washington was unswerving in his belief that the path to true equality led through hard work, patience, Christian humility, and a willingness to earn the respect of whites. He held fast to his view in spite of the fact that blacks were slipping still further in the legal and political arenas. By 1900 many states had laws mandating the segregation of races on public transportation, limiting black passengers to crowded, drafty, dirty accommodations—not separate but equal, as Plessy vs. Ferguson had ruled, but separate and woefully unequal. It was also the year the National Federation of Labor, precursor to the AFL-CIO, agreed to let local union authorities decide whether or not to admit blacks as members. Since its founding in 1881, there had been a national policy forbidding exclusion of applicants on the basis of race. Southern locals complained for years that they should have control over their own membership makeup. In 1900 they got it, and immediately expelled black union members.

In 1900, Washington founded the National Negro Business League as another forum for promoting the attitude of self-reliance that so characterized Tuskegee. His plan was to produce an organization whose aims complemented and paralleled those of the school. While the campus was turning out blacksmiths, dressmakers, and bricklayers, the League could be grooming a class of black merchant bankers, accountants, lawyers, and insurance underwriters—ambitious, talented men and women who were excluded from white commerce, but whose skills, once proven, should eventually earn them a place in the white business mainstream.

Operation of the League was nominally controlled by officers in local chapters, which eventually numbered more than six hundred. But as with everything else Washington was involved in, the League bore the stamp of his personality, and he directed it behind the scenes in every detail. It enjoyed modest success in helping establish fifty black-owned banks across the country, helping blacks start insurance companies (since white-owned insurers, almost without exception, refused to write policies for them) and even assisting black businesses that employed white workers.

The problem was that white clients generally refused to patronize them, and there were never enough black customers to generate the critical mass necessary to support an interconnected black professional economy.

The year 1900 was also the year Washington published his first autobiography, *The Story of My Life and Work.* Washington and a ghostwriter named Edgar Webber, whom one observer said "does as little as he can and complains as much as he can," wrote the manuscript in haste. Webber had attended Howard and Fisk and upon getting the job of writing the autobiography had promised to "enter most heartily into the work before me." He finished the manuscript in the summer of 1899 when Washington was in Europe, and it went to Washington's fellow writer (and former adversary) T. Thomas Fortune for editing. Preoccupied with editing his New York publication for Negroes titled the *Age,* Fortune gave the draft little attention. When the type was set and page proofs went to Fortune for his approval, he was appalled at the bad writing and the large number of errors. He marked up the typescript so badly that the publisher refused to send him the last two chapters, and complained that making all the revisions Fortune suggested would require resetting the whole manuscript, which the publisher insisted there was not time to do. (Webber's name was eventually deleted from the title page, and, to his outrage, even removed from the index.)

Not surprisingly, the book got a lukewarm reception from the critics and the public at large. Distribution was hampered by the fact that the publisher sold most of its books door-to-door to a black clientele.

Learning from his mistakes, Washington enjoyed far more success with *Up from Slavery*, published a year later by the respected New York firm of Doubleday, Page and Company. His new ghostwriter, Max Bennett Thrasher, was a former reporter, teacher, and school administrator who worked under Washington's close supervision. Thrasher accompanied his subject on his frequent trips, taking notes on trains and in hotel rooms. Washington then wrote the draft from Thrasher's notes and gave Thrasher his manuscript to edit.

Washington used the book to present an image the public loved: an impoverished former slave rises to national prominence through faith, hard work, and dedication to ideals. It was also a sounding board for underscoring the accomplishments of Tuskegee and Washington's hopes for the future of race relations.

In the closing pages of *Up from Slavery,* he wrote:

The only difficulty now is that the demand for our graduates from both white and black people in the South is so great that we cannot supply more than one-half the persons for whom applications come to us. Neither have we the buildings nor the money for current expenses to enable us to admit to the school more than one-half the young men and women who apply to us for admission....

While the institution is in no sense denominational, we have a department known as the Phelps Hall Bible Training School, in which a number of students are prepared for the ministry and other forms of Christian work.... What is equally important, each one of these students works half of each day at some industry, in order to get skill and the love of work, so that when he goes out from the institution he is prepared to set the people with whom he goes to labor a proper example in the matter of industry....

At least six thousand men and women from Tuskegee are now at work in different parts of the South; men and women who, by their own example or by direct effort, are showing the masses of our race how to improve their material, educational, and moral and religious life. What is equally important, they are exhibiting a degree of common sense and self-control which is causing better relations to exist between the races and is causing the Southern white man to learn to believe in the value of educating the men and women of my race....

The great human love that in the end recognizes and rewards merit is everlasting and universal. The outside world does not know, neither can it appreciate, the struggle that is constantly going on in the hearts of both the Southern white people and their former slaves to free themselves from racial prejudice; and while both races are thus struggling they should have the sympathy, the support, and the forbearance of the rest of the world.

Up from Slavery was widely acclaimed by reviewers, some of whom compared it favorably with the autobiography of Benjamin Franklin. In a review titled "An Exemplary Citizen," the prominent novelist, editor, and critic William Dean Howells applauded Washington's "constant common sense," and believed his cautious and accommodating approach to equality was "at present the only way for his race."

One reviewer who disagreed with Howells's glowing review was William Edward Burghardt Du Bois, a professor of sociology at Atlanta University and a prolific writer on race issues. In previous years, Du Bois had turned down numerous offers to teach at Tuskegee. He was the first black in America to earn a doctorate, receiving his Ph.D. from Harvard in 1895, and went on to positions at Wilberforce College and the University of Pennsylvania before arriving at Atlanta in 1897.

Du Bois had once shared Washington's view that over time blacks would earn their equality in the world and that patience and deference were the ultimate keys to success. Events over the intervening years prompted him to change his mind. As the twentieth century began, Du Bois became more convinced that passiveness and humility were forms of weakness, and that the only way to achieve equality was to demand it as a right, not hope for it as a privilege. His review of *Up from Slavery,* published in July of 1901, branded it as only "a partial history" insisting that Washington was not the universally recognized spokesman for his race the book presented him to be.

Du Bois's view to the contrary, Washington continued to consolidate his position as the nationally acknowledged representative of blacks considered responsible in the eyes of the white public and press. He generated a steady stream of articles and essays for the black press, some of which also found their way into large circulation white publications.

As the party of Lincoln, Republicans courted Washington as an ally and frequently asked his advice on the appointment of blacks to public offices traditionally held by blacks—particularly postmasters, port inspectors, customs officials, and foreign office employees assigned to African and Caribbean countries. Washington and Vice President Theodore Roosevelt

James and Elizabeth Burroughs owned Booker T. Washington's mother, Jane, and therefore by law were Booker's owners as well. An 1861 inventory valued Jane at $250 and Booker at $400. Booker's father was an unidentified white neighbor.

Washington strikes a debating society pose in a photo taken June 10, 1875, the day of his graduation from Hampton Institute. He won a debate that was presented as part of the graduation exercises.

Moses Carver, along with his wife, Susan, owned George Washington Carver, his mother, and brother James. After their mother was kidnapped by outlaws during the Civil War, Moses and Susan raised George and James as their own children.

Carver in costume for a theater production at Iowa State, c. 1894. His slender build and high-pitched voice, both probably caused by childhood illnesses, made him a natural for female or comedic roles.

Carver's drawing class at Simpson College, 1891. Carver is at far right. His teacher Etta Budd (center right) encouraged him as a painter and enthusiastically nurtured his interest in botany.

A formal portrait of Washington used for promoting his books and speaking tours near the turn of the century. He was concerned with presenting a respectable, cultured appearance, feeling that Negros should hold themselves to higher standards than whites to prove themselves worthy of equal treatment.

Carver with one of his paintings, similar in style to the work he displayed at the 1893 World's Columbian Exposition in Chicago.

The Washington family c. 1899: Ernest, Booker Jr., Margaret, BTW, and Portia.

Designed in 1896 by MIT's first black graduate, the Tuskegee Chapel was the center of campus life for generations.

Built almost completely by students, who also made the 1.2 million bricks used for construction, the chapel was the tallest building in the county and the first to have electric lights. It was destroyed by fire in 1957.

Fanny Norton Smith Washington, BTW's first wife. She was a student at the small community school in West Virginia where he first taught.

The tradition of marching to chapel services continued into the 1950s. Students wore special school uniforms, which were regularly inspected for neatness.

Tuskegee Executive Council, variously dated 1902 or 1906. BTW is seated center, with Carver standing at far right. Also pictured are Washington's longtime secretary, Emmett Scott (seated second from left), Tuskegee treasurer Warren Logan (seated second from right), and John Washington, BTW's brother (seated far right).

EQUALITY

This composite image combined separate photos of Washington and President Theodore Roosevelt to criticize Roosevelt for inviting BTW to dinner at the White House on October 16, 1901. People distributing buttons made from this picture were later arrested for possessing "obscene material."

George Washington Carver as head of the agriculture department at Tuskegee, 1906. He carefully placed a fresh flower in his lapel every day, often one he had grown himself.

President Roosevelt at Tuskegee, October 24, 1905. Washington was delighted at the attention and affirmation the president's visit produced, and Roosevelt used the trip to enhance his political position with Southern blacks and Northern white industrialists.

Carver teaching class during a Farmer's Conference. These annual events gave him the opportunity to explain improved agriculture methods directly to farmers, promoting simple, practical, inexpensive ways to improve crop yields.

Washington speaking to Farmer's Conference participants.

Carver in 1915. Though not well-known outside agriculture circles at this time, he would soon be world famous for his research on peanuts, which resulted in more than 200 possible commercial applications.

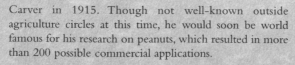

Carver in one of his early laboratories. The poor quality of his lab facilities was the source of frequent clashes with Washington. Carver insisted he needed better equipment to do the work expected of him, while Washington questioned the expense of a more elaborate setup.

After years of argument and cajoling, Carver finally received the fully equipped laboratory he insisted Tuskegee had promised him. Now relocated to the Carver Museum on campus, this is the lab Carver worked in for nearly thirty years.

During the celebration of Tuskegee's twenty-fifth anniversary in 1906, Washington hosted many of the school's most generous benefactors and supporters, including Andrew Carnegie (front row, second from right), and Harvard president Charles W. Eliot (far right).

Photo appearing with "A Boy Who Was Traded for a Horse" in the October 1932 issue of *American Magazine*. By this time, Carver's work with peanuts had made him a household name.

Carver with U.S. Secretary of Agriculture Henry A. Wallace, 1933. Carver had been a student of Wallace's father, also named Henry, at Iowa State, and had sometimes taken the younger Wallace on his hikes to collect plant specimens.

Washington speaking in Louisiana, Ap 1915, seven months before his death.

On December 30, 1933, the press reported that Carver had evidently developed a peanut-based treatment for polio. The announcement produced a deluge of letters from patients and their families desperate for help. Carver's treatment was never scientifically affirmed.

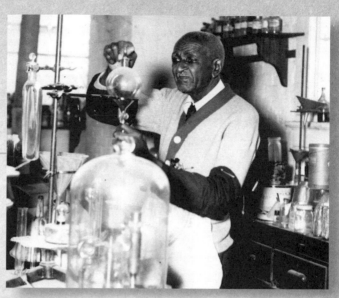

Carver in his beloved laboratory.

Even years after his arrival at Tuskegee, Carver continued to consider a career as a painter. Though he never painted professionally, he enjoyed it as a hobby for the rest of his life. Tragically, almost all of his paintings and sketches were destroyed in the museum he had established to preserve them.

Too weak to work in the fields with the rest of the boys, Carver had learned household chores instead of outdoor skills. All his life he enjoyed knitting, crocheting, and making lace.

Henry Ford was a great admirer of Carver's, and frequently invited him to visit. Carver's last trip away from Tuskegee, in December 1942, was to see Ford at his estate in Dearborn, Michigan. Near the time of Carver's death, there were reports that Ford had offered him a job as a research consultant.

Statue of Washington on the Tuskegee campus showing him lifting the veil of ignorance from the Negro race. Its dedication on April 5, 1922, was attended by a crowd of 5,000.

Statue of Carver as a boy at the George Washington Carver National Monument near Diamond Grove, Missouri.

were already friends when Roosevelt became president on September 14, 1901, following McKinley's assassination. They had spoken together at a celebration honoring Frederick Douglass two years before, and Roosevelt had sought Washington's advice on race matters even then. The day he became president, Roosevelt wrote Washington: "I must see you as soon as possible. I want to talk over the question of possible appointments in the South exactly on the lines of our last conversation together."

Washington traveled to the White House, and, true to his word, President Roosevelt queried his guest on prospects for a number of appointments. Washington was ready with a list of people he felt would support policies beneficial to Negroes—a range of candidates including Southern conservatives, black Republicans, a former governor of Alabama, and a black doctor from South Carolina. Scarcely a month later, while traveling in Mississippi, Washington received a request to return to the Capital. When he arrived on October 16, he found an invitation waiting for him to dine at the White House at eight o'clock that evening. He arrived at the appointed time and dined in the company of the president, his family, and Philip Bathell Stewart, a Republican businessman from Colorado who had been Roosevelt's hunting companion on several occasions.

The president hadn't intended to make a statement on his racial policy one way or the other by inviting Washington to dinner. "I did not devote very much thought to the matter one way or the other," he replied in a letter when congratulated on his courage. "I respect him greatly and believe in the work he has done." He went on to admit "a moment's qualm on inviting him because of his color," but that such a feeling "made me ashamed of myself and made me hasten to send the invitation."

Washington took the night train to New York, where he had dinner the following evening with the chairman of the Tuskegee Board of Trustees, William H. Baldwin Jr. Later the two of them spoke at John D. Rockefeller's Bible class at the Fifth Avenue Baptist Church. Washington noticed a two-line report of his White House visit in the New York papers, mentioned it briefly to Baldwin, and let the matter drop.

Everything changed the next morning, when front pages across the country carried the news that a black man had dined at the White House. Roosevelt had invited blacks to dinner when he was governor of New

York and on one occasion hosted a black Harvard classmate overnight at the governor's mansion. These precedents were lost in a flurry of editorials and bogus "interviews" in the days that followed. Some saw the beginnings of "social equality" for blacks, which would mean the end of the American social order and a rapid slide into debauchery and anarchy. Others saw Washington's role as a meek, ineffective supplicant to the white power structure further reinforced. Still others applauded the two for their courage and their apparent interest in a common goal.

The Richmond *Times* feared for the safety of white women. Seating a black man with the presidential family (including his spirited seventeen-year-old daughter, Alice) at the White House table "means the President is willing that negroes shall mingle freely with whites in the social circle— that white women may receive attentions from negro men. It means there is no racial reason in his opinion why whites and blacks may not marry and intermarry, why the Anglo-Saxon may not mix negro blood with his blood."

J. L. M. Curry, a representative of the Peabody Fund, which had made many generous gifts to Tuskegee, wrote from a different perspective:

> Perhaps it was a mistake, but a President or office holder ought to have the right to regulate his household affairs. It is not social equality with the negro race but an invitation to the chiefest and best representative of that race, whom I have found to be a gentleman. Few men, in this country, have been more useful.

The Montgomery *Advertiser* considered Washington's acceptance of the invitation a mistake that risked stirring up trouble, but that "in light of his record of bold opposition for years to any attempt at social recognition or political activity by his race, a solitary mistake, especially under the peculiar circumstances, should be overlooked."

One humorist reported no mark on the tablecloth where Washington's hands had rested, and that all the spoons were accounted for after he left.

The commotion was just dying down when Washington and Roosevelt marched together to receive their honorary degrees at the Yale Bicentennial. That event led to one final burst of editorial emotion, and then the matter dropped from public discourse. Years later, Roosevelt decided the invitation had been a mistake, not because of the invitation itself, but because it was so badly misinterpreted.

(A few days after Washington's death in 1915, Roosevelt wrote in response to a question about the event:

> On any rational theory of public and social life my action was absolutely proper.... Yet as a matter of fact what I did was a mistake.... It was misinterpreted by the white men of the South and by the black men of the South.... It was one of those cases where the application of a lofty and proper code of social observance to conditions which in actual fact were certain to cause the action to be misunderstood resulted badly.

In his autobiography, published two years earlier, Roosevelt had made no mention whatever of Booker T. Washington.)

During the presidential election of 1904, when Roosevelt was elected to a full term, two men were arrested in Indianola, Mississippi, for selling "obscene photographs" to residents of the black section of town. They were campaign buttons showing Roosevelt and Booker T. Washington dining together.

It was, as one historian noted, a generation before another Negro had dinner at the White House.

On the surface, Washington kept the same public profile as before. But after 1900 he began spending more time behind the scenes, working to advance his agenda by more private, more circuitous methods. One reason he changed tactics was that under constitutionally accepted states rights laws, individual state legislatures were systematically barring blacks from voting in one state after another. New registration laws set up simple but effective roadblocks to keep them out: literacy requirements, property ownership requirements, residency, poll taxes. Intimidations and lynchings served their purposes as well.

Some of Washington's efforts to stem the tide were laced with irony. Pullman railroad cars (named after the manufacturer in Chicago) were furnished with comfortable seats by day that were converted by porters into beds at night with individual sleeping spaces separated by heavy curtains. Around and shortly after 1900, states began requiring blacks and whites to have separate Pullman cars. The fact was that railroads were not likely to reserve a whole Pullman for whatever number of black passengers—if any—were on a particular trip. Banning them from white Pullman cars effectively denied them the only available means of comfortable cross-country transportation.

Since the Pullman Company leased their cars to the railroads rather than selling them, Washington and others sympathetic to the blacks' position (including W. E. B. Du Bois) petitioned the company to intercede on their behalf. The president of the company declined even to meet with them. He was Robert Todd Lincoln, President Lincoln's oldest son.

Eager to preserve his public image, Washington did not risk appearing defiant or angry. The Pullman incident and others like it prompted him to work even more diligently underground to stem the tide of legal discrimination washing over America's state houses. Masking his effort completely from public view, he became involved in a test case in the Alabama court over disenfranchisement, spending his own money to help pay legal fees. He did the same in Louisiana and in Maryland. In at least one case, his private secretary at Tuskegee, Emmett J. Scott, communicated with Washington's attorney in New York using pseudonyms and writing in code.

Though he never dined at the White House again, Washington remained a valuable informal advisor to President Roosevelt—and everyone in Washington's circle knew it. This influence, and the ability it conferred on Washington to recommend blacks for federal appointments, made his patronage a powerful persuasive tool. Disenfranchisement meant Republicans cared less and less about blacks, since fewer of them could vote every election, yet Roosevelt trusted Washington to nominate candidates for appointment—both black and, occasionally, white—who would keep the party's racial policy in balance. Roosevelt depended on Washington to help him carry out his plan of appointing fewer but better-qualified blacks. Practically speaking, Washington controlled a range of jobs all the way up to diplomatic postings and the register of the Treasury.

Ever mindful of the power of the press, Washington influenced publications behind the scenes, constantly aware he could never afford to upset the public appearance of neutrality. He made financial contributions to all the leading black publications, including the New York *Age,* the Washington *Colored American,* and the Boston *Colored Citizen.* He also advertised or contributed editorials and feature stories to friendly magazines, sometimes sponsoring a special "Tuskegee Issue," and used his clout to have writers and editors sympathetic to him placed in responsible positions. When challenged, Washington invariably denied subsidizing the black press.

There had always been prominent blacks who opposed Booker T. Washington and what they considered his acquiescence to white supremacy. As Washington fought a losing battle to preserve blacks' rights in the first years of the century, this once-flimsy chorus of opposition began to strengthen. T. Thomas Fortune, who had once opposed Washington but then edited his first autobiography, continued waffling back and forth, drifting further and further from him on the issue of what blacks should do. By 1903, Washington's most vocal opposition came from W. E. B. Du Bois, his former ally, once-prospective colleague, and occasional speaking partner.

The chorus started small, but it had been growing for years. Only months after Washington's Atlanta speech, John Hope, the president of Atlanta Baptist College, opposed Washington's ideas in a speech to a black debating society in Nashville. Like Washington, Hope was a mulatto—half Scot. Unlike his famous subject, Hope had no patience when it came to freedom:

> If we are not striving for equality, in heaven's name for what are we living? I regard it as cowardly and dishonest for any of our colored men to tell white people that we are not struggling for equality.... God forbid that we should get the implements with which to fashion our freedom, and then be too lazy or pusillanimous to fashion it. Let us not fool ourselves nor be fooled by others. If we cannot do what other free men do, then we are not free.... Rise, Brothers!

Come, let us possess this land. Never say, "Let well enough alone." Be dissatisfied. Let your discontent break mountain-high against the wall of prejudice, and swamp it to the very foundation. Then we shall not have to plead for justice nor on bended knee crave mercy; for we shall be men....

Two years after the Atlanta speech, a reporter, writer, and speaker named Victoria Earle Matthews spoke to the annual convention of the International Society of Christian Endeavor in San Francisco, pleading for the rights of black women in the South who had already done so much with so little.

Freed slave women, she said, "starting empty handed, were left to make Christian homes.... I believe the God who brought them out of the Valley of the Shadow, who snatched them from the hand of the white rapist, the base slave master whose unacknowledged children are to be found in every hamlet of the Republic, guided these women, and guides them in the supreme work of building their Christian homes."

Reverend Francis James Grimké, pastor of the Fifteenth Street Presbyterian Church in Washington, D.C., bristled at the sort of accommodation Booker T. Washington promoted. In 1898 he had published a scathing sermon condemning segregation:

The sentiment everywhere is: This is a white man's government. And that means, not only that the whites shall rule, but that the Negro shall have nothing whatever to do with governmental affairs. If he dares to think otherwise, or aspires to cast a ballot, or to become anything more than a servant, he is regarded as an impudent and dangerous Negro;... This is certainly a very discouraging condition of things, but the saddest aspect of it all is that there are members of our race—and not the ignorant, unthinking masses, who have had no advantages, and who might be excused for any seeming insensibility to their rights, but the intelligent, the educated—who are found condoning such offenses, justifying or excusing such a condition of things on the ground that in view of the great disparity in the condition of the two races, anything different from that could not reasonably be expected. Any Negro who takes that position is a traitor to his race, and shows that he is deficient in manhood, in true self-respect. If the time ever comes when the Negro himself acquiesces in the condition of things, then his fate is sealed and ought to be sealed. Such a race is not fit to be free.

CHAPTER TEN

An Inch of Progress

With the publication of *Up from Slavery*, Washington hit his stride as a fundraiser for Tuskegee and spokesman for racial harmony. After reading the book, George Eastman, founder of Eastman Kodak of the photography business, wrote to Washington that he had "come to the conclusion that I cannot dispose of five thousand dollars to any better advantage than to send it to you for your institute." Later, Eastman began sending regular gifts of ten thousand dollars year.

The book also caught Andrew Carnegie's attention. Washington had tried to call on the wealthy American during his 1899 European vacation when Carnegie was staying at his castle in Scotland. Carnegie's secretary declined Washington's request for an interview, insisting "he has come here for a much needed rest and would like a holiday until 1900."

Carnegie changed his attitude after *Up from Slavery* appeared. During a golf game, Washington's publisher, Frank Doubleday, entertained Carnegie with tidbits from the book. His interest piqued, Carnegie read the book and decided to give Tuskegee a library. Washington replied that, using student labor and Tuskegee bricks, they could build an adequate library for twenty thousand dollars. Impressed by their frugality, Carnegie immediately sent ten thousand dollars and followed it with an equal amount every year.

Henry Rogers, a partner in the Standard Oil monopoly, invited Washington to his office in New York the day after hearing Washington on a speaking tour there. He gave him ten one-thousand-dollar bills on the condition that the gift remain anonymous.

Soon afterward, Washington made a speech at a large fundraising meeting in Madison Square Garden. The festivities got off to an ominous start with the master of ceremonies, former President Grover Cleveland, pontificating on the "racial and slavery-bread imperfections" of the Negro race who endured down South in "a grievous amount of ignorance, a sad amount of laziness and thriftlessness"—and this in his introduction to Washington.

With dignity and aplomb, Washington redirected these coarse and thoughtless remarks, emphasizing the need black Southerners had on account of their condition, rather than the condition itself:

> The most fundamental and far-reaching deed that has been accomplished during the last quarter of a century has been that by which the Negro has been helped to find himself and to learn the secret of civilization—to learn that there are a few simple, cardinal principles upon which a race must start its upward course.... You of the North owe an unfulfilled duty to the Negro, and an equal duty to your white brethren in the South in assisting them to help remove the load of ignorance resting upon my race.

After the speech, Washington's supporters passed pledge forms among the audience. When they were tabulating the forms at the end of the evening, someone was astonished to read a slip that had been filled out by Andrew Carnegie pledging the jaw-dropping sum of $600,000, with the requirement that the interest income from $150,000 of the amount be used to provide for Washington and his family. In his acknowledgment of the gift, Washington said, "Your action will make me dedicate my life anew to the cause." And regarding his own windfall he wrote, "...my heart is so full that I can only say that we will try to repay you for what you have done in hard and earnest work."

Carnegie's gift letter continued:

To me he seems one of the greatest of living men, because his work is unique, the Modern Moses, who leads his race and lifts it through education, to even better and higher things than a land overflowing with milk and honey. History is to tell of two Washingtons, one white, the other black, both fathers of their people.

I am satisfied that the serious race problem of the South is to be solved wisely only through Mr. Washington's policy of education, which he seems to have been specially born—a slave among slaves, to establish and in his own day greatly to advance.

Ever practical, Washington was concerned that such a generous personal income would hamper his effectiveness as a fundraiser. He raised the question with Carnegie, who instructed Washington and two other Tuskegee trustees who had called on him at his New York townhouse to rewrite the bequest however they wanted and bring it to him to sign.

In the original document formally announcing the gift, Carnegie had said, "I wish that good man to be entirely free from pecuniary cares that he may be free to devote himself to his great mission," and specified the income from the $150,000. The new document instructed the Tuskegee trustees to make "suitable provision" for the Washington family, rather than give an amount. Washington kept Carnegie's first letter as a souvenir. Ultimately the university trustees earmarked the full $150,000 to endow Washington's salary, and he gave up his regular Institute paycheck. News of the $600,000 gift reached campus before Washington returned, and he was greeted by brass band, then processed through campus between two rows of cheering students who had been given a holiday in honor of the occasion.

Washington's success in raising money cemented his position as the leading black educator in the country. Other black institutions came to depend on him—directly or indirectly—for referrals and endorsements, while philanthropists more and more insisted on asking Washington where money should go when they wanted to donate for the benefit of Negroes.

As his influence grew, so did efforts among other influential blacks to slow the momentum of the Tuskegee Machine. Of all the black leaders who disagreed with his strategy, W. E. B. Du Bois emerged as Booker T. Washington's most articulate and well-known opposition. While Washington remained convinced that blacks would eventually prove they deserved equality with whites, Du Bois moved gradually from agreement with him to a point exactly opposite.

Back in 1891, Du Bois had agreed not all blacks should be allowed to vote. Washington had long promoted extending the vote to educated or property-owning men, whether black or white, and withholding it from the poor and unschooled of either race, reasoning that these people would be able to make informed choices at the polls. Du Bois had admitted that it had taken white Americans hundreds of years to reach the level of political sophistication necessary to make informed political decisions. At the time, Du Bois proposed limited voting rights to blacks who were intelligent, responsible, and law-abiding. In a widely quoted speech he explained:

> We must ever keep before us the fact that the South has some excuse for its present attitude. We must remember that a good many of our people...are not fit for the responsibility of republican government. When you have the right sort of black voters you will need no election laws. The battle of my people must be a moral one, not a legal or physical one.

Five years later when he was at the University of Pennsylvania, Du Bois wrote an analysis of the race issue titled *The Philadelphia Negro,* in which he still mirrored Washington's belief that the way to success was through self-help and cooperation. But by 1903 he had fundamentally altered his view. He concluded that in a culture that was obviously going to be segregated for the foreseeable future, blacks needed their own college-educated professionals: professors, publishers, philosophers, and businessmen who could serve as an inspiration to others of their race, and at the same time provide an infusion of intellectual and financial capital. Washington, on the other hand, believed blacks needed more practical education. That is why Tuskegee taught brickmaking and farming rather than philosophy and foreign language.

Du Bois felt the emphasis on industrial schools teaching practical skills to blacks was misguided. He insisted these schools produced relatively few true craftsmen and that too many of them were being trained in obsolete fields of employment. He thought people who supported the industrial school model should take a lesson from European history. He believed the history of education in the Old World proved that universities had to come first and industrial or trade schools later. Furthermore, Du Bois pointed out that Tuskegee depended on university graduates for their teachers. (Their own graduates were qualified to teach in rural primary schools but usually not at more advanced secondary schools like Tuskegee itself.) Without college level instruction, Du Bois insisted, black industrial schools would always struggle to find teachers.

Tuskegee's high profile as the largest and most successful black industrial school of its kind made it a frequent target of Du Bois's criticism. He hammered home his position that economic skills were being overemphasized at the expense of cultural and intellectual development. As the years passed, he also became more frustrated with the political and economic power of what he and other dissident black leaders called the Tuskegee Machine.

In the eyes of all the white politicians and benefactors who held the fate of the Negro man in their hands, Washington was the supreme and unchallenged symbol of success. In that role, he was the chief conduit for all the money, influence, prestige, and support that trickled down from the white power structure to the black. Washington's clandestine financial support of the black press gave him wide control over what they did and did not print. He was seen as a "safe" ally of white politicians—including President Roosevelt—whose position as a confidant and advisor seemed unassailable. In Du Bois's view, the Tuskegee Machine swept up all the money, influence, and public goodwill, and left blacks who championed other opinions with the crumbs.

In the spring of 1903, Du Bois seemed to break completely with Washington in an essay titled "Of Booker T. Washington and Others." He wrote that Washington's emergence as the apparent leader of black America was "easily the most striking thing in the history of the Negro" since Reconstruction. He claimed Washington "practically accepted the alleged inferiority of the Negro" and promoted a "submission of prejudice." Black businessmen and property owners, Du Bois insisted, would never be able to defend their interests without the vote. He said that self-respect and social discrimination would never coexist comfortably. Washington's passive stance, he asserted, was hurting, not helping, their case.

In 1898 the old Afro-American League that Du Bois had tried and failed to keep going was revived and rechristened the Afro-American Council. Though Washington himself was not a member, allies of his held all the important offices. In 1901 and 1902, Washington made significant secret financial contributions to the Council and helped engineer the election of a chairman sympathetic with his views. Du Bois and James Monroe Trotter—editor of the anti-Washington Boston *Guardian* and the first black member of Phi Beta Kappa at Harvard—fought unsuccessfully against Washington's powerful influence in the group. Trotter was arrested later in Boston for interrupting Washington during a speech with pointed questions about his policies.

Warned that there would be an attempt to take control away from pro-Washington forces in 1902, Washington decided to attend the meeting himself that year in St. Paul, Minnesota. His presence completely overshadowed the proceedings, prompting the Washington *Bee,* an anti-Washington black newspaper, to report glumly that "The 'Wizard of Tuskegee' was there.... His satellites were in the saddle.... They trotted and pranced as he pulled the reins and his ticket was elected and his namby-pamby policy...was incorporated into the address, which was nothing more than a pronouncement of his nibs, the boss of Negro beggars."

Washington wanted to steer the Afro-American Council and public opinion his way, but he still wanted friendship and cordiality among black public figures even if they disagreed on policy matters. He constantly sought compromise and reconciliation with people who opposed him. In January 1904, Washington held a meeting, financed by Andrew Carnegie, at Carnegie Hall in New York for the purpose of assembling a group that could work together effectively where the Afro-American Council had failed. Du Bois was invited and appeared for the discussions. (He had also accepted Washington's invitation to speak at Tuskegee the year before, in spite of the "On Booker T. Washington" essay.)

At the end of the meetings in New York, Washington affirmed his belief in "absolute civil, political, and public equality" between black and white, higher education for blacks, and access to Pullman cars. Du Bois added that, as long as Washington held to his positions, he was ready to join forces with him. Washington and Du Bois were pulling together again, at least temporarily.

The Carnegie Hall conference produced a group that optimistically named itself the Committee of Twelve for the Advancement of the Interests of the Negro Race. Once again, Washington, as chairman of the Committee, secretly supplied money to direct the work of the group, paying lobbyists to promote black interests in federal and state legislation. Though he continued to insist he agreed with the Committee's positions, Du Bois soon quit the group in disgust, citing Washington's overbearing influence on their actions. The collaboration between the two had lasted only a few months.

As the Tuskegee Machine grew stronger, those who considered Washington a traitor to his race became both bolder and more desperate. W. E. B. Du Bois and his followers believed Washington's program of appeasement had failed and wanted to take a more confrontational approach. Seeing disenfranchisement and Jim Crow laws growing up around them, they insisted to anyone who would listen that the Tuskegee ideal was a failure: Political activism and even social protest were the right tools to use now since the tools of patience and accommodation had failed.

Washington never veered away from his belief that once its value was proven and recognized, Negroes would be lifted up and respected by whites. He was willing to accept the position that after only half a century of freedom, blacks were not socially, politically, or educationally ready to be trusted with democracy, but that in time they would be. He was willing to wait. More important, his humility gave him credibility with and access to white politicians (such as President Roosevelt and Secretary Wilson) and white philanthropists (Carnegie and George Foster Peabody) whose help seemed absolutely essential for accomplishing anything at all in practical terms. And Booker T. Washington was a very practical man.

William Monroe Trotter, a Harvard graduate living in Boston, produced the weekly Boston *Guardian* beginning in 1901 mainly to publicize his adamant opposition to Washington's conciliatory tone and insist on the civil and political rights of blacks without qualification or delay. Like Du Bois, Trotter was convinced that blacks had to get college educations to lead their people.

(Washington did not disagree entirely with the idea of a college education. A number of Tuskegee graduates went on to college—his own daughter went to Wellesley—and many Tuskegee teachers were college graduates.)

Trotter thought Washington was the wrong black figurehead to be dining at the White House and said so stridently in his newspaper. His coeditor was George W. Forbes, who once declared publicly that "it would be a blessing to the race if the Tuskegee school should burn down."

The Tuskegee Machine went to work on Trotter and his publication through Robert Taylor, Tuskegee's Boston financial agent, and Roscoe Bruce, the dean of women. The two men saw Trotter as too fanatical to harness but felt Forbes could be muzzled through his connection with the Boston Public Library. Forbes earned most of his income as an assistant branch librarian, and the head of the library, Dr. James L. Whitney, was a friend and supporter of Tuskegee. Though under Civil Service rules Whitney couldn't threaten Forbes with losing his job, he could—and evidently did—blunt his enthusiasm for lashing out at Washington.

Other groups supported Trotter's opposition to Washington, including the Boston Literary and Historical Association and the Massachusetts Racial Protective Association, both of which were tailored to promoting anti-Washington viewpoints. They attacked Washington's attitudes toward college and his social relationships with white philanthropists, and they tried to dissuade invited guests from attending National Negro Business League functions in Washington's honor. When a group of black Harvard students rented a meeting room that had Washington's picture hanging on the wall, Trotter's men tried to persuade them to meet somewhere else.

Though he had been stopped by Washington's secret hirelings in the past, Trotter planned to make another run at taking control of the Council at its 1903 annual meeting in Louisville, Kentucky. Walking the racial tightrope with unequaled poise and faultless intuition, Washington used his network of informants to learn that Trotter planned to criticize him for his noncommittal stance on the state voting laws that were rapidly disenfranchising black citizens all across the country. In a preemptive strike, Washington unexpectedly endorsed a strong pro-suffrage statement and the planned confrontation fizzled.

On the other hand, Washington knew the president of the Council, a pro-Washington A. M. E. bishop named Alexander Walters, planned to deliver a speech underscoring President Roosevelt's support by black voters. The president sent word that too strong an endorsement could hurt his chances with white voters; Washington had the bishop tone down his remarks.

At the Louisville meeting, a Trotter supporter caused a stir by pointing to a huge picture of Washington on the platform and vehemently declaring:

I object to that picture being on the platform, unless placed opposite is some other black man who stands for the higher life and intellectual development. Booker Washington's propaganda has given color to the opinion that the Negro is mentally inferior, and his doctrine has been the most powerful argument to the country in favor of the disenfranchisement of the Negro, Washington arguing that the colored man should confine himself to labor and forego the ballot.

As in the year before, Washington's appearance at the convention was a triumph. After all the debate and posturing, his mere presence in the hall brought the meeting to a halt as the delegates enthusiastically cheered his arrival. That night during his speech, he encouraged them to support the new generation of Democrats President Roosevelt had appointed who were "more determined than ever before to see that the race is given opportunity to elevate itself." The results, he assured his audience, were the best argument for black political representation they had. "An inch of progress is worth more than a yard of complaint."

In an interview with the press the next day, one observer summed up the situation: "Samson slew the Philistines with the jawbone of an ass."

In the summer of the next year, Du Bois and other anti-Washington blacks met in Niagara Falls, Canada, and formed their own group. The Niagara Movement began with twenty-nine representatives who issued a position paper calling for freedom of speech, freedom of the press, and the abolition of all discrimination based on race or color, vowing "to assail the ears of America with the story of its shameful deeds toward us."

As soon as Washington's information network got wind of the organization, they set out to derail it. Learning of Du Bois's organizational meeting—originally planned for Buffalo but moved to Niagara Falls, Canada, when the stateside hotel refused them proper service—Washington sent a member of his staff on a sudden vacation there with orders to report on who came to the meeting and to sneak inside if he could. Another Washington ally went to the Associated Press office in Buffalo to persuade them not to report on the meeting. Even though he didn't know the meeting had been moved to Niagara Falls, he succeeded in squelching the story to the point where only one white newspaper in the United States outside of Buffalo, the Boston *Transcript,* carried any substantial account of Du Bois's activities.

Washington then turned his attention to the black newspapers, instructing his private secretary to telegraph "newspaper men you can absolutely trust to ignore Niagara movement." To a newspaperman he wrote, "The best of the white newspapers in the North have absolutely ignored it and have taken no account of its meetings or its protestations. I think, then, as I have intimated, if we shall consistently refuse to take the slightest notice of them that the whole thing will die aborning."

Only one black publication, the Atlanta *Age,* questioned Washington's position, and that not strongly. Even so, Washington suggested bringing a representative from the paper "to Tuskegee, at our expense, for a conference, without your letting him know the exact reason" which was to show him "the true inwardness of Du Bois." Washington continued, "I am very anxious that we lose not one of our friends on account of this new movement."

A writer for the Indianapolis *Freeman* ventured that his publication should avoid getting involved in "petty jealousies" and that it was "quite impossible for me to conceive of Mr. Washington's being vindictive to the point of wishing that this or any other matter be treated otherwise than on its merits."

Washington confided to his secretary, Emmett J. Scott, that such views "are all right when dealing with gentlemen, but not scoundrels, whose purposes are wholly known."

The Niagara Movement had its next meeting at Harper's Ferry, West Virginia, scene of the famous slave uprising led by John Brown. Because it was in a less isolated location, it was much better attended than the first one. Still, Washington had his inside man in the person of Richard T. Greener, Harvard's first black graduate and a member of the American consular service who had recently lost his job. Washington had helped him get a position in Bombay during the McKinley administration. When he complained of the heat there he was reassigned to Vladivostok in Siberia, then dismissed after the government changed is policy on blacks in the foreign service. Greener evidently failed to produce information Washington considered helpful.

Washington also had detectives shadow William Trotter's wife to find out where she worked, and infiltrate anti-Washington black newspapers. He hired an operative to get a job on the Washington *Bee* and convince the editor that though they both hated Booker T. Washington "as any upstanding lover of the race should," they should nevertheless accept financial support from him. The *Bee* eventually printed Washington speeches and pro-Washington editorials, infuriating Trotter and making the paper dependent on Washington's money for survival.

Chronically short of cash since Washington privately discouraged philanthropic donations to them, the Niagara Movement remained small. By 1910 it had faded completely away.

Washington developed a highly tuned network of informants among professional blacks—lawyers, doctors, editors, and political appointees—in major Northern cities. Some were not necessarily in agreement with

Washington's self-help philosophy but owed their position or appointment to him, or hoped to get one as a result of serving as an informant.

Washington, D.C., was a stronghold of Washington supporters, including the highest-ranking black appointees in the federal government: register of the Treasury, the ambassador to Liberia, and a judge in the District of Columbia. Black newspapers and local chapters of the National Negro Business League—a business association founded by Washington—became Washington's eyes and ears in every major Northern city, and served collectively as a mouthpiece for his views.

Washington helped found *The Voice of the Negro* in Atlanta in January 1904, but its editor, a member of Du Bois's Niagara Movement named J. Max Barber, began steering it toward being the voice of Niagara. Washington's own Emmett Scott was on staff at first as assistant editor, but quit over anti-Washington and anti-Tuskegee articles. In January 1905, Barber published accusations by Du Bois that Washington paid "hush money" to certain people in order to advance his position on the race question. Though the charge was absolutely true, Washington and Scott lobbied advertisers that the magazine was counter to the aims and efforts of the National Negro Business League and that they should withdraw their financial support.

In 1905 the Chicago *Conservator* published an editorial accusing Washington of buying "crippled Negro newspapers" to use for his own interests and especially to oppose Du Bois and the Niagara faction. Within months, Washington bought the *Conservator,* whose editor suddenly began printing pro-Washington news. Later, however, the editor was replaced by J. Max Barber, who redirected the paper away from Washington's views in the same way he had *The Voice of the Negro*.

A stockholder in the *Conservator* assured Washington the mistake would not be repeated; Washington responded that the new hire was "wholly dependent upon the position which he now holds. I happen to have information that he was to the point of nearly starving when you gave him something to do." The stockholder, Sandy W. Trice, telegraphed back, "Barber no longer editor *Conservator.*" When Barber sued the *Conservator* for damages, Trice wrote Washington pleading for "immediate financial assistance." Washington sent him money.

Barber was driven from Atlanta by telegraphing to a New York newspaper the truth that the terrible race riots that took place in Atlanta in 1906 were instigated by whites. A telegraph operator leaked his identity to the white press, which ran him out of town. He tried to resume publishing in Chicago but failed.

Desperate to earn a living, Barber moved to Philadelphia and took a job teaching in a manual labor school. When a trustee there asked Washington about him, Washington branded him a troublemaker "teaching colored people to hate white people" who was "about as unfitted for such work as is needed in Dr. Anderson's school as I can think of." Barber lost his job, worked his way through dental school, and spent the rest of his career practicing dentistry in Philadelphia.

All this complicated intrigue and political posturing was a world away from the hundreds of students and their parents who wrote to Tuskegee every year. And whether Washington was popular among America's black leadership or not, whether he was a savior or a villain, his school was a beacon of hope to young men and women who saw it as their one chance to transform their lives. Hardly a day passed without Washington or his school receiving a letter from an eager young applicant who had heard about Tuskegee and about how an industrious student could work off his expenses.

Some of the mail came from big cities. A woman in Dallas wrote:

> I am desirous of entering your school, very much so, but am unable to enter and pay my way through and write you to know if you can receive me as a night student to work my way through.... I am eager to attain a higher and better education and be of some benefit to my race. I feel proud that I have the opportunity to ask this favor of a man of my race of whom we all feel proud.

From Harrisburg, Pennsylvania:

> I was hired out to work for my living when I was eight years old and am now twenty-one.... I have never been in a school, but the people I lived with learnt me enough to read and write. And since

I have been hear I have several books given me. I came hear with the intention of earning money to go to school…. I feel satisfied that after my parents see my determination they will become more interested in me…. You can see my situation but I am not discourage. Where ever is faith there is hope.

Many more letters came from isolated communities, where the story of Tuskegee had penetrated even to the most distant and humble Negro settlements and neighborhoods—Yellow Bluff, Alabama; Shell Mound, Mississippi; Barton Station, Alabama; and to a boy from Greenwood, Mississippi, who wrote that he "would like to find out is there any way for a boy to learn a trade an work some part of the way an if so answer at once and let me no. I am not well educated at all but wants to learn the painters trade or the carpenters trade…. And I want to find out what my expense would be. I am not as yet 18 teen years of age an think I am just the right age to learn."

Some of those students eventually made their way to the Tuskegee Agriculture Experiment Station and Professor Carver. He had settled into a life of overseeing experiments, teaching classes, and doing what he could to keep up with Washington's endless directives on campus maintenance and repair. Like a marriage or a business partnership festering with the same problems and conflicts year after year, the relationship between Professor Carver and Mr. Washington retained a sense of chronic uneasiness. Carver loved his work and was clearly dedicated to it, but he continued to chafe at what he considered interference in his affairs, inadequate equipment and staffing, burdensome bureaucracy, and unreasonable expectations.

Washington's letters during one winter and spring were typical of the directives he sent Carver year in and year out. On January 14 he informed Carver he had received a letter "from a friend of the school" criticizing the condition of the grounds. "I often wish in the matter of roads and walks about the school grounds that Mr. Menafee [an agriculture department employee under Carver] might take notice of the water that lies in great ponds, and open up the sewers which are often clogged up with sand…."

The next month Washington turned his attention to the fruit trees, which would soon be budding, and the impression they made on visitors. "Have Mr. Warren [another department employee] put in half a day trimming the fruit trees and putting the grape vines in order near the new barn. I would rather for the people to see the old trees in good condition than to find us planting new trees."

Washington recommended "that a good strong man be put in charge of the horticultural work. This man should be married and a house built on or near the orchard site for him." Meanwhile, though, responsibility for the orchards and other trees remained on Carver's slender shoulders: "During the next few days I wish you would give special attention, personal attention if possible, to the condition of the peach orchard. I am very anxious that nothing be lost to the school in connection with the putting out of the peach trees."

Washington assigned a host of maintenance and repair duties for Carver to supervise or take care of himself:

> I note the embankment in front of the barns is gradually washing away. I wish you would give this immediate attention. The only way to keep such things in proper condition is to see that they are repaired at once when they begin to get out of order. We want to keep a good object lesson in this respect constantly before the students. I also wish you would see that the grounds around the old laundry are cleared; they are in bad condition now.

Carver was also supposed to prepare reports every morning on the number of pigs and fowls in the yards, and the amount of milk, butter, and eggs produced. "This report should reach me by 8:30 o'clock" every day, Washington reminded him. Rare was the day when all the reports were in by lunchtime.

When Washington was away, and sometimes when he wasn't, his brother John, now with the title General Superintendent of Industries, added his share to the flurry of memos and directives that ended up on Carver's desk.

He criticized Carver for allowing his workers to quit work too soon.

"This matter has been spoken of so many times that I feel it is almost useless to speak of it again," an obviously exasperated John Washington wrote. "It is understood that the bell rings for men to stop work, and that they have ample time to get ready for dinner between the work bell and the dinner bell."

John upbraided Carver for allowing parts of a harness to lie out in the rain for two days in plain sight beside the walkway to the new Carnegie library. "Hardly any one could pass without seeing this harness, and I am at a loss to know what the number of visitors who have been here for the last two days will think of an Institute like this for allowing a leather harness to remain out in that weather." He admonished Carver to find and punish the responsible parties, and sow oats in the mud around the library since visitors to its upcoming dedication would want to take pictures.

John was never shy about invoking his brother's image in trying to prod Carver into action. "I am sure that Mr. B. T. Washington would be greatly surprised and greatly distressed if he were to appear here and find things in their present condition," he warned on one occasion. "We know that he is going to have the improvement made when he comes and I see no use why we should wait and worry him about it. We should take it up as once." (Carver would surely have agreed with another member of the faculty, who, about their principal's frequent absences, frankly admitted, "Most teachers like to see the train puff out with him and dread to hear the engine whistling his return.")

Carver had different priorities. For one, he believed his beloved collection of botanical specimens was unappreciated and ignored. He had complained before about the amount of room he had to display them in. Now there was more space but leaks in the roof were ruining his collection. Repeated requests for repairs had gotten no results.

On November 5, 1902, Carver stiffly informed Washington that there were ten leaks in the roof over his display cases. "No one knows but myself how many specimens of my valuable collection from Iowa and the West have been ruined. I had hoped to leave this collection in toto for Tuskegee, but every rain brings partial destruction which in time means total destruction."

In another note written the same day, he admonished Washington that there were problems "relative to the conditions in the Agricultural Department which greatly militate against its progress. I assure I feel this matter keenly and feel that something radical must be done or else the department cannot prosper in any way as it should."

Weeks later, Washington and the school still hadn't made Carver's roof repairs a priority. On Christmas Eve he sent a detailed report to Washington's office with a chart showing the month, day, rainfall in inches, and number of specimens destroyed after each shower.

In trying to keep ahead of Washington's incessant calls for improvements in drainage, roads, fencing, toilet facilities, and other areas, Carver felt constantly stymied by the lack of money, men, and machinery to do the work. Sometimes he pressed his own staff as Washington pressed him but without results. Washington wanted the orchard cleared and cleaned up, and Carver gave a directive to his small staff to get it done. One of his hands patiently explained that they couldn't clean up the orchard without men to do the cleaning, couldn't plow without plows and teams, and couldn't haul brush away without wagons, none of which they had. The trees, he warned, "aren't apt to survive" without plowing, but there was nothing else he could do.

A frustrated Carver went to the administration to explain he had neither the men nor tools to do ordinary farm work, "the thing from which we expect to get our bread and butter," much less clean out the orchard. "I have reported this a number of times but do not see any improvement."

"From causes which I am unable to decipher," he said soon afterward, "I feel that I do not get the cooperation of the Council. Many times no attention is paid to my wishes and things passed over my head which work contrariwise to my efforts to carry out the school's wishes.... My work has been hampered and rendered unsatisfactory the entire school year from similar reasons."

Even though he complained about it, Carver worked diligently to keep costs down. Year after year Washington admonished Carver and the rest of the faculty and staff to be on the lookout for any way to save money. When he came up with a suggestion, he was quick to recommend it in hopes of beginning the savings immediately, and perhaps hopeful of a word of praise or encouragement from Washington as well. Since he had ended up with such wide-ranging responsibilities, Carver had ample opportunity to find ways to economize.

Based on his observations and experience, he feared some suggestions would fail. In those cases he precisely documented his argument and presented it to Washington. In a year when the dairy, under Carver's supervision, had supplied the school commissary with more than seven hundred dollars worth of milk, buttermilk, butter, and cream, Washington sent word he thought the department should start supplying cheese as well.

After some careful figuring, Carver saw that making cheese would be more expensive than buying it. The fresh milk, he explained to Washington, was worth five times the value of the cheese they could produce from it. Even worse, the cheese would be inferior quality because they would make it with skimmed milk—unless Washington wanted to give up supplying the dining hall with butter too. "However," he added, "if you want me to do so, I will make just as much cheese as you desire." The cheese making idea was quietly dropped.

One of many ideas he had to make the best possible use of available resources was to buy a bone mill instead of burning scraps from the livestock operation. The students could grind bones, treat them with sulfuric acid, and turn them into excellent fertilizer. It would use an otherwise wasted resource and save the school considerable expense in buying fertilizer. If the demand was there, they could even buy bones from townspeople and sell surplus fertilizer to Macon County farmers.

Another suggestion he made, though Washington didn't consider it at the time, showed Carver's ability to find innovative uses for mundane products. Carver valued cowpeas (later more widely known as black-eyed peas) as a crop because they were easy and inexpensive to grow and were good for the soil. Carver sent Washington two samples of cowpea meal ground in a coffee grinder for use as a hot beverage. The note attached affirmed that Carver had "always been in accord with your constant reminders that we do not make enough out of the things we can raise in abundance...." He went on to say he had found twenty-five different ways to prepare cowpeas as food.

He also proudly sent Washington samples of paint he had made out of clay taken from a drainage ditch on school property. He made ochre as well as a rich, deep blue that would make "a cheap but durable paint for poor people, to largely take the place of whitewash."

Another time, Carver suggested the school stop spending so much money buying rice and grits since their bumper crop of campus-grown turnips would make an excellent and inexpensive substitute.

No matter how many ideas Carver had for stretching the school's resources, it seemed Washington always came up with one or two more for him to look into. Among all his other work, Carver had studied the idea of planting nut trees and recommended the school set out twenty or thirty acres of chestnuts, almonds, and pecans. Washington agreed it was worth looking into and soon after sent Carver to find out what he could about keeping bees and raising angora goats as well.

In the summer of 1902, Carver sent his regular report to Washington, who was raising money in South Weymouth, Massachusetts. The agriculture department, he proudly noted, would have 170 acres in cultivation, including one hundred acres of sweet potatoes, forty of cowpeas, eleven of onions, five acres each of collard green and turnips, three acres each of beets and beans, two acres of squash, and half an acre each of lettuce and radishes. Whatever criticism Washington might have of his eccentric agriculture professor, he had to admit he was a hard worker.

The previous spring Carver had taken the school up on an offer to take over two rooms in the old library as soon as the new Carnegie Library was finished. Though he seldom painted any more, he still had plans to pursue an artistic career at some point and thought the new space might become his painting studio. "I greatly desire a place to do some historic painting" he wrote in a note of thanks to Washington for the additional room. "I greatly desire to do this that it may go down in the history of the race. The time is coming when I cannot do it."

The additional room, his success at economizing, and his growing reputation among the students as an exceptional and inspiring teacher, all made Carver optimistic. He told Washington he was "looking forward to a very profitable year, in fact, the most profitable of any since I have been here, as the number of changes which you have so kindly made from time to time have unfettered the work to such an extent that I think you will see the great and good results coming from it."

CHAPTER ELEVEN

THE NONSYMPATHETIC WORLD

As he had done since his days at Iowa State, Professor Carver went out early every morning to collect interesting plants to use as teaching tools or as specimens for the "museum collection" he so highly prized. Hauling the same bulky, cylindrical container he had carried as a graduate student, he wandered through the woods and creek beds on campus looking for noteworthy handiwork of his Creator.

He brought his discoveries into class, where students could see and touch them. That way, when he talked about how peas and peanuts fixed nitrogen in the soil, he could show students the delicate, spidery roots that produced this miracle of chemistry. He could use the same plant to demonstrate the effects of fertilization, the weather, erosion, and any number of other topics. Every condition and force in nature was interconnected, he explained, because they all came from the same divine source. To Carver, everything in nature was a gift from God and worthy of his admiration and praise.

Carver found inspiration in everything he saw in nature. For instance, a particular flower might inspire Carver to recite a Greek poem. Another rare blossom once kept him up all night because he didn't want to miss seeing it bloom.

Like all good teachers, Carver realized that his students naturally—if subconsciously—resisted being told what they ought to know and learned more when they felt they were discovering information on their own. Through experiments, field trips, and wide-ranging classroom discussions that sometimes drifted far from the day's lesson, he encouraged an individual spirit of inquiry and curiosity that whetted students' appetites for learning far beyond what lecturing alone could have done.

He encouraged students to collect specimens on their own and held contests to see which class could bring in the most. With his encyclopedic knowledge of plants and animals, he could identify even the strangest samples. Students made a game of trying to stump him, but it was almost impossible to do. One day a group of students constructed an insect specimen out of bits and pieces of various bugs and brought it to Carver, hoping to pass it off as an undiscovered type. This sparked the professor's sense of humor. After only a quick examination, the professor identified it with a smile as a "hum-bug."

Carver's success in teaching was all the more remarkable because so many of the students were ill prepared for Tuskegee. Few of them had any sort of advanced study; some were barely literate. Nevertheless, Carver showed them by action as well as word that God created the world for everyone's benefit and enjoyment regardless of race or education.

At the core of all Carver's teaching was his belief that the study of nature drew anyone who understood it closer to God. The more a student knew of the Creator's handiwork, the more fully he could appreciate his power. Carver unselfconsciously wove religious references into his classroom lectures, regardless of the topic at hand.

In spite of their ongoing differences, Washington recognized Carver's gift for teaching and praised him as "a great teacher, a great lecturer, a great inspirer of young men and old men." Washington often invited Carver to speak to other Tuskegee teachers on improving their teaching skills and even had him meet with the Institute's day laborers once to inspire them to higher standards.

Carver made a singular impression on students accustomed to other Tuskegee teachers meticulously turned out in suits, collars, and ties, their hair slicked back in the fashion of the day. He seemed to grow a little more rumpled with every passing year. His vest and trousers didn't always match; his lab coat was not always pressed; he wore a flower pinned to his left lapel every day, usually one he picked fresh that morning during his walk before breakfast.

Physically, he was a dramatic contrast to Washington, who in his appearance personified the Institute as well as the ideal of black educators and self-made men. Where Carver presented a haphazard appearance, Washington was always impeccably dressed with waistcoat and polished shoes. Washington had a rich baritone voice, well honed by many hundreds of public appearances, sometimes before ten thousand or more people. Carver, in contrast, still had the fluty contralto of a woman or a boy. Washington was a master of organization who placed great emphasis on appearance, while Carver had little talent for or interest in the mechanics of running a school and took a much more practical and realistic approach to the way things looked.

Carver rose early and worked a full, physically active day, but he continued to battle the same respiratory problems as an adult that he suffered as a child. He remained thin and frail looking, and though not much over forty he appeared older because he was so wiry and slight. His delicate appearance, lab coat and ever-present lapel flower marked him as a unique character in the minds of the students. By now they referred to him only as "the Professor." If you said something about the Professor, no last name was necessary. Everybody knew which professor it was.

As Carver approached his tenth year at Tuskegee, he was nowhere nearly as familiar to the general public as his famous employer. On the surface, their differences were far greater than their similarities. Booker T. Washington had dined at the White House, had tea with Queen Victoria, and earned the respect and support of the most powerful men in America. By contrast, Carver's influence was chiefly with audiences and institutions interested in agriculture. In addition to his enormous range of responsibilities at Tuskegee, he also traveled to symposiums, spoke to agricultural commissions and various meetings of farmers, and researched every sort of agricultural experiment and opportunity from raising silkworms to studing erosion-resistant plowing techniques.

A speech of Carver's at Georgia Industrial College in Savannah produced glowing reviews in the local press. The chancellor there claimed the professor's lecture on teaching agriculture was "the best he had ever heard" and wished Carver could repeat it for his teachers because his analysis of farming techniques was "applicable to and within reach of the farmer and housewife." Carver proudly told Washington about a speech in Athens, Georgia, that his hosts there said was "a magnificent hit and that the people are thoroughly stirred up over it."

Though Carver, along with the rest of Tuskegee, lived in the shadow of its principal, the professor was coming into his own. The two men, strong willed and proud, continued to disagree about administrative matters, but Carver began to enjoy wider recognition of his gifts to black education and his contribution to Tuskegee's success. On May 15, 1903, Washington officially notified Carver that "the institution values the services you have rendered it during the past year and desires you to remain in its employ."

One of Washington's first public acknowledgments of Carver's value to the school came in an article he wrote for *Atlantic Monthly* in the fall of 1903 that referred to Carver and his work as director of the agriculture department. It was interesting, Washington said of Carver, to see "how far above the horizon of the average individual one is permitted to rise, and how far into the future he is permitted to see, a sort of horoscope of God to foresee and work out the destiny of a great race of people." Carver was delighted with the mention because it meant to him that Washington was finally beginning to grant him some of the attention and status he longed for and felt he deserved.

Shrewd as he was, Washington also knew his mention of Carver was excellent publicity for the school agriculture department and programs. Requests for reprints of Professor Carver's experiment station bulletins were now coming from Cuba, Haiti, Mexico, and as far away as India, where a teacher at a one-room school with five pupils and one acre of arable land also requested a copy of "the Autobiography of Fred Douglas." Carver was inspiring teachers who had even less to work with than he did.

Several times over the years, Carver had requested a secretary to help him prepare the reports Washington expected him to submit, and submit on time. Citing a lack of money, the finance committee repeatedly denied his request, forcing Carver to write much of his correspondence himself in longhand, often at night after evening Bible study. In January 1904, yet another round of request and refusal inspired a heated letter from Carver summarizing all the difficulties he had been compelled to endure:

I fully appreciate the necessity of not increasing the school's expenses a single dollar or even less, but my work is of such a nature that I cannot do it without help regularly. I beg to say that this is my seventh year's connection with the school. I have not asked for an increase in salary or a vacation each year, and I have been wholly unobservant of office hours, beginning early and working late, also every night, for the school in one way or another.

My correspondence is constantly increasing, two bulletins are now ready except the typewritten work, and one has been on hand since last spring. Today my classes run thus: 8:00 to 9:00, agri. chemistry; 9:20 to 10:00, the foundation and harmony of color to the painter; 10:00 to 11:00, class of farmers and one in the afternoon. In addition to this I must try—and rather imperfectly—to overlook seven industrial classes scattered here and there over the grounds. I must test all the seeds, examine all the fertilizer—based upon the examination of the soil of the different plots. I must also personally look after every operation of the ten acre experiment station. I must endeavor to keep the poultry yard straight. In addition to the above I must daily inspect 104 cows that have been inoculated, looking carefully over the temperature of each one, making comparisons and prescribing whatever is necessary, besides looking after the sickness of other animals.

Again, the museum and laboratory (which hardly have an equal in the South for their specific work) are almost wholly the work of my own efforts, giving many things from my own private collection and securing others from various sources. If money were my only object I could not afford to stay at Tuskegee. I came here with the one idea of assisting you in building up the most difficult division of your great scheme. I came knowing that I would encounter more difficulties in the way of proper sympathy and support. I knew it would not be an easy life to live. I am not seeking that just now, neither am I seeking personal aggrandizement. I only want to give the school my best service.

By this time, the recitation of his snubs and hardships and of his accomplishments were standard themes in Carver's letters to Washington. He had also made a veiled threat to resign on numerous occasions. In spite of his complaining, though, Carver continued to support the school and worked diligently to meet Washington's lofty expectations as well as he could.

Along with his many other duties, Carver had for all practical purposes assumed responsibility for the annual Farmer's Conference and the Worker's Conference that had grown out of it. He was in charge of programs of lectures and demonstrations, as well as exhibits of farm machinery and essentially every detail of the conferences. There were also lower-key Farmer's Institute Days, special presentations for local black farmers on the latest experiments in crop rotation, fertilization, or plant development.

On July 20, 1904, he wrote proudly to Washington, then in Boston, that the recently completed Institute Day was

the most enthusiastic meeting that we have had. The room was filled to overflowing; many had to stand up.... I have not seen your brother so stirred up and pleased in a long while. The entire body...went to the Experiment Station and from there they went to the Orchard. I really wish you could have been here to hear their expressions and their determinations to do better farming, do away with the mortgage system and procure better homes.

In the public eye, Carver was becoming more closely associated with practical, manageable improvements directed specifically at farmers with limited education and limited capital. He offered simple advice that produced excellent results. Though they moved often in separate circles, Washington and Carver strengthened each other's best traits. Washington's vision, fundraising ability, and management skill combined with Carver's love of science, sincere empathy for people, and tireless energy yielded invaluable results.

Nonetheless, Carver continued to falter in managing day-to-day details. The pattern had become a familiar one: Washington or one of his immediate subordinates complaining to Carver about shabby fences or poor drainage or the fact that not enough eggs seemed to be in the incubators. Carver would reply that he was doing all he could with the chronically inadequate staff and underfunded budget he had to work with. He had never gotten comfortable with managing people and always considered poor performance from staff members in the agricultural school as prime causes for the calamity of the moment.

Pressured to reduce the cost of his departmental payroll in the spring of 1904, Carver replied in a memo to Washington that "the great difficulty with which money and supplies are gotten for the school, and the wisest and most economical use and expenditure of the same, are ever uppermost in my mind, therefore I do not see in a direct manner any way in which the expenses of my department can be cut down in the way of salaries." He went on to say the people he had to use weren't worth their salary as it was:

> We have now reached the point where we should rid ourselves as fast as possible of the great mass of ignorance the farm is carrying. These men are good in their way but know nothing about the fundamental principles which underlie their work, except by the "rule of thumb." They would do well on a plantation where labor with its corresponding results is the chief aim, but not in a great educational institution like Tuskegee.

What became the most demeaning, embarrassing, and disappointing episode in Carver's Tuskegee career, as well as the low point in his relationship with Washington, began with a letter from Washington on

September 28, 1899, soon after his return from Europe. It began:

> This is to say that I wish you as soon as possible to put in suc-
> cessful operation the teaching of poultry raising in all of its con-
> nections to as large a number of our girls as Mrs. Washington
> thinks well to take this industry. I wish you to let me have a list
> of whatever will be needed for you to carry on this work suc-
> cessfully.

Poultry raising was one agricultural job both Mr. and Mrs.
Washington considered appropriate for young ladies and one Booker
Washington was eager to add to his showcase department. In less than
three weeks, Carver sent Washington specifications for a chicken house
and for transferring chickens from a plot of school property known as the
Marshall Farm. The project was completed and grew along with the
enrollment in poultry raising and the demand on campus for eggs and
chicken dinners.

Some time around 1902, Carver put the operation of the chicken
yard in the hands of a newly arrived member of the agricultural department named George R. Bridgeforth. Carver had not particularly wanted
this confident new hire in his department. One member of the faculty
described Bridgeforth as "a big, energetic, blustery man with a flair and a
taste for administrative power." In other words, he was Carver's exact
opposite in many ways. The two began clashing early on.

The administrative and management skills Carver lacked were
Bridgeforth's strong suit. Sensing a growing appreciation of his abilities on
the part of Washington and other administrators, Bridgeforth soon
became openly disdainful of Carver and his orders. The new subordinate
complained about Carver to Washington in unflattering terms, suggesting
he could make the department run smoothly where Carver had failed.

Washington and Carver's relationship deteriorated more rapidly after
Bridgeforth earned a promotion. Moving a notch closer to his supervisor's
position, Bridgeforth found it easier than ever to criticize Carver's work in
general and his treatment of Bridgeforth in particular. Bridgeforth wrote
Carver on January 18 to complain that the agricultural enrollment was far
short of what it should be, partly because there was no separate catalog
for the agricultural program and prospective students overlooked it when

they read about Tuskegee. "In 1902–3 we had 82. Our recent enrollment is 86. We should have 300."

Furthermore, Bridgeforth was "greatly embarrassed by you telling me to do things and then could not back me up after I had done as you had commanded." Bridgeforth was restless and impatient under Carver's management and made a number of good recommendations, including allowing boys to join girls for the poultry classes instead of limiting them to girls alone.

In 1904, when Carver reduced the number of wagon teams Bridgeforth had to do his work in the agriculture department, Bridgeforth threatened to go to Washington and have the decision reversed. Carver wrote to Bridgeforth that his behavior was "very unsatisfactory to me, and of course, cannot continue." He further warned, "I want it clearly understood that I am not going to put up with such notes as [your threat to see Washington] coming into my office from you."

Bridgeforth answered Carver with a brash ultimatum of his own:

> I shall not stand another bit of this bluff and you must do business like a man and take some interest in the things that pertain to school. You seem to have lost all interest in all things at the school as it is noticed by all.... I am here to work as a man and I expect to be treated as such. I am not to be intimidated by your recent threats.

Washington seemed to give young Bridgeforth wide latitude in criticizing the professor—perhaps because he agreed at least in part with Bridgeforth's assessment. Still Washington warned, "I shall expect that respect and obedience must be given to the heads of the departments."

Some time during the winter of 1903–4, Carver transferred responsibility for the chicken yard from Bridgeforth to a man named Columbus Barrows. As reports of unsatisfactory conditions in the yard mounted, Washington became correspondingly more frustrated and dissatisfied. He could not understand why running a self-supporting poultry operation and keeping the facilities neat and orderly should be such a hard job.

From Carver's viewpoint, he was besieged with notes, memoranda, and directives from Washington about inadequate egg production, high chicken mortality rates, and the unkempt look of the chicken yard. Either the professor had delegated the work to an unreliable subordinate, or he was simply too busy and preoccupied with his many other duties and interests to notice the deteriorating conditions.

Bridgeforth was not the kind of person to let Carver's shortcomings go unreported. Washington knew about the poultry yard difficulties anyway, but Bridgeforth offered a steady stream of commentary on the poor performance and management of the operation and made suggestions for improving them. (Everyone seemed to have forgotten that Bridgeforth himself had had an unimpressive run as chicken yard manager a year or so before.)

Washington ordered a formal investigation into poultry yard practices in May 1904, which concluded that the flock was increasing but the chickens were improperly cared for, and instruction had deteriorated on Barrows's watch. In a broader context, such uproar over chickens seemed overblown. But it was the principle of the matter: Washington desperately wanted a showcase poultry operation that showed a path to black financial independence through agriculture. His suggestions and directives remained unanswered. Month after month, reports on the poultry operation failed to show significant improvements. And now, an eager and energetic young instructor seemed ready to take charge of a project the current head, Professor Carver, seemed hopelessly incapable of carrying out successfully.

Carver seriously wondered whether it was time for him to leave Tuskegee. There was a letter on his desk from Ralph W. McGranaham, whom Carver had met at Iowa State. He was the white president of Knoxville College, a black institution in Tennessee. McGranaham offered Carver a full-time faculty position teaching both art and agriculture.

For all his evident dissatisfaction, Carver hesitated to leave his beloved agriculture experiment station for another job. He wrote to his friend and former Iowa professor, Secretary of Agriculture James Wilson, to ask his advice.

Wilson was still secretary of agriculture (he would serve in that capacity under four presidents) and clearly admired Carver's sincerity while sympathizing with his frustration. In strictest confidence, Carver confided to Secretary Wilson that he was thinking of leaving Tuskegee for Knoxville College, or perhaps going to Puerto Rico. There he could benefit the black race, he hoped, without the distractions and disappointments that had become so much a part of his life at Tuskegee.

Wilson's reply, on July 25, was firm in its conviction:

[W]ith regard to leaving Tuskegee and going to Porto Rico[sic]. Don't do it. They can not spare you there yet, and the work you are doing in helping to educate future teachers is the best work you are doing and the best work Tuskegee is doing; and you should stick right to it. I hope the Tuskegee people will fully appreciate your value along these lines. But stay by Mr. Washington. He is doing a work that should be duplicated in many other places, not only for the colored people but also for the white. I hope I live to see the day when white people will be regarded as good as colored folk along these lines.

Carver also asked his friend if he thought he could get approval to start an experiment station in Knoxville like the one in Tuskegee. Wilson could not.

Matters came to a head on September 22, 1904, with a report from yet another investigative committee to the Executive Council—probably in Carver's presence since department heads were automatically members— that the poultry operation was in "very bad condition." The committee reported that the daily poultry reports Washington insisted on had been falsified. Columbus Barrows, the man Carver put in charge of the yard, had written that when a large number of chickens died, Carver warned him "not to report them all at one time as Mr. B. T. Washington would tare him to pieces." The committee decided Carver had instructed his staff to spread out large losses over several days so they wouldn't draw so much attention to the problem.

The investigators concluded that Carver had replaced some of the chickens without reporting their loss and bought them with his own money. The professor insisted he had done so out of his wish to see the poultry operation run as smoothly as possible. The committee—and Carver's detractors, especially Bridgeforth—suggested he was trying to hide his mistakes.

In early October, Bridgeforth and some other members of Carver's staff proposed reorganizing the agricultural department with John Washington as its head and five divisional supervisors, two of which would be Carver (as director of the experiment station and agricultural instruction) and Bridgeforth (as director of agricultural industries). Washington wrote to Carver, "There is no doubt in my mind a mistake has been made on your own part either in the direction of carelessness, or in the direction of being a party to the deception."

Carver wrote his reply to Washington on October 14, his manuscript uncharacteristically spidery and uneven on the page:

I beg to acknowledge receipt of your note, and come now to the most painful experience of my life.

For seven years I have labored with you: have built up one of the best Agl. laboratories in the south, so much so that the people of your own town recognize its value.

Only yesterday the Tuskegee Cotton Oil Co. submitted samples of cotton seed meal, and cake for analysis and have arranged to bring in samples every week.

The museum is the best of its kind in the south and constantly growing. The Experiment Station, in the nature of the problems chosen and the results obtained I am sure has no equal in the south. Now to be branded as a liar and party to such hellish deception is more than I can bear, and if your committee feel that I have willfully lied or party to such lies as were told my resignation is at your disposal.

I deeply regret to take this step but it seems to me the only manly thing to do.

I shall always feel kindly to your work and shall continue to be loyal to Tuskegee and its interests.

Five days later he wrote an even longer letter expanding on his thoughts, though the intervening days had given him a chance to calm down and reflect on his position and his future. More to the point, he had at Booker's suggestion spent valuable time with Margaret Washington, Booker's wife, seeking her assessment on the "unfortunate occurrence of recent date."

Washington valued his wife's opinion, and Margaret surely sensed Carver's bitterness and frustration. She also knew Carver's value to the school and could speak to him in a more conciliatory tone perhaps than Washington himself could do publicly; though in cases like this her voice was the voice of her husband.

At Washington's request, Margaret had asked the professor to reconsider resigning. Carver was unsure what to do. "I do not know what I can say to you more than I said in my former note," the one Carver wrote on October 19, his letters more controlled and more calmly formed this time. "If the school brands me as a liar and party to such hellish deceptions it would be best for me to go, my usefulness to Tuskegee would be at an end." Moreover, by the end of the three-page narrative, he reveals a change of heart. "If you have faith in me I will take hold of the [poultry] yard with renewed vigor and give you some chickens, a number that you will be proud of. If your committee wishes to retain me upon these terms I assure you I shall give them honest, faithful service and never let such an error again creep in."

Characteristically, Carver continued with his work even in the thick of all the charges, counter-charges, threats of resignations, and apologies of this busy October week. Between the two heartfelt letters to Washington on the topic of resignation, he submitted a typewritten report as director of agriculture reporting his experiment in Spanish peanuts had produced a crop of fifty bushels to the acre and noting that they were "one of the most valuable foods for hogs."

On November 3, Washington informed Carver that his new title would be Director of the Experiment Station and Agricultural Instruction, instead of Director of Agriculture. November 8 Carver replied, "I do not agree with the title, it is too far a drop downward, a few at Tuskegee might understand it but the public never."

Then, after challenging the committee's findings on a number of points:

> The above and much more which I will tell you if you grant me the privilege of a hearing, causes me to ask that you kindly accept my resignation to take effect just as soon as I can get the herborium and cabinets labeled and in place where they will be of the highest service to the school.

He affirmed he was leaving his collection of samples to the school. "Kindly permit me to make this request that what you have is kept intact the exclusive property of the Agrl. Dept. and one of the monuments to my seven and one half years labor at Tuskegee."

Washington appointed still another committee to make recommendations. Around the first of November, he sent Carver a copy of the committee's suggestions, none of which Carver agreed with. He particularly opposed changing his title from Director of Agriculture and objected to dividing his duties between himself and Mr. Bridgeforth even though he had complained so often in the past about being overworked. He was convinced that the division of labor "could not help but result in constant turmoil and final failure."

The committee's recommendation, he continued, would yield no department at all, but "a flimsy organization which cannot stand, and will furnish data for constant outside criticism."

Less than a week later Carver reconsidered his decision yet again and wrote a long letter to Washington filled with the familiar combination of complaints, suggestions, and wishes for success:

> In considering your note and the committee's report in detail, I think if there is to be no Dept. head I should bear, at least, an advisory relationship to it.... I was supposed to have held this advisory relationship but it was very often a farce and the advice ignored altogether at times and especially if a technicality could be found.... I spent much time in writing out suggestions and recommendations to be ignored afterward. I was often ignored

and am now wholly left out of the meetings pertaining to the farm, and no advice from me is sought except from those who are under me....

I should like to have a stenographer a half day or be given a machine [typewriter] and allowed to train a student to do my work. I think this is due me. I have never asked for a rise in my salary, have economized rigidly for the school and I fear to my detriment. An unanswered and unsolicited letter is on my desk now offering $200 more per year besides other tempting advantages. I bring this to your attention for no other purpose than to prove my interest in Tuskegee.

At the same time the poultry yard crisis was brewing, another conflict with Bridgeforth produced more disappointment for Professor Carver. Looking for more ways to carry education out to the community, Washington had come up with the idea of fitting out a mobile classroom and laboratory on a wagon and literally take Tuskegee directly to farmers in the field.

With Washington's encouragement, Carver—in the midst of being criticized and humiliated by the poultry committee—sketched a diagram of an enclosed wagon with canvas sides that rolled up to reveal displays, charts, a blackboard, and other teaching tools. Morris K. Jessup, a New York banker who was a member of the Slater Fund board of trust and a faithful contributor to Tuskegee, donated money for the project. The so-called Jessup Wagon was an agricultural classroom and demonstration unit on wheels, built into a mule-drawn wagon twelve feet long and twelve feet high.

Carver eagerly anticipated setting out with the wagon, and early announcements were that he would be in charge. Ultimately the honor of accompanying the Jessup Wagon went to Bridgeforth. He evidently did his work well, taking the wagon directly to workers in the field to explain the latest farm tools, experiment results, and announce upcoming Farmer Institute events and the "short course," an agricultural class for working farmers without the time to enroll in a regular course of study. Carver was particularly heartsick at this rejection since he had designed the wagon and since the program was the kind he thought most valuable to the community.

As the battle between Carver and Bridgeforth continued, both of them bombarded Washington with memos. From Boston, Washington wrote Professor Carver on December 14, 1904:

> Just as soon as I return, I shall take up the matter carefully, between you and Mr. Bridgeforth. I very much hope however, before I reach there, you and he can find a way to settle this matter in a satisfactory way.
>
> In order for people to work together, it is often the case that one must give up some of his own views, to have peace or a better understanding. I wonder if you should have a good frank talk with Mr. Bridgeforth, you could not settle the matter between yourselves.
>
> It requires a higher degree of ability often, to correct the weak points in an assistant and cause him to work in harmony, than to get rid of him.

Stung but still loyal to Tuskegee, Carver redoubled his involvement with the experiment station. His was the only all-black station in the nation to be supported by money from the Hatch Act, which provided federal money to states for agricultural research.

There were two stations in Alabama, one at Tuskegee and the other at Auburn. The Auburn station received the entire fifteen thousand dollars of federal money, and Tuskegee was awarded fifteen hundred dollars in state funds. In 1906 the federal grant to Alabama was doubled to thirty thousand dollars, after which Auburn received thirty thousand dollars while Tuskegee stayed at its previous fifteen hundred dollars. (By 1912, with Tuskegee's annual grant still unchanged, Auburn was receiving almost seventy thousand dollars in all for its experiment station.)

Agriculture Secretary Wilson helped Carver where he could and arranged for Tuskegee to receive regular federal farm publications, sample seeds, and other noncash help directly from his office. When he voluntarily filled out a form detailing how his budget was spent, Carver caused a minor stir back in the U.S. Agriculture Department. The clerk in

Wilson's office refused at first to believe Carver could run an experiment station on so little money.

Carver stayed busy writing experiment station bulletins and produced some of the most popular and often-requested literature of any of the stations. He dispensed practical advice to black farmers in simple terms and reported on experiments designed with them in mind: making low-cost fertilizer, improving the sweet potato crop, planting nitrogen-enriching crops such as peas and peanuts, and giving a portion of the cotton patch over to alfalfa and soybeans.

His work earned him both praise and criticism from Booker T. Washington: praise that his bulletins and programs were so well received and criticism that he wasn't producing bulletins frequently or fast enough. Washington had hoped to put out four bulletins per year, but most years only one or two were completed. Part of the problem was that Carver had so many responsibilities to attend to, plus new ones seemingly added all the time.

The rest of the delay was that there never seemed to be enough money to produce and print the booklets once Carver had them written. At least one bulletin was never printed at all because there was never the money to do it. Getting money for reprints was even more difficult; original printings of two to five thousand quickly disappeared, leaving Carver with nothing to send in reply to requests from the very farmers he was trying to help.

"I do not understand where the Experiment Station appropriation goes," he wrote to Washington on one occasion. "I am very confident I have not used it." He was right. A subsequent audit revealed other departments at the school had been charging their expenses against the experiment station account for years.

Carver and Washington still closed ranks for the sake of any project they thought would help Southern black farmers. When Secretary Wilson secured a grant to study growing silkworms in America, he directed that a portion of it go to Professor Carver. In 1902 and 1903, Carver set out three hundred mulberry tree cuttings—mulberry leaves being silkworms'

only food—and began production with about two dozen silkworms. The department of agriculture brought Carver to Washington, D.C., twice to discuss the project; on his second trip he brought a student along so the two of them could learn how to unravel the silk cocoons onto reels.

Whatever commercial prospects there might have been in silk went unrealized in Alabama. For better or worse it was cotton country, and Carver, with Washington prodding him, conducted numerous experiments on "king cotton" along with whatever else he happened to be working on. He developed a planting method that produced good yields of cotton without commercial fertilizers, which reduced the debt load of the constantly cash-strapped farmers. He encouraged them to plow under heavy growths of cowpeas, velvet beans, grass, and similar crops in the fall, followed by planting and plowing under grains such as rye, wheat, and oats. Another technique was to fertilize with a compost of leaves, mulch, and barnyard manure. These two systems produced noticeably large, healthy cotton bolls.

Carver also worked to develop his own strain of hybrid cotton. Named Carver's Hybrid, it had a long fiber for strength and easy ginning and grew rapidly so it could be harvested before boll weevils could do too much damage. (Boll weevils, which were spreading like a plague across the American South, would not reach Alabama until 1910. Carver realized their arrival was inevitable and developed his fast-growing strain five years early.) Farmers who received Carver's Hybrid seeds at the annual Tuskegee Farmer's Conferences reported excellent results. However, the strain was never marketed on a commercial scale.

As much as he relished experimentation and research, Carver still enjoyed interaction with his students even more. It wasn't the teaching he enjoyed so much—preparing lectures, scraping materials and supplies together, and so forth—but the interaction with students in and out of class. In 1902, in an introduction he wrote to a Tuskegee booklet, he reminded teachers that education was not limited to the classroom.

In the beginning, every teacher should realize that a very large proportion of every student's work must lie outside the class room.... The study of Nature is both entertaining and instructive, and it is the only true method that leads up to a clear understanding of the great natural principles which surround every branch of business in which we may engage. Aside from this, it encourages investigation and stimulates originality.

Later, in a booklet titled "Nature Study and Gardening for Rural Schools," Carver expanded on his theme:

The thoughtful educator realizes that a very large part of the child's education must be gotten outside of the four walls designated as class room. He also understands that the most effective and lasting education is the one that makes the pupil handle, discuss and familiarize himself with real things about him, of which the majority are surprisingly ignorant.

His widely ranging interests involved Carver in a number of outside enterprises. One of the longest running of all began with a letter from the National Building and Loan Association of Montgomery, Alabama. Like many other businesses and individuals, National sent Carver soil samples to analyze for them. Landowners curious to know what kind of fertilizer their soil needed or what it was best suited to grow or how valuable a particular rock, mineral, or ore was, could send a sample to Tuskegee, where Carver would analyze it and give them a report.

In 1902, the National Building and Loan Company sent Carver clay samples they thought might be commercially valuable as paint pigment for a bright, rich tone of blue known as Prussian blue. Carver's preliminary analysis showed great commercial potential. Combining a painter's eye and a scientist's curiosity, he performed chemical tests, then mixed up batches of paint himself on the spot, applying it side by side with commercial pigments to compare them.

If he were right and the blue pigment had commercial possibilities, National Building and Loan could sell the clay for $280 per ton wholesale. Elated, they acknowledged their debt to Carver and assured him they would be "glad to have you enjoy with us any benefits which may accrue to us as the result of your discovery."

Flushed with success, National informed Carver that they owned large tracts of land covered in these clays and that on his recommendation they would send samples, along with his report, to paint and pigment dealers. Results from the professionals dashed their hopes; they pronounced the clays less brilliant and less true than their present sources, adding that they received such samples "several times a week" from all over the country and gave these special attention only because they were submitted by "Professor George W. Carver, the Chemist and Commissioner of Agriculture of the famous Tuskegee Normal and Industrial School [colored] of which Mr. Booker T. Washington is Principal."

National Building and Loan sent samples to another company and got much the same answer. The samples, they said, were less true and brilliant than the sources they already had. "We would have given them no more attention had it not been for the fact that they were from Mr. Booker T. Washington, and we are interested in the Tuskegee Institute."

Undaunted, the secretary and treasurer of the National Building and Loan, Alva Fitzpatrick, formed a company of his own with word to Carver that he had reserved "a nice block of stock" for him, the Montgomery Paint & Dry Color Works, in the new corporation. He was convinced Carver could overcome the defects the analysts pointed out. A few months later, he wrote Carver again with encouraging news. The Ohio Paint and Varnish Company had offered ten thousand dollars in their company's stock for stock in the new venture. Not only was the potential financial gain impressive, but the discovery was made, company officers proclaimed, "by a negro, which would be a further proof of the wonderful strides this race is making in the onward march of civilization."

The venture seemed promising, but Fitzpatrick never could raise the money to get production of the pigment underway. He kept up a brave front. "All discouragement & doubts lie in the past," he wrote to Carver on September 19, 1902. "Don't for one moment think that we *remotely dream* of giving up."

By the spring of 1904, however, the excitement was over. The new company informed Carver that they were planning to sell their land holdings "at what it cost us which is about forty dollars per acre.... Now as

you were the discoverer of this mineral and have been so intimately associated with it and interested in it, we feel that we should give you an
opportunity to purchase it should we not we able to bring our scheme to
a successful issue. There are two hundred and twenty acres and a loan for
about half the amount could be negotiated if desired."

So much for the paint and pigment business.

Carver saw far greater success in the students who were graduating from
Tuskegee and beginning their careers as teachers or skilled tradesmen all
across the country. Carver carried on correspondence with a number of
students; and though most of them only wrote a few letters, they were sincere in their appreciation for Carver's lessons and his personal interest in
them.

From Hartsville, South Carolina, one student proudly informed
Carver he had put up a brick building twenty-five feet by forty-three feet
for a local matron, and was now laying bricks for the new post office in
town. "On the third day I went to work at my trade and I've been working ever since," the student wrote.

A new poultry farming instructor wrote from Raleigh, North
Carolina, to express her delight at getting a good price on laying hens
(twenty-one cents each), building a chicken house, and coaxing more
milk out of her school's Jersey cows. "Prof. it is through you and Mr. Gus
Owens [one of Carver's assistants] that I am able to do this work. My
thanks to youal is, you are great." As so many correspondents did, she
also asked for more advice, this time on how to teach a nature study class
for young children.

And from Bolivar, Tennessee, a graduate student wrote with advice for
the students who would follow him: "I should advise every Tuskegee student to get everything out of Tuskegee that is possible for his head, heart,
and hand to secure. Don't throw away time. The getting of diplomas and
certificates should be secondary to the getting of knowledge wherewith to
meet the nonsympathetic world."

Students shared their fears and frustrations with Carver as they would
a close friend. One young man who was forced to leave school for lack of

funds wrote from Montgomery to thank him for his encouraging letter, but admitted:

> One thing is on my mine that is school thinking day and night if I will be able to return and enter the day school. but by having your good thoughts with my sorry ones I think we can plan the way out. Above all I am comming trusting in God that I may be successful. Prof where shall I work after I get there that I may ern anuff to get through day school? I wash I was able to return now but I can't get there before the second week in Oct. and it will take my best to return then. I shall be glad to hear from you at your erlyest date.

Other alumni wrote to Carver of how dirty and careless other schools seemed compared with Tuskegee. They also wrote to lighten burdens by sharing them with their revered teacher so many miles away. A graduate arriving at a new job teaching in Prairie View, Texas, wrote that students were refusing to attend classes taught by a man everyone knew had had intimate relations with a female student. He boldly refused to resign, and his friends in the administration refused to fire him. Carver's correspondent knew what was right and had a calm confidence of his view on the matter. "I wish it to be distinctly understood that I will not sacrifice my honor as a man for the right to hold any position here." Tuskegee prepared its pupils to have a secure knowledge of right even in situations they could never have anticipated.

Carver also increasingly received invitations to submit scientific papers for publication both in America and abroad (chiefly in Germany, home of a world-renowned scientific community at the turn of the century) and requests to assess new seeds, farm machinery, and other products. Since analyses were usually requested in exchange for a free sample of the item—plow, incubator, separator, or similar machine—Carver was always willing to do it for the benefit of his eternally cash-strapped department.

He also received solicitations from businessmen looking for qualified workers. One businessman and landowner from Coatopa, Alabama, inquired about the availability of men to work his thousand acres of cropland and pasture, assuring him they would receive a cordial welcome: "There has never been any race trouble here, & colored men who try to better their condition & live decently receive every encouragement from the whites.... I am in sympathy with every movement looking to the progress of the South and the betterment of her people—be their color what it may."

The 1904 school year had begun with an enrollment of 2,042 including 1,455 boys and 587 girls. Of the total there were 491 in night school, working off their expenses during the day. Tuition was still free; board was $8.50 per month, which the night school students reduced by up to $3.00 per month with work credits. There were also books and the school uniform to buy, and a five-dollar entrance fee. Students had to be at least fourteen years old and "strong, healthy and well grown for their age." In addition, they had to be able to pass the entrance exam, and they were "required to bring two letters of recommendation as to their moral character from well-known persons of their community."

One hopeful applicant wrote the school from Westminster, North Carolina:

> I am a poor fatherless girl wishing an education. My Mother cairs nothing of education therefore I have no help at all. I live with my grandfather who have sent me to school a little, but he being very old and decripted he is not able to school me, and I have no way to educate myself it takes all I make to live on. I farmed this year with the expectation of making money enough to enter your school but did not do so.... My reason for writing you in this way is I red in the book, *The Life of Booker T. Washington,* where you said that aney one that wanted an education you could educate them. I don't want you to take me and educate me for nothing. Give me a chance and I will educate myself. I want you to let me enter cheaper and I will work and pay you afterwards. I have not the money now and I want to go to school so bad...

A prospect from Kingston, Jamaica, saw an advertisement in *The Colored American* saying any Christian wishing to obtain Bible training can do so by applying to Tuskegee. He later wrote:

I sincerely thank my great and good Lord for this, one of his greatest blessings to mankind, especially to us the colored race...for it is my fondest ambition to know all there is to be known in the blessed scripture of truth.

CHAPTER TWELVE

TUG-OF-WAR

Washington spent a good deal of time defending industrial education against attacks by opponents who insisted blacks should educate an upper class of businessmen and professionals in college. A version of the argument went on at Tuskegee as well. Most faculty members who taught academic classes were college graduates and generally favored intellectual pursuits and "pure" learning—literature, philosophy, and French. The industrial teachers, on the other hand, had an eye for the more practical learning and felt more at home in the brickyard, dairy barn, or livery stable.

At the beginning of the 1903–4 school year, Washington hired a new academic department head named Roscoe Conkling Bruce, a Harvard graduate and son of a black Reconstruction-era senator from Mississippi. That year also, John Washington headed a committee that recommended a series of changes in the schedule that sent all the students to classes every morning under academic department supervision, then to work assignments in the industrial department every afternoon.

The academic and industrial departments competed with one another, each wanting to prove to Washington they could get the most out of their students. The result was that students—suddenly and without explanation—were pulled in both directions and had vastly more job responsibilities and academic coursework.

When the new program began, Washington was on vacation in France courtesy of his Carnegie legacy. It was his first vacation since the European tour of 1899. This time he went alone and was out of the country only about three weeks, returning on the same ship he sailed out on, the luxury liner *Kaiser Wilhelm II*. The German liners of the time were recognized as the best in the world; they also delighted in having such a celebrity on board; among the international clientele, Washington's race was a nonissue.

Washington was in Europe scarcely a week, from October 1 to October 7, and though he had no agenda, his hosts showered him with reception and speaking invitations. He found anonymity by taking an assumed name, Homer P. Jones.

Meanwhile, there were problems brewing at home.

In Washington's absence, the male students at Tuskegee staged a protest over the new working and classroom conditions. They marched from the breakfast table to the chapel, locked themselves in and voted to not work or study until the policy was changed. Faced with an ultimatum, the Executive Council, chaired by John Washington in his brother's absence, decided to take no action for the time being. After two days the revolt collapsed, and the students returned to their routines.

When Booker Washington learned of the revolt, he and Roscoe Bruce thought the students who led the rebellion should be punished. Margaret Washington countered that "the feeling is so general that it would be difficult to locate the leaders." The council considered reducing chapel services from every night to twice a week in order to give students more time to work and study, but decided against it.

When Washington returned, he praised the teachers' actions and admitted that "the students were crowded pretty hard in both their studies and in their industrial work." To the dismay of the academic teachers, he issued a new directive the next year: "Every Academic teacher is appreciably to diminish the amount of time required of his students for the preparation of his subjects. This arrangement goes into effect at once."

This, he said, brought the two departments into proper balance and made the academic department "more effective for the special purposes of the Institution." Arithmetic, he insisted, was best taught on the job in the carpentry shop or in dressmaking class.

Though he appeared evenhanded on the surface, Washington was protective of Tuskegee's reputation, sometimes to a fault. He could send his detective network into action quickly if he felt the school was being slandered. A faculty member named G. David Houston later complained about Washington and Tuskegee in private letters to his home pastor in Boston. Tipped off by a friend and former student, Washington arranged to have the letters stolen, then copied and returned. Washington confronted Houston, who admitted he had complained and apologized for it. Having made an example of him, Washington helped him get a job he wanted teaching in a Washington, D.C., high school and later endorsed his joining the faculty of Howard University, where Washington was a trustee.

In 1906, Tuskegee celebrated its twenty-fifth anniversary with a graduation gala. Dr. Charles Eliot, president of Harvard University, addressed the assembly, along with Andrew Carnegie, Secretary of War William Howard Taft, and other distinguished guests. Taking a moment to look back at how far they had come, the faculty and students considered the statistics. From the first day of class in a leaky shack, the Tuskegee campus and farmland combined now totaled more than 2,300 acres. The school owned 83 buildings, many of them designed and built by the students. There were 1,590 students enrolled, about a third of them girls, and a staff of 156 teachers. The endowment stood at more than a million dollars; the land and buildings were worth almost a million more. During the previous year the school had helped offset its $117 per student operating cost by producing, among other things, almost 200,000 pounds of meat, 8,000 bushels of sweet potatoes, and 970,000 bricks.

An organization the size of Tuskegee was bound to have occasional crises, such as the two-day student protest in 1903. A more serious example was in 1907 with the dismissal of Edgar J. Penney, dean of the Phelps Hall Bible School at Tuskegee. Penney was charged with sexually molesting a female student boarding in his home. He categorically denied the charges, but two additional facts cast his protestations in a suspicious light. First, he had been accused—and cleared—of a similar charge several years earlier; second, letters from a white New Orleans doctor indicated the woman was no innocent, but was in fact the doctor's mistress.

Though Penney insisted he was falsely charged, Washington told him he had the choice of resigning or being fired. Penney accused his employer of listening to only one side of the story and acting "prematurely and hastily in not granting me the asked for interview; and in demanding my resignation and in taking my work from me before knowing all the facts."

True to form, Washington was extremely anxious about how the incident might affect the public perception of Tuskegee. As president of the institution, he saw his responsibility not in finding the truth—that was the court's job—but in protecting the school's reputation. As he explained to the president of Atlanta University, where Penney was a trustee, "We have already taken the position that a school is not a court of law, that it is the duty of the court to prove a person guilty; in the case of a school we take the position that whenever a student or teacher gets into a position where his influence is hurtful that the school has a right to part with such an individual."

In spite of this momentary upheaval in the Bible school, Tuskegee's dedication to nondenominational Christianity remained strong, and one of its most effective religious programs was turning out to be Professor Carver's agricultural classes. Carver laced his demonstrations and lectures with references to the Creator, whose handiwork, Carver said, made everything from flowers to chemical solutions possible.

In his classroom presentations, Carver affirmed his belief that Christianity and science supported and reinforced each other: that the more mankind could learn about the physical world, the more it would know about the Creator who made it. Some students questioned his use of the name "Creator" instead of "God." Carver insisted they were one in the same, and that, as he once said in one of his Bible studies, "our Creator never changes despite the names given Him by people here and in all parts of the world. Even if we gave Him no name at all, He would still be there, within us, waiting to give us good on this earth."

Carver's position matched Washington's nondenominational approach to religion. And though he was no match for Washington on the speaker's podium, it was Carver who perhaps best articulated the position they shared on the issue of civil rights. He had no doubt that God worked for good in the world and that evil was caused by man's refusal to embrace that goodness. In response to calls for resisting oppression and confronting their white tormentors, Carver cautioned members of his race who sought restitution or revenge:

When our thoughts—which bring actions—are filled with hate against anyone, Negro or white, we are in a living hell. That is as real as hell will ever be. While hate for our fellow man puts us in a living hell, holding good thoughts for them brings us an opposite state of living, one of happiness, success, peace. We are then in heaven.

Carver's easy command of the classroom and laboratory, coupled with his genuine interest in students and their spiritual welfare, led him to craft impromptu sermons that touched committed Christians and the nominally religious alike. The first group enjoyed the way he brought spiritual ideas down to a practical level, talking about the Creator as he examined his creations. The second often admitted a personal connection with religion they had never felt before. Carver made religion not only palatable and relevant, but appealing.

In 1907, a group of Carver's agriculture students who enjoyed his class commentaries on the Creator, asked him to organize a Sunday evening Bible study to be held between the end of supper and the beginning of evening chapel. Carver gladly agreed and held the first session in a room at the Carnegie Library on campus. Though the thirty-five minutes after Sunday supper was one of the few unstructured times in the students' entire week, fifty or so boys came the first night to hear Carver's presentation on the creation story, complete with maps, rock and plant samples, and other illustrations.

In spite of his experience and education, Carver took the same back-to-basics approach to Bible study as he did in explaining cowpeas to a farmer who had grown cotton all his life. He preached messages that were as easy to grasp as the lessons in his old McGuffey speller, the precious blue-backed book his mother had somehow gotten for him. He could almost lift the essence of his religious belief from selections in the speller such as "The Cool Shade":

> The grass is soft to our feet, and the clear brook washes the roots of the trees. The sheep and cows can lie down to sleep in the cool shade, but we can do better; we can praise the great God who made us. He made the warm sun, and the cool shade; the trees that grow upward, and the brooks that run along.... All that live get life from God. He made the poor man as well as the rich man. He made the dark man as well as the fair man.... All that move on the land are his; and so are all that fly in the air, and all that swim in the sea....

After three months, attendance at the professor's Bible class topped a hundred; eager participants wolfed down their supper so they could get to the library early and get a good seat. Carver's optimistic, beneficent view of the world presented religion in a way some students had never seen. One later remembered his first night in the class: "For the first time in my life I was witnessing no gloom surrounding the Bible. I began to feel as I had back home when we went to a candy-pulling party—happy that I had come."

For all his success with the students and his growing notoriety outside Tuskegee through his Experiment Station Bulletins and speeches at agricultural conferences, Carver remained mired in difficulties with the school administration. George Bridgeforth continued angling for Carver's job and had come within a chicken feather of getting it in 1904. Carver's threat to resign then had convinced Washington not to carry out the recommendation to remove Carver as head of the department at the time.

In 1908 another round of serious complaints about the poultry operation caught Washington's attention and fanned the flames of Bridgeforth's ambition. This time Carver lost. Bridgeforth became Washington's political equal as head of the newly formed Department of Agricultural Industries. Instead of Director of Agriculture, Carver's new title was Director of Agricultural Instruction and Experiment Station, the very title he had refused and threatened to resign over four years before. Soon Carver was using his own money to replace missing chickens again, chickens a manager under his supervision claimed had been sold to a "traveling poultry peddler."

By the fall of 1910, still another inquiry reported 765 chickens missing. John Washington and Bridgeforth recommended recombining the industrial and instructional sections of the agriculture department under Bridgeforth. Of course Carver objected since this would leave Bridgeforth as the sole department head and place him firmly and unmistakably under the control of his former subordinate. Washington offered Carver the honorary title of dean and supervisor of the experiment station but made it clear that in all teaching and administrative matters, Bridgeforth was in charge.

Carver responded by tendering his resignation. Once again he wrote to his old friend, Secretary of Agriculture James Wilson, for leads on a new position. Earlier in the year they had discussed the prospect of the U.S. Agriculture Department sending Carver to Liberia to teach farming methods. (Perhaps revealing the depth of his frustration, Washington had approved the move, but Wilson evidently could not secure a position for his friend.) Now Wilson sympathized with Carver's circumstance but had nothing specific to offer:

What in the world they want to put anybody over your head for is more than I can understand, unless you are developing characteristics that are new to me. You will have to be the judge of what is right for you to do. I do not happen to know of a place where your services would be wanted at the present time, but nobody has ever suspected that you would care to leave there.

Meanwhile, Washington tried to find a permanent solution that would rid him of Carver's poor management without losing him altogether. Every time Carver had tendered his resignation over the years, Washington had always found a way to entice him back. In the past, Washington had always relented and let Carver remain as a department head. This time the principal held his ground.

A particular visitor raised Carver still higher in Washington's eyes, making him all the more eager to accommodate his eccentric but gifted teacher. In 1910 an English nobleman named Sir Harry Johnson visited the Tuskegee campus during an American tour and made special note of Carver in the book he wrote about his journey, *The Negro in the New World*. In describing Professor Carver he wrote:

> He is, as regards complexion and features, an absolute Negro; but in the cut of his clothes, the accent of his speech, the soundness of his science, he might be professor of Botany not at Tuskegee, but Oxford or Cambridge. Any European botanist of distinction, after ten minutes' conversation with this man, instinctively would deal with him "de puissance en puissance."

Apart from the description of his clothes, which would have surprised most anyone who saw Carver regularly, it was a picture that seemed to make Washington suddenly more aware of Carver's gifts as a teacher and of his growing value to Tuskegee.

Sir Harry's comment about Carver prompted Washington to look at his longtime faculty member in a new light. With a few exceptions, most notably the *Atlantic Monthly* article of 1903, he had given Carver scant attention or mention in his writing and speaking. When President McKinley visited the Tuskegee campus in December 1898, Carver's special responsibility had been to make sure all the farm machinery in the welcoming parade was freshly painted. In his books up to that time, Washington had scarcely mentioned Carver at all. But in *My Larger Education*, published in 1911, he quoted Sir Harry's impression of Carver in full and added considerable praise of his own.

Washington's praise revealed the value he placed on Carver's career, particularly his acceptance by whites. Translating Sir Harry's French as meaning a European botanist would treat Carver "as a man on a level with himself" [the literal translation is "from power to power"], he barely touched on Carver's work and research for the benefit of black farmers.

Instead, he emphasized the accolades Carver received from whites: his friendship with Secretary Wilson and the international visitors he received. "I have always said that the best means...for destroying race prejudice is to make [oneself] a useful and, if possible, an indispensable member of the community in which he lives. I do not know of a better illustration of this than may be found in the case of Professor Carver."

Nonetheless, when the agriculture department was reorganized with George Bridgeforth as its head in October 1910, Carver was affronted and once again tendered his resignation. He wrote Washington on November 19, 1910, his spelling and syntax revealing the distraction and emotion of the moment:

> I have read, thought and pondered very carefully over your scheme for the reorganization of the Agriculture Dept.
>
> As this seems the best thing to do I beg of you to carry it out, but I cannot be honest with you and true to the course for which I have given manly 15 years of the best of my life. So therefore I tender to you my resignation to take effect as soon as my work can be put in order and the Dept. inventoried over.
>
> Trusting the work will grow and prosper as never before, I shall always be greatful to you for past favors.

Washington replied three days later, revising the departmental organization to finesse Carver out of responsibilities he performed poorly while allowing him to save face with Bridgeforth. Carver was designated the head of a Department of Research, excused from teaching classes in the academic department, and promised a "first class laboratory to be fitted up, so as to enable him to carry out whatever investigations he may wish to undertake...."

Carver stayed. But by the following February none of the promises had been fulfilled, and Carver once again protested his treatment at the hands of the Tuskegee staff. On February 21 he told Washington that "the new Department is not going to receive the sympathy or the support of the school.... I am not satisfied and cannot be under the existing conditions."

A week later Washington answered him with a five-page letter meant to put the conflict between Carver and the school administration behind them one way or another:

Perhaps in the past we have done ourselves as well as you an injustice by pursuing a policy of trying to please everybody. This policy has not resulted in success.... We cannot stand any further or pursue a policy which permits you or anyone else to argue at length every order that is given, and to lay down the conditions upon which you will [carry them out]....

From the first it has been the settled policy of this institution to give each individual head of a department all the liberty possible. We realize fully that it is not possible to keep in the employment of the school strong men and women unless we give them liberty of action.... Once in a while, however, [direct] orders must be issued and when they are issued we expect them to be complied with without hesitation and in a sympathetic manner.

For example: You have had charge of the experiment station some twelve or fifteen years; during this time I think you will agree with me that the school has never suggested, except on two or three occasions, how the experiment station should be conducted.... The rule has been to leave you in absolute control....

This year the school has thought it wise...to give you a definite order as to what should be planted in the experiment station during the next twelve months. Instead of complying with this order in a sympathetic and prompt manner you are dilly-dallying with it, and have tried in many ways to bring influences to bear through officers of the school and students to get us to change this order. This is not the proper way to act: and instead of gaining you lose in influence and power by such actions.

I think I ought to say to you again that everyone here recognizes that your great fort [sic] is in teaching and lecturing. There are few people anywhere who have greater ability to inspire and instruct as a teacher and as a lecturer than is true of yourself....

When it comes to the organization of classes, the ability required to secure a properly organized and large school or section of a school, you are wanting in ability. When it comes to the matter of practical farm managing which will secure definite, practical, financial results, you are wanting again in ability. You are not to be blamed for this. It is very rare that one individual anywhere combines all the elements of success. You are a great teacher, a great lecturer, a great inspirer of young men and old men: that is your fort and we have all been trying as best we could to help you do the work for which you are best fitted and to leave aside that for which you are least fitted....

I was greatly surprised...to find that you wish a laboratory fitted up for your exclusive use and that you do not mean to give instruction to any students in this laboratory.... We have no right to expend so large a sum of money in the fitting up of a laboratory which is not to be used as frequently as possible in the instruction of students. We are all here to help the students, to instruct them, and there is no justification for the presence of any teacher here except as that teacher is to serve the students.

You seem to have made up your mind that you are to give no instruction; that you are to teach no classes whatever. Here, again, the school cannot agree to have any person here in the capacity that you are serving unless he gives instruction to classes when the school requests that such instruction shall be given.

You do not help yourself when you assume the attitude that when you make a request that many hundred dollars shall be spent for chemicals, that there must be no modification of your requisition, that the last dollar you request for chemicals, etc., shall be spent, nothing must be cut down, that you must have all or nothing: that is an attitude, again, which the school cannot comply with.

My own requests for supplies go before the Finance Committee the same as yours. Very often the Finance Committee refuses to give me what I want. The same is true for every officer of the institution. We can make no exception in your case....

Now, I do not mean to be unkind in making these statements. In fact, in putting the matter before you as I do, I am acting in the greatest charity and with the greatest degree of kindness. The longer we go on treating you as we are, the worse conditions are going to be....

I repeat that all of us recognize your great ability, recognize

255

your rare talents in certain directions, and we should be sorry to part with your service, but the time has now come for perfect frankness and for definite action.

We want to allow you the largest amount of liberty. But all this does mean that when an order is given it is to be complied with without objection and difficulty being thrown in the way to the extent that has been true in the past.

As the leader of an institution approaching two thousand people, and as an international spokesman for Negro rights and opportunities, Washington could still focus his attention on something as specific and limited in scope as Carver's laboratory and give it a considerable amount of his time. Again he found himself wrestling with how to make the best use of Carver's obvious skills and his growing public popularity while keeping him from making a mess of things administratively. In his view, he was willing to meet Carver more than halfway.

Carver, for his part, saw the whole matter as the last and worst in a long line of broken promises. It was his understanding that he would not have to teach classes under the academic department (meaning no classes that were out of his control and under Bridgeforth's) and that he would have a completely equipped laboratory—which he had never had, even though Washington had led him to believe he would find one waiting for him when he arrived at Tuskegee fifteen years before.

With as many issues as Washington had competing for his time, it is likely he had no idea how primitive Carver's laboratory setup was and how much he was doing for the benefit of the school in spite of its limitations. The professor was still using cast-offs to make laboratory ware. He was also still using alcohol lamps and gasoline burners for heat in his tests and experiments, though gas-fired Bunsen burners were available and much safer to use. But they cost money, and Carver had none to spend. Besides, he had no natural gas piped into the building.

The laboratory became the center of a new tug-of-war between Carver and Washington that lasted almost a year. Carver was convinced his laboratory was essential for analyzing soil samples for farmers and landowners; experimenting with cowpeas, Spanish peanuts, cotton, and other crops; and preparing charts and tables for his Experiment Station Bulletins. To fulfill his duties he had to have the right tools. Washington was equally convinced that every dollar Tuskegee spent must be spent as carefully as possible with the greatest benefit possible to the students. The idea of a research laboratory for the exclusive use of one faculty member, where no teaching would be done and no students involved, directly opposed Washington's fundamental understanding of the Tuskegee mission.

Gradually, Carver began to see his laboratory take shape, though he still had to make concessions in teaching other classes, and he prodded Washington regularly about delays in getting the work done. For his part, Washington saw the laboratory as a way to keep Carver within the Tuskegee fold and agreed to his specific requests as long as the budget permitted them.

By September the laboratory was under construction but still had no supplies because the Finance Committee had not authorized any appropriation to buy them. The committee replied that it needed to know what the various items requested were for. Carver sent back a four-page letter explaining what every piece of equipment was for: the Sartorius Analytical Balance, "indispensable" for all forms of delicate weighing; Parr's Calorimeter for analysis of coal and sulfur gas; Soxhlet's Apparatus for analyzing soil; Koening's Apparatus for detecting adulteration in butter made by the dairy classes; all the way down to clamps, crucibles, and glass stirring rods.

In his own summary of events, Carver sent a letter to Washington on September 14 that underscored his exasperation with bureaucratic procedures and his disappointment at the disturbing string of broken promises:

> Nearly eleven months ago [when Bridgeforth became a department head and Carver assumed directorship of the Department of Research] my work was arbitrarily changed, I was asked to sever my connection with a work that 15 years of my life's blood had gone into, pioneer years in which no one wanted it: I reluctantly did, but accepted the promise [not to have to teach classes under Bridgeforth's supervision].

Afterward it was modified to the extend that I must yet teach classes. This I did, with the understanding that my laboratory would be hurried long.

Here it was September, Carver went on, and he had "absolutely no equipment."

He continued:

I am being annoyed by committees that sometimes say very unhandsome and unbecoming things which causes me to indulge in the same spirit, with the result that the laboratory is yet empty.

My mind is not in condition to do good work, and if it was I could not do it because I have nothing to do with.

Carver resubmitted his equipment list divided into thirds, "which I trust you will allow to come sufficiently far apart so as not to press you for the means."

He concluded: "Kindly excuse me from meeting any more committees on this as my nerves will not stand it."

Their disagreement over the laboratory continued through the spring. On May 4, 1912, Carver sent Washington a long summary of grievances, beginning with his reassignment and Bridgeforth's promotion at the beginning of the 1910 school year, and ending with Carver's claim that he still didn't have his laboratory, still didn't have a stenographer, and took exception to having his teaching ability questioned by people in the academic department.

Moreover, he was being hampered in one area where he was an unqualified success, which was in publishing his Experiment Station Bulletins. Two manuscripts were completed and ready to go, but he couldn't get approval to spend money on having them printed. It was, he fumed, "practically impossible to get matter published. If a 50¢ rake is asked for it must go to the budget committee, which means it will not be gotten at all or delayed beyond the point of usefulness."

Along with his own summary, Carver sent a sheaf of letters and office memos, all signed by Washington, pointing out where he himself had endorsed various proposals and promises, none of which had come to pass. "I interpret the above to mean that the school is really tired of my services and wishes me to resign. I see no other alternative, am I correct?"

Once again Washington was caught in the position of needing to rein in Carver without prompting him to act on his threat to resign. On June 12, 1912, Washington spelled out in unmistakable yet conciliatory terms exactly what Carver could do and what he could not:

> From now on until further notice I think it well for you to understand that your work will consist of the following:
> 1. In charge of the Experiment Station.
> 2. Poultry Yard.
> 3. Research.
> 4. Teaching agriculture or botany in the Academic Department.
> 5. Teaching the girls cooking, etc., whenever Mrs. Washington desires it in connection with her department.
>
> We shall go on as fast as we can in fitting up your research laboratory. You are authorized to spend $400.00 in the immediate present in perfecting this laboratory.

This gave Carver the Experiment Station, which was his greatest triumph; it left him in charge of the poultry yard, which he managed poorly but did not want to leave in a state of failure; and it gave him the first position at Tuskegee to focus on research rather than teaching, though he still would be required to teach in some capacity.

With Carver continuing to be demonstrably unhappy, Washington expanded on his position a few days later.

> Mr. Carver
> I think, unconscious to yourself, that there is growing within you a disposition to take in an unkind way the orders or request which are made in the council and elsewhere in reference to the Experiment Station work.
> I fear that you, like some other members of the Council, are inclined to misinterpret my suggestions which in many cases, in fact most cases, are but a polite way of giving orders.
> I do not want the Council to become a debating club, where

every member feels that he must either object to or debate every order or suggestion given by the Principal. I have reasons for every order I give and suggestions that I make in reference to any department, and it is not necessary for any head to feel that when I do make suggestions that it is because he is not doing his duty or trying to do it. We can all make improvements and changes by hearing suggestions from other people, and I should dislike very much to see you get to the point where you feel that it is a personal affront for suggestions to be made to you in reference to the improvement of your work.

The conflict continued through the summer and into the next academic year, with Carver teaching under protest in the academic department, and Washington, when he was in town, spending as much time as he could spare smoothing Carver's feathers. Further misunderstandings in summer school generated more complaints from Carver about his classroom responsibilities.

The last week of 1912, Carver once more tendered his resignation, requesting a month to see to his affairs, "as it will take quite that long to put my department in order, get my things packed, find storage for them, and incidentally get myself located." The words were remarkably similar to the ones Carver used more than eight years before, in the wake of the first disturbing and demeaning report on the poultry yard, when he threatened to resign rather than face the thought of serving under George Bridgeforth.

Now the practical management of the agriculture department had been taken away, and he was a department head in name only. He had been invited to consider heading either one of two new experiment stations planned by the U.S. Department of Agriculture. But somehow he felt Tuskegee still gave him the best possible opportunity to carry out his life's work—in spite of the disappointing turn the politics of the job had taken.

Other offers notwithstanding, Carver's heart was at Tuskegee. And there he stayed.

CHAPTER THIRTEEN

DETERMINED
TO RISE

By the time of Tuskegee's twenty-fifth anniversary in 1906, Booker T. Washington was internationally recognized as the leading spokesman for his race. Against all naysayers, he held fast to his long-established position that the best way to achieve political and financial equality with whites was to demonstrate that their fears of blacks as a group were unfounded.

Early in his career he had had to soothe those who carried haunting memories of Reconstruction. According to the *Negro Year Book,* as quoted in *Tuskegee Institute: The First Fifty Years* (1931), only 30 percent of black Americans could read by 1881, the year Tuskegee opened its doors. Candidates elected since the end of the war had been all the proof some Southerners needed to insist that blacks must be kept out of politics, out of the economy, and out of the way of white progress.

The years following Reconstruction saw a backlash against the early promises of Emancipation. Public policies, which, by and large, had not separated the races nor defined their rights, began to grow steadily more burdensome to anyone who was black. By the time of Tuskegee's silver anniversary, blacks were effectively prevented from voting by state laws, denied seats on public transportation, denied service in hotels and restaurants, and denied jobs except those that traditionally went to blacks, such as masons, teamsters, and certain positions in the civil service including assistant postmasters and customs inspectors.

The legal and political status of blacks had headed steadily downhill the whole time Washington was at Tuskegee. By 1906 the black voting power that brought Tuskegee into existence had entirely disappeared. If anyone had come to Lewis Adams for election support that year, he would have been unable to provide it. The constituency of black voters—the bargaining chip that had brought the school into existence in 1881—had ceased to exist.

Against this historical backdrop, Washington was accepted—though sometimes grudgingly—as the most important black man in America. As the laws bore down on civil rights, W. E. B. Du Bois, William Monroe Trotter, and others grew more impatient, persistent, and threatening, calling for blacks to stop waiting for equality and insisting on it *now*, even if it meant civil disobedience. Washington was unswerving in his commitment to humility and self-help. He never abandoned his belief that the best way to a better life for blacks was to become indispensable to whites, the reasoning being that once white people saw the benefit of working with blacks, they would welcome the opportunity. He had proven it early on at Tuskegee with his brickyard. If the bricks were good, he had said, white people would buy them because they wanted good bricks regardless of the color of the hands that molded them. He was right; the school steadily sold about a million bricks a year.

If dairymen, seamstresses, blacksmiths, or estate managers were good enough, Washington thought, they would be hired and respected whatever race they were because they provided a valuable service. The letters that came to Tuskegee offering respectable jobs at higher than prevailing wages for their graduates satisfied Washington that his theory was correct.

In addition to Washington's complete separation from racial confrontation, another characteristic that made him popular with whites was that he never promoted social equality between white and black. Washington clearly and consistently separated his call for economic and political parity from any suggestion of social equality. In the often-quoted phrase from his Cotton States speech, the two races could work together like fingers on a hand, but still be separate fingers—by this he meant socially separate.

This was a message many whites were encouraged and relieved to hear. Many Southern whites feared social equality with blacks on several levels, one being they believed black men, if given the chance, would retaliate for the common practice of white slaveowners' using of attractive slave girls as "concubines" by sleeping with white women (this often led to lynchings of black men in the South). In addition, many wrongly saw blacks as genetically inferior to whites and feared the dilution of white bloodlines.

Washington's approach continued to make him by far the most visible and successful black money raiser of his time. Rockefeller, Carnegie, Slater, and the other wealthy Northern industrialists were eager to send money to Tuskegee out of a combination of respect, conscience, guilt, and relief that here was a place their money would be well and wisely spent.

Washington's detractors continued to fume at his success in fundraising because every dollar that went to him or to Tuskegee was one dollar that would never go to support their point of view. As the tide turned against racial equality after 1900, Du Bois and Monroe spoke for an increasingly large and vocal constituency that considered it demeaning for blacks to try to "earn" rights that should have been theirs to start with. Why, they asked, should they have to prove they "deserved" to vote or ride on Pullman cars?

The Afro-American Council had been formed to give voice to black leaders other than Washington who wanted a say in public affairs. Partly on account of Washington's power, the Council failed to attract any significant publicity or high profile leader. Then the Niagara Movement began, again to coalesce and concentrate the power of the fractured anti-Washington groups into a single force. Washington rose to the challenge by getting his allies elected to leadership positions, stifling coverage in the white newspapers, and manipulating black publications to keep news about Niagara quiet or negative.

Washington's distaste for the Niagara organization discouraged many prospective members, both white and black, from joining. Knowing his influence in securing jobs for blacks and his power behind the scenes in controlling publications, they were simply afraid to go on record opposing him. This incensed Du Bois and his cohorts.

In March 1908, *Horizon*, the unofficial mouthpiece of Niagara, complained that Washington "has accepted the revised constitutions [state constitutions that in effect deprived blacks of the vote];…he has acquiesced in the 'Jim Crow' car policy [banning blacks from Pullman cars];…he has kept dumb as an oyster as to peonage [an oppressive landowner/tenant arrangement];…he has even discovered that colored people can better afford to be lynched than the white people can afford to lynch them.…"

Washington had defeated his ideological enemies in the Afro-American Council and the Niagara Movement for years just by attending annual conventions and angling for his slate of officers. But his influence over the organizations steadily weakened after Washington took an opposing stance on two racial incidents in 1906. By 1908, Niagara's leaders were convinced Washington's way was a dead end and would go on to form yet another organization that finally gave them the Washington-free base of operation they wanted.

The first crisis came weeks after the 1906 annual meeting of the Negro Business League in Atlanta. Hoping to head off any racial tension caused by a large assembly of black businessmen in a Southern city, Washington wrote to his white friend Charles A. Wickersham, general manager of the Atlanta and West Point Railroad, asking him to suspend the prevailing policy that black railroad passengers had to enter and leave the terminal by a side door. Delegates from thirty or more states would be coming for the meeting, some of whom would not even think of having to go to the side entrance of the train station.

As Washington explained, "No matter how well-intentioned the visitor may be, the arrangements are such that persons who have not lived in Atlanta and learned by experience where to enter and leave would [not] think of going to the side door." He feared whites would get angry at NNBL delegates, unfamiliar with local custom, using the front door.

Wickersham insisted the Atlanta terminal did not have a front door and side door but only a white entrance and one for blacks. All he offered was to put a sign up on the side door that said "Main Colored Entrance." In the margin of the letter, Emmett Scott penciled, "Will do more harm than good."

Racial tension in the city was high when Washington arrived in late August, and he submitted copies of his keynote address to the local newspapers. The Atlanta press had done its share to stir up racial feelings in reporting on the Georgia governor's race. Each candidate was trying to outdo the other in promising to keep blacks out of politics, and the three city newspapers were milking the story for all the circulation they could get.

Washington's speech was an affirmation that the South was still the best place for industrious blacks who wanted to work. Reporting on his speech, the *Atlanta Constitution* headed its story, "Law-Breaking Negroes Worst Menace to Race."

The NNBL meeting went off without incident, but less than a month later, on September 22, an armed mob of whites attacked blacks in the city, touching off five days of riots that left at least eleven people dead. Negroes were attacked on the streets, dragged out of bars and restaurants, and hauled off streetcars and beaten.

T. Thomas Fortune, the New York publisher who had edited Washington's first book, wrote confidentially to Emmett Scott that the whole scene made his blood boil, and he wished he could be there "with a good force of armed men." From his New York hotel, Washington encouraged patience even in the face of such raw lawlessness and evil. In an open letter to the New York *World,* Washington admonished Atlanta's blacks to "exercise self-control and not make the fatal mistake of attempting to retaliate, but to rely on the efforts of the proper authorities to bring order and security out of confusion." He urged a meeting of the "best white people and the best colored people" to reach a solution around a table rather than on the street. "While there is disorder in one community," Washington observed, "there is peace and harmony in thousands of others."

Many more blacks sympathized with Fortune, who insisted in a letter to the New York *World,* "I cannot believe that the policy of non-resistance in a situation like that of Atlanta can result in anything but contempt and massacre of the race."

Another incident that cost Washington credibility among other black leaders was President Roosevelt's reaction to a disturbance in Brownsville, Texas, on the night of August 13, 1906. A shooting spree outside a bar near an army installation killed a white man and wounded a police officer. The townspeople thought black soldiers stationed there were retaliating for past attacks on blacks, while the blacks thought a white mob was coming after them. Despite the fact that the shooting lasted only about ten minutes and the guilty parties were never identified, local citizens demanded the Negro soldiers be punished.

President Roosevelt approved the summary dismissal of all the black soldiers, though not their white officers. In a letter, Roosevelt invited Washington for a personal consultation on the matter but refused his advice to consider additional information. "I could not possibly refrain from acting as regards those colored soldiers," he wrote. "You can not have any information to give me privately to which I could pay heed, my dear Mr. Washington, because the information on which I act is that which came out in the investigation itself."

When organizations formed to oppose him, Washington made it his business to find out some way to influence them or else put them out of business. The Afro-American Council and the Niagara Movement followed similar trajectories. They each began as a forum for blacks who disagreed with Booker T. Washington's methods. Washington got wind of them, eventually gained a measure of control, saw his influence beaten back and expelled, and withdrew his support. Lacking publicity and financial support, the organizations faded.

There was a fair amount of movement back and forth between the Washington and anti-Washington camps, prompted both by honest changes of heart and the realization that opposing the country's leading black spokesman and moneymaker was a very tall order. Du Bois, after all, had himself been offered a faculty position at Tuskegee and spoke favorably about Washington as late as 1903. Bishop Alexander Walters, still straddling the fence even after the rise and decline of Niagara, spoke for many when he addressed the Niagara Movement convention of 1906 to say, "It is nonsense for us to say Peace! Peace! when there is no peace.... We use diplomatic language and all kinds of subterfuges, but the fact remains that the enemy is trying to keep us down and we are determined to rise or die in the attempt."

The more radical the movement's position became, the less notice it commanded. By the following year the tactical niceties were all but gone with the group denouncing "bitter and relentless race hatred and contempt" and the "base" blacks in high places who accepted the inequalities of "American colorphobia."

In 1908 a race riot in Springfield, Illinois, led to the deaths of six Negro residents at the hands of white mobs; two thousand black residents were driven from the city. Such outrageous lawlessness, coming particularly as it did in the place where Abraham Lincoln lived, practiced law, and bought the only house he ever owned, inspired the formation of a new organization for the black leaders who strained at further peacemaking and longed for a more forceful stance against discrimination.

Their opportunity came with a meeting in Springfield on the centennial of Lincoln's birth, February 12, 1909, organized by a white businessman named Oswald Garrison Villard, editor of the *New York Evening Post* and biographer of John Brown. Villard's grandfather, William Lloyd Garrison, had been a leading abolitionist; his father was a railroad millionaire. He had raised more than $150,000 for the Tuskegee endowment over the years but saw merit in a movement that went beyond Washington's methods and addressed "the race question" more directly and with higher expectations of results.

Three white socialists also interested in racial equality—William English Walling, a writer, and Dr. Henry Moskowitz and Mary White Ovington, both social workers—encouraged Villard to convene the meeting to find a way for Negroes to take a more active role in claiming the political and economic freedom they were entitled to. Villard agreed to organize the meeting in New York and invited virtually every prominent black in the country to attend, including Washington, Du Bois, Bishop Walters, Reverend Francis J. Grimké, and a host of others.

Villard sincerely thought this opportunity would bring Washington and Du Bois together for a common purpose at last. Anticipating Washington's reluctance to attend, he laced his invitation with assurances of fairness and balance:

> It is not to be a Washington movement or a Du Bois movement. The idea is that there shall grow out of it, first, an annual conference...for the discussion by men of both races of the conditions

of the colored people, politically, socially, industrially, and educationally.

He went on to explain that the organizers:

[D]o not wish to embarrass you; they do not wish to seem to ignore you, or to leave you out, or to show any disrespect whatever. On the other hand, they do not wish to tie you up with what may prove to be a radical political movement. Hence, they have not felt like urging you very hard to join the new movement, but have wanted you to know that you would be welcome at the conference, or if you decided you could not attend, the conference would least of all misrepresent your absence.

Villard's concern that the meeting could lead to a "radical political movement" was well founded. Within months, W. E. B. Du Bois, who would become the new organization's director of publications and research, issued the caveat that his magazine *Horizon* had taken off the kid gloves. "THIS IS A RADICAL PAPER" the November 1909, issue proclaimed. It further asserted:

It advocates Negro equality and human equality; it stands for universal manhood suffrage, including votes for women; it believes in the abolition of war, the taxation of monopoly values, the gradual socialization of capital and the overthrow of persecution and despotism in the name of religion.

Washington declined Villard's invitation, reinforcing his ever-present position that it was "through progressive, constructive work that we are to succeed rather than by depending too largely upon agitation or criticism." Washington's critics were relieved he would not be coming. They knew only too well the power of his presence.

Having sent his regrets, Washington dispatched his trusted lieutenant Charles Anderson, head of the New York Republican Club, to spy on the proceedings and see how he might throw a wrench into the machinery. Anderson promised to "do all I can to discredit this affair."

Washington's staunchest critics were there, and when someone suggested Washington be nominated for membership on the steering committee to set up a formal organization on account of his high profile and ability to attract contributors, the protestations were so loud that his name was quickly withdrawn.

In a letter to the Boston *Transcript,* published March 19, 1910, Du Bois later explained his differences with Washington in a more accommodating tone:

> Mr. Washington has long and earnestly counseled his race to let politics alone, acquiesce temporarily in disenfranchisement and pay attention chiefly to industrial development and efficiency. I do not think this a wise programme, but it is a logical one and deserving of thought. In the face of this, however, Mr. Washington has for the last eight years allowed himself to be made the sole referee for all political action concerning 10,000,000 Americans.

The result, Du Bois concluded, was to effect "a substitution of monarchy for democracy among a population twice as large as that of all New England."

Washington did not reply directly to the charge, but a "well-known educator"—very likely Emmett Scott—published a response suggesting that "it would be entirely out of place for Dr. Washington [Doctor was a commonly used courtesy title] to enter into any discussion with a man occupying the place that Dr. Du Bois does, for the reason that Dr. Washington is at the head of a large institution.... Dr. Du Bois, on the other hand, is a mere hired man, as it were, in an institution completely controlled by white people."

Within a year of their organizational meeting in New York, Oswald Garrison Villard and his group of like-minded men formally organized themselves as the National Association for the Advancement of Colored People (NAACP). Their stated purpose was "to make 11,000,000 Americans physically free from peonage, mentally free from ignorance, and socially free from insult." Villard was installed as treasurer. All the founding officers were white with a single exception: W. E. B. Du Bois, who as director of publications and research launched the monthly organizational magazine *Crisis*.

The NAACP was set up as the Afro-American League and the Niagara Movement had been with a national leadership group coordinating local chapters where the bulk of the work was done. Villard was a dedicated and energetic supporter of the new organization. Du Bois attracted national attention with *Crisis,* which quickly gained a core of loyal subscribers. Together with the rest of the group at their New York organizational meeting, they achieved a critical mass with the NAACP that they had never managed in the past.

Another reason for the success of the NAACP where its predecessors had failed was that sympathy for the rights of Negroes at the national level continued to slide. In 1901, Booker T. Washington could point to his dinner at the White House as proof that the president and his government were sympathetic to the needs of the race in general and that they recognized Washington as the representative and spokesman for African Americans.

By 1906 the situation had fundamentally changed. Roosevelt reacted tepidly to the white-instigated riots in Atlanta that September, then, a month later, summarily dismissed the three companies of black American soldiers in Brownsville.

Roosevelt declined entreaties by the Republicans to run for a second full term, and his Secretary of War, William Howard Taft, succeeded him as president in 1908. The decline in Washington's influence continued under the new administration. Just after he was elected, Taft spoke at the North Carolina Society of New York, and Washington was invited to edit his speech. Taft used many of Washington's suggestions, promoting equal education for all children and equal privileges for men of equal property, education, and character regardless of race; unfortunately he also interjected ideas of his own that somewhat undercut Washington's, saying that "the best friend that the Southern Negro can have is the Southern white man" and that the "Federal Government has nothing to do with social equality."

Taft insisted he wanted to use Washington as a confidant and advisor on race issues in the same way Roosevelt had. Though Washington and

Taft had several meetings before the inauguration in March 1909, Taft was already working to have black office holders appointed under Roosevelt removed from their posts. In his inaugural address he avowed he would not appoint blacks to offices anywhere their race might cause local friction or affect their ability to perform their official duties. The result of this was that whites throughout the South complained about "local friction" caused by black appointees, some of whom had been at their jobs since before the turn of the century, and had them removed from office in droves.

Taft's removal of John C. Dancy, recorder of deeds for the District of Columbia and one of the most highly placed blacks in the country, was a particular blow to Washington's influence and credibility. At the news of Dancy's dismissal, one Washington ally, P. B. S. Pinchback, admitted, "Man! I am so mad I can scarcely write. It is all over the city that Dancy's defeat is Washington's defeat."

Washington found a silver lining even in this ominous cloud. To Dancy he wrote: "You will have now a rare chance to set an example in the way of commercial and business leadership and I very much hope that you will seize on to this opportunity." To James C. Napier, a black pro-Washington businessman and civic leader in Nashville, he confided, "Taft in my opinion is a good, well-meaning man, but it seems impossible for him to hold out against strong men, who want to use him for selfish purposes."

Still, Washington saw a liability in allowing Taft to be too self-satisfied with his policies on race. In a letter dated April 1, 1910, he warned his advisors:

Unless one is perfectly frank with the President, he may go on feeling that the Negroes are satisfied, when they are not and when the time comes to expect their support, he will be disappointed, hence it is disloyalty for any person to deal in a manner that is not frank with the President.

In an ironic twist, Washington's diminishing access to the White House made it easier for him and his supporters to insist he was not the black kingmaker his adversaries made him out to be. They soon realized, however, that without Washington at the president's side, blacks had no direct access to the president at all. In a letter to Washington that June, Pinchback described the "jubilant" state of Washington's enemies "at what they call the fall of one man power etc. To a bunch of them some time since I remarked—under the so called one man power you all got your places and the race some recognition. What are we getting now? Better one man power than no power at all. A dead silence for some moments."

Certainly no president would risk the political liability of consulting with Du Bois or Trotter, who were on record as socialist-leaning radicals ("THIS IS A RADICAL PAPER"). White leadership within the NAACP or among the Northern philanthropists could not bring the same insights or connections to the table. They were delighted to see Washington begin to slip, but they were horrified to realize there was no one to take his place.

Taft's systematic purging of federal black office holders quickened the pace of a change that had been transforming the relationship between blacks and the party of Lincoln. The Great Emancipator had been the first Republican president; Republicans had engineered and carried out Reconstruction; black officeholders of the time, including governors and senators, were Republican virtually without exception. But by the time of the 1910 midterm elections, black voters had been demoted from asset to annoyance.

Blacks, who had heavily supported their Republican emancipators and benefactors at the polls, were rewarded after Reconstruction with appointments that recognized both their political loyalty and their qualifications to serve. The relentless progress of disenfranchisement meant that by 1910 blacks had precious little influence in politics because so few of them were allowed to vote. Poll taxes, residency requirements, literacy tests, and the notorious "grandfather" clauses in state laws (which held that a man's grandfather had to have been qualified to vote in order for the man to qualify) had been widely instituted under the banner of states' rights.

Aware of their helplessness and eager for Southern white approval, Taft turned away from his black constituents. An informal group known as the Black Cabinet—which included J. C. Napier, Taft's most senior black appointment as register of the treasury—began to meet and occasionally got the opportunity to advise Taft on race issues. But their influence was weak. Taft appointed a few blacks to offices, typically those dealing with minorities—superintendent of Indian schools or collector of internal revenue for Hawaii, for example.

The Black Cabinet's only clear victory was in dissuading Taft from appointing Judge William C. Hook of Kansas to a vacancy on the United States Supreme Court. Taft had already added two former Confederates to the Court and made a third Chief Justice. As the judge in a high-profile discrimination case, Hook had ruled that Oklahoma railroads did not have to allow black passengers access to sleeping cars, dining cars, or club cars, nor did they have to provide separate cars of those types for blacks. Such cars, Hook ruled, were "luxuries" and therefore not required for Negroes under the separate but equal rule.

By the time nominations came around for the 1912 presidential election, Theodore Roosevelt was ready to take the reins of government back from his former cabinet secretary. When he lost the Republican nomination to Taft, Roosevelt formed his own third party, the Progressives, which quickly gained the nickname "The Bull Moose Party." This turn of events put Washington in a difficult spot. He had been an advisor to Taft and promised to help him win a second term. However, for at least the first part of his presidency, Roosevelt had been far closer to Washington and more willing to act on his advice than Taft ever was and was still, in fact, a member of the Tuskegee board of trustees.

Another member of the Black Cabinet, Ralph Tyler, drafted a statement supporting the appointment of qualified blacks to federal posts and encouraged President Taft to include it in an upcoming speech in order to rally black political support. The paragraph also denounced segregation on railroads, lynchings, and disenfranchisement. On the page, which he initialed after reading it, Taft wrote to his secretary, "I am not going to say anything on many of the subjects here set out. I think it cheeky to ask it. What I have said I have said and it can be quoted but if the negroes want to vote for Roosevelt or a Democrat let them."

At the request of the Tuskegee board, Washington played no active part in the 1912 presidential campaign. Roosevelt and Taft divided their electorate while the Democrats, united behind New Jersey Governor Woodrow Wilson, after a long and bitter convention battle carried the electoral college.

The Democrats reclaimed the White House with only 42 percent of the popular vote. The Democrats also gained majorities in both houses of Congress. Except for Grover Cleveland, it was the first time a Democrat had been elected president since the Republican Party was founded in 1860.

Wilson was the son of a Presbyterian minister and was himself a Presbyterian elder who read the Bible daily. But his Christianity had brought him to far different conclusions about race relations than Washington's faith had. When Washington was a guest at Wilson's inauguration as president of Princeton University in 1902, he had been the only podium guest who was not invited to stay in a faculty house. Wilson was a Virginia native whose father had once been chaplain of the South Carolina legislature. Under Wilson, Princeton remained the only Ivy League school that categorically excluded Negroes.

After he became president, Wilson stood by while subordinates in the post office and treasury began segregating black workers, designating offices in a specific area for blacks. Lunchrooms and rest rooms were divided as well. Beginning in May 1914, civil service applicants had to submit a photo of themselves to take the civil service exam, making discrimination easier and more routine.

Washington put the best face possible on this political turn of events. Wilson had been the candidate of Du Bois and Trotter, but after the election the *Nashville Banner* reported that Washington

> ...stated his belief the next President of the United States is one of the best friends of negro education who has occupied the presidential chair, and that he will favor at all times all things that will prove beneficial to the people of his [Washington's] race. He said he had known President-elect Wilson for many years, and that he had greatest confidence in his willingness to hear any just cause that might be presented on behalf of the negro. Being Southern born, he had the knowledge of conditions in the South that would give him a thorough understanding of things that would tend to their advancement in the true sense.

In private, Washington was more frank, telling his Boston colleague William Lewis, "I fear the President's high-sounding phrases regarding justice do not include the Negro."

Before William Howard Taft went down in defeat, Washington had been through a dramatic first-person demonstration of what justice for the Negro truly meant. On the night of March 9, 1911, Washington stood in the first floor vestibule of an apartment building at 11½ Sixty-third Street in New York City. He was there at the suggestion of Emmett Scott, who had written him from Alabama that D. C. Smith, the auditor for Tuskegee, would be visiting friends at that address. There was some school business he and the principal needed to discuss, and Scott wrote Washington that it would be well for him to call at the apartment while he was in the city.

When no one answered Washington's ring, he walked back out into the street. It was Sunday night and thinking the residents might be at church, he walked around the neighborhood a while and returned to the vestibule. He rang the doorbell again but still no one answered. He left the building again and was gone about an hour. Entering the vestibule a third time, he put on his reading glasses to take a closer look at the names beside the row of doorbell buttons.

Suddenly a disheveled, powerfully built white man rushed in from the street shouting, "What are you doing here? Are you breaking into my house? You've been hanging around here four or five weeks!" Instead of waiting for a reply, the man hit Washington on the side of the head with his fist. Washington tried to explain his presence, but the man started hitting him again. Washington ran out into the street; his assailant followed, grabbing a walking stick from a passerby.

The stocky man caught up with Washington and began hitting him repeatedly with the head of the walking stick. Between blows, Washington tried to reason with him. "Don't beat me like this!" he shouted. "If I'm breaking the law, call an officer and have him arrest me if I'm doing anything wrong!"

The beating continued. Washington fled down the street, his assailant and the owner of the stick in close pursuit. Again they caught up with Washington, who was now bleeding profusely from the head, and beat him as he ran. Washington caught his foot in the trolley tracks and sprawled on the pavement near Sixty-third Street and Central Park West, almost at the feet of a plainclothes policeman standing at the curb. The owner of the stick ran on; the other man pointed to the dirty, bleeding Negro with torn clothes who lay panting and exhausted on the ground and shouted, "This man is a thief! I found him with his hand on the doorknob and his eye at the keyhole!"

A uniformed policeman appeared and escorted Washington and his accuser to the station house. The accuser's name was Henry Ulrich, a carpenter by trade who was currently running a dog kennel. Ulrich testified that he was eating dinner when his wife came in. "She was very much excited and said that a negro was lurking about the front of the building," he explained. He said he went out into the vestibule and saw the accused peeking through the keyhole of an apartment. He said he challenged the man to explain himself, and "when I got no answer I started to throw him out of the building. He resisted and I gave him the best beating I could." He denied hitting Washington with a walking stick and insisted Washington had hit him first. He explained the two large gashes in Washington's head and his torn ear by saying he had run into a fire hydrant when he tried to escape, then hurt himself again when he stumbled and fell on the trolley tracks.

A police lieutenant began to book Washington on suspicion of theft, and, for the first time, asked his name. When Washington gave it, the lieutenant refused to believe him. It was only after Washington produced a calling card, a letter addressed to him, and other evidence that the police believed he was who he said he was. Charges were dropped at once, and, to Ulrich's astonishment, he himself was charged with felonious assault. Doctors at nearby Flower Hospital closed Washington's wounds with sixteen stitches, bandaged his head, and sent him back to his hotel.

While Washington was being treated, Ulrich's wife appeared at the police station and indignantly demanded her husband be released, accusing Washington of threatening her before her husband attacked him. "It is strange that a man cannot protect his wife and daughter from insult and keep out of jail, while the Negro who insulted them is free," she declared, then stormed out to collect fifteen hundred dollars for her husband's bail.

Two days after the attack, Washington appeared in court to press assault charges against Ulrich, offering to lower the charge from felonious assault to simple assault. Ulrich and his wife insisted Washington was guilty. Mrs. Ulrich testified that Washington had seen her in the vestibule earlier and said, "Hello, sweetheart," to her. Ulrich testified that when he asked Washington why he was there, he answered, "None of your damned business," then hit him in the jaw. Washington stumbled not because Ulrich had beaten him, he insisted, but because he was drunk.

Newspapers across the country carried accounts of the assault and the court proceedings; editorials strongly supported Washington's version of the story. Andrew Carnegie visited Washington at his New York hotel to offer encouragement, and even W. E. B. Du Bois and Monroe Trotter closed ranks. In an editorial in the Boston *Guardian,* Trotter said:

> Our opposition to Mr. Washington because of his propaganda and methods, even to his method of treating reputable Colored men who get into trouble, as he has now, is well known, but we do not desire to take any advantage of his present troubles. We want to fight men when standing up.

President Taft wrote a letter of encouragement; Theodore Roosevelt insisted Washington should defend his name against the "utterly wanton" attack. (During the presidential campaign next year, Wilson emphatically denied having sent Washington any letter of encouragement, as some Southerners accused him of doing.) Washington sent a telegram to his sons reporting, "Judges, lawyers and everybody most kind."

By the time the trial was held the following November, Ulrich and his legal advisors had turned up several inconsistencies in Washington's story. First and foremost, the letter Washington claimed directed him to the address on Sixty-third Street had been destroyed. Washington explained that it had been handwritten by Scott, no copy had been kept, and that he destroyed it after reading because it also contained confidential information about Tuskegee faculty members. For someone as organized and detail oriented as Washington, destroying letters of any kind was highly unusual, especially one that contained an unfamiliar name and address he needed and was in fact not sure he had right when the assault took place.

Moreover, D. C. Smith, who lived in New Jersey, had no memory of expecting a meeting with Washington on March 19, and no one living at the apartment building knew him. Also, when he was interviewed in the

hospital on the night of the attack, Washington made statements incon-
sistent with his later testimony. (The inconsistencies could be explained
by the fact that Washington had just had his head beaten in with a
heavy-handled walking stick. Smith's story was harder to track. There
was private speculation later that Washington may have been on his way
to visit a prospective donor who wished to remain anonymous and was
embarrassed to be meeting him in an admittedly run-down part of the
city on the edge of the Tenderloin District.)

Washington went to work on Ulrich as he did on his black opponents, hiring reporters and detectives to find out what they could about
him. Raising questions about Ulrich's truthfulness proved to be remarkably easy. First, he had been accused—but not convicted—of stealing a
prize Pomeranian from one of his kennel customers. Second, Mrs. Ulrich
was not Mrs. Ulrich. She was Mrs. Laura Page Alvarez, separated from her
husband, and the mother of a ten-year-old daughter. The real Mrs. Ulrich
lived in Orange, New Jersey, with children of her own. Reading newspaper accounts of the trial, she offered to testify on Washington's behalf with
the hope Ulrich would then be extradited to New Jersey and tried for
nonsupport. Washington's men also learned that Mrs. Alvarez's husband,
with a black companion, had previously attempted to kidnap their
daughter, which might help explain his rabid reaction to seeing
Washington at the door.

At the trial the two sides stood by their respective stories. After a five-
minute consultation, the three-judge panel voted two to one to acquit
Ulrich. The New York *Age* reported the courtroom audience was
"astounded" by the verdict and that evidence proving Washington had
been beaten was overwhelming. Beaming, Ulrich strode from the courtroom—and was arrested in the hall for extradition to New Jersey to stand
trial for deserting his wife and children.

Oswald Garrison Villard saw Washington's defeat as an opportunity to
invite him to join forces with the NAACP and resolve the differences that
had separated him from its leadership. Washington answered that the
good wishes he had received even from his enemies as a result of the New

York assault convinced him that "this business of having a divided race must cease." Villard confided that Washington wanted him "to help him bury the hatchet and bring about a cordial union of both factions on a mutually satisfactory basis." Villard also suggested the NAACP pass a resolution in support of Washington. After much discussion and talking between the two camps, Washington said he would welcome a resolution, and Villard hammered one together that eventually passed. By the time it met with everyone's approval, however, its language was tepid and noncommittal, more a comment on the event than praise for its victim:

> Resolved that we put on record our profound regret at the recent assault on Dr. Booker T. Washington in New York City in which the Association finds renewed evidence of racial discrimination and increased necessity for the awakening of the public conscience.

The Atlanta *Constitution,* which had generally supported Washington over the years, suggested in an editorial that Washington was simply trying to do too much. "He goes about all over the country, flitting here and there like a butterfly, but what has he accomplished for the negro schools, except to raise money, some of which goes to the schools, and some does not?" By staying closer to Tuskegee, the editorial continued, Washington "will certainly not be found in New York, in the night time, 'hunting keyholes,' and attending police courts, with himself on the criminal side of the docket."

Washington's standing among his friends, his peers, his Northern donors, and the Tuskegee community at large was not compromised by the New York court case. But there were telltale changes that acknowledged something had happened. The Hotel Manhattan, where Washington had been a guest the night of the assault and where he had stayed many times, informed him he could no longer be accommodated. At least one Tuskegee trustee harbored continuing doubts about Washington's reasons for being at 11½ Sixty-third Street late on a Sunday night—reasons Washington never fully or clearly articulated to anyone. Charles F. Dole, a Congregational minister whose son later built the great pineapple fortune in Hawaii, continued to press Washington and others for specifics. Why would Washington destroy the letter from Emmett

Scott before locating the address? Why would Smith have met anyone on a Sunday night at a friend's apartment instead of in his own home or office? Under the circumstances, why didn't Washington call ahead on the telephone?

Reflecting on a meeting with Washington to discuss his concerns, Dole said in a letter to Seth Low, chairman of the Tuskegee board of trust, "It seemed to me that he was evasive rather than straightforward.... It puzzles me why an innocent man, who has good ground on which to stand, should decline himself, or be advised by any true friends to decline to tell his story just as it was."

The story gradually disappeared from the public stage. To those who remained dissatisfied with Washington's explanation, he might have repeated one of his favorite quotations from Abraham Lincoln:

If I were to try to read, much less answer, all the attacks made on me, this shop might as well be closed for other business.... If the end brings me out all right, what is said against me won't amount to anything. If the end brings me out wrong, ten angels swearing I was right would make no difference.

CHAPTER FOURTEEN

OUR OWN
HEAVEN

T hroughout the Taft Administration, Washington had direct access to
the president and saw him more or less regularly. The most important difference between his relationship with Taft and the one with
Roosevelt was that Roosevelt had taken his advice seriously and valued
his friendship, while Taft did neither. Roosevelt seemed to genuinely
respect Washington, while Taft seemed interested only in getting the
black vote. Wilson's election in 1912 diminished Washington's influence
even more. As the Reconstruction era faded further into history, the black
vote became more and more marginalized. Post-Reconstruction laws
steadily made it harder for blacks to vote or hold public office. By the time
Wilson was elected, he didn't have to worry about the black vote very
much because as a group, blacks had very little influence. After his inauguration, President Wilson corresponded with Washington only twice.

As always, no matter how much money Washington brought in, Tuskegee's
financial condition remained precarious. The larger the campus and enrollment, the more money they required, and the thinner the margin for error.

Of the many proposals the Tuskegee finance committee had to pass judgment upon, Professor Carver's research laboratory continued to be one of the most drawn out. From the time the agriculture department was reorganized in October 1910, well into the following year, Washington and the administration struggled with the idea of spending scarce resources on what seemed to some of them a lavish and unnecessary facility. Carver continued to insist that he had been promised the lab as a condition of accepting the reorganization and that questions about it now amounted to reneging on a promise.

Carver's repeated threats to resign may have lost some of their value as bargaining chips by then, but one point that remained potent was that, in the long term, his laboratory could save the school money. The committee, Carver reasoned, should look at his laboratory as more than keeping a promise and giving him his due. It was also an investment in self-sufficiency. He used his lab to inspect shipments of grain to the school, test the purity of dairy products and canned goods made by the students, and perform soil analyses on farmland to advise farmers what to grow and how best to prepare the soil.

A new laboratory would make it possible for Carver to make more detailed and specific recommendations to farmers. It would also make all his other work easier and more accurate. He shared Washington's vision for making the school self-sufficient in food and in fertilizer, both of which were expensive and used in large quantities. He insisted that new testing equipment would benefit the whole institution and not just himself.

At the same time Booker T. Washington was recovering from his New York beating, Carver was renewing an old interest in the properties and composition of paint. His experience with Alva Kirkpatrick and the proposed Montgomery Paint & Dry Color Works had come to nothing. But in the spring of 1911, Carver began working with his chemistry students on processing local clays into whitewash, paint, and wood stain.

After reviewing Carver's progress, Washington suggested he set up an exhibit of products at the Tuskegee post office. Carver was delighted because he felt producing colors from local materials would make them cheap enough for poor farmers to afford. "When I began this work," he explained, "I had in mind primarily the rural school-teacher and farmer how easily, effectively and inexpensively" they could decorate and protect schoolhouses, churches, homes, barns, and fences.

Carver tried out his products on buildings at Tuskegee. Several students painted their dormitory rooms with his color wash, and the result impressed everyone who saw it. Within a year the school was using Carver's paint for applications all over campus instead of buying it from outside. A white Episcopal congregation in town ordered Carver's stain for the interior woodwork in their new church. They were elated with the result, and Carver cheerfully pointed out that it had cost the church one-tenth the price of commercially available stain. That year Carver devoted one of his popular Experiment Station Bulletins to instructions for making paint and whitewash easily from native clays.

Continuing his experiments on food, Carver concluded that three crops in particular showed great promise for Southern farmers because they were inexpensive to grow, thrived under local weather and soil conditions, were nutritious and filling, and could be prepared in a number of different ways: cowpeas, sweet potatoes, and peanuts. These three also stored easily for months, solving another chronic problem for poor farmers, which was how to feed themselves in the winter without much store-bought food.

Carver set up a demonstration of the peanut's potential. Under his direction, a class of senior Tuskegee girls prepared a complete meal for Washington from peanuts, including the main dish and beverage. Washington was impressed and delighted. Carver also presented Washington with samples of meat that had been pickled months before, which Washington pronounced excellent and ordered that the school stop buying canned meat since obviously Carver could supply it.

Carver got an unexpected benefit from his success at preserving meat. Washington assigned George Bridgeforth to help Carver with the slaughtering, butchering, and pickling of hogs under Carver's direction. Predictably, Bridgeforth resisted Washington's directive, prompting Washington to reply somewhat wearily, "The records in my office show that I spend more time in dealing with your Department and trying to get orders carried out…than I do with all the other departments combined."

Later on, Carver prepared a complete week's worth of recipes for the dining hall using only foods the agriculture department could supply cheaply and in quantity. The same foods appeared almost every day, but the recipes were varied to keep students from getting tired of them. Cowpeas were served plain, as pea soup, peas with pork roast, Granada stew (peas, white potatoes, sweet potatoes, and cabbage), hopping John (a traditional Southern combination of rice and cowpeas), and boiled peas with bacon. True to form, Carver's recipes were simple, inexpensive, wasted nothing, and tasted delicious.

Another line of products Carver was interested in was an offshoot of his interest in paint and pigments. Working with local clay, he discovered he could easily make a fine grade of face powder or talcum powder from it. At one time he and Emmett Scott discussed the possibility of forming a company to manufacture and sell toiletries and cosmetics, but, like Carver's abortive attempt with the Montgomery Paint and Dry Color Company, nothing ever came of it.

Other experiments were equally short lived, such as Carver's demonstration that Tuskegee girls could enjoy "lucrative employment" by making and selling some of the fifty-three products he had developed using discarded chicken feathers from the Tuskegee poultry yard. At the time, he pronounced it "the most valuable and astonishing" experimental exhibit he ever produced.

His successes notwithstanding, Carver continued his administrative skirmishing. In order to save money, the Executive Council voted to furlough teachers during the summer of 1914 on a rotating basis for one month each. Carver was finishing his eighteenth year at Tuskegee and was incensed at the idea he would be without a job even for a month.

On May 26, Carver sent Washington a curt note reminding the principal that he had saved the school almost four hundred dollars the previous summer "by manufacturing things it would have had to pay a much higher price for." He also considered it "too much trouble" to find work elsewhere for one month. However, "if the school has reached the point where it cannot pay me and doesn't need my services any more, I shall abide by that decision and seek employment elsewhere." Eight days later he impatiently prodded Warren Logan to find out what Washington was going to do.

Washington answered him at last on June 6, patiently explaining the circumstances surrounding Carver's involuntary vacation: "In the interest of economy, it becomes necessary, from year to year, for us to lay off certain teachers for certain months, and I do not see how you can complain about losing one month within a period of 18 years." He also told Carver the summer school director expected to have some work for Carver during the month he would be off.

As had been the case so often, at the same time Carver was enmeshed in disagreements with Washington, Bridgeforth, and other Tuskegee faculty and staff, he was working with genuine dedication on the school's behalf. While he was feuding with Washington about his summer layoff, he was busy completing a detailed analysis of the food pantry and refrigerator in the dining hall for John Washington. Among his recommendations were to mend torn screens because "the whole place swarmed with flies," and to patch some large rat holes in the refrigerator that let in both rats and mice.

Carver also continued to charm his students with his innovative lectures. He complained often to Washington and others about having to teach, saying he preferred research to teaching. But his students universally agreed that he was an exceptionally gifted teacher who could literally mesmerize classroom audiences with his presentations of botany lessons, soil experiments, and chemical analysis. Carver bristled at being forced to teach in the academic department. There he had to teach under someone else's oversight in a building managed by another department, while in the agriculture department he was much more on his own, even during the years he was officially under Bridgeforth's direction.

He adored his students, and they returned the compliment; but the politics of Tuskegee soured him, encouraging him to retreat to his laboratory where there were no committees, no memos to write, no turf wars to fight, and Carver was free to do whatever he wanted.

Carver carried on extensive correspondence with a number of students after they graduated or left school for some other reason—often because their money ran out. Students asked him for advice, thanked him for preparing them so well for their new jobs, and shared their triumphs, fears, and failures with him to an extent that showed they deeply admired and appreciated him. The tone of the letters was more than one of pupil to teacher; it was closer to that between a master and an admiring apprentice.

Many of them referred to the natural way he combined science and faith. In one explanation of the relationship, Carver said:

> To me nature in its varied forms are the little windows through which God permits me to commune with him, and to see much of his glory, by simply lifting the curtain, and looking in. I love to think of nature as wireless telegraph stations through which God speaks to us every day, every hour, and every moment of our lives.

The Bible class Carver's office boy had started in 1906, and which Carver began teaching soon after, had become a campus institution by 1915. Attendance regularly topped 150 every Sunday night. The caustic attitude that characterized his working relationship with Washington completely disappeared in the classroom or chapel when his focus was on his students. He considered them his children and even addressed them that way sometimes in his letters; many of them in turn began their letters to him, "Dear Father."

One of Carver's Bible students, Alvin D. Smith, later recalled that for all the teaching, speaking, and experimental work Carver did, it was in his Bible class teaching "that he gave the key to all that he had been able to do. Busy as he was with duties in his laboratory and botany curricular classes, he did not have to add a Bible class. But knowing the backgrounds from which students of the rural South, Africa, and other lands came, he was anxious that they have this key, without which they could not unlock the kingdom of good things they desired, or that they deserved, regardless of race, color, or creed." By taking Carver's Bible lessons to heart, Smith said, "one is assured good out of every situation."

At the beginning of each school year, one of the students made an announcement in the dining hall after Sunday supper that Professor Carver's Bible class would meet in the assembly room of the Carnegie Library. That first class always started late because returning students came down front to greet Carver and exchange a few words about their experiences over the summer.

As a new student, Alvin Smith noticed several odd things his first night in Carver's Bible class. The professor's appearance was striking. His coat and pants were mismatched and wrinkled. He only buttoned the top button on his coat, leaving the rest to splay open, and in his lapel was a large red poppy blossom. Overhearing him speaking with students before class began, Smith also noticed Carver's high voice—like a boy's, though richly articulate and expressive. There was a warmth about his presence, particularly his smile, that drew students to him.

Though Carver was about to begin a Bible class, he did not have a Bible nearby. In fact, none of the students in the room had a Bible. Bracing himself for the accustomed warnings about the evil of sin and damnation of the unrepentant, Smith was greeted instead with words of comfort. When all the boys were seated (Carver's class was only for boys), Carver stood at the front of the classroom and began.

> Your faces are beaming with happiness tonight. Your lives will be filled with happiness if you contact thy Creator and keep tuned in with him.
>
> Each of you came to Tuskegee to learn a trade, to study the academic courses and graduate and then go out into the world. You are enthusiastic about that now, but if you do not know how to turn the key to the storehouse of happiness—how to contact and keep tuned in with our Creator—you are in for many unhappy situations.
>
> The advice of Solomon can come in handy here. With all thy getting, get understanding—understanding that our Creator is Law and he will give us the happiness our hearts desire, if we follow his Laws.

The hundred and fifty students sat silent and entranced. The short class seemed to be over in a heartbeat, leaving the students hungry for more.

Between one Sunday night and the next, students thought of questions for Carver and made a game of trying to stump him. After several weeks of hearing about the Creator, several students asked him to explain exactly who and what the Creator was. "He is Spirit," Carver answered without hesitation and quoted John 4:24 from memory:

> "God is a Spirit, and they that worship him must worship him in spirit and in truth." To refer to him as God or to call him our Creator is one and the same.
>
> Our Creator, being Spirit, is Principle—Law—and by keeping his laws, we get from him good, for he is good. The things we go to our Creator for must be good things; he has nothing else to give us and through us for the benefit of mankind—regardless of race—except good. Persons who attempt to contact him with a selfish and mean motive in mind are defeated before they start and are driven from the temple to failure.

A student asked that if God were Spirit, did that mean they would never be able to see him? Carver touched the flower in his lapel. "When you look at this flower, you see thy Creator. Students at Tuskegee who are studying to be electricians are not able to see electricity, but when they make the proper contact—fulfill the laws of their trade—a bulb lights the way, not only for them, but for all of us."

Carver looked straight at the boy who had asked the question. "As I look at you, I see our Creator just itching for you to contact him." A chuckle rippled through the room; Carver and the boy both joined in.

At another session a student wanted to know, if the Creator was a spirit who could be seen in flowers and even in each of them as Carver had told them, then how could they contact him?

"The promise is that he who prayeth in secret is awarded openly," Carver explained. "Pray in silence. Ask him for guidance. Keep your thoughts pure. Forget yourself. Know that you are an instrument through which your Creator wishes to pour out some blessing for others. Be not overanxious. Keep your mind on him after you have come out of your secret contact prayer, while alone. See the good in all things. See the good in your classmates, in your instructors, in your parents, in both colored and white people. The moment you fail to see the good in any situation which is seemingly bad—that moment you are out of contact. If, in any situation you find yourself, your mind strays from the fact that he—the Good—is in all things, wrestle with yourself and get back on the track. It behooves us to stay in contact with him, because we know not the minute, hour, day, or year when he is ready to reveal to us a wonder of his universe.

"Having good wishes for others, doing good deeds for others, listening to good singing and instrumental music, studying to master some trade, saying words of cheer, and above all, doing to others as you wish to be done by all—all are a part of how you contact and keep in tune with thy Creator."

Carver's concern for his students made him an unusually perceptive and capable teacher. His skill and experience were valuable benefits; but everything he did in class, in the laboratory, or in the field embraced the importance of faith over all else. His religious conviction, coupled with his interest in the personal well-being of the boys and girls he instructed, nurtured an interest in introducing all his young charges to their Creator. Not only in Bible class but in the chemistry laboratory, the dairy barn, or in a field of experimental peanuts, Carver made a point of drawing attention to God's goodness and his handiwork in nature.

Washington was a far more private man than Carver in discussing his personal thoughts and feelings. In their various exchanges through the years, Carver was invariably the more emotional and subjective of the two, while Washington was more analytical and businesslike. Based on his actions, however, Washington clearly shared Carver's fundamental belief that everything God did was for good, and that there was good even in what seemed to be the worst possible situation.

In *Up from Slavery*, Washington wrote, "I would permit no man, no matter what his colour might be, to narrow and degrade my soul by making me hate him." He would surely have agreed with Carver's advice to his Bible class:

We make our own hell or heaven. We bring upon ourselves little moments of hell when we think and act a little meanly toward a fellow student or a fellow American, black or white. When our thoughts—which bring actions—are filled with hate against anyone, Negro or white, we are in a living hell. That is as real as hell will ever be.

Booker T. Washington and George Washington Carver had spent almost twenty years sparring over Carver's position, treatment, and responsibilities. Though he advised his Bible class to find the good in everything, he himself found little good in the broken promises and oppressive criticism Washington sent his way.

In Carver's mind, he was not "done well" at all by Washington and the seemingly endless procession of committees that interfered with his work: insisting he make more and better efforts for the good of the school and never giving him enough resources with which to do it. He had had respect at Iowa State and never really came to terms with the lack of deference he felt at Tuskegee.

Professor Carver was certainly not singled out for mistreatment. It was just Washington's way. Many teachers withstood the endless criticism without complaining, but there were others who strained against Washington's tight control and considered him overbearing and unfair. Responding to the principal's remarks, one physics teacher said, "If my work is not satisfactory I think there are more rational methods of informing me than such a lewd one as you used last evening. It is just such remarks as those referred to which cause many of your instructors to do only what they are 'hired' to do. You will never get the best work from your teachers until they find that you are at least in sympathy with and leave no encouraging word for whatever they do to help build up your institution."

On another occasion, a teacher who had spent nine years at Tuskegee wrote to Washington, "Your statement with regard to my not being in sympathy with any policy which tends to help the school in any way, I think both unjust and unfounded. I cannot think that you believe so." Her experience, she thought, had been ignored in the matter "now that I do not bow down and fawn where I do not care to."

Washington was a relentless taskmaster who criticized faults in his faculty and students far more often than he complimented their successes. But as hard as he pushed them, he pushed himself even harder. Washington's long hours and extensive travel began taking a toll on him.

The single-mindedness that breathed life into Tuskegee year after year kept Washington from taking regular vacations, spending time with his family, or cultivating social friendships. Everything he did was with the promotion and survival of Tuskegee in mind.

Into his middle fifties, Washington kept up his furious pace almost without stopping. His health remained reasonably good with the exception of indigestion, which bothered him more and more frequently, especially when he traveled. By the time of Tuskegee's thirty-fourth anniversary on July 4, 1915, Washington was ordering stomach pills by hundreds at a time.

Most mornings, Washington rose early and went for a walk or horseback ride alone around the campus. Whether in Alabama or at his summer home in New York, he scheduled a full day of speaking engagements and appointments even if he had ridden all night on the train the night before. Sometimes he would finish a speech, board a train, and ride half the day or night to reach his next engagement just in time to mount the podium.

Some time in his middle years, Washington developed kidney stones. They combined with the indigestion from time to time to make traveling an unpredictably painful ordeal. Still he kept up the pace.

In 1914, as Professor Carver reminded him so forcefully, Washington was forced to pare down expenses to the point of furloughing teachers in the summer. The principal had to keep up his visits to Tuskegee's present and prospective benefactors. And he stood alone as the spokesman and symbol of the black man who preached reconciliation and patience in the drive for economic and legal equality with the white man. If he should falter, there was no one standing in the wings to take his place.

Washington well knew there were many opponents eager to see him fall. A correspondent named J. C. Waters spoke for many of them when he wrote to the editor of the *New York Times:*

The most prominent Negro in the world today, he is also the most pathetic figure in our national life. Slowly but surely the clouds of a race's indignation are gathering about Booker Washington's head and he may well wish to be dead before the storm breaks. For I give it as my most solemn belief that the day will come when Booker Washington's name will be cursed wherever an American Negro sets his foot, and the best that his most sanguine friends can hope for is that posterity will at least temper its judgment of him by conceding that he really and truly believed that the ends justified the means.

What this disgruntled writer could not have known is that Washington, as he had for many years, continued to work actively behind the scenes supplying money, information, and moral support to slow the spread of segregation. It was impossible to take this action publicly because it would cost him the access he alone enjoyed to the white political power structure. Moreover, it would also cost him the financial support of many of his Northern friends. Even though a significant number of them agreed privately with him that the trend toward segregation must be reversed, they would not feel able to support the position directly and publicly for fear of the reaction by their families, friends, associates, clients, and stockholders.

By 1915, Washington's most effective work in opposing segregation was strictly behind the scenes. This kept his lines of communication open to whites but gave his opponents ample ammunition against him for apparently standing on the sidelines. A vivid example had taken place two years earlier in South Carolina when the editor of *Progressive Farmer* magazine, Clarence H. Poe, instigated a plan to segregate farmland to the same extent urban residential and business areas were separated. His plan was to promote state legislation in several states to pass, in his words, "a simple law which will say that whenever the greater part of the land acreage in any given district…is owned by one race, a majority of the voters in such a district may say (if they wish) that in future no land shall be sold to a person of a different race."

This plan would keep farmland from black owners. Poe insisted his plan would promote harmony between the races by limiting contact between them; it would also attract white immigrants to farm and eventually own the land instead.

Gilbert T. Stephenson, a Winston-Salem lawyer, invited Washington to supply a response to this proposal. Washington wrote Stephenson a long, well-reasoned, eloquent letter underscoring the fact that there was "no sentiment among the substantial white landowners in this section of the South in favor of such a proposition." On the contrary, with all the work to be done on a farm and blacks eager to do it, the "average Southern white man, as perhaps you know, likes to have just as many black people in 'calling distance' as possible."

Washington went on to make a number of other related points, many of which Stephenson included in his response to Poe's ominous proposition. He also wrote to a friend that "the time has come in all these matters when we have got to take a position and stand by it. We cannot, in my opinion, without great loss to the cause, attempt to please everybody or attempt to straddle."

Washington, however, got no credit in the public forum for his strong, unwavering opposition to Poe (whose suggestion was eventually ruled illegal by the South Carolina Supreme Court). Oswald Garrison Villard, organizer of the NAACP, wrote a letter to the nephew of William J. Baldwin Jr., president of the Tuskegee board of trust, comparing Washington to Nero

> ...fiddling while Rome burns. One right after another is being taken away from the colored people, one injustice after another being perpetrated, and Booker Washington is silent. There has developed in North Carolina the greatest menace yet, a movement under the leadership of Clarence Poe, which will undoubtedly result in legislation, segregating the Negro on the farm lands, thus giving the lie to Washington's advice to his people that if they will only be good and buy land they will be let alone and will flourish.

The race debate entered a new medium in 1915 with the release of *The Birth of a Nation,* a motion picture based on a white supremacist novel,

The Clansman. In a time when films often lasted no more than ten or fifteen minutes, this one ran an unheard-of three hours. Moreover, it was filled with innovative techniques such as close-ups, intercutting between one story and another, dramatic lighting, and sophisticated editing that greatly enhanced its emotional impact. Its producer, D. W. Griffith, had begun his career working for Thomas Edison and had used a professional pseudonym because he was so ashamed of being associated with an unsavory profession like the "flickers." Now he had spent the then incredible sum of $125,000 on a film that revolutionized the industry.

Unfortunately, *The Birth of a Nation* also pictured Negroes as little more than savages.

The author of *The Clansman,* Thomas Dixon Jr., wrote a scathing article in the *Saturday Evening Post* accusing Booker T. Washington of prodding black people to compete with whites, which would bring on a race war that would annihilate the Negro race. He brashly offered Washington ten thousand dollars to give "complete and satisfactory proof" that he was opposed to social equality for blacks and that his school was "opposed to the amalgamation of the races."

Washington declined to answer, saying any response from him would only give the film more exposure.

William Monroe Trotter organized a boycott of Boston theaters showing *The Birth of a Nation* when it opened there in April and was soon arrested. Washington was speaking in Louisiana at the time, and his colleagues telegraphed him there to ask whether they should support the boycott. Again he replied that "any direct opposition will result in further advertisement of the play." The next day, however, Washington wrote that he thought an appeal should be made to Griffith and Dixon to change the film and portray the black characters in a more favorable light and that he hoped the boycott would be successful. Washington often brought up the fact that segregation did not relieve racial tension; it intensified it. This he also mentioned in his wire, then closed on a hopeful note: "Particularly unfortunate to have this play at present time when we were entering upon era of good racial feeling throughout the country such as we have not experienced lately."

At various times Washington considered making a motion picture of his own. There had been short films about Tuskegee produced in 1910 and 1913, but neither was widely distributed or financially successful. With the unprecedented popularity of *The Birth of a Nation*, the motion picture business suddenly recognized the public's intense interest in the race issue. Producers flooded Washington and Emmett Scott with requests to make a film based on Washington's bestselling book *Up from Slavery*. Washington saw only too clearly the power of film to sway public opinion, but he was worried that no matter what the producers and screenwriters told him, the finished piece would not accurately depict his book.

For evidence he pointed to a prologue for *The Birth of a Nation*, filmed with students from Hampton Institute, that had been added to the finished film to counterbalance the stark racial stereotypes portrayed in the picture. While it helped somewhat when it was shown, the film was often run with the prologue deleted. "The moving picture people are not keeping faith with Hampton," Washington confided in a letter.

As early as 1911, Washington's friends began to express private concerns about his health even though he appeared hale in public. Just before his fateful trip to New York in 1911, Washington had visited a sanitarium in Battle Creek, Michigan, run by the wealthy and eccentric Kellogg family. The Kelloggs, who made their fortunes first in grain and then by virtually inventing breakfast cereal, were contributors to Tuskegee. Washington went there for a few days to see if they could help his indigestion. Though they found no cure, the relaxation was a relief to him. His wife conspired with the Kelloggs to have one of their male nurses installed for six months in the Washington home. At the end of that time, Washington reported he was "a new man, and not only a new man, but I knew more about living and enjoying life than I had ever known before."

Over the next several years, Washington's friends and benefactors became more creative and more insistent in their requests for him to join them on fishing and hunting trips, camping excursions, and day sailing on their yachts. Washington accepted many of their invitations but seldom missed an opportunity to meet with any possible benefactor. But by the summer of 1915, Washington's indigestion had grown worse and more frequent. He tried various remedies including papaya pills and radium water. Some of them seemed to give short-term relief, but his discomfort continued.

At the 1915 meeting of the National Negro Business League, Washington was too sick to hide the fact any longer. Soon after, he wrote to George E. Vincent, president of the University of Minnesota, asking for a letter of introduction to Drs. William and Charles Mayo. Their father, William, had helped found St. Mary's Hospital in Rochester, where the brothers in turn established a clinic that was already developing an international reputation for the quality of its care. Vincent quickly supplied the letter, but Washington put off the trip insisting he had too much to do.

On October 25, Washington arrived in New Haven, Connecticut, to begin a series of speeches and meetings at Yale and in New York. Emmett Scott noted that Washington was "greatly improved in every way," and suggested to another of Washington's doctors, George C. Hall, that postponing his Mayo Clinic visit had been a wise move, as it allowed him to keep his busy schedule of meetings.

On the same day Scott wrote Dr. Hall, however, Hall wrote to Washington's friend and benefactor Julius Rosenwald that Washington must be relieved of all work for six months to a year. Dr. Hall recounted a fifteen-day trip with Washington when he had three "severe attacks of kidney trouble" and was "taking a chance" every time he exerted himself physically or mentally. He also warned that Washington's blood pressure was "extremely high."

In his speech at Woosley Hall on the Yale campus before the American Missionary Association and the National Council of Congregational Churches, Washington praised their work on behalf of Negroes. Later he spoke at the African Methodist Episcopal Zion Church in New Haven.

A man who had heard both addresses shared his reaction to them with Washington:

Eloquent as your address was at Woosley Hall I enjoyed your heart to heart talk at Zion Church more. Why? Because you were among you own people and you could appeal direct to them in a confidential manner better than you could in a great meeting.

Washington had encouraged the church audience to take advantage of the opportunities for higher education that literally surrounded them in New Haven. Yale was there and Harvard was in Cambridge, another Boston suburb, only a few minutes away by rail. Five thousand black people lived in the area, but only two local blacks were enrolled at Yale.

Washington promised Robert Russa Moton, a Hampton graduate and head of the Negro Organization Society of Virginia in Petersburg, that he would give a speech in Petersburg on November 5 between his appearances in New Haven. Then he planned to go back to Tuskegee to meet Julius Rosenwald, who was visiting the campus with friends from Chicago, and to the inauguration of a new president of Fisk University in Nashville. His wife telegraphed her advice that he should stay in New York and rest. Washington tried to cancel his appearance in Petersburg without admitting he was ill and exhausted, saying he had to speak in North Dakota (from where he could reach the Mayo Clinic with a minimum of publicity). Moton insisted Washington keep his promise to come. On November 4, Washington finally realized he was too weak to keep either commitment.

While he was in New York, Washington's doctors called an abdominal specialist for consultation. Dr. Walter A. Bastedo was a teacher of pharmacology at Columbia Medical School and practiced at St. Luke's Hospital in New York. His examination confirmed that Washington had "pretty serious kidney trouble" and a blood pressure reading of 215. The doctors' recommendation, reported confidentially by one of the Tuskegee trustees, was that the school should expect "an almost complete cessation of his trips about the country and of public addresses." In perhaps a more telling message, Washington wired his wife to come to New York at once. Admitted to the hospital, he also sent for a current statement on his personal finances. His business agent promptly wired back, "Macon County Bank eight thousand two hundred thirty two. Securities thirty four hundred. Property value forty thousand."

Continuing a habit formed over more than thirty years, Washington fired off a steady stream of telegrams from his bed at St. Luke's on everything from substitutes for his speaking appointments to keeping his lawn picked up.

On November 10, five days after Washington was admitted to the hospital in New York, the *Tribune* reported he was "suffering from a nervous breakdown." Dr. Bastedo reported Washington "has been suffering from severe headaches for more than a month." (This was the first public mention of headaches and may have been intended to shield the truth. There was no evidence of any permanent injury resulting from his 1911 assault.)

Bastedo continued his interview, revealing details of Washington's condition far beyond what the patient and his trustees doubtless would have wished. Washington was "completely worn out," "aging rapidly," had "noticeable hardening of the arteries," and was "extremely nervous."

All those observations, thoughtlessly revealed as they were, were nothing compared with the bombshell that followed: "Racial characteristics are, I think, in part responsible for Dr. Washington's breakdown." Dr. Bastedo could have meant high blood pressure or some other symptom Washington had that was more likely to occur in blacks. Bastedo was Canadian; what he might not have known was that "racial characteristics" was often code for "a history of syphilis."

To add fuel to the speculative fire, Dr. Bastedo consulted with Dr. Rufus Cole, head of the Rockefeller Institute Hospital, on Washington's case. It would be routine to consult with such an experienced and highly regarded physician when treating someone as prominent as Booker T. Washington. Cole was a logical choice; but he also happened to be a recognized authority and textbook author on gonococcus infections.

Trustees and others called for Bastedo to be relieved of his duties on the spot for breaching Washington's privacy. Others who had treated Washington insisted there were no signs whatever of syphilis. Bastedo retreated from the public spotlight, though he later clarified his diagnosis without mentioning syphilis.

By the time Margaret Washington arrived at St. Luke's, it was clear her husband was dying. He insisted on returning to Tuskegee immediately, even though doctors warned him he would never survive the day and a half rail journey. "I was born in the South," Washington replied, "I have lived in the South, and I expect to die and be buried in the South." To the doctors' astonishment, Washington got out of bed that afternoon, dressed, and, leaning heavily on his wife's arm, made his way to Pennsylvania Station and boarded his coach, ignoring the wheelchair waiting at the curb.

From Charlotte, North Carolina, Margaret Washington wired Emmett Scott: "Send ambulance to Chechaw tonight nine o'clock with plenty of blankets and sheets. Also send two automobiles. Wish you, Booker [Washington's son] and J. H. Washington meet train." When the gleaming Southern Railway coach pulled into Chechaw that night, the party was waiting anxiously. The little spur station on the main line was the same one Washington had arrived at that summer in 1881 expecting a school but finding only a vision for a school. He had spent his life bringing shape to that vision; and in doing so he had left Alabama for the great industrial cities of the North and the capitals of Europe hundreds of times from this same platform. He was coming home for the last time.

He recognized his son Booker as he helped lift his father off the train. "How is Booker?" he asked, meaning his grandson and second namesake. Bundled into the vehicles, the group slowly made its way the five miles to the campus. By the time they reached the house, Washington had drifted into unconsciousness. At home in the South and at peace, he died the next morning, November 14, 1915.

Letters and telegrams poured into Tuskegee from around the world. Typical of the thousands was one from a friend of Washington's who was "shocked—overwhelmed with sorrow."

"There is the feeling of personal loss," reported the Montgomery *Advertiser*. "Nobody is hiding his tears. Nobody is free from gloom."

Washington's body lay in state for a day in the Tuskegee chapel, drawing one of the largest crowds in the school's history. Eight thousand people came for the funeral, though only three thousand could squeeze inside. As described by a Tuskegee graduate named Isaac Fisher, the Episcopal funeral service was a simple one:

No labored eulogies; no boastings of his great work; no gorgeous trappings of horses; no streaming banners; no mysterious ceremonies of lodges—just the usual line of teachers, trustees, graduates, students and visitors which so often marched to the chapel just as it did Wednesday, and the simple and impressive—impressive because simple—service for the dead, said for the humblest, and so often for those who die, in all walks of life.

Flags at every school in the District of Columbia flew at half mast during the funeral, and teachers spent the time telling their classes about Washington's life and work.

As he had requested, Washington was buried on the Tuskegee campus with only his name and years of birth and death on his gravestone.

Throughout nineteen sometimes stormy years, George Washington Carver had always gone out of his way to compliment Washington personally for his work and achievements on behalf of their race. Carver was devastated by Washington's death and asked to be relieved temporarily of his teaching assignments. Emmett Scott, as acting principal, quickly granted Carver's request, reassigning him to monitor students in study hall while continuing with his laboratory research.

The school organized a memorial fund to accept gifts in Washington's honor. Carver gave a thousand dollars—a year's salary—and energetically promoted the fund to students in his classes and on his trips away from campus. On the following February 25, he wrote to Emmett Scott from Denmark, South Carolina, where he was visiting the Voorhees Industrial School. Scott had thanked Carver for his generous support of the fund and acknowledged what a sacrifice it must have been for him to give such a large amount.

"True it is," Carver replied, "it was a sacrifice in one way but a blessed privilege in another.

"I am sure Mr. Washington never knew how much I loved him, and the cause for which he gave his life."

CHAPTER FIFTEEN

SCIENCE SHALL MAKE YOU FREE

The *New York Times,* which had reported Washington's illness "not serious" on November 10, carried a page 1 account of his death five days later. Former President Roosevelt described him as "one of the most distinguished citizens of the United States." Julius Rosenwald, president of Sears, Roebuck & Company and a generous supporter of Tuskegee, said of him, "By emphasizing the dignity of labor he has rendered a great service not only to his own race but to the white race as well.... The injustices he was made to suffer never embittered him. Those who knew him best were proudest of his friendship. His life enriched not only this country but the entire world."

Clearly no one could literally pick up where Washington left off; he was a vanguard, an innovator of ideas and positions. Others could only hope to follow him as closely as possible.

Three men who had been associated with Washington and Tuskegee almost from the beginning began the search for a new Tuskegee president. Warren Logan, Emmett Scott, and John H. Washington settled on Robert Russa Moton of Hampton Institute, who had known Washington for years and served as an officer of the National Negro Business League as Washington's successor. Moton was inaugurated on May 25, 1916.

Moton was a capable and visionary leader, but as any replacement inevitably would, he lacked Washington's personal charisma and sense of drive. Tuskegee certainly lost a measure of public exposure that had come through its association with Washington. At the same time, though, the school benefited from Moton's relatively easygoing personality. Moton set about to mend fences with faculty members who had felt battered and bruised by Washington's hard-charging and ever-demanding ways. And one of his first orders of business was to shore up the relationship between Tuskegee and George Washington Carver.

If Moton lacked Washington's drive, vision, and relentless pursuit of perfection, he was also more accommodating, particularly in Carver's case. Perhaps to test the waters, Carver informed Moton that he did not think he would be able to teach botany at the beginning of the next school year. Washington would have patiently but firmly called on Carver to do the job required of him, pulling his fair share of the load for the good of the school and its goals. Moton's reply underscored the difference in his approach.

Beginning with the salutation, "My dear Professor Carver" (no one in official correspondence had ever addressed him as either "dear" or "Professor"), Moton answered, "I wish you would withhold your definite decision until I have a chance to talk with you.... I need not tell you that it will be impossible to get anybody to teach this subject as you have done, and I do not like to think of the students losing the inspiration and help that would come by your teaching."

Though he never asked for it, Moton also gave Carver the first raise he had ever received at Tuskegee. At the beginning of the school year in the fall of 1915, Carver earned the same one thousand dollars per year that had been his starting salary in 1896.

Carver appreciated the increase, but not because he needed more money. On the contrary, he sometimes stashed paychecks in his desk drawer and left them there for months until someone from the business office called to ask him to cash them so they could reconcile their books. His assistants would find checks in his lab coat pockets, worn and crumpled by all the other items that had come and gone from the same pocket over several weeks.

What pleased him about his raise far more than having more money to spend was that it was an indication the Tuskegee administration was paying more attention to him and recognizing his value. He had felt underappreciated his whole career there. At Iowa he had been a celebrity; at Tuskegee he too often felt like a beleaguered schoolteacher among a hundred others. Washington hired Carver because he saw him as the best and most highly qualified black to head the agriculture department, yet always saw him as a subordinate. When Moton arrived at Tuskegee, Carver was the most popular professor on campus and was beginning to gain notoriety outside the South and outside the field of agricultural research. Moton knew Carver's value to the school, and he planned to protect this invaluable asset.

Booker T. Washington had freely acknowledged Carver's abilities in his 1911 book *My Larger Education*. Though he had scarcely mentioned Carver in any of his previous books, including *Up from Slavery,* he went out of his way to praise him personally and professionally. This was in spite of the fact that he was writing the manuscript during the time his special committee was investigating Carver's mismanagement of the poultry yard and recommending he be demoted.

The extended passage about Carver from *My Larger Education* was reprinted in 1913 in the Iowa State *Alumnus* under the title "Work of Gifted Negro Teacher Praised by Dr. Washington." The same extract also appeared that year in the *Christian Science Monitor*.

In it Washington began, "One of the most gifted men of the negro race whom I ever happened to meet is George W. Carver, Professor Carver, as he is called at Tuskegee, where he has for many years been connected with the scientific work in agriculture...." Washington emphasized Carver's acceptance by mainline white institutions such as Iowa State and the convention of Alabama teachers. He also held Carver up as an example of a quiet, capable man—"quite the most modest man I have ever met"—whose universally recognized ability was overcoming discrimination.

I have always said that the best means which the negro has for destroying race prejudice is to make himself a useful and, if possible, an indispensable member of the community in which he lives. Every man and every community is bound to respect the man or woman who has some form of superior knowledge or ability, no matter in what direction it is. I do not know of a better illustration of this than may be found in the case of Professor Carver.

Others associated with Tuskegee began to recognize and honor Carver's work more publicly. On May 5, 1915, Julius Rosenwald sent Carver $125 "in recognition of your valued service" in honor of the Rosenwalds' twenty-fifth wedding anniversary.

Carver began to blossom outside Tuskegee and the agricultural fraternity of teachers and experiment station directors. *My Larger Education* went on sale the year the boll weevil reached Alabama. Cotton farmers desperate for a new way to earn a living were suddenly much more interested in sweet potatoes, cowpeas, and peanuts than they had been before. Carver's years of dogged research, his insatiable curiosity, and his commitment to bringing scientific farming knowledge "within the reach of the one-horse farmer" prepared him well for the attention that began to come his way. In a pattern that would become common later, Carver actually published little new information on fighting boll weevils or growing alternate crops. His great contribution was in seeing the need, then meeting it by transforming scientific research and data into practical step-by-step advice any "one-horse farmer" could implement.

It was a gradual flowering at first. At the same time he was researching weevil-resistant cotton, he wrote several detailed reports on how to make best and most sanitary use of "night soil" (a euphemism for solid human waste collected overnight from chamber pots in the dormitories). He made beautiful mahogany stain out of clay taken from the drainage ditch outside the teachers' dining room.

As late as 1916, the year after Washington's death, George Washington Carver was still a somewhat mysterious and unknown figure to the general public. One columnist who planned a weekly feature called

"Men Making Good" wrote to Tuskegee requesting information for an installment about a "Mr. Carter. I am not absolutely clear about Mr. Carter but it seems to me he has made distinguished contributions to the race...." This distinguished "Mr. Carter" would soon be much easier to identify.

That same year, an article in the Baltimore *Afro-American* described Carver in a way that would surely have delighted his old principal:

> This is Prof. Carver's theory: For many years to come the individual who can produce the most milk, make the best butter, raise the finest and cheapest beef, pork, mutton, fowl, etc., put upon the market superior fruits, grains, and in short gilt edge products of every kind, and at the least expense and the least injury to the soil, will be in constant demand, regardless to the color of his skin or the texture of his hair.

Accolades awarded to Carver in 1916 proved the accuracy of the *Afro-American* statement. He accepted an invitation to serve on the advisory board of the National Agricultural Society. He was also elected a Fellow of the Royal Society for the Encouragement of Arts, Manufactures, and Commerce in London. At first he hesitated to answer the invitation of the Royal Society, confiding in Emmett Scott on September 7 that he had "not as yet decided to accept." The nomination was probably secured through his old friend and former Secretary of Agriculture James Wilson. At last he did decide to join and was elected a member on November 29.

On April 6, 1917, the United States entered the Great War in Europe. Though America was never threatened, and its resources were never dangerously stretched, there was a surge of interest in food conservation and in replacing products from abroad that could no longer be imported. First in the South and then in an ever-widening circle, George Washington Carver began to emerge as a practical scientist bursting with ideas that would help win the war.

In November, Carver announced he had developed a type of rubber from sweet potatoes and a way of making rope from peanut hulls. He also continued working on stains, paints, and dyes. Many of the best pigments came from Germany. They were now unavailable, and no one knew when they might be imported again. Besides, after the war, as one article noted, "The chances are strong that Germany will try again to push her remarkable color combinations into the markets of the world." The United States must take advantage of her natural resources as the Germans had done. "Is German science to dominate the world of scientific achievement after the war?" Carver's was the kind of fertile mind that could keep the unthinkable from happening.

He demonstrated dyes developed from a variety of local Alabama clays, as well as from tomato plants, Osage oranges, radishes, maple bark, peanuts, and onions. He made flour from sweet potatoes too, so American doughboys could have plenty of wheat for their bread.

Attempting to categorize Carver concisely, newspapers began referring to him as a chemist or research scientist even though his work through the years had been almost entirely focused on botany. Photographs of Carver at work in his Tuskegee laboratory showed a spacious room filled with neat rows of glassware and equipment—the up-to-date and fully-equipped laboratory he had waited so long for.

Around 1917, Carver stopped teaching regular classes and began spending all his time in the lab working on soil analyses and chemical experiments with plants. Though they had not yet produced any commercially viable products, Carver's work with food, stains, paint, dyes, cosmetics, and crops brought him more and more into the public eye.

Carver was a captivating public figure. Shy and unkempt as always, he continued to appear in mismatched clothing with only the top button of his jacket or lab coat buttoned, always with a fresh flower or cedar sprig in his lapel. His thinning hair was gray now, as was his still-luxuriant moustache. His quick step was a little slower, and his back a little stooped. But he was articulate, confident in his subject, and eager to share what he knew, his dark eyes sparkling as he explained his latest discovery.

Carver had long been interested in a family of plants known as legumes. Legumes are valuable to farmers in that they restore nitrogen to the soil.

Nitrogen is a crucial component of productive soil, and a major ingredient in most types of fertilizers. Cotton and tobacco, two of the South's biggest crops at the time, stripped large amounts of nitrogen from the soil. Cultivating a crop that replaced nitrogen produced food or a cash return while at the same time naturally fertilizing the soil and reducing the expense of fertilizer or the time and effort spent on manuring.

In his work with legumes, Carver studied clover, cowpeas, lentils, and various kinds of beans. Of all the legumes Carver grew or tested, he gradually became most interested in the peanut. It thrived in the local soil, was inexpensive to cultivate, and had a ready market. The Greater Four County Fair in North Carolina was in fact an annual international marketplace for buying and selling peanuts.

The first public connection between peanuts and Professor Carver came in 1906 with the publication of his Experiment Station Bulletin Thirty-One, "Planting, Cultivating, Harvesting and Cooking Peanuts." In it he promoted peanuts as an inexpensive way to build up the soil, a versatile and nutritious food, and a cost-effective cash crop. Bulletin Thirty-One also included 105 recipes for everything from a coffee substitute to peanut pie. Carver worked as well on peanut talcum powder, face cream, rope, dye, and a wide range of other products. Many of them had little practical application or were more expensive to produce commercially with peanuts than with conventional raw materials. But they showed Carver's one-horse farmer how independent he could be.

After the defeat of Germany in 1918, world trade once again flowed freely. For the first time in history, the center of economic power began a shift from the Old World to the United States. America was the new economic engine of the world, with steel, railroad, and petroleum interests fueling a worldwide economic boom. What American agricultural interests soon learned was that the rest of the world could produce food products much more cheaply than American farmers could. They began to seek protection of tariffs—import fees on foreign produce—to keep cheap foreign goods out of the marketplace and protect American growers.

The United Peanut Grower's Association was the chief proponent of a bill introduced in the House of Representatives to set a hefty tariff on imported peanuts. The bill was debated in the House Ways and Means Committee over several weeks as the Grower's Association struggled to convince the committee that peanuts were important to the nation and worthy of tariff protection. Apparently the representatives made little headway. Every day the committee met in its ornate chamber and listened to a parade of witnesses, each limited to ten minutes, explaining the value of peanuts to the American people. One winter day the routine was shattered by a shuffling old man who transformed the proceedings. Peanuts would never be the same. Nor would the life of George Washington Carver.

On January 20, 1921, as he had so many other days, Representative Joseph W. Fordney, a Republican from Michigan, sat waiting with the rest of the committee for the next witness on behalf of the Peanut Grower's Association. He was amazed suddenly to see an aging black gentleman with a large box under his arm come in and take his seat. Carver was introduced to the committee, and Chairman Fordney reminded him that he had ten minutes to speak.

Calling the peanut "one of the most remarkable crops that we are all acquainted with," Carver asked if he could make room on the table in front of him for some of the exhibits he had brought. He had spoken to audiences about agriculture for a quarter of a century, and he knew the power of compelling visual examples, whether the audience was students, farmers, or U.S. congressmen in a Washington committee chamber.

Carver showed the committee representatives blocks of crushed peanut meats he called "crushed cake," good for making breakfast cereals and "a great many things I have not time to touch upon" in ten minutes. He showed them ground peanut hulls, which were excellent for burnishing tin plate.

Warming to the witness, Chairman Fordney asked Carver if he had brought anything to drink (in reference to Prohibition, which had been in effect a little over a year). "If you do," said the chairman, "don't put it under the table."

Carver replied, "I am not ready to use them just now. They will come later if my ten minutes are extended." The chamber, including Chairman Fordney, burst into laughter. Fordney had to gavel for order before Carver could continue.

Carver showed the committee chocolate-covered peanuts, then a breakfast food made from peanuts. "I am very sorry that you can not taste this," he said, "so I will taste it for you." Again laughter rolled through the ornate chamber.

He explained that the cereal was a combination of peanuts and sweet potatoes, "two of the greatest products that God has ever given us," which could be made into a "perfectly balanced ration." If all other vegetables on earth were destroyed, Carver affirmed, "a perfectly balanced ration with all of the nutrients in it could be made with the sweet potato and the peanut. From the sweet potato we get starches and carbohydrates, and from the peanut we get all the muscle-building properties."

John Q. Tilson, a Republican from Connecticut, interrupted Carver. "Do you want a watermelon to go along with that?"

Carver took the racial jibe in stride. He had long since grown accustomed to such thoughtless remarks and went on in the same quiet tone as before, giving the senator the benefit of the doubt by answering the question as though it had been a legitimate one: "Of course, if you want a dessert, that comes in very well, but you know we can get along pretty well without dessert. The recent war [when sugar and other staples were in short supply] has taught us that."

Carver continued, pulling a seemingly incredible number of examples out of what he called his "Pandora's box": peanut bars with peanuts held together by sweet potato syrup; peanut hay ground into livestock food; five kinds of breakfast cereal in all; peanut skins, which could be made into dyes and a substitute for quinine. He spoke for the rest of his allotted time without any more questions from the committee. When his ten minutes were up, the chairman offered him more time. John Nance Garner, a Texas Democrat who would later become Franklin D. Roosevelt's vice president, agreed. "Yes, I think this is very interesting. I think his time should be extended."

Republican Congressman Henry Rainey from Illinois asked whether, in light of its versatility, there was any need to put a tariff on the peanut at all. That depended, answered Carver, "upon the problems that these gentlemen [of the Grower's Association] have brought before you.... I wish to say here in all sincerity that America produces better peanuts than any part of the world, as far as I have been able to test them out."

The committee drifted into a discussion of other substitute food products, particularly oleomargarine. Congressman Garner pointed out that dairy interests lobbied for a tax "to put it out of business."

"Oh yes," Carver said eagerly, "yes, sir. That is all the tariff means—to put the other fellow out of business." The room rocked with laughter again. Crusty Washington insiders were unaccustomed to such transparent honesty.

As the laughter and applause subsided, Fordney spoke to the witness. "Go ahead, brother. Your time is unlimited."

Carver went on to show the committee a bottle of "peanut milk" alongside a bottle of cow's milk. The liquids looked nearly identical; both had a layer of cream on top. Peanut milk could be used to make buttermilk, curds, evaporated milk, instant coffee substitute, Worcestershire sauce, soy sauce substitute for Chinese cooking, Neufchatel and Edam cheeses, salad oil, face cream, ink, fruit punch, relish, and a main dish Carver called "mock oysters."

In conclusion, Carver testified that peanuts were part of a "natural diet" that was meant for everyone. "If you go to the first chapter of Genesis, we can interpret very clearly, I think, what God intended when he said, 'Behold, I have given you every herb that bears seed upon the face of the earth, and every tree bearing a seed. To you it shall be meat.' That is what he means about it. It shall be meat. There is everything there to strengthen and nourish and keep the body alive and healthy."

John Carew, a New York Democrat, declared Carver had "rendered the committee a great service." Once again the chamber echoed with heartfelt applause. Carver told the men that he had produced everything he brought in his research laboratory at Tuskegee. He had come up with 107 uses for the sweet potato but had just begun on the peanut and did not know how many he would eventually find.

"You have seen, gentlemen, just about half" of the peanut applications he had identified so far. Massachusetts Republican Allen Treadway shot back, "Well, come again and bring the rest."

Eventually, the Fordney Committee approved the highest protective tariff ever on peanuts up to that time, three cents a pound shelled, four cents unshelled.

Carver's appearance in Washington, D.C., was an unqualified triumph. Robert Russa Moton praised his "modest, unassuming manner." Carver's natural warmth, transparent honesty, and mastery of his subject combined with carefully honed teaching skills made an unforgettable impression on the most prominent audience he had ever addressed.

Carver's testimony did for him what the 1895 Cotton States Exposition had done for Booker T. Washington: elevate him suddenly, after years of preparation, into the national arena. In this case the public spotlight fell on a genuinely endearing and captivating figure. As different as their personalities were, Washington and Carver entered the public eye in similar positions. They were articulate, accomplished black men who were experts in their fields, who demanded little (or in Washington's case, seemed on the surface to demand little), and who posed no threat to whites. Carver and Washington shared a belief that the path to genuine and lasting equality was through hard work and self-help. Protest, public confrontation, or violence were, to them, counter-productive and ultimately destructive.

The summer after his House committee testimony, Carver welcomed his old Iowa State professor Louis Pammel to Tuskegee. Carver had hoped for years that Dr. Pammel could visit him. The two had kept in touch over the twenty-five years since Carver left Iowa, and Carver had also written to Pammel's wife and family regularly. This was the first time Pammel had been able to make time for a visit to his old student, and both of them relished every minute. One of Carver's regrets was that he hadn't had the chance to show Pammel the suit, hat, and gloves Pammel had bought for him to wear to the Cedar Rapids art exhibit when he was a student. They were, he wrote, "nearly as good as new," and he still wore them when he wanted to look his best.

After Pammel returned to Iowa, Carver wrote a letter expressing the sincere affection and concern he felt toward him and a few other of his closest friends:

> I was so glad to see that God had dealt so kindly with you, by giving you increased bodily vigor, great mental attainments etc. When you were going out of your way to help a poor insignificant black boy, you were giving many 'cups of cold water' in his name. The memory of yourself, Mrs. Pammel and the children are more dear to me than words can express. They have served as lamps unto my feet and lights along my pathway....

Carver began attracting the attention of writers and reporters eager to learn more about this shy and singular-looking scientist. One hopeful biographer was another old friend and longtime correspondent, Helen Milholland. She had been the "prima donna" in the church choir in Winterset, Iowa, who befriended Carver when he was a young man and encouraged him to enroll at Simpson College, where he studied before going to Iowa State.

Retiring by nature, Carver encouraged would-be writers to tell his story. As he counseled Mrs. Milholland in a letter in 1920, "When I pass from earth to my reward there will be a great demand for [my biography], and it will be a source of revenue for you, possibly in your declining years. To give it more value I might give to it my endorsement. I am also wondering if magazines would not pay for certain popular parts of it as an article that would be of interest to science or popular reading."

In 1916 a writer inquiring at Tuskegee about "Mr. Carter" was unsure of exactly what he had done to be worth writing about. Five years later, after his committee appearance, George Washington Carver was swept up in a tide of national publicity. Features based on his testimony before the Fordney Committee appeared in print for a year or more. They reported how typically jaded and impatient congressmen sat transfixed for an hour and forty minutes as Carver displayed his peanut products. He was widely quoted as saying a pound of peanuts had "a little more of the body-building nutrients than a pound of sirloin steak, while the heat and energy producing nutrients are more than twice as much."

His kidnapping as a small boy, his early quest for knowledge beginning with elementary school in Neosho, his struggles for acceptance in college, his genuine disinterest in money, and his friendship with two Iowa professors who became Secretaries of Agriculture—James Wilson (under McKinley, Roosevelt, and Taft) and Henry C. Wallace (serving at the time under Harding)—made his life story a public relations dream, "a tragedy and a romance," as one writer described it. Invariably the articles pointed out that his work accomplished good for everyone, transcended the issue of race. Said one, "His service has been to no class, but to the nation."

To the news media, Carver became a "great specialist in foods and food values," and a "great chemist." Booker T. Washington had once been hailed as the "Wizard of Tuskegee." Now Carver was the "wizard chemist," the "goober wizard," and eventually assumed the title as "Wizard of Tuskegee" himself. Washington had largely missed the first great media age of radio, mass circulation magazines, and theater newsreels. Children of the twentieth century knew of him from books and old newspaper articles and little else.

Without irony, the writers and reporters crowned a new wizard in the first years of the Roaring Twenties. For more than thirty years, news reports about Washington virtually never mentioned George Washington Carver. As Carver's star rose in the early 1920s and stories about him proliferated, Washington's name faded from view.

Carver did nothing to challenge stories that were untrue and watched them pass from one publication to another without comment. Strangers took to calling him "Dr. Carver." To anyone who asked, he freely admitted he never earned a doctorate, but he never corrected anyone who assumed he had. Even the *Tuskegee Alumni Bulletin* reported in 1922, shortly after Carver's retirement, that he had been a "professor of chemistry" rather than the more pedestrian sounding "director of agriculture."

One of the most tantalizing stories that came to light was that, during the Great War, Thomas Edison secretly offered Carver a job at a salary variously reported as one hundred thousand dollars per year, two hundred thousand dollars, or "five times the salary of the President of the United States." On one hand Carver insisted the matter was private, but on the other, he himself kept it before the public by mentioning it in his speeches and interviews, beginning as early as 1917. In *Success* magazine, Carver said of the offer, "there was nothing to talk over, and I thanked Mr. Edison in a letter." Carver made it clear that he would rather stay among "his people" in the South and help them improve themselves than move to New Jersey and work under another wizard, the Wizard of Menlo Park. Carver loved the publicity news the offer generated, but was typically coy in revealing the details.

Thomas Edison, the great genius who invented the phonograph and made electric light, motion pictures, and the telephone practical, never met Carver, but an associate of his named Hutchinson evidently came to Tuskegee to make the offer on his behalf. Edison could not make the trip; he was redesigning the electrical systems of American submarines. Carver steadfastly refused to reveal the terms of Edison's offer. (Years after Edison's death in 1931, the curator of the Edison Laboratory wrote to Carver saying he continued to get inquiries about the offer. "I do not know why confirmation should be required of us when the story was apparently told by you.... It seems to be altogether consistent with Mr. Edison's ways." Carver recalled the initial contact was by telegram from Edison, but he could never produce the telegram, and the Edison Laboratory had no written record of the offer.)

Speculation about the amount of his salary offer, Carver insisted, came from a driver who took him to the Tuskegee train station and overheard his conversation with Hutchinson. Whatever the actual amount, it was unassailable proof to Carver that he was appreciated, and by a fellow researcher no less. The money meant nothing to a man who habitually forgot to cash his monthly paychecks. The public recognition was priceless.

The accolades continued to mount. Carver was called the "Columbus of the Soil," "God's Ebony Scientist," and "a colored Horatio Alger," after the prolific novelist whose characters became symbols of success in the face of adversity. An increasing tide of visitors arrived at the Chechaw station, then took the spur line to Tuskegee to call on Professor Carver.

Visitors frequently mistook Professor Carver for a gardener or hired man. His shuffling gait, eccentric appearance, and retiring personality was not what they expected from a man who had accomplished so much. He received invitations to speak all over the United States and was received as a celebrity wherever he went. When he was at Tuskegee, he spent his days in his beloved laboratory looking for more ways to use peanuts and other economical crops. He identified more than 130 uses for the peanut, forty-five for the pecan, and he continued his work with sweet potatoes. Other than his one unsuccessful attempt at forming a dry pigment company, he never demonstrated any interest in commercial development of his ideas or applications for his own gain.

Carver's humility and lack of interest in financial reward drove writers to heights of hyperbole. A Tuskegee alumni publication declared:

> He does not expect to withhold from the world the benefit of his remarkable discoveries, but he declares that when they are commercialized, his race shall receive full credit for them. He is almost daily turning down offers to market his products with the Negro racial identity eliminated.... The invention of the automobile, the cotton gin, spindle and loom will have no greater importance than Professor Carver's discoveries.

An article in *Success* magazine echoed the same enthusiasm:

> The magic colors which adorned the works of art in Tutankhamen's tomb and stand resplendent and unfaded after thirty centuries, an art lost to modern workers in pigments, this magician has reproduced in cold water paints compounded from the clays he has dug out of the hills and pits of the South.

Time and again questioners asked Carver how he managed to come up with such innovative and unusual ideas for using peanuts and sweet potatoes. Easily and without hesitation, he always gave the glory to God. "I didn't make these discoveries," he would say. "God has only worked through me to reveal to his children some of his wonderful providence."

Carver's scientific method was equal parts chemistry, motivation, curiosity, and prayer. He went even further, defining the whole of scientific discipline in terms of the Creator: "They say that science is classified knowledge. I know that science is truth. Jesus said 'Ye shall know the Truth and the Truth shall make ye free.' It seems to me that he meant, 'You shall know science and science shall make you free.'"

Professor Carver was an unexpected combination of scientific skill and childlike simplicity. His transparent personality and sensitivity to criticism had made it hard for him to deal with the politics and relentless attention to detail of the Washington years. Now, that same transparency and sensitivity amidst all the attention he was receiving made him all the more endearing.

Carver's eclectic yet friendly personality made him especially popular with the students, even though he no longer taught regular classes. From his earliest years at Tuskegee, Carver had taken a special interest in everyone who attended his lectures and his Bible class. Many of them were young, in their mid or late teens, though a few were thirty or older. Most of them came from poor families; many had never been away from home before. Carver befriended them and stayed in touch even after they graduated or left to take a job. They wrote him eagerly to announce they had gotten a job or built a building or helped their family pay off a debt. They also wrote of their fears and failures.

Carver invariably replied with kind and comforting words. He called his favorite students his sons, and they addressed him as Father, Daddy, or My Only Dad in their letters. It wasn't botany or soil science that changed their lives so much as it was Carver's example of patience and persistence and his unfailing reliance on his faith. The admiration went both ways: the students relished his counsel, and he delighted in their attention and friendship. They were the only family he had.

Students often asked Carver's advice in personal or career matters, and the Professor was a fountain of advice. Answering a letter from a student in Virginia, Carver observed:

> You are now in the midst of a great struggle. You are fighting for freedom, you will win, God is on your side.... My friend I love you for what you are and what you hope to be through Jesus Christ.

There are times when I am surely tried and am compelled to hide away with Jesus for strength to overcome. God alone knows what I have suffered, in trying to do as best I could the job he has given me in trust to do, most of the time I had to work without the sympathy or support of those with whom I associated. Many are the strange paths God led me into. He is and will lead you likewise.

A number of Carver's students went on to found schools of their own based on the Tuskegee model. They were modest institutions, and many lasted only a few years. But they carried Carver's spirit into poor backwaters of the South, transforming—at least for a time—the lives of all they touched. A student of Carver's named H. B. Bennett set up a school in Stallo, Mississippi, and wrote an exultant letter to Carver with details of his progress.

If you had any idea what you have done in this community through me, I am sure you could die happy. Think of a community five years ago that was on its way to destruction, and today it is on its way to the Promised Land. Its humble servant, your son, is so very happy because of the change.

Prof., the reason I give you credit for what little I have tried to do, is because it was you who laid the right foundation for my life's journey. I can look back and see how I would have failed time and time again had it not been for your good instruction.

He goes on to describe a local man who "bitterly opposed" him. But, he continued,

I never retaliated one bit; I used righteousness, patience, and self-control, and won out.... He comes to my house now, sits down and talks about how to get through life. He is a completely converted man.... This little verse comes to me now, from the Bible: "The righteous shall never be moved." Now, this is not my victory; it is yours; because, had you not impressed my whole life, I am sure I would have retaliated....

For Christmas in 1921 the senior class at Tuskegee gave Professor Carver a fountain pen. In his acknowledgment to the class president, Carver took advantage of the opportunity to remind his "children" of virtues he considered vital.

> As your father, it is needless for me to keep saying, I hope, except for emphasis, that each one of my children will rise to the full height of your possibilities, which means the possession of these eight cardinal virtues which constitutes a lady or a gentleman.
>
> 1st. Be clean both inside and outside.
>
> 2nd. Who neither looks up to the rich or down on the poor.
>
> 3rd. Who loses, if need be, without squealing.
>
> 4th. Who wins without bragging.
>
> 5th. Who is always considerate of women, children, and old people.
>
> 6th. Who is too brave to lie.
>
> 7th. Who is too generous to cheat.
>
> 8th. Who takes his share of the world and lets other people have theirs.

Because Carver had no public political agenda he got along well with prominent blacks who had opposed and despised Washington. He did not necessarily agree with them, it was just that he had no real interest in their political pursuits. In 1923 the National Association for the Advancement of Colored People, founded to challenge Washington's power and influence, bestowed a signal honor on Washington's now famous associate.

Each year the NAACP awarded the Spingarn Medal—named in honor of Joel Spingarn, a white publisher and early chairman of the organization—to "the man or woman of African descent and American citizenship who during the year shall have made the highest achievement in any field of human endeavor." Carver received the award in recognition of his work with the sweet potato and the peanut. By then his peanut products numbered 145, with 107 for the sweet potato.

The NAACP acknowledged that not all the products would prove commercially feasible, "yet they indicate a racial genius devoted to practical ends which men of all races must admire." Those words would have sounded perfectly natural coming from Booker T. Washington, which made it all the more remarkable that they came from the award presentation committee, which included Oswald Garrison Villard, founder of the NAACP, and Washington's old nemesis, W. E. B. Du Bois.

CHAPTER SIXTEEN

STANDING
BEFORE KINGS

In the NAACP, Villard, Du Bois and their associates had an organization that thrived in the decade after Booker T. Washington's death.
Their rhetoric opposing segregation and disenfranchisement was welcomed by blacks who began the Roaring Twenties on an ominous note.

The tension was caused in part by an unprecedented migration. During
the Great War, immigration came to a standstill, creating a shortage of semi-
skilled workers, laborers, and domestic servants in Northern cities. At the
same time, the skilled workers there left their jobs for military service.
Desperate for replacements, Northern factory owners sent agents south to
offer jobs to blacks, often paying their rail fare back to Detroit, Chicago,
Cleveland, Pittsburgh, and other great factory cities. Blacks eagerly accepted
the offers and moved north by the tens of thousands.

The drain on the Southern labor market was so severe that some
communities refused to sell blacks northbound railroad tickets. Rumors
circulated in the South that blacks who went north risked freezing and
starvation. But still they came.

Then when the war ended and four and a half million soldiers, mostly
white, came home, the transplanted blacks were fired or demoted to
lower skilled, lower paying jobs. Unable to afford train fare home or

unwilling to return to farming, many of them stayed in the North. White military veterans found their neighborhoods crowded with black people who competed for low-paying jobs and often worked for less than whites would. Blacks felt isolated and alone; whites felt they had been invaded.

As the doughboys returned from France in the spring and summer of 1919, one Northern metropolis after another endured some of the worst race riots in their history up to that time. In Chicago, a young black boy drifted alone off the beach on Lake Michigan into an area used only by whites. When white boys threw rocks at him, he fell off his raft and drowned. The outrage by the black community at his senseless death was met by seething resentment of the white population. Armed mobs commandeered the streets for two days and nights until the state militia was called in to restore order. In the end 38 people were killed and 537 wounded.

Washington's voice of reconciliation and reason had long been silent, and there was no one to take his place. Carver never commented publicly on the incidents. Robert Russa Moton, Washington's successor at Tuskegee, was an effective administrator and a national figure in his own right, but even he had no real chance of keeping the once-awesome Tuskegee Machine alive.

As the public memory of Washington began to lapse, Carver took care never to discuss the conflict that had characterized their professional relationship. All of Carver's disappointments and administrative shortcomings had been strictly private matters between him, Washington, and the Tuskegee faculty.

Administrative difficulties aside, Carver had cast down his bucket and brought it up brimful and running over with the joy he felt in helping students improve their lives. His great reward was in the attention and love that came from his students over the years, reading about their victories great and small and counseling them on their problems. He had never felt that emotional satisfaction in his relationship with Washington.

Had he been more subjective and emotional, however, Booker T. Washington would hardly have been able to breathe life into Tuskegee as he did. Had Carver been more businesslike and precise, he could never have connected with students as he did. Moreover, he could scarcely have made the discoveries he did, as they came as a result of intuition and informed curiosity rather than scientific precision.

Each man had needed the other, particularly in Carver's case. Without Washington, Carver would never have had the opportunity to conduct the kind of experiments that later made him famous. Yet it was only after Washington's death that the spotlight shifted from the articulate, immaculate, supremely confident figure of Tuskegee's first president to a quiet, shuffling genius in mismatched clothes who made his own neckties.

Carver's election to the Royal Society elevated his stature in the public mind, and the honor was still being reported as news more than five years after he accepted it. In an editorial on March 28, 1923, the *St. Louis Globe Democrat* began:

> There is the interest which surrounds occurrences highly extraordinary in an account stating that a Negro born in Missouri as a slave, has been made a Fellow of the Royal Society of Great Britain.... He is honored by British scientists for having made a number of very remarkable chemical discoveries....

Other publications described him as "a man of international repute," "acceded to be one of the world's greatest scientists," "a genius who lives in closest touch with nature," and a "wizard of organic chemistry." His vision brought hope to Southern boosters and businessmen so long frustrated by the underused land and manpower they saw around them. Some confidently predicted Carver's discoveries would add a hundred million dollars a year to the wealth of the South.

His appearance in any city brought a standing room only crowd that became spellbound by his presentation skills just as the Ways and Means Committee had been. A thousand people or more sat nearly motionless and silent for up to two hours as Carver showed them the products he fashioned in his Tuskegee laboratory from peanuts, sweet potatoes, and pecans. After a lecture at the Cecil Hotel, the *Atlanta*

Constitution concluded, "The Scripture was literally fulfilled: 'See thou a man diligent in business, he shall stand before kings.'"

Perhaps the most remarkable endorsement Carver received was from the Atlanta Chapter of the United Daughters of the Confederacy. During an exhibit of his work in Atlanta in March 1923, the chapter passed a resolution to send Carver, born a slave, "a written expression of their interest and appreciation of you in your efforts to exhibit the products and possible industries of our South, and the Chapter wishes you God-Speed in any endeavor looking to the development of any project in which we are naturally interested."

In his presentations, as he had in his class lectures, Carver turned again and again to the image of God as the Creator who reveals his goodness through his creations. Nature was full of mysteries, Carver told his audiences, wonders of creation that God reveals to anyone patient enough to look for them. God's goodness, he said, was mankind's for the taking as a gift, if only we would accept it. He had not strayed from this belief in all his life. But in November 1924, he was surprised to find his belief directly challenged on the national stage.

That month he spoke at the Marble Collegiate Church in New York and explained to his audience that his scientific discoveries were the result of divine revelation. He did not follow the accepted scientific practice of starting with existing knowledge and building from there. On the contrary, he admitted "no books ever go into my laboratory."

"I never have to grope for methods," he said. "The method is revealed at the moment I am inspired to create something new." This was consistent with his belief that God would reveal his mysteries to him if he would look for them.

The *New York Times* took issue with Carver's position. Two days later on November 20, an editorial headed "Men of Science Never Talk That Way" upbraided Carver for his "complete lack of scientific spirit," claiming it discredited him, his race, and Tuskegee. Real chemists, the commentator insisted, "do not scorn books out of which they can learn what other chemists have done, and they do not ascribe their successes, when they have any, to 'inspiration.'" Vigorously defending his position, Carver wrote to the editor expanding on his view of Divine inspiration and, for good measure, highlighting his legitimate scientific education, awards, and accomplishments:

I regret exceedingly that such a gross misunderstanding should arise as to what was meant by "Divine inspiration." Inspiration is never at variance with information; in fact, the more information one has, the greater will be the inspiration.

Paul, the great Scholar, says, Second Timothy 2:15, "Study to show thyself approved unto God, a Workman that needeth not to be ashamed, rightly dividing the word of truth."

Again he says in Galatians 1:12: "For I neither received it of man, neither was I taught it, but by the revelation of Jesus Christ...."

I receive the leading scientific publications. I thoroughly understand that there are scientists to whom the world is merely the result of chemical forces or material electrons. I do not belong to this class.... The master analysist needs no book....

An Example: While in your beautiful city, I was struck with the large number of Taros and Yautias displayed in many of your markets; they are edible roots imported to this country. Just as soon as I saw them, I marveled at the wonderful possibilities for their expansion. Dozens of things came to me while standing there looking at them. I would follow the same or similar lines I have pursued in developing products from the white potato. I know of no one who has ever worked with these roots in this way. I know of no book from which I can get this information, yet I will have no trouble in doing it.

If this is not inspiration and information from a source greater than myself, or greater than any one has wrought up to the present time, kindly tell me what it is.

"And ye shall know the truth and the truth shall make you free." John 8:32.

Science is simply the truth about anything.

The *Times* editorial generated a flood of letters in defense of Carver. These quickly lifted his spirits, which had been dashed, he said, not because the editorial had been critical of him personally, but because it had criticized Christianity. The negative comments eventually produced an overwhelming show of support for Carver through articles in other publications and letters to Carver. Many more sent their own letters to the *Times* with a copy to Carver. In the end he saw the whole episode as an illustration of God's providence. "After all, God moves in a mysterious way His wonders to perform," he said.

In a letter to one of his former students, Carver reinforced his belief that God revealed himself in nature:

> As soon as you begin to read the great and loving God out of all forms of existence he has created, both animate and inanimate, then you will be able to Converse with him, anywhere, every-where, and at all times. Oh, what a fullness of joy will come to you. My dear friend, get the significance. God is speaking.

Carver steadfastly insisted that he had no interest in personal gain from his experiments. However, he began to believe more strongly that, prop-erly managed, businesses based on his peanut or sweet potato products could help the South become more self-sufficient. Ralston-Purina con-tacted him and expressed interest in developing a new breakfast cereal, but Carver did not pursue a business arrangement with them. Instead, with the help of a new business manager, he decided to start a company of his own.

Ernest Thompson was a local white admirer of Carver's who had con-tributed money and supplies to his projects over the years. He was not particularly well qualified to be a business manager—he was from a wealthy Tuskegee family and lived on his inheritance—but he shared Carver's vision for a business enterprise dedicated to the public good and not to making a profit.

The two began their business with high expectations, inviting a wide range of prospective investors to Tuskegee for consultations. It was soon clear, however, that the most enthusiastic prospects had the least money, and the ones with significant capital insisted on more facts about the products and their potential than Carver and Thompson could give them.

Carver was proud of the fact that he never had reference books in his laboratory. It was also true that, in another break with accepted scientific procedure, he seldom wrote anything down. There were no notebooks full of formulas or processes, no records of results an investor could look at and feel confident his investment would eventually yield profits. (Years later when an archivist came to Tuskegee to help Carver organize his records, she was astonished to learn that he didn't have any.)

When he did write about his work, Carver tended to use indistinct or pseudo-scientific language that prompted people to investigate further, causing Carver to bristle with indignation. In one case he described a paint as a "sextuple oxide." It described the form of a chemical compound which, based on accepted usage of chemistry nomenclature, could not exist. Carver later explained he used the term to describe the process he used to make the compound and not the compound itself. "I call it sextuple oxide," he said, "because after three years of work I am able to produce this beautiful blue only by oxidizing it six times.... After we protect our formulas, I will be glad to show them everything I know about it."

Thompson arranged a visit to Atlanta for Carver as a guest of the Atlanta and West Point Railway, which provided a private railroad car both for Carver's transportation and for lodging in the city. The gesture delighted Carver for two reasons. First, it was the sort of gesture that made Carver feel appreciated. Second, it allowed him to avoid the elaborate preparations necessary for a black man, even a famous one, to find decent lodging in Atlanta.

He spoke there to enthusiastic audiences about his new venture. After such an encouraging reception, Carver expected his company would attract plenty of interest. The Carver Products Company issued a prospectus announcing a capitalization of $125,000. Carver may have invested in the company himself and was reported to be receiving 10 percent of the net income with a portion of his earnings going to Tuskegee.

Unfortunately, there never were any earnings. Carver filed three patent applications, all of which were eventually registered, but none of which led to any marketable product. The first, U.S. Patent No. 1,522,176, a formula and manufacturing process for cosmetics, was registered January 6, 1925; Patent No. 1,541,478, for pigments derived from clay and iron, was registered June 9, 1925; and Patent No. 1,632,365, for paint and stain pigments, was registered June 14, 1927.

They were the only three patents Carver ever filed, and by the time the last one was registered, the Carver Products Company had all but disappeared. The company had established its headquarters in the Healey Building in Atlanta, drawn up plans for a paint factory near Chechaw, and come near winning a contract to paint Coca-Cola barrels. In September 1925, Carver declared he had "practically retired from the nominal work of the Institute and will devote the remainder of my life trying to get these industries going and leave them for the benefit of our race especially, I hope."

By the spring of 1927, Carver and Thompson had learned there were existing food and cosmetic patents that made pursuing their business impractical. They also found out how hard it would be to get peanut oil or meal economically. Besides, no significant investor had stepped up with the money they would need to start production.

The only one of Carver's products to find any commercial application was Penol, a medicine marketed as a treatment for tuberculosis and other respiratory problems. Creosote was widely used to treat pulmonary disease; Penol was an emulsion of creosote and peanuts, which Carver believed made the creosote taste better and work more effectively. Carver began mentioning Penol in his speeches, fanning the flames of public interest, prompting one newspaper to report he had announced a new cure for tuberculosis. Carver hastily explained the newspaper report was in error and that he would make no claims until after it was thoroughly tested.

Ernest Thompson and a group of Tuskegee businessmen incorporated the Carver Penol Company, and by the summer of 1926 production was under way on a very small scale. The company produced a pamphlet assuring patients that Penol was "composed of some of the best known and most proven remedies for Coughs, Sore Throat, Bronchitis, Catarrh, Pulmonary and Stomach Troubles," and that furthermore it was a "Tissue Builder, Intestinal Cleanser, Germ Arrester, Nerve Food and Intestinal Antiseptic."

The medicine was never a financial success, though in one form or another it nearly outlived its inventor. After complaints surfaced about Penol's quality in 1929, Ernest Thompson sold the manufacturing rights to a company in Virginia for one hundred dollars a month plus a two-and-a-half cent royalty per bottle. As shipments dwindled, the monthly fee was cut to fifty dollars and then eliminated in 1937. The same year, the Food and Drug Administration challenged Penol's nutritional claims, and later the curative properties of creosote as well. Carver had never allowed his name to be used in advertising Penol, and some time in the early 1940s the trickle of sales stopped completely.

Business failures notwithstanding, George Washington Carver moved steadily from scientist to celebrity. In 1923, the same year he received the Spingarn Medal, Carver attended the Southern regional conference of the YMCA in Blue Ridge, North Carolina. The conference was supported by an Atlanta-based organization called the Commission on Interracial Cooperation. One of CIC's most active members, Will B. Alexander, had heard Carver speak and thought his singular presentation style would warm Southern audiences and promote racial harmony.

Dr. Moton had spoken at Blue Ridge in 1920. Even though he had eaten and slept in segregated facilities, the YMCA participants received Moton well. Carver arrived at Blue Ridge in the summer of 1923 to discover he had met the camp director, Willis D. Weatherford, when they were both summer YMCA delegates thirty years before. Carver's accommodations at the center were separate, as Dr. Moton's had been. The arrangement angered Weatherford, but he was afraid Carver's appearance in the dining hall would anger the students and make them unreceptive to his message. Carver kindly admonished him not to worry about it.

Though the point of Carver's appearance was to foster better race relations, he never mentioned the subject in his presentation. Instead, he talked about the miracles of nature and how they could be used for the benefit of mankind. He brought samples of products made from peanuts, sweet potatoes, and Alabama clays, and showed the students what could be accomplished using only the most meager resources. As he always did, Carver held the room captivated; his own innocence and wonder encouraged the audience to drop its cynicism and look at the miracle of creation with new eyes.

When he finished, the silence of the room was shattered by a roar of applause. The students Weatherford feared would shun Carver waited in line to shake his hand instead. A number of them invited him to their campuses, and in the fall, Carver was back in South Carolina for a whirlwind tour of colleges, with appearances on six campuses in seven days. The student newspaper at one of them concluded:

> He is probably the one colored man out of a million who could have held the attention of the Clemson boys.... To see a man as black as Doctor Carver and yet as able as he is, comes as a distinct shock to Southern boys, and jars them out of their conviction of the Negro's absolute inferiority.

The next year, Carver was invited back to Blue Ridge, and this time he shared a cottage with students from Lynchburg College at their invitation. However, he still avoided the dining hall; his cottage hosts, whom he called his "Virginia boys," served him meals in his quarters. When they heard Carver would be speaking to them, groups from Florida and Louisiana threatened to walk out at the beginning of his speech. But when the Professor began to speak, an "almost unbelievable silence" enveloped the room, and not a single student rose from his seat.

After Carver finished, the leader of the Florida delegation stood and told the assembly what they had planned to do and offered Carver an apology.

The only real disappointment in an otherwise stellar year for Carver was a disagreement over who should manage the new Veteran's Administration hospital that opened on the Tuskegee campus. Black war veterans had faced daunting levels of discrimination in existing VA hospitals, and the Harding administration agreed to build a hospital for Negroes at Tuskegee. Local white residents had been assured the hospital would be run by whites, but Dr. Moton wanted black management. The hospital opened with a predominantly white staff and all white management. Even the nurses were white; since they were forbidden by state law from touching "colored" patients, black maids did most of the work the nurses would normally have done.

Taking a lesson from his predecessor at Tuskegee, Dr. Moton worked behind the scenes to make sure the new hospital also provided employment for black doctors, nurses, and managers. President Harding and the VA supported Moton's position, and in July 1923, the first black manager had arrived in town. White residents, feeling betrayed by their government, announced a march by the Ku Klux Klan. A wave of protest from blacks kept the marchers off campus, but the black hospital administrator quickly left town. Eventually Moton and his supporters stood fast, the unhappy whites relented, and by the following July the hospital was all black.

Carver's appearances at Blue Ridge in 1924–25 produced a bumper crop of what the Professor called "my boys," young men Carver considered to be bright, energetic, open minded, and receptive to his belief in the relationship between Christianity and natural science; men who in turn admired Carver's personality, knowledge, gentleness, and his sincere interest in their well-being.

One of them wrote an article about Carver for *World Tomorrow*, proclaiming:

> The man who had been and is to this day the greatest inspiration in my life is a Negro.
>
> In the whole life of this saintly man I see the future of a great race. In his eyes I see the soul of a people who experienced God and understand the meaning of the Cross.
>
> The unique contribution George Carver has made in the field of science and religion is symbolical of the contribution the Negro race is destined to make to our civilization is all unequal relationships are abolished and the Negro is given every opportunity fully to develop his personality.

Carver unfailingly gave the credit to God. A letter to Jimmy Hardwick on March 9, 1928, was typical of his frequent comments on the divine guidance he received. "O if you could right now step into 'God's little Work Shop' and see what he has permitted me to do, and its effect upon the south, you would marvel."

Always eager for recognition and praise, Carver began dropping hints after receiving the Spingarn Award that he would particularly like an honorary doctorate from Iowa State. He wrote to his old friend Dr. Pammel to see whether he thought an award might be possible. Whatever Pammel's connections were, they were not enough to get Carver the acknowledgment he wanted.

There was also a practical side to a doctorate for Carver. For years people had addressed him as "Doctor Carver," and recognition from his alma mater would make the title legitimate. Also, many Southerners hesitated—or refused—to refer to a black man as "Mr." Carver, reserving that courtesy title for whites only. Of course, "Professor Carver" was both correct and socially acceptable.

Though Iowa State never came through with the degree, Simpson College gladly honored its most famous alumnus with an honorary doctorate. With the encouragement of the Milhollands, Carver had studied music and art at Simpson before he began his botanical studies at Iowa. In 1928, the college bestowed the award Carver longed for.

To the nation and the world, George Washington Carver had become the Peanut Man. In the public eye, his research to develop commercial applications for peanuts outshone all his other accomplishments. His thirty-year academic career, his research into pigments, paints, and stains, his artistic and musical gifts, his scientific study of fungi, even his experiments with sweet potatoes, which caught his attention before peanuts did, were swallowed up in the popular image of a stooped, graying Negro man, often wearing a shop apron over his jacket or sweater, who made a miraculous list of products from the humble peanut in the laboratory he called "God's Little Work Shop."

As an artist, Carver had shown enough promise to have his paintings exhibited at the Chicago World's Fair. As a botanist, he made important contributions to mycology, the study of fungi. As a teacher, he inspired thousands of young men and women to persevere in the face of adversity. As a Christian, he was a living embodiment of patience, frugality, industry, humility (more or less), selflessness, and concern for others. As a Negro he inspired his race to rise above unfair conditions rather than complain about them, and proved undeniably to whites that a black man could be their intellectual equal.

But, ironically, as the Peanut Man, Carver added little that was new. His list of peanut-derived products had grown to 165. In theory the peanut's versatility and food value made it a valuable commodity, a promising replacement for cotton to farmers who had grown nothing else all their lives and who were being bankrupted by the boll weevil. But practically, Carver's specific products were not commercially viable. He had learned that himself firsthand with the Carver Products Company and his disappointing experience with Penol. Capitalization, transportation, manufacturing, supply, and marketing challenges all stood in the way of helping the "one-horse farmer" make a living from Carver's peanut products. And some of the products cost more to make with peanuts than with the raw materials they were supposed to replace.

By this time, however, George Washington Carver had become more than a scientist. The Peanut Man was not a man who helped farmers save their farms by growing peanuts. He was a shining symbol of victory over centuries of crushing oppression and slavery followed by decades of discrimination. He was a man who, like Booker T. Washington, met hatred with respect, disdain with courtesy, and resentment with gratitude. He was a man who fought a war of attrition against racism with faith in God and trust in mankind. He earned the respect of whites who grew up believing that blacks were genetically inferior to them by quietly and irrefutably proving he was smarter than they were. His peanut experiments had limited scientific and commercial value. But as a bridge between white and black, they were priceless.

Like Washington, though to a lesser extent, Carver had a public and a private side resulting from opposing forces deep within him. On one side, he was genuinely humble before God and mankind, invariably giving credit for his accomplishments to the Creator. On the other, he craved attention and was attracted to it like a moth to a flame. His years as an orphan, then as a homesteader in Kansas, then as an often-criticized member of the Tuskegee faculty, whetted his appetite for praise all the more. He was a retiring man who nevertheless loved to be loved.

In his presentations and correspondence, Carver brought his religion ever more into the forefront. He saw God as the Creator of all but believed mankind had the free will to accept God or not. In a letter to Jim Hardwick, Carver said, "I am happy because God is [with your permission] drawing nearer and nearer to you." Yet he could also write to a Canadian friend named Robert Johnson saying, "I have the assurance that God will take care of me. He blesses me with the ability to earn a living, and gives me wisdom and understanding enough to lay a little by from time to time for the proverbial 'rainy day.'"

Carver's admirers represented a wide variety of denominations and faiths, from the Baptist beliefs of John D. Rockefeller to Baha'i and the Rosicrucian Fellowship. The Divine Philosophy Group, the Theosophical Society, the Unity Farm, and the Universal Group of Intuitives also sought his position on spiritual matters, along with groups attracted by Carver's strongly nondenominational views.

On numerous occasions, Carver corresponded with followers of Mahatma Gandhi, the great Eastern Indian leader who was protesting British sovereignty over India. Like Carver, Gandhi rejected direct conflict in favor of patience and gradual success. Gandhi was physically frail and inclined to hunger strikes in order to attract the attention of the British and sympathy for his cause. Fearing for his health, one of his followers visited Carver at Tuskegee for a recommendation on a vegetarian diet that would keep up Gandhi's strength.

Years later another supporter requested some of Carver's agricultural bulletins on behalf of Gandhi. Carver had them sent and received a personal note of appreciation from Gandhi. Delighted, Carver wrote back saying he would pray for Gandhi "in the marvelous work you are doing." From then on Carver mentioned the correspondence frequently in his speeches.

During much of the 1920s, Carver continued as a consultant to the peanut industry, numerous individuals and institutions, and the U.S. Department of Agriculture. His most important collaboration was with the Tom Huston Company, maker of Tom's Peanuts and other snacks. Carver and Huston first met at the Montgomery State Fair in 1924, when Huston was searching for a new way to make salt stick to peanuts without oil.

Huston consulted Carver regularly after that and in 1929 offered him a job in his newly-expanded research laboratory. Though the offer caught his attention, Carver declined, explaining, "My work is a great publicity asset for the school and my race.... I, with others, am clannish enough to want my people to receive full credit for my work."

Working with the Tom Huston Company in the years that followed, Carver melded his public celebrity with genuine scientific insight. The company was trying to discover how they could grow Virginia peanuts on land that previously supported only cheaper, less popular varieties. Virginia peanuts harvested from fields in Georgia, Alabama, and Florida were immature or rotten. Tom Huston Company researchers found evidence that a fungus was causing the plants to fail. The senior horticulturist at the USDA disagreed, insisting the fungus was a result of the unknown problem, not the problem itself.

The company turned to Carver for advice. After inspecting some of the ruined peanuts in the field, he agreed that fungi were the cause and identified several different varieties that were producing both root rot and leaf spot. Bob Barry, a researcher for Huston, leaned toward believing Carver over the government, fearing the USDA "would boo at the situation because somebody else found out" the truth. "Then too," Barry went on, "people in political jobs are not looking for hard work as a rule. If they did attempt to do something the chances are they would scare the farmer to death...."

Barry and his colleague at Huston, Grady Porter, decided to print and circulate five thousand copies of Carver's report, "Some Peanut Diseases," along with a cover letter describing him as "a mycologist of International fame." Even if it was a little exaggerated, the statement was defensible. Carver had had a lifelong interest in the study of fungi, and his formal scientific training and research had been concentrated there.

But others, ignorant of Carver's early life and career, bristled at the thought the Peanut Man could be a legitimate scientist. A botanist at a government experiment station in Georgia fumed that Carver was not "a mycologist of any kind." Doggedly pursuing their idea, Barry and Porter eventually persuaded a well-known researcher named Charles Miller to present Carver's findings on behalf of the Tom Huston Company.

At last the USDA agreed to conduct a survey of peanut fields and discovered more than 20 percent of the peanut crop, Virginia peanuts as well as others, was being lost. Based on their findings, the agency developed treatments that dramatically improved yield and cut the peanut farmers' losses due to fungi. Charles Miller was particularly impressed with Carver's detailed knowledge of fungi and his intuitive ability to find valuable specimens of the different varieties. His admiration was redoubled when he learned Carver worked with so little equipment and money compared with what was available to other researchers on the project.

Eventually the USDA recognized him as a "collaborator" with its Plant Disease Survey, inviting him to collect and submit specimens to the department of agriculture in Washington, and awarding him franking privileges for his samples.

The Tom Huston Company considered Carver a major factor in the success of their effort to identify and treat peanut fungi. Huston had already offered Carver a job; later Carver declined a cash reward. He had no interest in material things, but Huston bought him a few items he thought the elderly scientist might enjoy: a typewriter, a fine blanket, and a small gold peanut. Thoughtful as they were, Huston thought these tokens still fell short.

Riches never appealed to Carver, but praise meant everything to him. At last Huston hit on the idea of commissioning a special medallion honoring Carver. He had a clay image of Carver made by Baltimore sculptor

Isabelle Schultz and had it cast in Italy as a bronze bas-relief. It showed Carver in left profile writing notes at a table. In the background was a rack of test tubes, and on his left lapel, a sprig of cedar. Two copies were made, one for the Tom Huston laboratory and the other for Tuskegee, to be presented during commencement exercises in the spring of 1931.

Carver was absolutely delighted at the recognition and wrote stacks of letters to friends, many of them white, inviting them to attend the ceremony on May 28. Bob Barry from the Huston company presided at the unveiling. In his speech, which doubtless elated Carver as well, he warned the Tuskegee audience not to overlook the great figure who lived and worked among them:

> You know him so well. But do you really know him? I see many young people here today. Do you, whom he can help so much, really know him as he is? If you live beside a mountain and see it every day, it does not seem high to you; but someone who does not see it often knows that it is high.

Certainly Tuskegee and the peanut industry knew the value of the mountain among them. From about 1930 on, Carver traveled frequently, speaking at both white and black schools, state assemblies, teacher and farmer organizations, YMCA groups, agricultural expositions, state fairs, and many other audiences. His presentation was much the same from one place to the next, but he always had plenty to say about the benefits of Tuskegee and of peanuts. Carver sincerely believed in both and proved to be a public relations bonanza for them. They sponsored most of the trips if the host organizations could not afford the cost.

With stooping shoulders and shuffling gait, he made his way to the lectern. He spoke in a high, articulate, quiet voice his audience had to strain to hear. In their concentration to catch his words they fell completely silent: Many public accounts of his appearances marveled at how he captured and held the attention of his listeners.

Newspapers and magazines also frequently repeated Carver's version of his conversation with the Creator about the peanut. One story Carver told often in public appearances was a somewhat fictionalized account. In it, Carver asked God for knowledge about all of creation, but God declined. Then Carver asked to know just about the peanut, to which

God answered, "All about the peanut is infinite and you are finite." At last the Creator said, "I'd be glad to give you a few peanuts. I've given you a few brains. Take the peanuts into the laboratory and pull them into pieces."

"Can I make milk out of peanuts?" Carver asked God.

"Do you have the constituents of milk?" the Creator countered. Then from behind the lectern Carver pulled out a bottle of peanut milk. He held up other products in turn, more than a dozen in all, to the growing amazement and admiration of the audience. It was part science, part religion, and part showmanship, all wrapped up in an engaging—and famous—person.

Carver never brought up the issue of his race directly, but the implied message was always there: Through hard work, humility, and faith, black people could succeed, even by white standards.

By and large, the country embraced Carver without taking his message to heart. Lynchings still took place—fifty had been reported during the Harding administration—and segregation was the law in practice if not in fact. As his traveling schedule became more crowded, Carver began traveling with H. O. Abbott, a secretary from Tuskegee who went along to assist Carver and make travel arrangements. On a fifteen-day trip through Kansas, Oklahoma, and Texas, Abbott made Pullman reservations for the two of them between Oklahoma City and Dallas. But when they arrived at the platform in Oklahoma City, the passenger agent there refused to let them aboard. Instead they were forced to ride in the segregated coach, which had no sleeping accommodations.

The Oklahoma City *Black Dispatch* reported that "George Washington Carver, the latches of whose shoes few white men in Oklahoma are worthy to unlatch, must warm himself in the corner of a Jim Crow coach and suffer." The railroad agent insisted he was just following company policy; furthermore, the railroad argued, it was too expensive to maintain a Pullman car for blacks under the "separate but equal" state transportation law. Said the *Black Dispatch,* "White folk should have surveyed this phase of the question before they acted so hurriedly in 1907."

Abbott sent a letter of protest to the Atchison, Topeka, and Santa Fe management; they promised an investigation not only of Carver's mistreatment but of the general policy on accommodating Negroes in states such as Texas and Oklahoma that required segregated coaches. The president of the railroad wrote a personal letter to Carver affirming that the company would "be guided by what will best and most certainly insure our black passengers against disturbance and possible danger of violence or arrest and I believe that your knowledge of existing conditions...will enable you to understand how great is the problem and how hard it is to meet this situation wisely at all times."

Carver accepted the apology, such as it was, with characteristic grace, grateful that "every courtesy possible will be extended to colored patrons." Some blacks encouraged Carver to sue the railroad, but Abbott explained they were more interested in "better traveling accommodations for our people, rather than any petty gains or notoriety."

When another Negro was denied Pullman access in Oklahoma a month later, the *Black Dispatch* wondered aloud why Carver had not sued. Abbott sent the publication copies of the correspondence between Carver and the railroad, hoping it would settle the issue. Instead, the editor took the letters to mean "Carver can ride in a Pullman, but the rest of the niggers can't."

Abbott pressed the railroad for a clear public statement on its Pullman policy. The railroad declined, hinting darkly that Abbott should feel fortunate to win even a limited victory: "The same elements that caused the enactment of the separate coach laws may easily bring pressure to bear on the railways to prevent more liberal interpretation of them."

It was a strange position for Carver. The only parents he ever knew were white. His early friends, fellow churchgoers, and college classmates were white. His professors and oldest friends were white. Many of his hosts and most ardent admirers were white. He was in every way their peer. To a white railroad agent, however, he was anything but.

CHAPTER SEVENTEEN

A BLAZER
OF TRAILS

The 1920s were prosperous years for American business and years of dramatic change for American culture. Women, white ones at least, won the right to vote in 1920. In 1923 the first commercial radio station went on the air in Pittsburgh. Charles Lindbergh flew solo across the Atlantic in 1927, the same year the first talking picture was released. Henry Ford cranked out Model Ts so fast they accounted at one point for half the cars on American roads.

Between 1924 and 1929 stock values rose an average of 22 percent per year. Yet the rosy figures hid underlying problems that eventually pulled the world economy into steep decline. In 1929, a faltering stock market revealed how delicate the prosperity had been. For years businesses and farmers had been producing more goods than their markets demanded, but the mismatch between supply and demand was hidden by easy credit and continuing market growth. By 1931 the American economy was in desperate straits, and George Washington Carver's "one-horse farmers," the "men farthest down"—terms Carver used frequently to describe the poor farmers he most wanted to help—were among the most desperate of all.

The twenties had never been prosperous times for farmers. Prices had remained more or less depressed throughout the decade. The South had recovered from the boll weevil through new strains of cotton plants, new farming techniques, and pesticides. Even though farmers were beginning to plant other crops such as soybeans, they struggled nevertheless. When crops were plentiful, it drove down prices; when they were scarce, the harvest was too small to be profitable. Industrial growth elevated the price of machinery and equipment. Many workers who left the South during the war had never returned. Farmers, especially small independents in the South, never knew that the twenties were supposed to roar.

By 1931, the year Carver received his elegant bas-relief portrait from the Tom Huston Company, farm prices were in a free fall. Between 1929 and 1932 they fell 53 percent. Tenants and sharecroppers were "tractored off the land" as landowners struggled to cut costs by replacing farm workers with modern labor-saving machinery.

In the face of such hopelessness, Carver's presentations took on a new level of meaning. He was born poor and had made do with little for most of his life. His products and discoveries were based on one of the simplest and most inexpensive of all crops, the humble peanut. Carver's spirit of achievement in the face of adversity struck a chord with farmers of both races in their struggle to survive.

Carver quietly donated money to organizations set up to help farmers and gave food, clothing, and cash both to individuals he knew and to destitute strangers. Though he never had a large salary, he had begun depositing money in a Missouri savings bank while he was still a student and had saved regularly through the years. He probably lost some of his money in the Carver Products Company and the Penol misadventures but had a comfortable reserve to share with others nonetheless.

Friends of his who knew of his generosity sometimes gave him money in turn. In responding to one such gift from his friend Jimmy Hardwick, Carver returned a check from him, explaining:

I knelt down by the bedside…and prayed for light and direction.
All day today I have made a survey of the destitute conditions and found that every family, both white and colored, had been helped and was receiving enough to keep the wolf from the door, and if they will work they will get along.

I said, "O God, this is your money. What shall I do with it that will bring the greatest returns for him?"

The urge comes to return it and let you place it where God will direct it.... I so thoroughly believe that this check is bread cast upon the waters and will return to you many fold.

Looking beyond the stock market, the failing banks (eleven thousand in four years), and the floundering policies of President Hoover, Carver saw hope in frugality and diligence, with a special role for the peanut. He expressed his simple optimism in the January 1932 issue of the *Peanut Journal* titled "Are We Starving in the Midst of Plenty? If So Why?"

In Proverbs the thirteenth chapter and twenty-third verse, we have this statement: "Much food is in the tillage of the poor; but there is that which is destroyed for want of judgment." I doubt if this verse has ever had a greater significance than at the present time.

We have become 99 percent money mad. The method of living at home modestly and within our income, laying a little by systematically for the proverbial rainy day which is sure to come, can almost be listed among the lost arts.

To illustrate—A few weeks ago I was visiting a large city and was entertained in a very luxuriant home of the latest style of architecture furnished with every modern convenience, and Lincoln car of the latest model.... Yet, when the subject of making a little sacrifice in giving and receiving Christmas presents in favor of the vast hordes of the unemployed, they were not willing to do it and showed very conclusively by their system of reasoning why they needed presents this year more than ever before.

Last summer, we had an unusually large fruit and vegetable crop. Peaches, plums, figs, pears, etc., were often fed to the hogs.... Anyone could get all the fruit they wanted for the asking, yet many families put up absolutely nothing for the winter. Their excuse being too poor to buy jars or cans. It had never occurred to them that peaches, apples, plums, pears, figs, cherries, etc., are delicious when properly dried....

Since 1928, welfare agencies...have sensed the need and have begun to study in a thoroughly scientific and systematic way the whole food problem as it relates to feeding the family, laying special stress upon food expenditures for low-income families, in order to give them the maximum amount of nourishment at the minimum cost....

Taking the peanut pound for pound, I know of no other farm, or garden, or field crop that contains as many digestible nutrients.... The enterprising and resourceful housewife will be agreeably surprised how perfectly and cheaply she can feed the entire family.... It is hoped that the billion pound peanut crop will be utilized in a way that will bring 100 percent nourishment, comfort, and joy especially to the many thousand jobless, under-nourished people within our borders...."

By this time Carver had identified 265 uses for peanuts, 118 for sweet potatoes, and 85 for another bountiful Southern crop, pecans. The length of his lists was somewhat misleading since each of a group of related items was counted separately. For example, hand cream, face cream, and night cream, all nearly identical, were considered three different products. Still the sheer variety and imagination of them—from sweet potato rubber to peanut skin dye—was encouraging to people who looked around and saw only despair.

In another *Peanut Journal* essay published in November 1932, Carver encouraged "constructive thinking" as a way to promote economic development in the South, which would "in all probability be the greatest beneficiary from the development of [creative minds] by reason of its vast wealth of undeveloped resources."

"Strike while the iron is hot" and "Take time by the forelock" were trite sayings, he admitted, but never more applicable.

Now is the psychological time for the creative mind to work out the many, many new uses from the inexhaustible deposits of our fine Southern clays; vegetable dye stuffs; mineral deposits, new and old; various and varied mineral waters; Southern fiber plants;

material for paper pulp, and many, many other things too numerous to mention in an article of this kind.

Among the hungry and destitute people around him, Carver saw a horn of plenty filled with the Creator's providence. He tirelessly continued trying to reveal it to others, but the more desperately they needed it, the less inclined they seemed to see it.

Enrollment at Tuskegee remained high throughout the Great Depression of the 1930s. The families who supplied its students had always been poor, so they suffered less in relative terms than many who were better off to begin with. In 1931, Tuskegee's fiftieth anniversary, student enrollment was at more than 2,250, the second largest in school history. On April 14 the entire campus celebrated the "semi-centennial" event with a day of looking back over past accomplishments and looking ahead into the future.

Lewis Adams's vision for a school for blacks and Booker T. Washington's long years of service claimed center stage, though George Washington Carver was honored especially for his receiving the Spingarn Award eight years previously. (His bas-relief medallion was awarded at the end of the school year six weeks later.)

Tuskegee was in robust financial health, with a paid endowment of more than $7.7 million. With one exception, its goals were unchanged since the day Booker Washington taught its first class. The school still gave poor blacks an alternative to subsistence living on the farm or a lifetime of menial service jobs. Students left the school armed with practical skills, moral training, and a sense of self-worth. The most important asset they had was the Tuskegee stamp of approval. Tuskegee was arguably the most famous and successful school for blacks in the country; its aura of excellence and expectation followed them from then on.

The exception was that since 1927, Tuskegee had been offering college classes. Booker T. Washington had steadfastly refused to establish a college on the Tuskegee campus, maintaining that what blacks needed was education in a trade, not Latin or trigonometry. Twelve years after his death, the trustees of Tuskegee decided to open a college department with the idea of training black teachers. Other disciplines were gradually added, and by the time of the fiftieth anniversary celebration more than five hundred pupils were enrolled in college courses.

As in Washington's time, religious training was still an integral part of the Tuskegee experience. Students also had to uphold strict rules of decorum everywhere on campus, in class or out. Female students went into town only with a chaperone, and male students had to wear the distinctive Tuskegee cap whenever they went out. All students had a special Tuskegee uniform, which they wore on special occasions such as Founder's Day and commencement.

Students also wore their uniforms to chapel every Sunday morning. There were religious services every day except Saturday (two on Sunday), but the Sunday morning march into chapel had evolved into a major production. Many locals, dressed in their own Sunday best, came to the campus every Sunday morning to watch it.

One student later recalled the spectacle:

After roll call and inspection, the students were assembled in formation. The cadets assembled in military formation, by company, on Campus Road in front of Carnegie Hall [which was the library until a larger one was built in 1931] with the Institute Band in front. The girls were grouped by dormitory, in columns of fours, in front of White Hall for uniform inspection by the Dean of Women's staff.

At the appointed time, the Band struck up ["Onward Christian Soldiers"] and led the march down Campus Road, past the Reviewing Stand to a designated position along the line of march. The band was followed by the girl students, then the Cadet Corps.

That was some sight, one usually enjoyed by the numerous visitors who flanked the line of march. There was something about those uniforms. We ROTC cadets looked forward to the formation but many others did not share the feeling. [A junior Reserve Officer Training Corps unit had been on campus since 1919].

Certainly some students dreaded the whole Sunday morning program—uniforms, inspections, marching, and all the rest. One female student spoke for many when she candidly admitted, "Oh! How the students hated Sunday mornings, preparation for mandatory Chapel attendance, uniform inspection by the Dean's Staff in front of White Hall; and the line of march to Chapel." However she also admitted "it was a beautiful sight to behold, if you were watching from the sideline."

Though Booker T. Washington was active in the religious training of Tuskegee students, the school also had a chaplain. The first, John W. Whittaker, came in 1888 and served forty years. After five years without a chaplain, the school called Dr. Henry V. Richardson, a Harvard Divinity School graduate, to the position in 1933. Richardson had come to teach history for a faculty member on sabbatical, was appointed chaplain, and remained in the position for sixteen years.

Dr. Richardson had no direct connection with Booker T. Washington and the Tuskegee tradition. As a result, he soon made changes Washington would have been surprised to see. Realizing "students hated Sunday mornings," Richardson modified formerly ironclad rules, cutting weekday vesper services from five days a week to three, and later to one. Eventually the uniform requirement was relaxed as well, requiring formal school dress less and less often. Washington considered strict control and discipline essential in managing young men and women in close proximity on an otherwise isolated campus, but Richardson's policy revealed he thought a change was in order.

One element of religious training that stayed comfortably constant through these times was George Washington Carver's Sunday school class. Its legendary status brought standing room only crowds every Sunday the old professor was in town.

Visitors of every sort streamed into Carver's laboratory or sought him out on campus. Some had scientific questions to ask, others invited him to speaking engagements or reinforced invitations sent earlier by mail, and a growing number of them simply wanted to meet the most famous living black man in the world. He took at least a moment to talk with anyone who came to see him, even if he were busy. He would carry on a conversation with them as he worked. Many guests used the term "childlike" in describing him, and were flattered when he proudly showed them something he had made—a chalk sketch, a crocheted blanket, or a pair of gloves.

Stories about him began to take on a life of their own. Carver had published research on peanuts at least fifteen years before his 1921 Ways and Means testimony and had made careful studies of sweet potatoes even earlier. Even so, a long article in *The Friend, A Religious and Literary Journal,* described his research in far more dramatic terms.

> For days and days he shut himself in his laboratory, saying little but working steadily. One day he spoke. What he said aroused the nation. "I have discovered," he said, "that out of the clays and sands which are in our hills in great abundance it is possible to make dyes such as the world has not seen since the days of the Egyptians...."
>
> Once more he shut himself in his laboratory. People awaited his results with considerable interest. This time his discoveries were hardly short of being miracles. The sweet potato was a real Aladdin's lamp, and Carver was Aladdin. At his magic touch what a concourse of products poured forth!...
>
> "What next, Mr. Carver?" the world asked. "Just wait," he said, "and I will show you that the South had another lowly product out of which scores and scores of worthwhile articles can be developed to take the place of the cotton which the boll weevil is destroying." He went back to his laboratory.... This time he took a few peanuts, the food we give to elephants and monkeys at the circus. Lo! at his magic touch the peanut was changed into products which men never dreamed could be so developed.

When he was not speaking out of town, Carver still lived simply in two rooms of Rockefeller Hall, a men's dormitory on campus. One room was his bedroom and the other, a combination living room, library, gallery, and museum he called his "little den." Books were stacked from floor to ceiling with magazines and journals heaped in the corners. Along one wall was a large glass case four feet wide and six feet high filled with his own expertly done embroidery, tatting, and crocheting. A large table in the middle of the room held rock samples and stalactites. Outside, window boxes were jammed with dozens of plants and flowers.

Carver was an early riser, often up by four in the morning to walk in the woods before sunrise, collecting samples of whatever caught his attention. By nine o'clock he was at his laboratory in a building nearby. He often prayed briefly before entering the lab, "Open thou mine eyes that I may behold wondrous things out of thy law. My help cometh from the Lord who made heaven and earth, and all that in them is." Throughout the day he met with visitors, answered his voluminous correspondence from around the world, and visited with students. Evenings he spent quietly reading, sketching, or crocheting, and retired by nine.

Carver added gradually to the long list of items he could derive from the peanut, sweet potato, and pecan. He also continued experiments on wheat (which he thought would be a good raw material for paper), okra (which he made into matting and rope), and artichokes (a source of commercial starch).

He explained he was interested in them because "God told me to look there."

Feature articles about him took on a mythical tone. Incidents in his early life were reduced to popular formulas that were picked up and repeated time and again. By way of his childhood kidnapping he became the orphan child who was "traded for a $300 horse" since Moses Carver had gratefully bestowed a horse on his rescuer. Though Carver began his peanut research well before the boll weevil became established, popular accounts claimed he started experimenting on peanuts in response to the threat to Southern cotton.

Perhaps the most widely read description of George Washington Carver at the time was written by James Saxon Childers for the October 1932 issue of *The American Magazine*. Later reprinted in *Reader's Digest*, it painted a detailed portrait of an endearing old man who, guided by God, uncovered all sorts of natural wonders for the good of mankind.

Childers's description of his first glimpse of Carver was both unforgettable and consistent with what others said about their own first meetings:

> The stooped old Negro shuffled along through the dust of an Alabama road at a curiously rapid rate. He was carrying an armful of sticks and wild flowers.
>
> The sticks I could understand—he would use them for kindling—but I had never before seen an old black man ambling along the road at nine o'clock in the morning with swamp roses, wild geranium, and creeping buttercups mingled with a lot of dry sticks.
>
> When I got a little closer to him I saw that he was wearing a saggy coat which originally might have been a green alpaca, but which the sun had faded until I couldn't be sure about the color; there were so many patches that I couldn't even be certain about the material.
>
> The old man was walking towards a large brick building, one of the buildings of Tuskegee Institute, the famous school for Negroes at Tuskegee, Ala. His thin body bent by the years, his hair white beneath a ragged cap, he seemed pathetically lost on the campus of a great modern educational institution. Poor old fellow; I had seen hundreds just like him. Totally ignorant, unable even to read and write, they shamble along through the dust of Southern roads in search of any little odd job that will earn enough food to keep them alive, enough clothes to cover their tired old bones.
>
> At the entrance of the building toward which we were both walking, the old Negro turned in. "He's probably the janitor," I told myself, "and I'm sincerely glad that they've given him a job of some kind."
>
> I stepped into the hallway. I saw a trim little secretary hurry toward the bent old Negro. I heard her say to him, "That delegation from Washington is waiting for you, Doctor Carver."

Carver's prominence produced a burst of publicity in 1933 at the news that one of his peanut oil preparations had "evidently" cured polio.

Though it had been identified in 1908, doctors and scientists had made little progress in treating the polio virus. Ironically the disease seemed to do its worst damage in relatively clean, advanced environments. In undeveloped areas where sanitary facilities were primitive, the virus was rampant; many people there developed mild cases which they recovered from completely, resulting in permanent natural immunity to further, more serious infection. In countries like the United States, natural immunity was less common. While many victims did recover, others suffered permanent weakness or deformity in their limbs. The fact that many of the sufferers were children made the disease even more sinister and frightening.

In 1932, America had elected a president with polio. Franklin D. Roosevelt had caught polio at the age of thirty-nine but had gone on to serve two terms as governor of New York before defeating Calvin Coolidge to become president during the depths of the Great Depression. Though Roosevelt almost never mentioned his paralysis after becoming president and was rarely photographed in a wheelchair or with his leg braces visible, his condition naturally gave polio a high profile.

When he was in college, George Washington Carver had been the "rubber," or masseur, for the football team. Throughout his life, Carver used massage to help friends alleviate insomnia, poor appetite, and other ills. As word of his skill spread, friends brought other friends to Carver for help. By all accounts he was an excellent massage therapist, and one of his outstanding success stories was an eleven-year-old boy named Foy Thompson. Foy's family were prominent in the Tuskegee community, and they brought him to Carver hoping to improve his health. Little Foy was weak and underweight when Carver first saw him, and Carver gave him "muscle building" massages with peanut oil three times a week.

Within a month, Foy gained thirty-one pounds. Carver decided that the protein-building qualities of peanut oil had strengthened the boy's muscles by being absorbed through the skin. Carver then tried the oil on two polio patients and concluded that his treatment had helped them tremendously. As he was inclined to do, Carver began mentioning his oil massage in speeches as a possible treatment for polio. Questioned by the newspaper wire services, Carver replied, "Do not want any further publicity at this time. Am making more demonstrations of its efficacy."

T. M. Davenport, a reporter for the Associated Press, visited Carver at

Tuskegee late in 1933 to learn more details. Carver insisted—and Davenport's story began—"It has been given out that I have found a cure. I have not, but it looks hopeful." The rest of the article, however, focused on the question of how close Carver actually was to a cure.

Carver explained that his formula was derived from a beauty oil base he had made. "I gave it to some ladies to use," he said, "and those inclined to be fat brought it back to me" because it made them gain weight.

The article went on to quote Carver as saying, "I have used it on 250 persons, and it has never failed, so far as I can find out." What Carver had meant was that in the various applications he had tried, the peanut oil massage always helped. He did not intend to say he had treated 250 people with polio.

Davenport's article appeared on December 30, 1933. Immediately, Carver was swamped with inquiries and requests for help from sufferers of everything from leprosy and multiple sclerosis to baldness and weak arches. By the end of January he had received more than eleven hundred letters about peanut oil treatments. A long line of cars appeared on the Tuskegee campus, many carrying patients arriving unannounced hoping for a miracle.

The Associated Press story caused a severe shortage of peanut oil nationwide. Carver himself could scarcely find enough for his work. Tuskegee had no press powerful enough to extract oil from peanuts, and he had to scramble along with the general public to find a reliable source. Carver emphasized that peanut oil could be used in its natural form. Even so, entrepreneurs rushed to market with a host of preparations aimed at satisfying the new market.

Carver carefully and specifically positioned his treatment as a way to restore damaged limbs and not as a cure for the polio virus. A number of doctors expressed interest in his idea, but Carver was characteristically vague in describing his restorative process. The fact that he had no notes on his work raised the suspicions of some and made it impossible to test his treatment scientifically.

Carver did describe his treatment process to a few friends who were doctors. He began massages only after the disease had run its course and any necessary corrective surgery had been completed. He suggested for-mulating oil based on how quickly the patient's skin absorbed it, and at one time had nine different formulas which he spent about a week test-ing on a patient before settling on one for long-term treatment.

"Five or six drops only of this oil should be used at a time," he explained, "massaged in until every trace has disappeared. Repeat this as long as the skin and weak muscles will take it up, then stop until the next day. Treatment should alternate nine days of oil massage with nine days of massage without oil."

One of Carver's most dramatic successes was with a young man named Emmett Cox Jr., who had been crippled by polio at age two. After four operations as a child, he could walk with difficulty and only when wearing two heavy leg braces that extended up to his waist. He began Carver's treatments in September 1934 and within six months he could walk without braces.

The *Reader's Digest* agreed to carry a story on Carver's treatment if the medical community would endorse it. After a protracted series of letters, visits, inquiries, and interviews among various groups, the endorsement never materialized. Instead, the magazine reran James Saxon Childers's 1932 article from *The American Magazine*. Even though the article avoided the subject of polio treatment, other publications reprinted it with stories and photographs of polio patients, unleashing another wave of letters.

In 1939, President Franklin D. Roosevelt visited Carver at Tuskegee and received a bottle of peanut oil for treating polio. The next week Carver received a letter of thanks from the president, saying "I do use peanut oil from time to time and I am sure that it helps." As war clouds gathered in Europe, and the medical community remained skeptical, public interest in Carver's polio treatment gradually faded.

Because Carver never kept any records, it is impossible to follow his line of research on polio treatment. Peanut oil has no properties that could restore damaged muscles. However, Carver obviously achieved dramatic results in some patients. In some cases, polio victims did con-tinue to improve slowly over time after the virus was gone. This may account for some results, but not all. In cases like Emmett Cox Jr., Carver's treatments clearly made a difference. These improvements were likely the result of expert massage techniques and unwavering encouragement. Peanut oil was the least important ingredient.

Carver himself had been in delicate health all his life. He was probably born prematurely, nearly died from illness after his kidnapping as a young boy, and was invariably described by those who met him as slender, delicate, or frail. Beginning in the late 1930s, Carver dramatically scaled back his traveling and speechmaking. He lent his name to one more beauty products company, Carvoline, but had no direct involvement in its operation. From New York or Chicago he appeared on numerous coast-to-coast radio broadcasts.

Most of all he wanted to make some provision for preserving his work and continuing it after his death. He chafed at the thought his agricultural experiments would not go forward. "I am not a finisher," he said, "I am a blazer of trails."

Carver grew weaker and suffered from potentially fatal pernicious anemia, spending weeks in the hospital. Vitamin B_{12} shots allowed him to recover, but from about 1938, he began a slow, steady decline.

He moved into the Tuskegee guest house, Dorothy Hall. The building adjacent to it had been built as the school laundry, and plans were made to convert it into the George Washington Carver Museum. Carver's laboratory equipment, specimen collection, and even his paintings would be on display. The scientist himself would have a research laboratory on the premises. The Tuskegee president, Frederick Douglass Patterson, who had succeeded President Moton in 1935, recognized Carver's inestimable value as publicity for the Institute and pushed ahead to solicit funding for the project.

Carver hoped for a museum that presented a complete and detailed chronicle of his life, but there were seemingly endless delays caused by discussions over what the museum should contain and by lack of money to buy display cases and repair roof leaks in the old laundry building, which had been built in 1915. At times he was convinced some members of the faculty wanted to see the project fail, and it was true that recently hired teachers, as well as some students, made fun of him and considered him a fussy old man. Feeling his time was growing short, Carver agreed to settle for a more modest facility. The George Washington Carver

Museum was opened on July 25, 1939, with more than two thousand guests attending the inaugural festivities.

As famous and beloved a public figure as Carver had become, he was never far from reminders that he was still a member of a race many considered to be second class. Six weeks after the museum opening, Carver traveled to New York to appear on the radio program *Strange as It Seems*. His assistant had made hotel reservations, but when the two arrived at the New Yorker Hotel, the clerk insisted they had no vacancies.

The assistant, Austin Curtis, refused to leave. Carver, near eighty and exhausted after a night and day on the train, was offered a chair near the men's washroom where he could wait "in case any other guests checked out." Curtis called Doubleday, Doran & Company, which was preparing a biography on Carver. The publishing firm sent an employee over to ask about a room. When he was given one immediately, he insisted it be given to Carver instead. The hotel manager again claimed there were no rooms after all.

The vice president of Doubleday called the hotel and threatened to sue. At that point, after sitting six hours in the washroom hallway, Dr. George Washington Carver, Fellow of the Royal Society, was shown to his room.

One honor came on top of another. He was awarded one of three Roosevelt Medals in 1939 (one of the others went to Carl Sandburg); honorary membership in the American Inventors Society, the Mark Twain Society, and the National Technical Society. Metro-Goldwyn-Mayer approached him about making a film of his life. Carver considered the movie offer because he thought it would provide money for the Carver Creative Research Laboratory he was trying to fund. When M-G-M offered him only a five-hundred-dollar honorarium, he declined and the project was dropped.

Late in life, Carver had become friends with Henry Ford, and beginning about 1937, had visited him several times in Dearborn, near Detroit, where the gigantic River Rouge Plant churned out hundreds of Ford cars a day. Ford, himself a self-made success story and lifelong tinkerer, genuinely admired Carver. Ford built a Carver cabin at his Greenfield Village farm, set up a nutritional laboratory in his honor, and established the George Washington Carver School on his Georgia plantation, persuading Carver to attend the dedication and personally escorting him throughout the day.

Ford also paid to install an elevator in Dorothy Hall at Tuskegee, so Carver could more easily come down for meals and to work in his laboratory. Carver still hoped for a larger museum exhibit, especially room to hang his paintings. Many people had no idea Carver was a painter, and the sight of his vibrant still lifes was a revelation to them.

By the fall of 1939, Carver was going into the hospital for progressively longer stays. A doctor told him once he shouldn't expect to live to be twenty-one, and now he was approaching his eightieth year. But he walked only with difficulty and spent weeks at a time in a wheelchair.

Carver repeatedly requested his museum expanded so all his available paintings could be hung in one place. He also wanted some assurance that the experimental work he had spent so many years on would be preserved and continued. The old professor sensed his time was growing short, and on February 10, 1940, Carver incorporated the George Washington Carver Foundation to help ensure his legacy would be preserved. He endowed the organization with his life savings of $32,374.19.

Still, Carver sensed the Tuskegee authorities were dragging their feet when they insisted there was still not enough money to make the museum improvements he envisioned. Frustrated and fearing he would die before the matter was resolved, Carver informed the school administration he was considering donating his paintings to the Alabama state archives in Montgomery.

His threat produced results. The school hastily came up with money to expand the George Washington Carver Museum and add exhibit space for more paintings, seventy-one in all. The new facilities were opened by Henry Ford on November 17, 1941.

Carver's universal appeal was apparent in the variety of the crowd that viewed the Carver collection that first afternoon. One eyewitness vividly captured the scene:

There were ladies in furs, student chefs in tall white cook caps; carpenters, with hammer heads sticking from the long pockets of their brown coveralls; student architects with rolls of drawings; white school children and grown ups; farm boys in blue overalls, nurses in uniform, a washer-woman, a dressmaker, the wife of a state senator, a telephone operator, a cotton warehouseman; colored people and white people.

One other project Carver wanted to see through to completion was a biography of himself by Rackham Holt. Mrs. Holt had finished her first draft of the book by the summer of 1940 and had a publication agreement with Doubleday, Doran & Company before she even started work. She visited Carver several times and corresponded regularly with him as she refined and polished her manuscript. A year passed, and then another, while she gathered more reminiscences from Carver about his early life and accomplishments.

Holt's book portrayed George Washington Carver in exactly the way he wanted the world to remember him: a humble genius, often maligned but never bitter, virtually flawless in every way. On October 14, 1942, he wrote hoping she would push on with the book and get it to press as soon as possible. "May I urge again to please finish the book as I would like to have it come out while I am still able to see it."

Henry Ford spent part of the summers at his enormous eighteenth-century estate, Richmond Hill, in Georgia. The last several years, he had made it a point to stop by Tuskegee both on his way South and on the way back to Dearborn to visit with Carver. In June 1942, Carver went to Dearborn, as he had numerous times over the past seven or eight years, to see Ford and look over his research and engineering facilities. The two spent almost every waking hour together with Ford personally escorting the feeble scientist from place to place throughout the day. Newspapers everywhere published a photo of Carver serving his host a weed salad with a wry smile.

There had been rumors that Carver would stay and work for Ford in the Dearborn experimental lab, but he returned to Tuskegee shortly before the new year. He was physically spent, and his doctors warned him to keep activity to a minimum. To his way of thinking, he still had a lot left to do and little time remaining to do it.

A few days later he slipped on a patch of ice and fell while trying to open the door to his museum. After a couple of days' bed rest, he was on his feet again but kept feeling sore and uncomfortable. He never really recovered and drifted gradually into a deep sleep. George Washington Carver died at 7:30 P.M., January 5, 1943.

War news kept news of George Washington Carver's death off the front page of the *New York Times* the next morning, but his death was announced all over the world. His picture headed the obituary section of the *Times* with the headline, "Dr. Carver is Dead; Negro Scientist."

The notice reported Carver's discoveries, his early life (including his kidnapping), and his many honors and awards. Then a surprising insight into this popular but enigmatic man:

> A less known side of Professor Carver's activity was his Bible class at Tuskegee, started in 1906, when his office boy and seven other students asked him to teach them the Bible on Sundays. He taught the Bible by impersonating the characters himself. On one occasion he astonished his class when it reached the story of the manna-fed Israelites by producing a variety of the original manna, which he had gathered in the woods about Tuskegee.

Three days after his death, Carver was buried near the grave of Booker T. Washington on the Tuskegee campus. At the funeral service in the Tuskegee Chapel, Reverend C. W. Kelly read messages of tribute and condolence from around the world.

Carver left his entire estate to his foundation. Combined with his initial gift, the total contribution was more than sixty thousand dollars, nearly equal to his total earnings in forty-six years at Tuskegee. He had faithfully kept a savings account since his student·days. He lost at least part of it during the bank failures of the Great Depression but gradually rebuilt his account over the years—and evidently never made a significant withdrawal.

Of the many commentaries on Carver's life, few had the simple eloquence of a letter one man wrote him after visiting him for polio treatments:

Upon leaving your office I remarked to my wife that I could well conceive the fact that Jesus was a man of color after knowing you. Your spirit of deep humility moved me and has made me resolve to be a better man and to attempt to live more accurately the teachings and principles of the lowly Nazarene.

CHAPTER EIGHTEEN

UNSHAKABLE FAITH

Geoge Washington Carver was buried near the Tuskegee Chapel in the small campus cemetery where Booker T. Washington had lain since 1915. Business leaders, politicians, and commentators across the country praised his lifetime of quiet devotion to his goal of uplifting "the man farthest down."

After his death the swirl of mythology surrounding his life and career continued to mount. History somewhat distorted the details of his scientific accomplishments and found causes and effects where none had actually existed. Carver was an expert mycologist, who added to that field of knowledge, and a gifted artist, who until the last weeks of his life enjoyed sketching, painting, finger painting, knitting, crocheting, tatting lace, and embroidering. He achieved limited but impressive results treating polio patients. He was a singular teacher whose students admired and loved him deeply and drew life-changing inspiration from him.

There was less solid science in his work with peanuts than almost anything else he did, yet it was as the Peanut Man he achieved international fame. Carver's techniques for making cosmetics, cereal, dye, and so forth from peanuts were not distinctive. For the most part, the products themselves were ultimately impractical, and none of them was ever successful in the marketplace.

Part of Carver's fame came from the public's desperate need for good news during the Depression. As Carver became more prominent, his notoriety fed on itself, generating ever more news for radio, newsreels, and wire services hungry for a great human interest story.

His success also came from his personality. Shy, quiet, and self-depreciating, he endeared himself to his audiences as a grandfatherly storyteller who made miraculous discoveries from the simplest plants.

Furthermore, like Booker T. Washington, Carver infused everything he did with a sincere spiritual element. From his earliest days, Carver looked to his Creator to lead his life and work. Like Washington, he chose a nonconfrontational approach to discrimination. The both of them could have spent their lives railing against the inequality of segregation, disenfranchisement, and Jim Crow. Instead, they spent their lives resolutely proving them wrong.

In 1920, Tuskegee was still very much the school Booker T. Washington had envisioned, but during the decade that followed, its new leadership gradually began loosening the institution's historically strong ties with the past. The most dramatic change was the establishment of the college department in 1927. Washington had always been firm in his conviction that practical education—farming, bricklaying, harness making, backsmithing—gave blacks the best chance for becoming self-sufficient. With Washington gone, those who for years had insisted Tuskegee should offer a fully-rounded educational opportunity finally prevailed. Alongside the traditional vocational training, new college-level courses in English, mathematics, and other subjects were added.

The pace of change was modest at first. Washington's successor as president of Tuskegee, Robert Russa Moton, was, like Washington, born on a Virginia plantation and a graduate of Hampton. When he came to Tuskegee in 1915, Moton had been the commandant in charge of discipline at Hampton for a quarter of a century—a job he had taken upon graduation and held ever since.

While moving deliberately ahead, Major Moton (a title that followed him from his position at Hampton) also revered and preserved the memory of the past. In 1922 he presided at the unveiling of a statue of Booker T. Washington on the campus. The larger-than-life bronze monument, cast in Italy, portrayed Washington lifting the veil of ignorance from a crouching black man, symbolizing Washington bringing light and hope to his race.

Changes came more quickly under Frederick Douglass Patterson, who served as president from 1935 until 1953. Vespers, which had been held every weeknight since Washington's time, were reduced to once a week, on Wednesday. School uniforms, so much a part of the Tuskegee image for more than half a century, were discontinued in 1948. Washington had felt it important that needy students work off the cost of their uniforms as a lesson in the rewards of labor and considered uniforms a part of teaching the value of grooming and personal hygiene. By the 1940s few students agreed with him (and may have silently opposed uniforms well before), and at last the school administration did away with the "blues" as an idea whose time was past.

In a historic echo of the 1903 student dining hall protest, hundreds of students refused to enter the dining hall or attend class on January 15, 1941. Inflamed by an editorial in the Tuskegee *Student* criticizing the food, students demanded more variety in their menus. Dr. Patterson "dropped in" to the dining hall for dinner that night for liver and onions, cabbage cooked with bacon, peas, cornbread, salad, and a choice of apple cobbler or Jell-O for dessert. He pronounced it "palatable and wholesome." Though the protest coincided with the opening of Dr. Carver's polio research center, Patterson insisted that "the student difficulty interfered in no way with the ceremonies."

With America's declaration of war against Japan on December 8, 1941, Tuskegee students had more to worry about than liver and onions. Earlier, in the spring of 1941, Tuskegee received authorization to replace the junior ROTC unit, which had been on campus since 1919, with a senior unit, whose members would qualify for commissions in the U.S. Army. In July, after intensive lobbying from Dr. Patterson and other friends of the school, Tuskegee was authorized to set up an Army Air Force facility to train African-American pilots. The center was a "civil contract school" operated by Tuskegee under military supervision with cadets from Tuskegee, Hampton Institute, Howard University, West Virginia State College, and North Carolina Agricultural and Technical College. In October the AAF supplied Tuskegee with training aircraft.

Five cadets out of the first class of thirteen successfully completed their training and received commissions in the 99th and 100th Pursuit Squadrons, the first two black AAF units.

The first American of African descent to become a licensed pilot had earned her wings in 1921. Bessie Coleman, a Texas native, had not been allowed to fly in the United States, so she took her lessons in France. After earning her pilot certificate there, she returned home and received her American license in 1922.

After the War, students returned to a world that was changing more rapidly than ever. As the Cold War era began, President Harry Truman ordered desegregation of the U.S. military, one of the first wide-scale efforts at legally assuring equal treatment for black Americans. The Congress of Racial Equality (CORE), organized in Chicago in 1942, developed a pattern of nonviolent direct action such as sit-ins and boycotts, which was adopted over the next several years by members of both races seeking a middle ground between violence and acceptance of the status quo. In 1947, Jackie Robinson, a star college athlete and former World War II army officer, became the first black man to play major league baseball. In his first season, he helped lead the Brooklyn Dodgers to the World Series and was voted Rookie of the Year. The logjam of segregation Washington and Carver had spent their lifetime trying to untangle was breaking loose at last.

The year 1947 brought tragedy to the George Washington Carver Museum. A fire gutted the former laundry building and all the exhibits. The building—of sturdy Tuskegee brick—survived, as did much of Carver's scientific equipment and memorabilia, including the telescope he had received as a parting gift from his friends at Iowa State in 1896. The great loss was Carver's paintings. Virtually every known work by Carver, some painted during his days as an art student at Simpson College, was on display there, and all but a handful were destroyed. The building was refurbished, enlarged, and reopened in 1951.

On January 23, 1957, fire destroyed the Tuskegee Chapel. The building, designed by Harvard graduate Robert Taylor, had been the tallest building in Macon County when it was completed, and the first building on campus to have electric lights. It originally held twenty-five hundred people, but galleries added in the transepts increased the capacity to three thousand in 1906. In 1933 the school had installed the Singing Windows, a series of ten large stained glass panels from the studios of J. & R. Lamb of New York City depicting stories from Negro spirituals including "Swing Low, Sweet Chariot," "Go Down, Moses," "Deep River," "Steal Away," and others.

With the loss of the chapel, the issue of mandatory church attendance, which had been questioned by students from time to time, returned to the forefront. Young veterans fresh from World War II had seen little point in school administrators making them go to church. Uniforms had been discontinued in 1948; the march into chapel Sunday services, another long-standing tradition, was abandoned in 1956 except for special occasions. Though in announcing the end of the chapel march, President Luther Foster reminded the students of its place in Tuskegee history and its "unifying force and symbol of oneness," he nevertheless oversaw the dismantling of one of the school's most visible links with the past. Chapel attendance, however, remained mandatory.

After the chapel fire, religious services were moved to Logan Hall, the campus gym. The administration immediately began planning for a new chapel, but it would be ten years before funds would be available for its construction. In the meantime, sitting on bleachers, inhaling the smell of stale socks, students' minds wandered and interest in religious life continued its decline. Of course none of the students remembered the Pavilion, the leaky, ramshackle, homemade building their predecessors had cobbled together seventy-five years before to hold services in, where Tuskegee's first students had worshiped with such gratitude and enthusiasm.

No doubt Washington would have dealt with the situation in his precise and unequivocal way: Religion was essential to proper character development, which was essential to being accepted by society and achieving success.

In his day, no student would have even considered suggesting that religion was no longer relevant or that a student's preferences should hold any sway over school policies. But times were changing faster and more dramatically than ever.

Students arrived on campus in the 1960s with far different expectations than their predecessors. Their view of the world—and of themselves—had been transformed by the 1954 United States Supreme Court decision known as *Brown vs. Board of Education*, which ruled that the "separate but equal" segregation of blacks legalized by the court in *Plessy vs. Ferguson* fifty-eight years before was, in the court's words, "inherently unequal" and therefore unconstitutional. With the reversal of *Plessy*, the Supreme Court demolished the foundation of legal segregation with a single blow. Passage of the Voting Rights Act and the Civil Rights Act during the next decade brought blacks even more fully into the social and political mainstream of American life.

Blacks were demanding their rights, and one of the rights Tuskegee students were demanding was the right not to go to chapel. After numerous meetings among themselves and with student representatives, the administration agreed to make chapel attendance voluntary for a trial period. So many students began skipping services that by 1965 the administration, still insisting the rule was only temporarily suspended, assigned seats to freshmen and sophomores.

The next year, during Religious Emphasis Week, one chapel service was attended by only seventy-five students out of an enrollment of almost twenty-eight hundred. Leon S. White, editor of the student *Campus Digest*, expressed the thoughts of many disgruntled students when he wrote, "Chapel will not meet the requirements of any students as long as some are compelled to attend.... No horizons are going to become broader if a student is...compelled to sit through a half hour or forty-five minutes of something that does not *relate*." Students had become judges of what was relevant for them to learn and expected to play a part in shaping their own scholastic experience.

Among other things, this attitude led to a 1968 student protest during which students locked trustees of the school in Georgia Hall and insisted they consider the students' wishes in formulating school policies. Compulsory chapel was completely and permanently discontinued that year.

A new chapel was eventually built in 1969 and named in honor of Air Force General Daniel "Chappie" James, a Tuskegee alumnus. A starkly modern building with angular brick walls, it has a capacity of eighteen hundred, less than two-thirds the size of the original.

In February 1956, President Luther Foster admonished the campus community that "Tuskegee Institute must devote its major efforts to strengthening its educational services. It is not our place to become enmeshed in the skirmishes that naturally accompany the broad movement toward a fully implemented democracy." This point of view, printed in the faculty newsletter, could have easily come from the mouth of Washington himself. But in only a few years the institution would be faced with cultural and social changes that would dramatically alter its position.

The 1960s was a time of unprecedented, sometimes shocking confrontations along racial lines. By the time he spoke at Tuskegee commencement in 1965, Dr. Martin Luther King Jr. was already a national symbol of hope for equality among black Americans. Two years before, King had been arrested in Birmingham for defying an injunction against public demonstrations. From his jail cell, he wrote a long letter to a group of clergymen who admonished him for his behavior and urged patience:

> For years now I have heard the word "Wait!" It rings in the ear of every Negro with piercing familiarity. This "Wait" has almost always meant "Never".... There comes a time when the cup of endurance runs over, and men are no longer willing to be plunged into the abyss of despair.

In the summer of 1965 impatience turned to tragedy in Los Angeles, where two days of riots in the Watts section of the city resulted in thirty-four deaths and four thousand arrests. In 1967 a total of nearly one hundred people were killed and two thousand injured in riots in Detroit, Newark, and other American cities.

Tuskegee had its own taste of conflict during these bitter times. Late on the night of January 3, 1966, a Tuskegee student named Samuel Younge Jr. got out of his car at the Standard Oil gas station in town and asked to use the rest room. Younge was a United States Navy veteran, who had taken part in the Bay of Pigs invasion, and a leader of a local civil rights organization called the Tuskegee Institute Advancement League. When he tried to use the facilities reserved for whites, the attendant threatened him with a pistol. Younge ran away but returned a few minutes later to retrieve his car. The two argued again, and the attendant, a sixty-seven-year-old segregationist named Marvin Segrest, shot Younge once in the temple. He was found dead in an alley later that evening.

Both the campus and the city were horrified at the news of Younge's death. In the community, which was 80 percent black, the police force, city hall staff, VA hospital, and downtown stores were all integrated; and a racially-motivated killing seemed almost impossible to imagine. More than two thousand people marched quietly and respectfully through town and past the gas station without incident. On January 6, Tuskegee President Foster called a meeting in Logan Hall attended by virtually everyone on campus, in which he officially encouraged the staff, students, and citizens to get personally involved in the Civil Rights Movement, expressing his "expectation that people will so involve themselves."

Thus, Tuskegee moved publicly and officially from a stance proclaiming involvement in civil rights "skirmishes" was "not our place," to the position that it was each person's duty to get involved and that the school expected each person to do so.

Certainly Washington and Carver would be shocked at many of the changes that have rocked the school that was their life's work. Today's students enjoy a level of prosperity their predecessors could hardly have dreamed of. Clothing inspections and chapel roll call are distant memories. The dining hall, where some of Washington's first students earned their education and where Carver spent so much time looking for efficiency and savings, is no longer even run by the school. The food is catered by Marriott.

Yet in many important respects, the school has remained on the same track. Members of the class of 1908 posed proudly to show their diversity: that year there were students from Puerto Rico, West Africa, Japan, South America, Haiti, and Cuba. Today's student body, one-third white, one-third black, and one-third foreign, is more diverse than ever.

An engineering student from the American Southwest recently chose Tuskegee because it had the best combination of high engineering credentials and moderate tuition cost. It wasn't until he got off the bus at the campus entrance that he learned the school was traditionally black. He was attracted by reputation, not racial policy. Observes one administrator, "That would have made Booker T. Washington very proud."

Various science-oriented departments would have made Dr. Carver proud as well. The school of veterinary medicine, founded in 1945, has trained 70 percent of the black veterinarians in practice today and many white ones besides. (Some years only 20 percent of the vet school applicants have been black.) After Jonas Salk announced the development of an experimental polio vaccine in 1953, more than six hundred thousand cultures used worldwide in testing the Salk vaccine were produced at Tuskegee, fulfilling Carver's dream of prevailing against this tragic, crippling disease.

The work continues as well at Carver's beloved agriculture station. Student scientists, working under a contract from NASA, are developing ways to grow the sweet potato in outer space as food for astronauts on their way to Mars.

As different as they were from one another, Booker T. Washington and George Washington Carver lived their lives in pursuit of the same goal of political and social equality for their race. They faced centuries of slavery and the decades of legal discrimination that followed with the same unshakable faith in God. They believed too in a divine spark—sometimes buried very deep—inside even their most sinister oppressors and never faltered in their resolve to touch that divinity with kindness, patience, humility, and understanding.

Humility made these men great; without it they would have never gained access to the white corridors of power where political decisions were made from the end of Reconstruction until the 1960s. Confrontation was useless then as everyone from John Brown to W. E. B. Du Bois found out. Only by fighting a patient war of attrition could Washington and Carver accomplish what they did.

These men were intellectual giants. They were keen enough to realize they could not mount a frontal assault on three hundred years of convention. Moreover, that was not their style. They were not interested in fighting; they were devoted to proving themselves to a skeptical society. Compelling and persuading the culture on the culture's own terms, they made progress that was permanent.

Washington and Carver were strong, and strongly nondenominational, Christians. Washington's faith was reflected in his approach to education, basing everything as he did on a foundation of moral absolutes grounded in biblical teaching. Circumspect as he was and eager to promote harmony among his supporters, Washington did not wear his faith on his sleeve. He was a man of business and efficiency, not a man who made a point of expressing his emotions. Carver was Washington's opposite in that he wove religion forthrightly through everything he did: his classroom lectures, his speeches, his letters, and of course his long-running Sunday night Bible study.

Curiously, one blind spot in their feelings of Christian brotherhood and humility from time to time seemed to be in their relationship with each other. Washington used Tuskegee as a base to spring out into the business, political, and social world. During Washington's lifetime, Carver used it as a perimeter from which to look inward into the lives and beliefs of individual students, nurturing, encouraging, and inspiring. In the early years of the school, Washington was much more the nurturer than he was later; still it is hard to imagine Professor Carver inspecting students' fingernails on the first day of class. After Washington's death, Carver became much more outwardly focused, though he never abandoned his deep personal interest in his friends and Tuskegee relationships.

Their realms were overlapping circles: Washington's going outward and Carver's in, with the overlap representing their Tuskegee relationship. Because they were both so intelligent, so well educated, and so strong willed, yet had such opposite personalities, they clashed almost from the first day Carver arrived. Washington was convinced Tuskegee had to appear flawless to prove blacks could run a school and educate themselves. He was a man of order and precision. Carver was more subjective and intuitive with a heart for people and little interest in managerial or administrative details. He really couldn't manage the poultry yard and wondered why it mattered so much. At the same time, Washington saw a tidy chicken run as essential to the impression he felt Tuskegee had to make in order to succeed and wondered why following such simple orders was so impossible.

Their differences touched on assumptions and the way each man dealt with them. Washington came to Tuskegee expecting to take over a school and discovered there was no school to take over. He set about building one. Carver followed fifteen years later, expecting to take over an agriculture department but soon learning he would have to build one from scratch. He expected a certain level of respect and deference, coming from a well-funded and well-equipped state college where he was an excellent student as well as a celebrity of sorts as the only black on campus. At Tuskegee he was just another of the talented black men and women who shared its founder's vision for an exemplary school.

Carver had legitimate complaints about the shortage of funds, poorly trained and ill-supervised student labor, and Washington's obsession with details. But during his teaching years, through about 1916, he was no worse off than any other department or faculty member. Carver had lived much of his life as a distinctively different member of an all-white group, whether it was the Moses Carver household, the plains of western Kansas, the Milhollands' church, or the classroom at Iowa State. At Tuskegee, Carver was not a novelty. That situation was compounded by the fact that Washington was naturally reserved and unemotional, while Carver was emotionally transparent sometimes to a fault. Carver craved the praise and attention he had become accustomed to; Washington was not inclined to praise. The hunger for attention frustrated Carver even more.

Somehow in all of this, the spirit of Christian brotherhood that so defined their relationships with others disappeared in their memos and letters back and forth, Carver's threatening and shrill, and Washington's mostly patient but sometimes exasperated and always direct. Nonetheless, a current of Christian fellowship ran deep between them as shown in Carver's reaction to Washington's death. Had Carver died first, Washington would very likely have felt the same way, though he would have hardly written it in a letter.

Both in their own time and later, Washington and Carver were accused by blacks and some whites of being far too docile and accommodating. Succeeding generations of blacks would accuse their kind of being "Uncle Toms," by which they derisively meant sniveling, cowering

Negroes only too happy to succumb to oppressive white rule. (Harriet Beecher Stowe's Uncle Tom was actually nothing like that.) They were neither cowards nor weaklings; they were realists. It was only by working within the all-powerful white political and financial structure that they could hope to accomplish anything.

Two ingredients made their success possible. The first was a consuming evangelical desire to improve opportunities for black Americans against the tide of three centuries of slavery. The second was a powerful, unquenchable humility patterned after the humility of Christ. Both men claimed lifelong, heartfelt spiritual beliefs that propelled, sustained, and encouraged them in the face of seemingly insurmountable odds. Without this unshakable faith, they could never have achieved what they did. This they admitted freely and often.

Over the years various commentators and biographers have accused each other of trying to spin the facts to portray Washington or Carver as "Christian," or more particularly as Presbyterian, Methodist, deist, pantheist, or some other denominational stripe. Some have discounted religion as a force in these men's lives, while others have tried to paint them as strict Presbyterians (Carver belonged to a Presbyterian church), Episcopalians (Washington's funeral service was Episcopalian), or whatever else fits that chronicler's needs.

The facts support the view that these two men themselves gave credit for their accomplishments to God. From their earliest years they embraced basic beliefs often associated with Christianity, though not exclusive to it, such as moral absolutes, honesty, humility, generosity, and submission to authority. They did what they could and had faith that God would do the rest.

Rather than railing against the profoundly unfair laws and traditions that confronted them, Washington and Carver spent a lifetime proving to the world that everyone who thought blacks were inferior was wrong. Blacks could do as well as whites—in fact they could do better than most. This was the attitude that gained Booker T. Washington tea with Queen Victoria and dinner at the White House; it got George Washington Carver the Roosevelt Prize and membership in the Royal Society. These shining examples told the world black people were people of great potential and great achievement.

Change on a larger scale was long in coming and came in part because of the kinds of confrontations Washington and Carver so carefully avoided. Yet it was the pioneering strides made by these two that cracked open the door to racial equality in the first place. They are the ones who stemmed the tide and allowed more aggressive action to succeed generations later. They, far more than W. E. B. Du Bois and other of their opponents, are the spiritual ancestors of later historical figures in the Civil Rights Movement who made great gains—against almost unimaginable odds—preaching of peace and reconciliation, not of retribution and revenge. Washington and Carver left an undeniable legacy for white and black alike, partly in brick and mortar, partly by way of inspiring example, and partly through the graduates who complete their Tuskegee education every year. Du Bois, in contrast, was awarded the Lenin Prize by the Communist government of the Soviet Union and retreated to Africa, where he died all but forgotten in 1963, one day before Dr. Martin Luther King Jr. electrified America with a speech on the Washington Mall telling his fellow countrymen, "I have a dream."

Washington and Carver were not black heroes; they were not Christian heroes; they were heroes for everyone and every time. Their faith made their accomplishments possible. And any of us who would look for a better world in our future will look down to find ourselves standing on their shoulders.

AUTHOR'S NOTE
ON SOURCES

Like everyone else who has written about Booker T. Washington in the past twenty-five years, I owe a debt of gratitude to Louis R. Harlan. His two-volume biography of Washington, the second volume of which was awarded the Pulitzer Prize in 1984, is the most complete source of information about Washington ever assembled. Harlan also prepared Washington's papers for publication, and the resulting thirteen-volume collection is a blessing for researchers, or for anyone interested in going deeper into Washington's life, times, and ideas.

Washington's own writings were also particularly helpful, especially *Up from Slavery,* which was recently placed third on the list of the 100 best nonfiction books of the twentieth century according to the Random House Modern Library. Editors and ghost writers actually produced the books for the most part, yet Washington's personality and philosophy are clear and consistent.

Though there is no work on George Washington Carver comparable to Harlan's on Washington, three sources stand out. The first is *George Washington Carver: An American Biography,* by Rackham Holt. Its value lies not in its degree of accuracy (rather low), but in that it was written during Carver's lifetime and with his cooperation. Mrs. Holt had almost unlimited access to Carver during his last years, and this book reflects the famous, almost mythical scientist as he wanted the world to remember him. However, there is a substantial amount of fictional dramatization and factual misinformation in the book. Holt relied on Carver's memory and her own imagination for much of her story, and the results are clearer and more accurate on some points than on others.

Fourteen years after Mrs. Holt's book was published, the National Park Service completed research on Carver in conjunction with establishing a national monument to mark his birthplace in Missouri. This research includes letters and transcripts of detailed interviews, recorded in the early 1950s, with friends, neighbors, and classmates of young Carver—men and women who were then in their 80s and 90s—who remembered Carver as a boy. These memoirs are a priceless living link with the past, and uncovered many facts that had become scrambled or enhanced over time.

Another source on Carver of special note is *George Washington Carver: Scientist & Symbol* by Linda O. McMurry. It is the most complete biography of Carver in print. If it lacks some of Rackham Holt's swashbuckling storytelling technique, this book is far more responsible with the facts.

Allhoff, Fred. "Black Man's Miracles: The Story of a Great and Good American." *Liberty Magazine* (8 January 1938): 19f.

"Andrew Carnegie." *New York Times*, 21 May 1906, p. 12, col. 3.

"Asks Aid for Tuskegee." *New York Times*, 13 February 1909, p. 4, col. 5.

"Atlanta Mobs Kill Ten Negroes." *New York Times*, 23 September 1906, p. 1, col. 1.

Battey, George M., Jr. "Wanted—New Uses for Wheat." *The Western Home Monthly* (October 1930): 18f.

"Booker T. Washington." *New York Times*, 17 November 1915, p. 11, col. 6.

"Booker T. Washington Ill." *New York Times*, 10 November 1915, p. 6, col. 6.

"Booker T. Washington Speaks." *New York Times*, 15 April 1899, p. 10, col. 4.

"Booker T. Washington's Position." *New York Times*, 28 November 1902, p. 1, col. 2.

"Booker T. Washington's Views." *New York Times*, 23 November 1900, p. 2, col. 5.

"B. T. Washington on Riots." *New York Times*, 12 October 1906, p. 5, col. 2.

"B. T. Washington Speaks." *New York Times*, 19 March 1905, p. 9, col. 2.

"B. Washington at Home." *New York Times*, 22 August 1913, p. 18, col. 4.

Butler, Addie Louise Joyner. *The Distinctive Black College: Talladega, Tuskegee and Morehouse*. Metuchen, N.J.: The Scarecrow Press, Inc., 1977.

Campbell, Thomas Monroe. *The Movable School Goes to the Negro Farmer.* Tuskegee, Ala.: Tuskegee Institute Press, 1992.

Carroll, William R., and Merle E. Muhrer. *The Scientific Contributions of George Washington Carver.* University of Missouri, 1962.

Carver, George Washington. "Experiment Station Bulletin No. 1: Feeding Acorns." Tuskegee, Ala.: Normal School Steam Press, 1898.

"Carver Gives Fund to Spur Search." *New York Times,* 14 February 1940, p. 19, col. 6.

"Carver Memorial—A Tribute to Genius." *Peanut Journal and Nut World* 16, no. 5 (6 March 1937), 5f.

"Carver to Work for Ford." *New York Times,* 12 June 1942, p. 38, col. 8.

"Catalogue of the Tuskegee State Normal School at Tuskegee, Alabama, for the Academic Year, 1881–82." Hampton, Va.: Normal School Steam Press, 1882.

Caudill, Rebecca. "A Scientist in God's Workshop." *Our Young People* (16 January 1927), 3f.

Childers, James Saxon. "A Boy Who Was Traded for a Horse." *The American Magazine* (October 1932): 24f.

"Colored Men's Dinner for B. T. Washington." *New York Times,* 16 April 1903, p. 3, col. 4.

Curtis, A. W., Jr. "A New Horizon." *The Science Counselor* 6, no. 3. Pittsburgh: Duquesne University Press (September 1940).

"Destiny of the Negro." *New York Times,* 16 April 1899, p. 12, col. 1.

Didier, Roger. "Milk and Ink from Sweet Potatoes and Peanuts." *The Alumnus* (1922): 238f.

Dilebo, Getahun. "The Life and Character of George Washington Carver 1860–1943." Washington, D.C.: National Park Service, 1972.

Dozier, Richard K. "From Humble Beginnings to National Shrine: Tuskegee Institute." *Historic Preservation* 33, no. 1 (January/February 1981): 40–45.

"Dr. B. T. Washington, Negro Leader, Dead." *New York Times,* 15 November 1915, p. 1, col. 4.

"Dr. Carver Is Dead; Negro Scientist." *New York Times,* 6 January 1943, p. 25, col. 1.

"Dr. Washington Buried." *New York Times,* 18 November 1915, p. 7, col. 3.

"Effect of Negro Education." *New York Times,* 16 February 1904, p. 8, col. 6.

Eleazer, R. B. "The 'Goober Wizard.'" *Intercollegian* magazine (1924): 10.

Elliott, Lawrence. *George Washington Carver: The Man Who Overcame.* Englewood Cliffs: Prentice-Hall, 1971.

Ellison, Ralph. *Invisible Man.* New York: Vintage Books, 1995.

"Ex-Slave Aids Paralytics." *New York Times,* 20 July 1937, p. 1, col. 21.

"Facts of Interest About Dr. George W. Carver, Director of Research and Experiment Station, Tuskegee Institute." Tuskegee, Ala.: Tuskegee Institute Press, 1937.

Fauset, Arthur Huff. "George Washington Carver." *The Friend* 101, no. 44 (26 April 1928): 541f.

Foner, Philip S., and Robert James Branham, eds. *Lift Every Voice: African American Oratory, 1787–1900.* Tuscaloosa, Ala.: University of Alabama Press, 1998.

"Form Company to Market Products of Plant Wizard." *Atlanta Constitution,* 20 September 1923.

Franklin, John Hope. *From Slavery to Freedom: A History of Negro Americans,* 6th ed. New York: Alfred A. Knopf, Inc., 1988.

Fuller, Robert P. "The Early Life of George Washington Carver." Washington. D.C.: National Park Service, 26 November 1957.

"Geo W. Carver Takes Interest in Llano Eats." *The Llano Colonist* (26 August 1922).

"George Washington Carver." *The Friend* 101, no. 44 (26 April 1928).

"Gifts to Fisk University." *New York Times,* 29 March 1911, p. 8, col. 5.

Harlan, Louis R. *Booker T. Washington: The Making of a Black Leader, 1856–1901.* New York: Oxford University Press, 1972.

———.*Booker T. Washington: The Wizard of Tuskegee, 1901–1915.* New York: Oxford University Press, 1983.

———.*The Booker T. Washington Papers: Volume 1: The Autobiographical Writings.* Chicago: University of Illinois Press, 1972.

———.*The Booker T. Washington Papers: Volume 2: 1860–89.* Chicago: University of Illinois Press, 1972.

———.*The Booker T. Washington Papers: Volume 3: 1889–95.* Chicago: University of Illinois Press, 1974.

Harlan, Louis R., and Raymond W. Smock, eds. *The Booker T. Washington Papers: Volume 5: 1899–1900.* Chicago: University of Illinois Press, 1976.

———.*The Booker T. Washington Papers: Volume 6: 1901–2.* Chicago: University of Illinois Press, 1977.

Harris, Julia Collier. "Lions Honor Guest Tonight Is Chemist of World-Wide Fame." Columbus *Enquirer Sun,* 12 June 1929.

Hobbs, Ruth. "God, Why Did You Make a Peanut?" *Boys and Girls Comrade* 9, no. 17 (25 April 1937).

"Honors Negro Scientist." *New York Times,* 15 June 1942, p. 17, col. 3.

Hunter, J. H. "Prayer and Peanuts." *The Evangelical Christian* (June 1938).

Kaufman, Arnold S. "Murder in Tuskegee: Day of Wrath in the Model Town." *The Nation* 202, no. 5 (31 January 1966): 118–125.

King, Martin Luther, Jr. *Why We Can't Wait.* New York: Penguin Books Inc., 1964.

Kremer, Gary R., ed. *George Washington Carver In His Own Words.* Columbia, Mo.: University of Missouri Press, 1987.

"The Latest Contribution to the Negro Problem." *The Tuskegee Alumni Bulletin* 2, no. 4 (January–March 1914).

"Leadership and Learning: An Interpretive History of Historically Black Land-Grant Colleges and Universities–A Centennial Study." 79.

Lewis, David Levering. *W. E. B. Du Bois: Biography of a Race.* New York: Henry Holt and Company, 1993.

"Lynching Is Disappearing." *New York Times,* 12 March 1907, p. 6, col. 2.

Marable, Manning. *W .E. B. Du Bois: Black Radical Democrat.* Boston: Twayne Publishers, 1986.

Massey, James Earl. "A Bridge Between: A Centennial History of Campus Ministry at Tuskegee University 1888–1988." Tuskegee, Ala.: Tuskegee University Press, 1988.

Mayberry, B. D. *The Role of Tuskegee University in the Origin, Growth, and Development of the Negro Cooperative Extension System, 1881–1990.* Montgomery, Ala.: Brown Printing Company, 1989.

McClung, Littell. "A Glimpse of the Remarkable Work of George W. Carver, the Negro Scientist." Montgomery *Advertiser,* 25 November 1917.

McMurray, Linda O. *George Washington Carver: Scientist and Symbol.* New York: Oxford University Press, 1981.

Meier, August. *Negro Thought in America, 1880–1915.* Ann Arbor: University of Michigan Press, 1966.

"Men of Science Never Talk That Way." *New York Times*, 20 November 1924, p. 22, col. 6.

Mills, Marjorie. "The George Washington Carver Memorial Cabin." *Herald* 9, no. 14 (14 August 1942).

Moss, W. Wade. "The Wizard of Tuskegee." *The Chemist* 8, no. 7 (October 1936): 688f.

"Mr. Taft Pleads for Negro Schools." *New York Times*, 24 February 1909, p. 1, col. 7.

"Negro History Week." *New York Times,* 15 February 1940, p. 18, col. 3.

"Negro in the South, The." *New York Times,* 20 November 1900, p. 2, col. 4.

"Negro Leader on Lynching." *New York Times,* 29 February 1904, p. 5, col. 1.

"Negro Regiment Arrested, A." *New York Times,* 21 November 1898, p. 1, col. 7.

"Negro Scientist Honored." *New York Times,* 20 June 1923, p. 19, col. 5.

"Negro's Chemistry Astounds Audience." *New York Times,* 19 November 1924, p. 5, col. 1.

"Nineteen Negroes Shot to Death." *New York Times,* 11 November 1898, p. 1, col. 2.

Nurney, Daisy. "A Patient Scientist Works Out New Destinies for the Peanut." *Virginia-Pilot and the Norfolk Landmark,* 5 November 1922, p. 8, col. 1.

"Object to B. T. Washington." *New York Times,* 14 February 1902, p. 9, col. 6.

"Ovation from Crowds for B. T. Washington." *New York Times,* 6 March 1905, p. 7, col. 1.

Ovington, Mary White. "How the NAACP Began." 1914.

————.*The Walls Came Tumbling Down.* New York: Harcourt, Brace and Company, Inc., 1947.

"A Plea for His Race." Atlanta *Constitution,* 19 September 1895, p. 1, col. 1.

"Paper Blamed for Riots." *New York Times,* 28 September 1906, p. 1, col. 4.

"Pick Negro Winners of Spingarn Medals." *New York Times,* 2 May 1926, p. 30, col. 4.

"Prof. George Washington Carver." *The Negro American* 6, no. 8 (December 1928): 4f.

"Profile: Tuskegee Institute." *The Black Collegian* 2, no. 1 (September/October 1971): 12f.

Quarles, Benjamin. *The Negro in the Making of America.* New York: Simon & Schuster, 1987.

Ridout, Rev. G. W. "I went to Tuskegee Institute...." (From a sermon delivered 17 July 1935).

"Riots Helped Negroes, Says Booker Washington." *New York Times,* 27 November 1906, p. 6, col. 2.

Scipio, L. Albert II. *Pre-War Days at Tuskegee: Historical Essay on Tuskegee Institute (1881–1943).* Silver Springs, Md.: Roman Publications, 1987.

Scott, Emmett J., and Lyman Beecher Stowe. *Booker T. Washington: Builder of a Civilization.* New York: Doubleday, Page & Company, 1917.

Seely, Walter Hoff. "Carver of Tuskegee." *Success* magazine (1923).

"Shakespeare." *New York Times,* 23 April 1914, p. 12, col. 6.

Shoffelmayer, Victor. *Here Comes Tomorrow.* Evanston, Ill.: Row, Peterson & Co., 1942.

Slatter, Horace D. "Men I Have Known." *The Afro-American.* Baltimore (14 October 1916).

Smith, Alvin D. *George Washington Carver: Man of God.* New York: Exposition Press, 1954.

"South Calls Negro, Says Washington." *New York Times,* 21 August 1913, p. 6, col. 6.

"South Carolina Riots, The." *New York Times,* 17 November 1898, p. 1, col. 2.

Sparks, Edwin E. "The Wizard of the Goober and the Yam." *American Life* 1, no. 6 (November 1926).

Stewart, Ollie A. "Carver of Tuskegee." *Scribner's Commentator* 10, no. 1 (May 1941): 12f.

————. "Carver of Tuskegee: The Wizard Who Is Trying to Cure Infantile Paralysis with Lowly Peanut Oil." Cleveland *Plain Dealer*, 25 March 1934, Magazine section, p. 6, col. 1.

Stokes, Anson Phelps. *Tuskegee Institute: The First Fifty Years*. Tuskegee, Ala.: Tuskegee Institute Press, 1931.

Tarpley, Willie Hughes. "He Never Thought of Quitting." *Abbot's Monthly* (November 1932): 14f.

"Thanks Cotton Exchange for Aid." *New York Times*, 14 May 1925, p. 27, col. 3.

Thrasher, Max Bennett. *Tuskegee: Its Story and Its Work*. 1900. Reprint, Freeport, N.Y.: Books for Libraries Press, 1971.

"To Suppress Race Wars." *New York Times*, 18 November 1898, p. 1, col. 8.

Turner, Thomas W. "Dr. George W. Carver: A Pioneer in Scientific Research." *The Southern Workman* 68, no. 5 (May 1939): 151f.

"Tuskegee and Its Principal." *New York Times*, 24 April 1903, p. 1, col. 4.

"Tuskegee Annual Report." Tuskegee, Ala.: Tuskegee Institute, 31 May 1888.

"Tuskegee Institute Centennial Celebration." Tuskegee, Ala.: Tuskegee Institute, 1981.

"Tuskegee Student Slain." *The Campus Digest* 34, no. 13 (8 January 1966): 1, 3.

"United States Commission to the Paris Exposition of 1900: The American Negro Exhibit." n.d.

"Wants a White Color Line." *New York Times*, 20 April 1914, p. 11, col. 6.

"Wants Negroes to Protest." *New York Times,* 18 April 1914, p. 17, col. 2.

"Wants Negro Troops Removed." *New York Times,* 22 November 1898, p. 1, col. 2.

Warren, Vincent. "An Appreciation: Dr. George Washington Carver." *The Colored Harvest* 29, no. 3. Baltimore: St. Joseph's Society of the Sacred Heart (June/July, 1941).

Washington, Booker T., "The Fruits of Industrial Training." *Atlantic Monthly* 92 (October 1903): 453–62.

Washington, Booker T., et al. *The Negro Problem.* New York: Arnot Press (1903) and the *New York Times* (reprinted 1969).

Washington, Booker T., ed. *Tuskegee & Its People: Their Ideals and Achievements.* Freeport, N.Y.: Books for Libraries Press, 1971.

Washington, Booker T. *Up from Slavery.* New York: Viking Penguin, Inc., 1986.

Washington, Booker T. *Working with the Hands.* New York: Negro Universities Press, 1969.

Washington, Booker T. "Work of Gifted Negro Teacher Praised by Dr. Washington." *The Alumnus* 8, no. 5 (February 1913): 3f.

"White Man Assaults Booker Washington." *New York Times,* 20 March 1911, p. 1, col. 5.

"Whites and Negroes Killed at Atlanta." *New York Times,* 25 September 1906, p. 1, col. 1.

Wilkins, Lou. *George Washington Carver: The World's Greatest Chemist.* Fort Worth, Tex.: 1929.

"Wilmington Race Riots, The." *New York Times,* 21 November 1898, p. 10, col. 2.

"Woman Bequeaths Tuskegee $1,000,000." *New York Times,* 27 August 1910, p. 1, col. 4.

Young, Pauline A. "George Washington Carver." *The Tuskegee Alumni Bulletin* 4, no. 12 (December 1922): 5f.

Zuber, Osburn. "Negro Scientist Shows 'Way Out' for Southern Farmers." 1930.